Family Ties

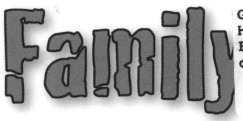

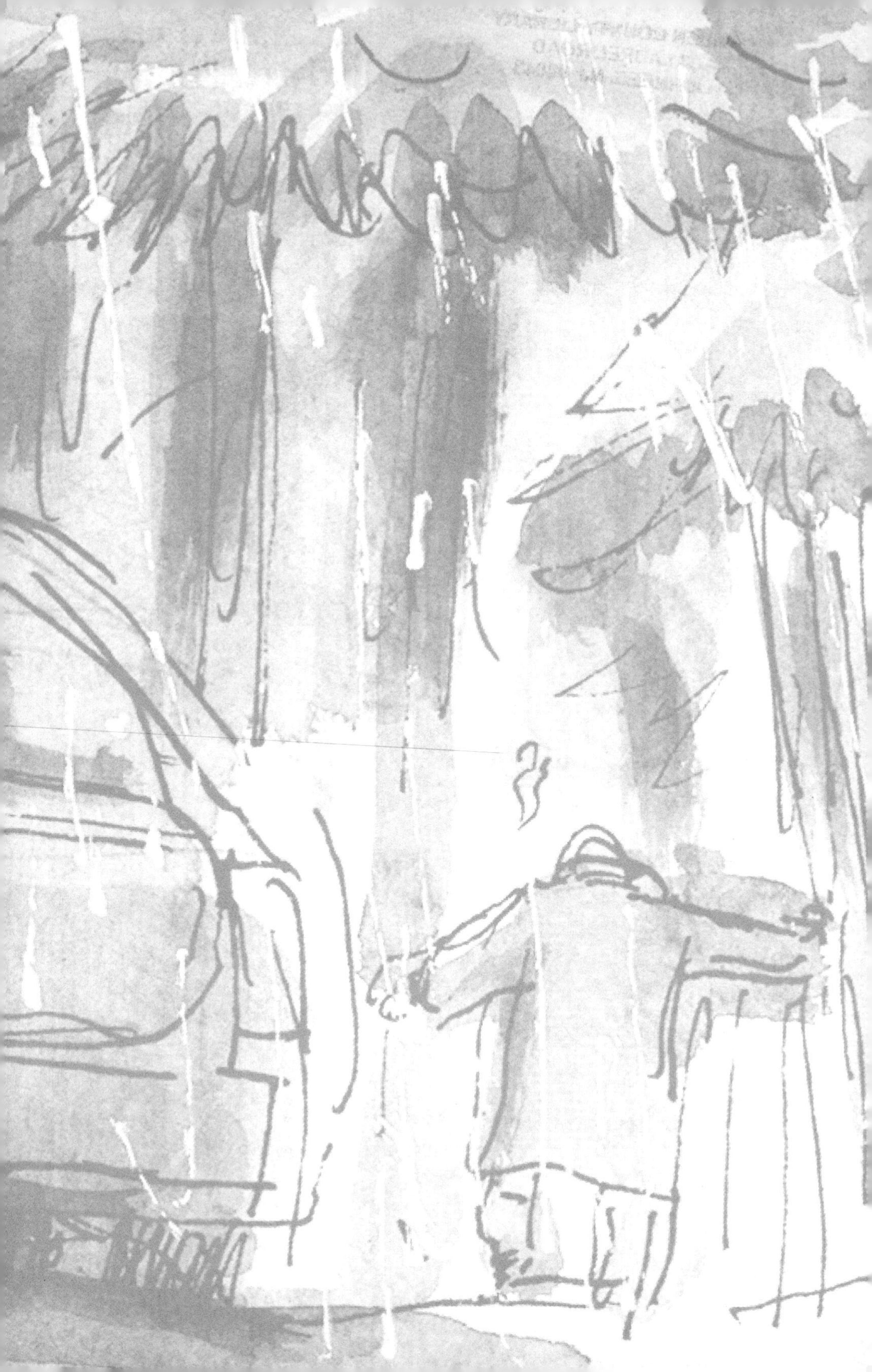

Family Ties

An Alaskan Crime Drama

Eric HOBBS, writer
Noel TUAZON, artist
Jaymes REED, letterer

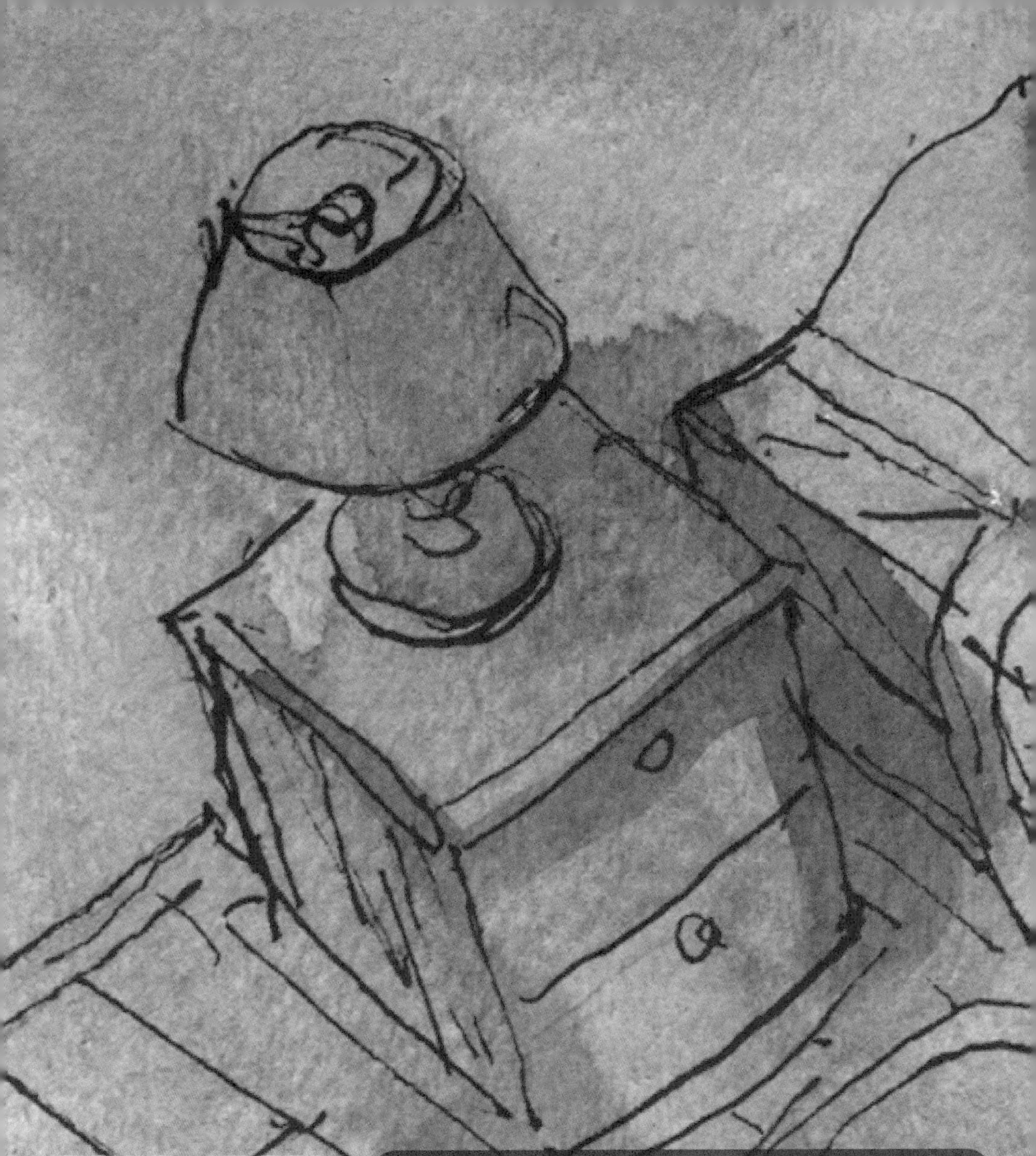

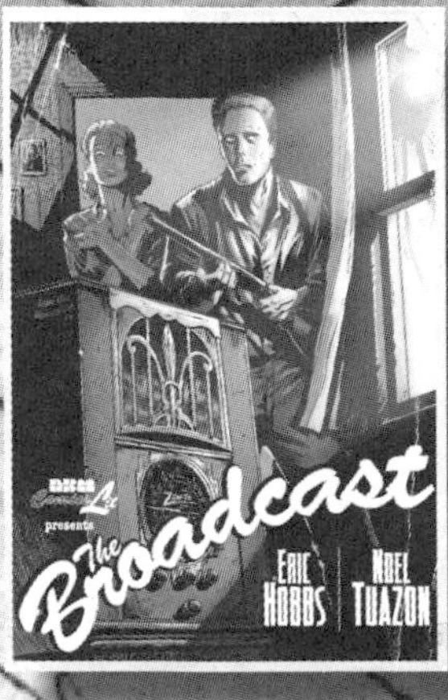
presents
The Broadcast
Eric Hobbs
Noel Tuazon

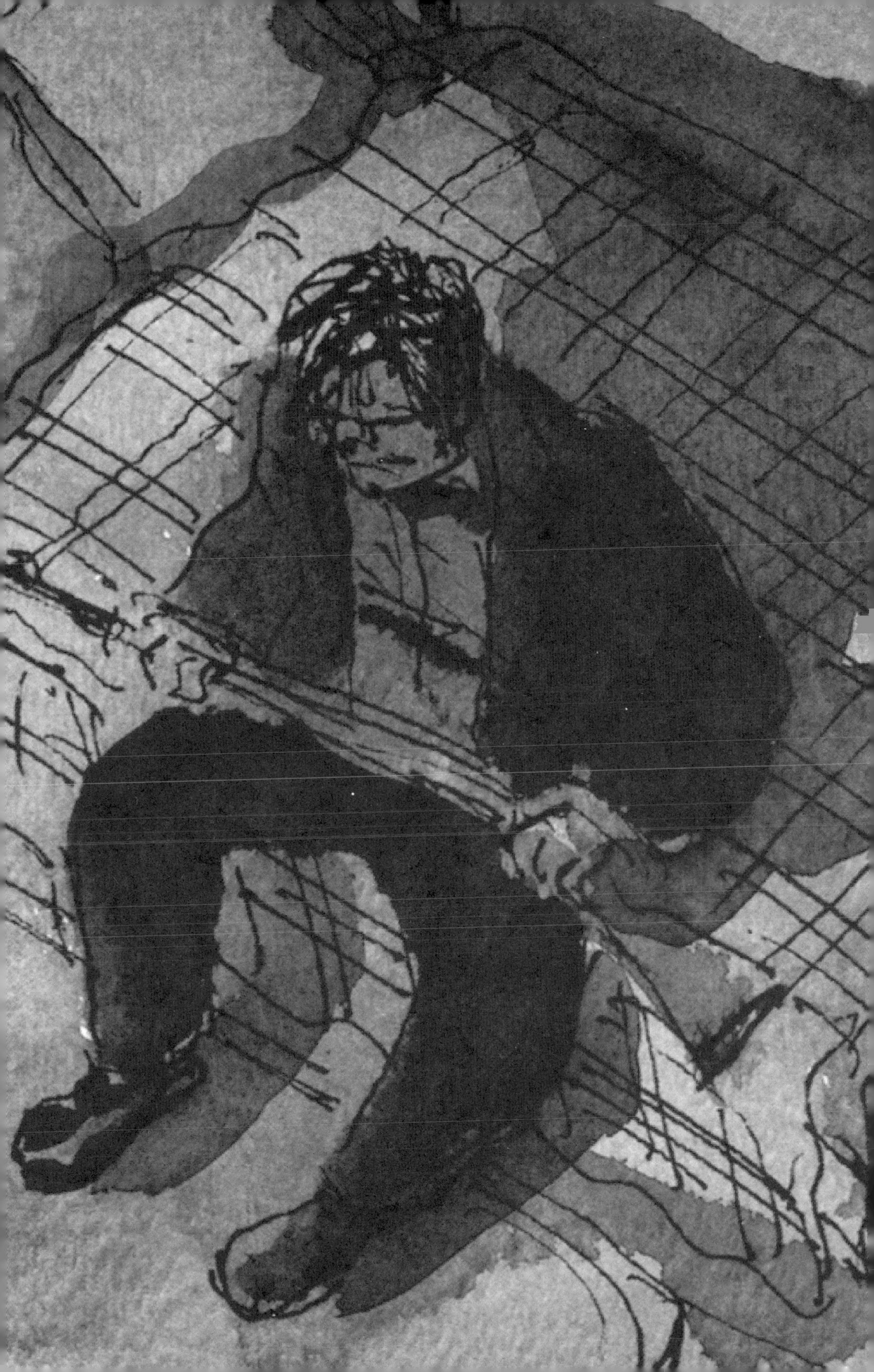

ISBN: 978-1-56163-729-4
© 2014 Eric Hobbs and Noel Tuazon
Library of Congress Control Number: 2014934447
1st printing May 2014

Also available digitally wherever e-books are sold.

ComicsLit is an imprint
and trademark of

NANTIER · BEALL · MINOUSTCHINE
Publishing inc.
new york

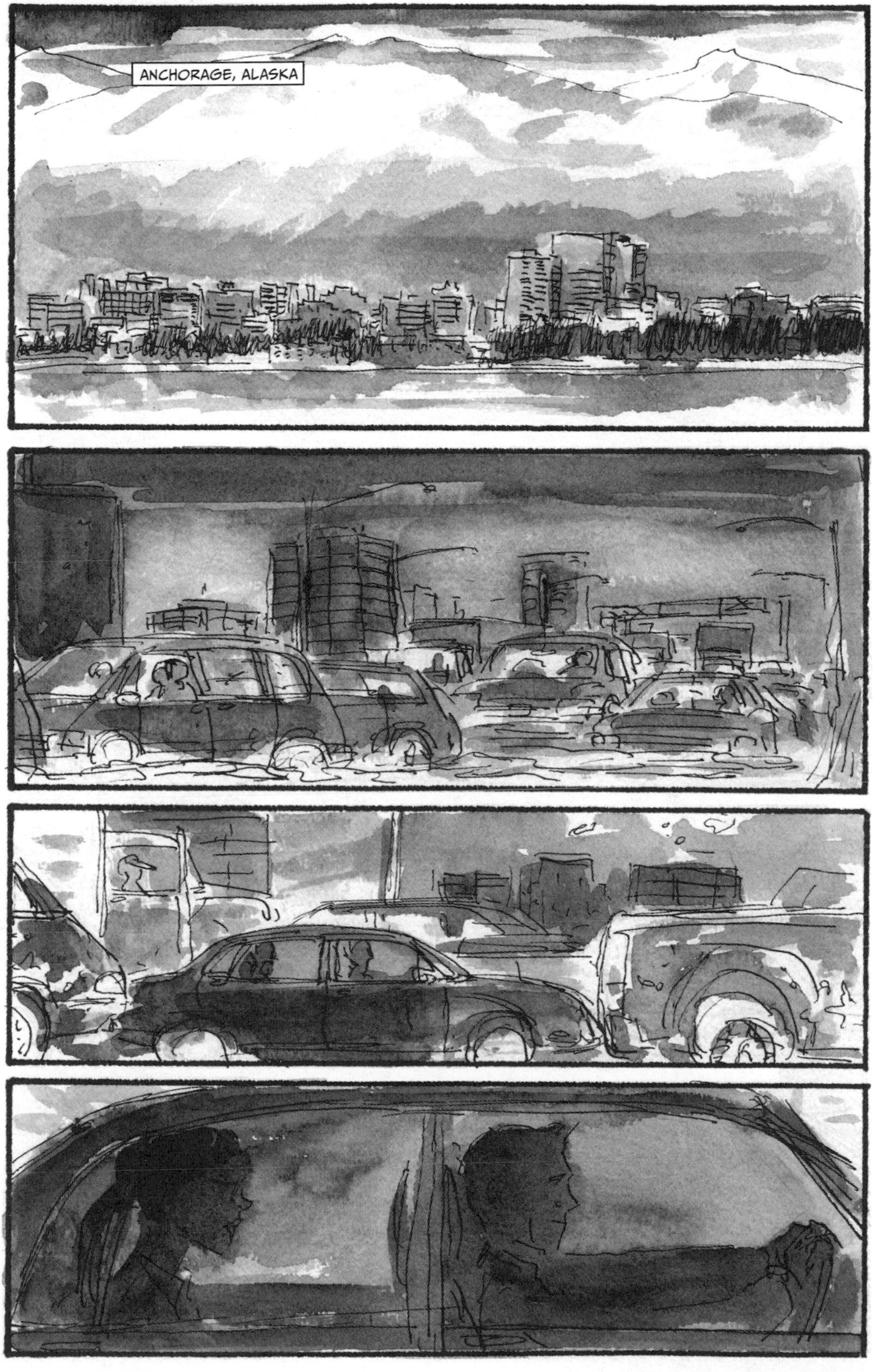
ANCHORAGE, ALASKA

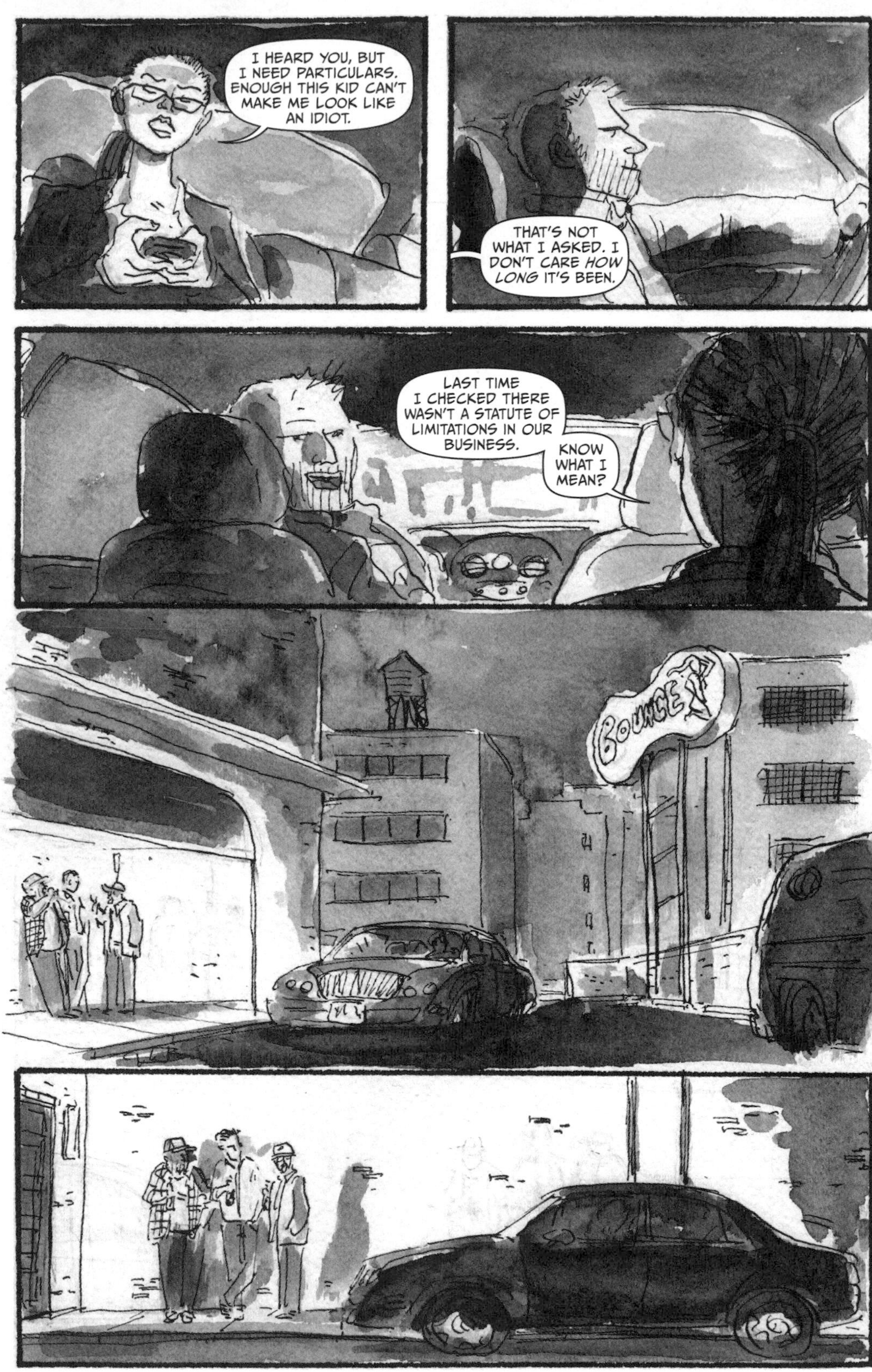
I HEARD YOU, BUT I NEED PARTICULARS. ENOUGH THIS KID CAN'T MAKE ME LOOK LIKE AN IDIOT.
THAT'S NOT WHAT I ASKED. I DON'T CARE *HOW LONG* IT'S BEEN.
LAST TIME I CHECKED THERE WASN'T A STATUTE OF LIMITATIONS IN OUR BUSINESS.
KNOW WHAT I MEAN?
BOUNCE

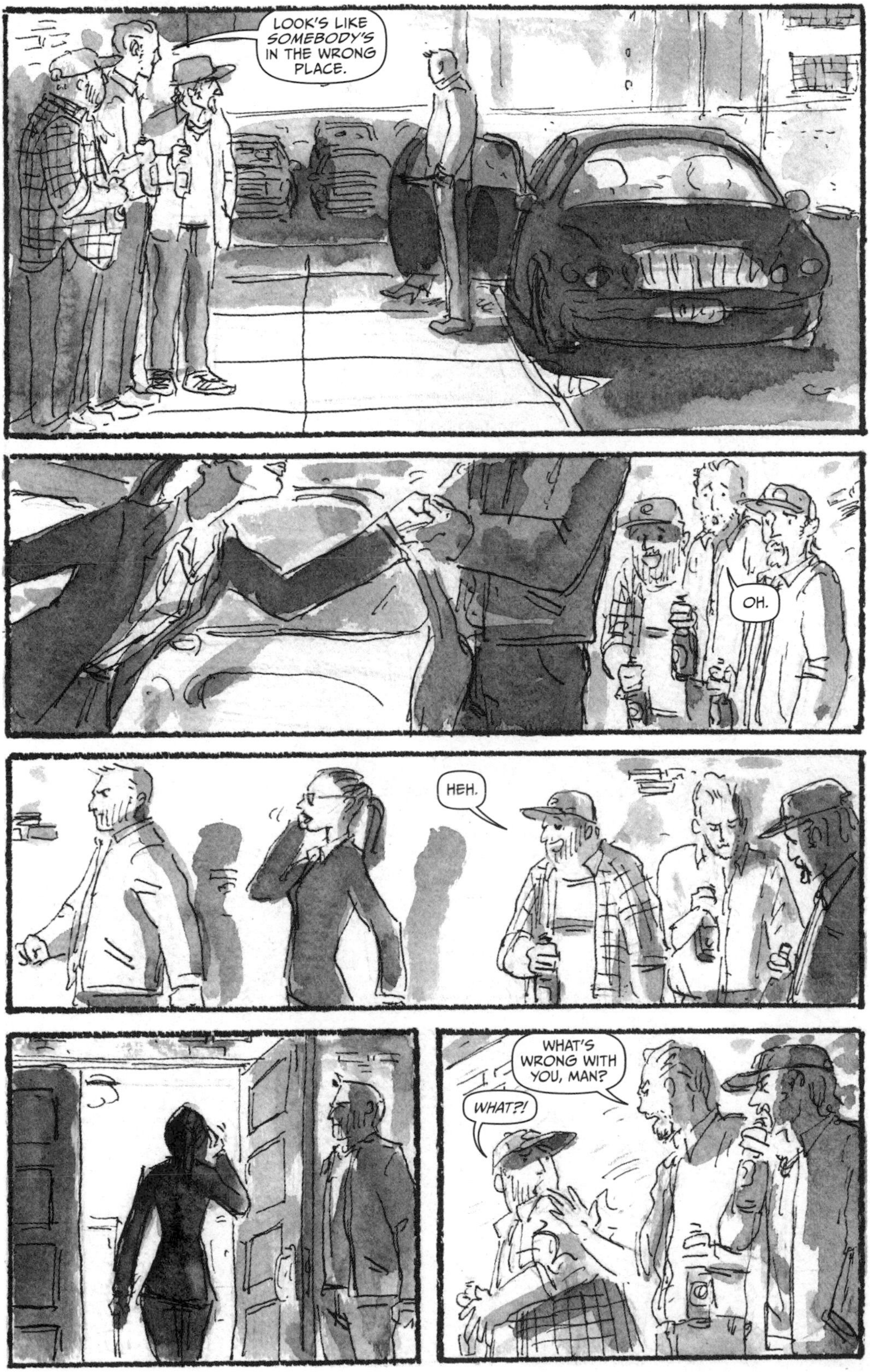
LOOK'S LIKE SOMEBODY'S IN THE WRONG PLACE.
OH.
HEH.
WHAT'S WRONG WITH YOU, MAN?
WHAT?!

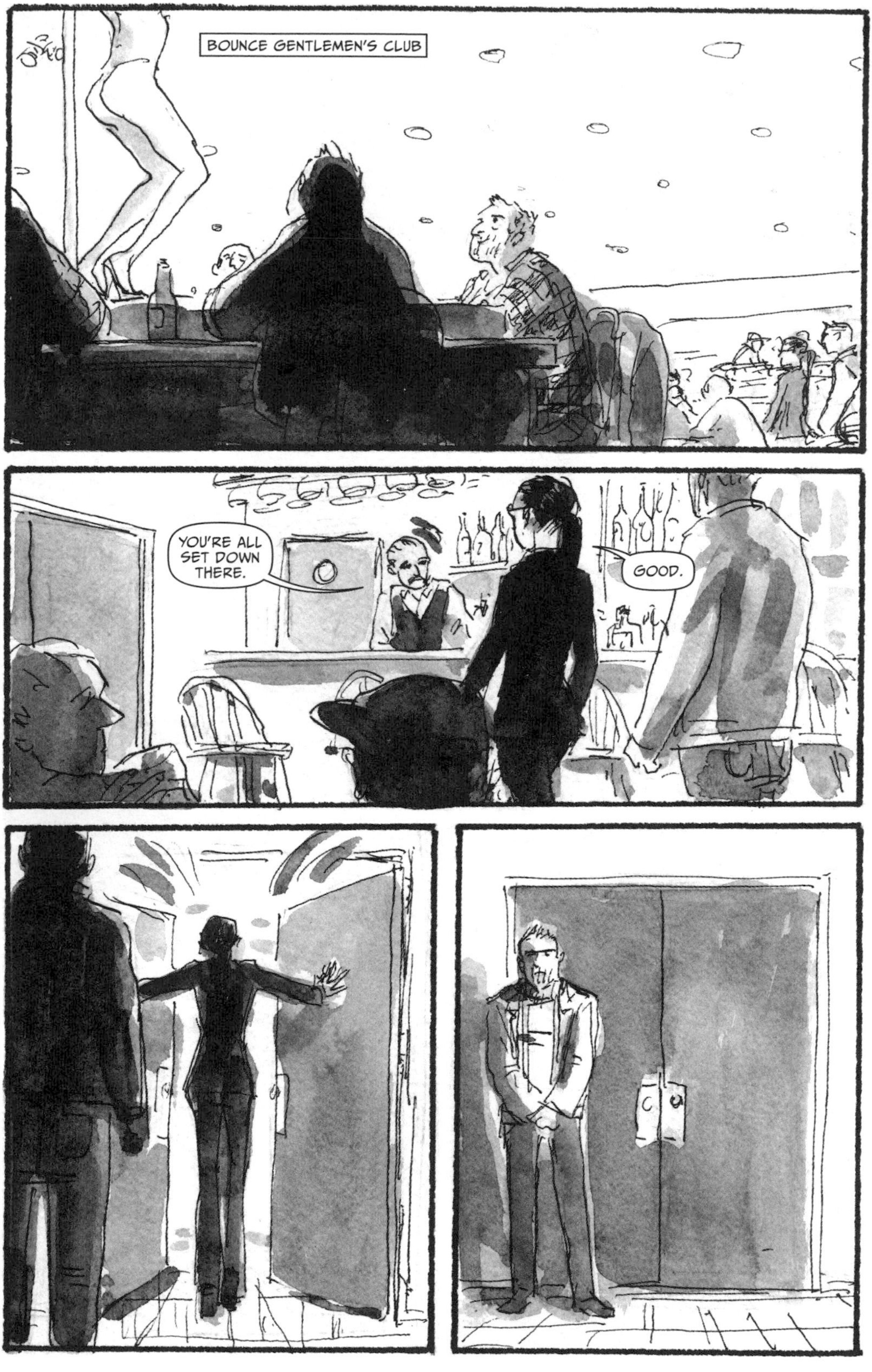
BOUNCE GENTLEMEN'S CLUB
YOU'RE ALL SET DOWN THERE.
GOOD.

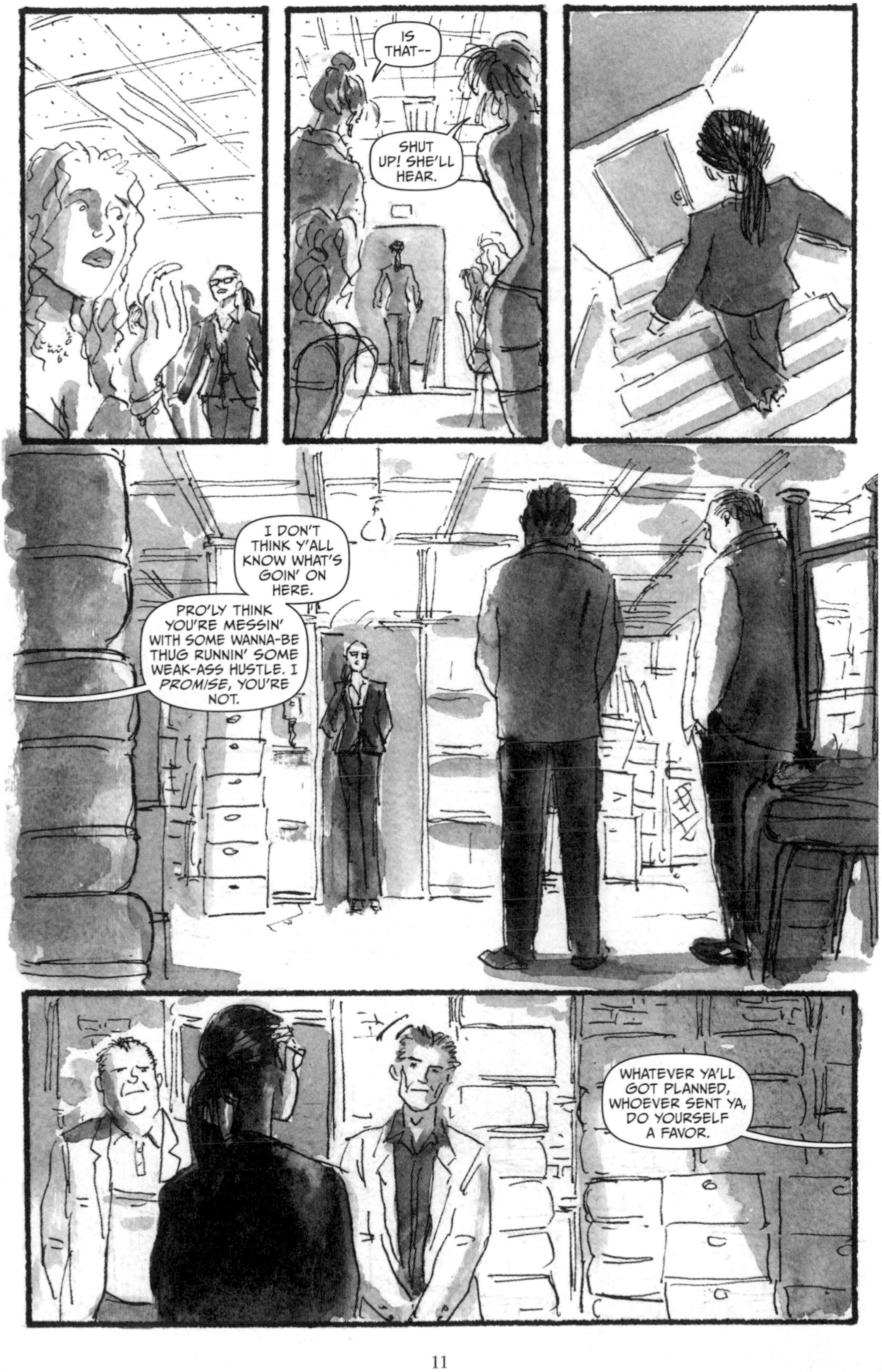
IS THAT--
SHUT UP! SHE'LL HEAR.
I DON'T THINK Y'ALL KNOW WHAT'S GOIN' ON HERE.
PRO'LY THINK YOU'RE MESSIN' WITH SOME WANNA-BE THUG RUNNIN' SOME WEAK-ASS HUSTLE. I *PROMISE*, YOU'RE NOT.
WHATEVER YA'LL GOT PLANNED, WHOEVER SENT YA, DO YOURSELF A FAVOR.

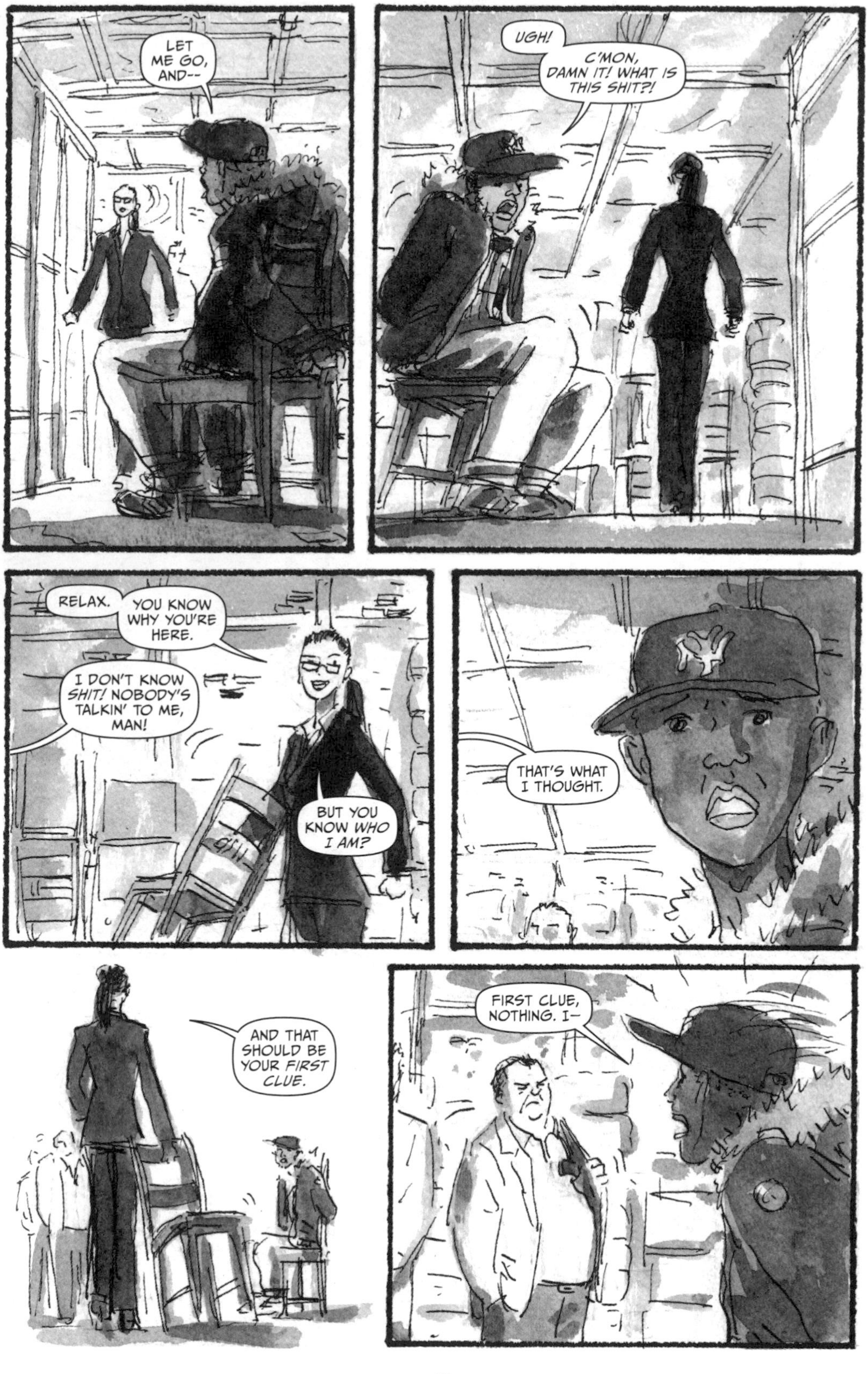
LET ME GO, AND--
UGH!
C'MON, DAMN IT! WHAT IS THIS SHIT?!
RELAX.
YOU KNOW WHY YOU'RE HERE.
I DON'T KNOW SHIT! NOBODY'S TALKIN' TO ME, MAN!
BUT YOU KNOW WHO I AM?
THAT'S WHAT I THOUGHT.
AND THAT SHOULD BE YOUR FIRST CLUE.
FIRST CLUE, NOTHING. I—

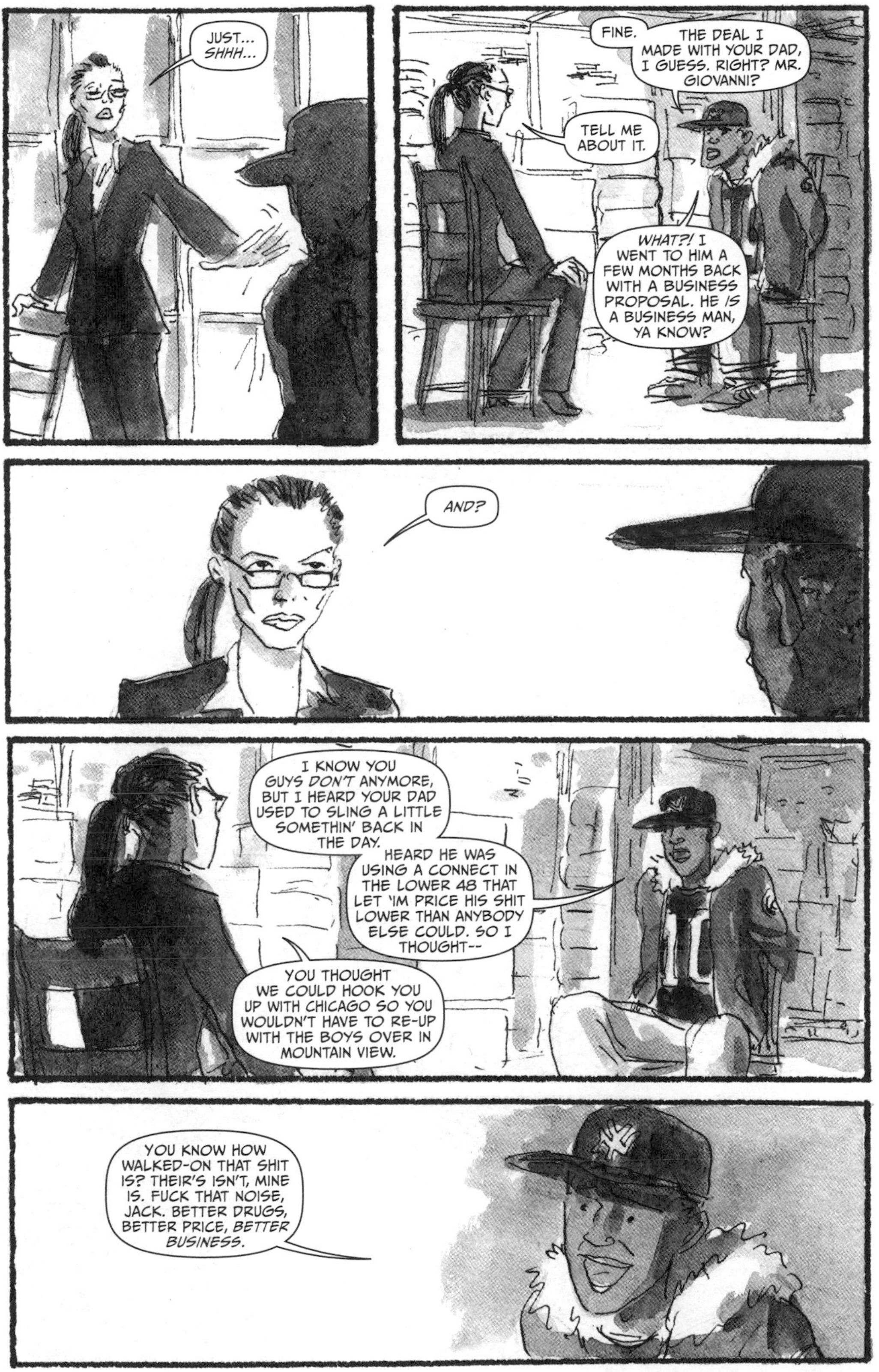
JUST... SHHH...
FINE.
THE DEAL I MADE WITH YOUR DAD, I GUESS. RIGHT? MR. GIOVANNI?
TELL ME ABOUT IT.
WHAT?! I WENT TO HIM A FEW MONTHS BACK WITH A BUSINESS PROPOSAL. HE IS A BUSINESS MAN, YA KNOW?
AND?
I KNOW YOU GUYS DON'T ANYMORE, BUT I HEARD YOUR DAD USED TO SLING A LITTLE SOMETHIN' BACK IN THE DAY.
HEARD HE WAS USING A CONNECT IN THE LOWER 48 THAT LET 'IM PRICE HIS SHIT LOWER THAN ANYBODY ELSE COULD. SO I THOUGHT--
YOU THOUGHT WE COULD HOOK YOU UP WITH CHICAGO SO YOU WOULDN'T HAVE TO RE-UP WITH THE BOYS OVER IN MOUNTAIN VIEW.
YOU KNOW HOW WALKED-ON THAT SHIT IS? THEIR'S ISN'T, MINE IS. FUCK THAT NOISE, JACK. BETTER DRUGS, BETTER PRICE, BETTER BUSINESS.

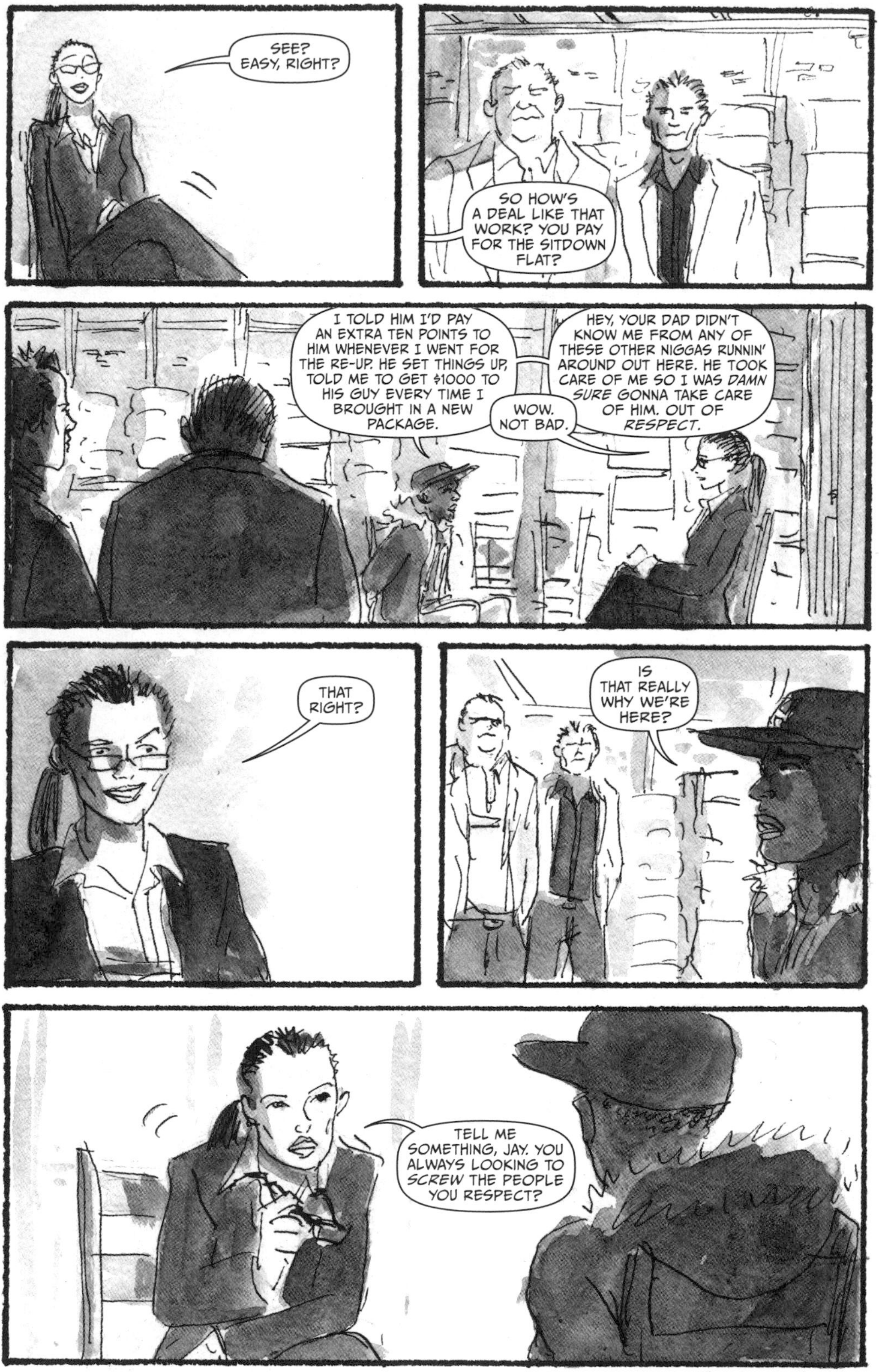
SEE? EASY, RIGHT?
SO HOW'S A DEAL LIKE THAT WORK? YOU PAY FOR THE SITDOWN FLAT?
I TOLD HIM I'D PAY AN EXTRA TEN POINTS TO HIM WHENEVER I WENT FOR THE RE-UP. HE SET THINGS UP, TOLD ME TO GET $1000 TO HIS GUY EVERY TIME I BROUGHT IN A NEW PACKAGE.
WOW. NOT BAD.
HEY, YOUR DAD DIDN'T KNOW ME FROM ANY OF THESE OTHER NIGGAS RUNNIN' AROUND OUT HERE. HE TOOK CARE OF ME SO I WAS *DAMN SURE* GONNA TAKE CARE OF HIM. OUT OF *RESPECT*.
THAT RIGHT?
IS THAT REALLY WHY WE'RE HERE?
TELL ME SOMETHING, JAY. YOU ALWAYS LOOKING TO *SCREW* THE PEOPLE YOU RESPECT?

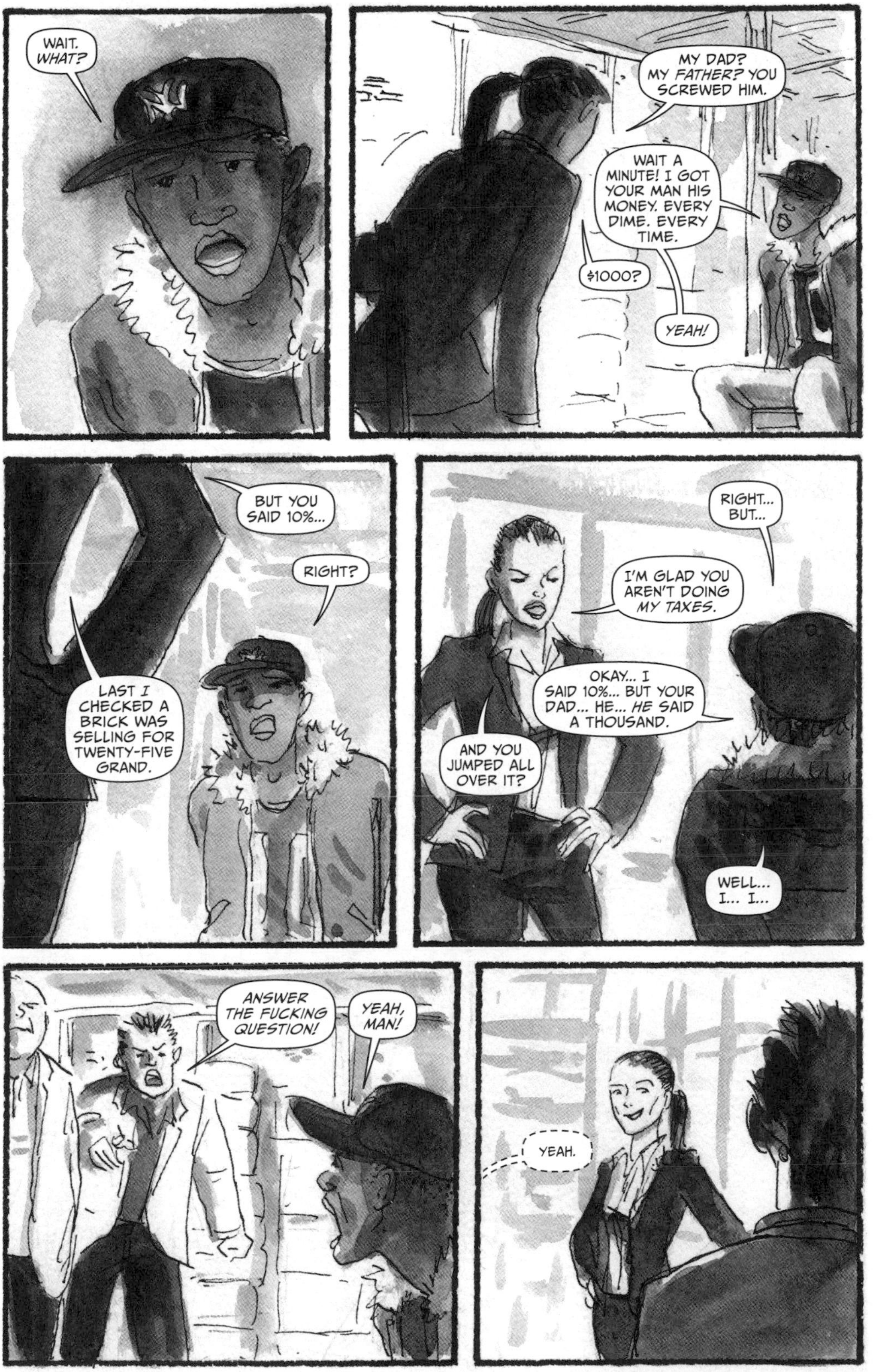
WAIT. *WHAT?*
MY DAD? MY *FATHER?* YOU SCREWED HIM.
WAIT A MINUTE! I GOT YOUR MAN HIS MONEY. EVERY DIME. EVERY TIME.
$1000?
YEAH!
BUT YOU SAID 10%...
RIGHT?
LAST *I* CHECKED A BRICK WAS SELLING FOR TWENTY-FIVE GRAND.
RIGHT... BUT...
I'M GLAD YOU AREN'T DOING *MY TAXES.*
OKAY... I SAID 10%... BUT YOUR DAD... HE... *HE* SAID A THOUSAND.
AND YOU JUMPED ALL OVER IT?
WELL... I... I...
ANSWER THE FUCKING QUESTION!
YEAH, MAN!
YEAH.

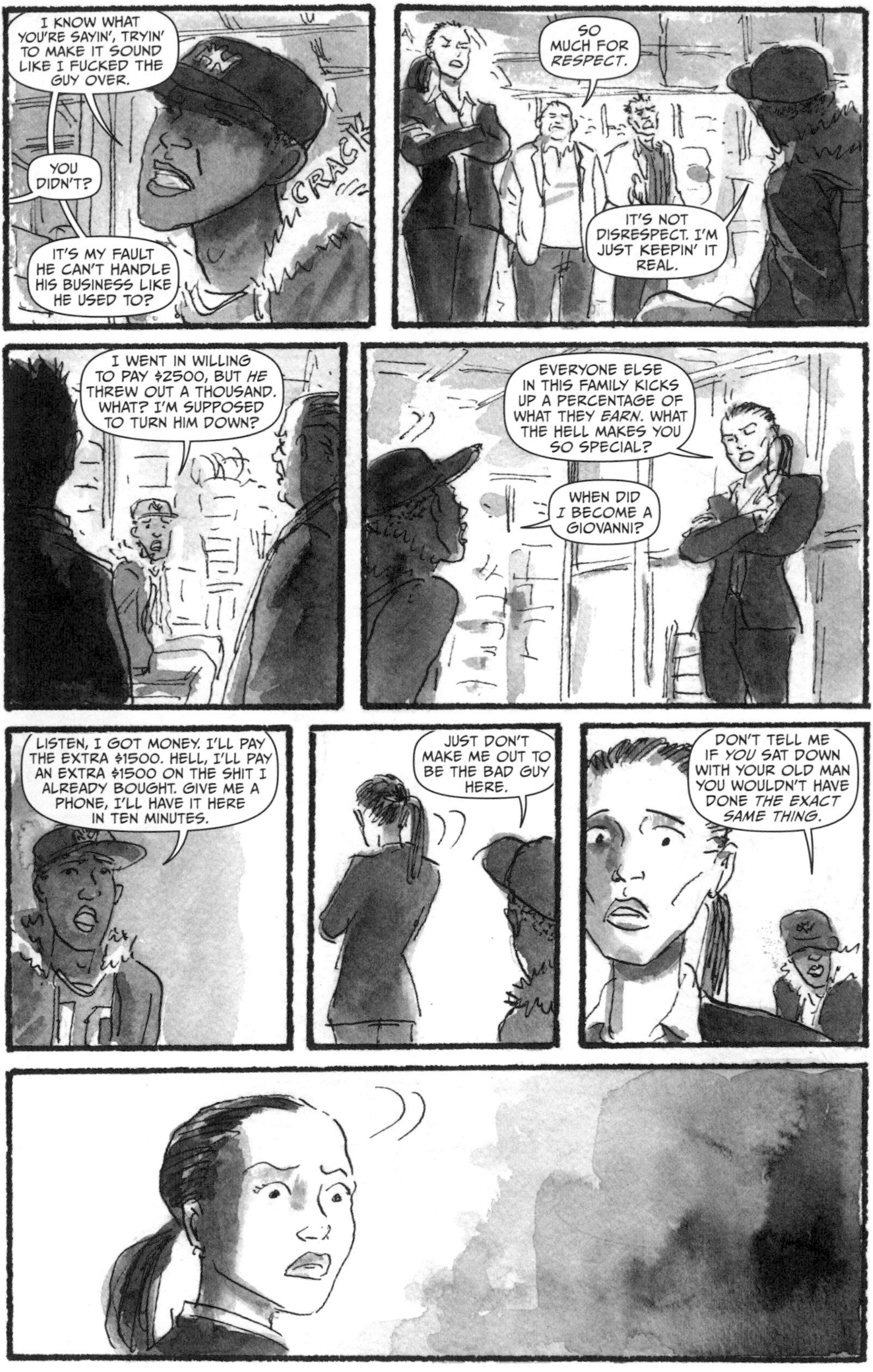
I KNOW WHAT YOU'RE SAYIN', TRYIN' TO MAKE IT SOUND LIKE I FUCKED THE GUY OVER.
YOU DIDN'T?
IT'S MY FAULT HE CAN'T HANDLE HIS BUSINESS LIKE HE USED TO?
CRACK
SO MUCH FOR *RESPECT*.
IT'S NOT DISRESPECT. I'M JUST KEEPIN' IT REAL.
I WENT IN WILLING TO PAY $2500, BUT *HE* THREW OUT A THOUSAND. WHAT? I'M SUPPOSED TO TURN HIM DOWN?
EVERYONE ELSE IN THIS FAMILY KICKS UP A PERCENTAGE OF WHAT THEY *EARN*. WHAT THE HELL MAKES YOU SO SPECIAL?
WHEN DID *I* BECOME A GIOVANNI?
LISTEN, I GOT MONEY. I'LL PAY THE EXTRA $1500. HELL, I'LL PAY AN EXTRA $1500 ON THE SHIT I ALREADY BOUGHT. GIVE ME A PHONE, I'LL HAVE IT HERE IN TEN MINUTES.
JUST DON'T MAKE ME OUT TO BE THE BAD GUY HERE.
DON'T TELL ME IF *YOU* SAT DOWN WITH YOUR OLD MAN YOU WOULDN'T HAVE DONE *THE EXACT SAME THING*.

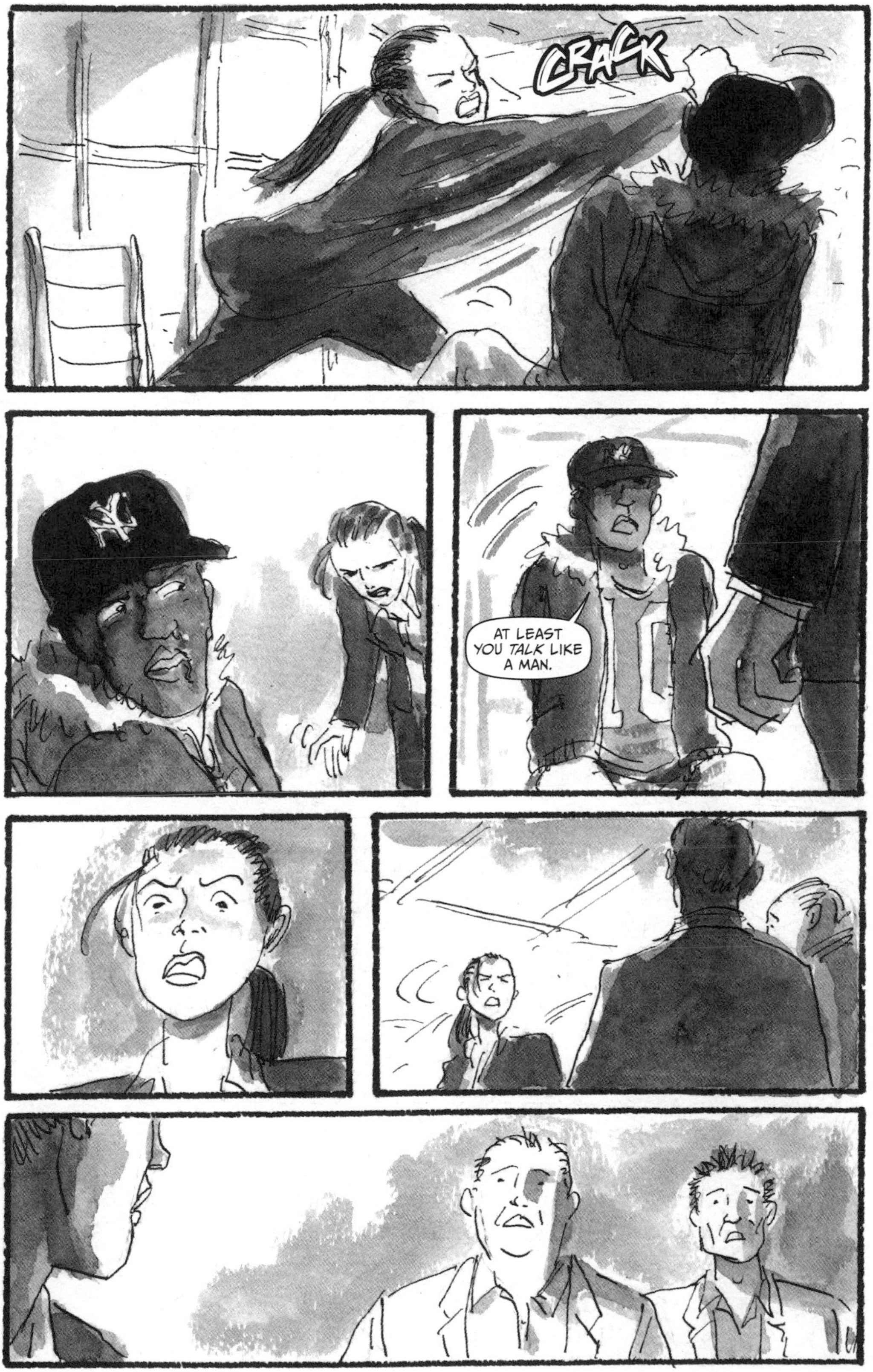
CRACK
AT LEAST YOU *TALK* LIKE A MAN.

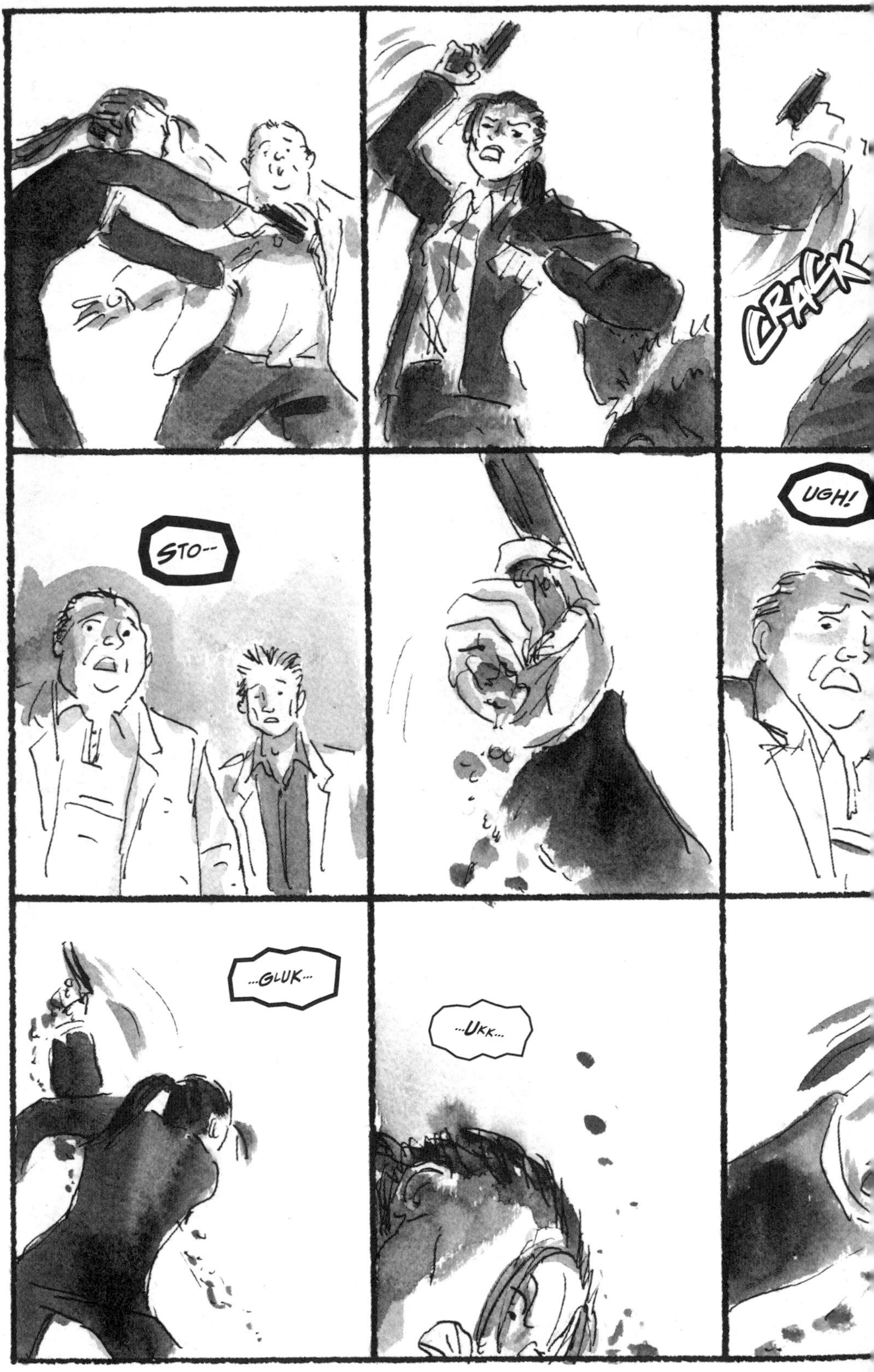
CRACK
STO--
UGH!
...GLUK...
...UKK...

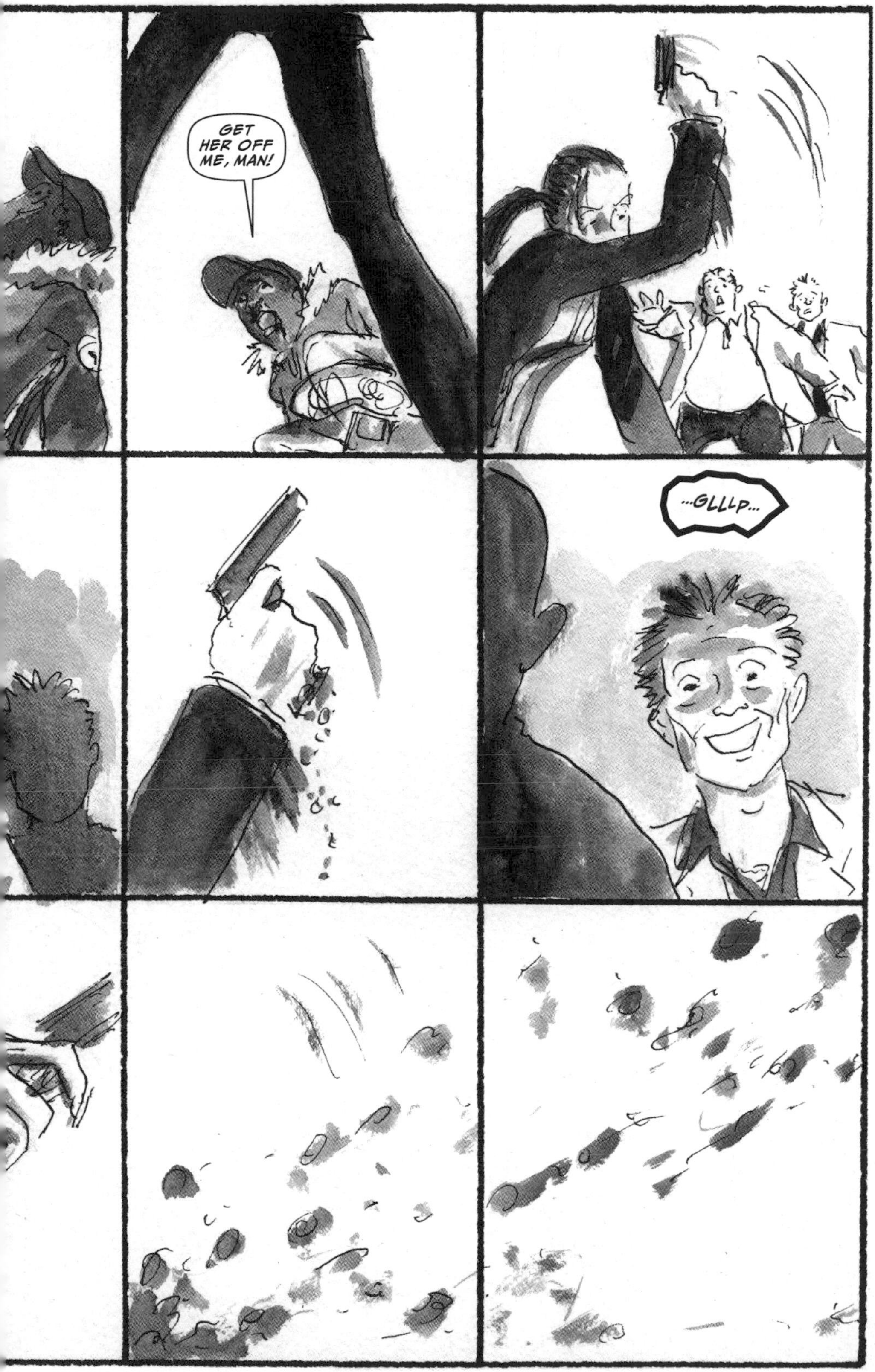
GET HER OFF ME, MAN!
...GLLLP...

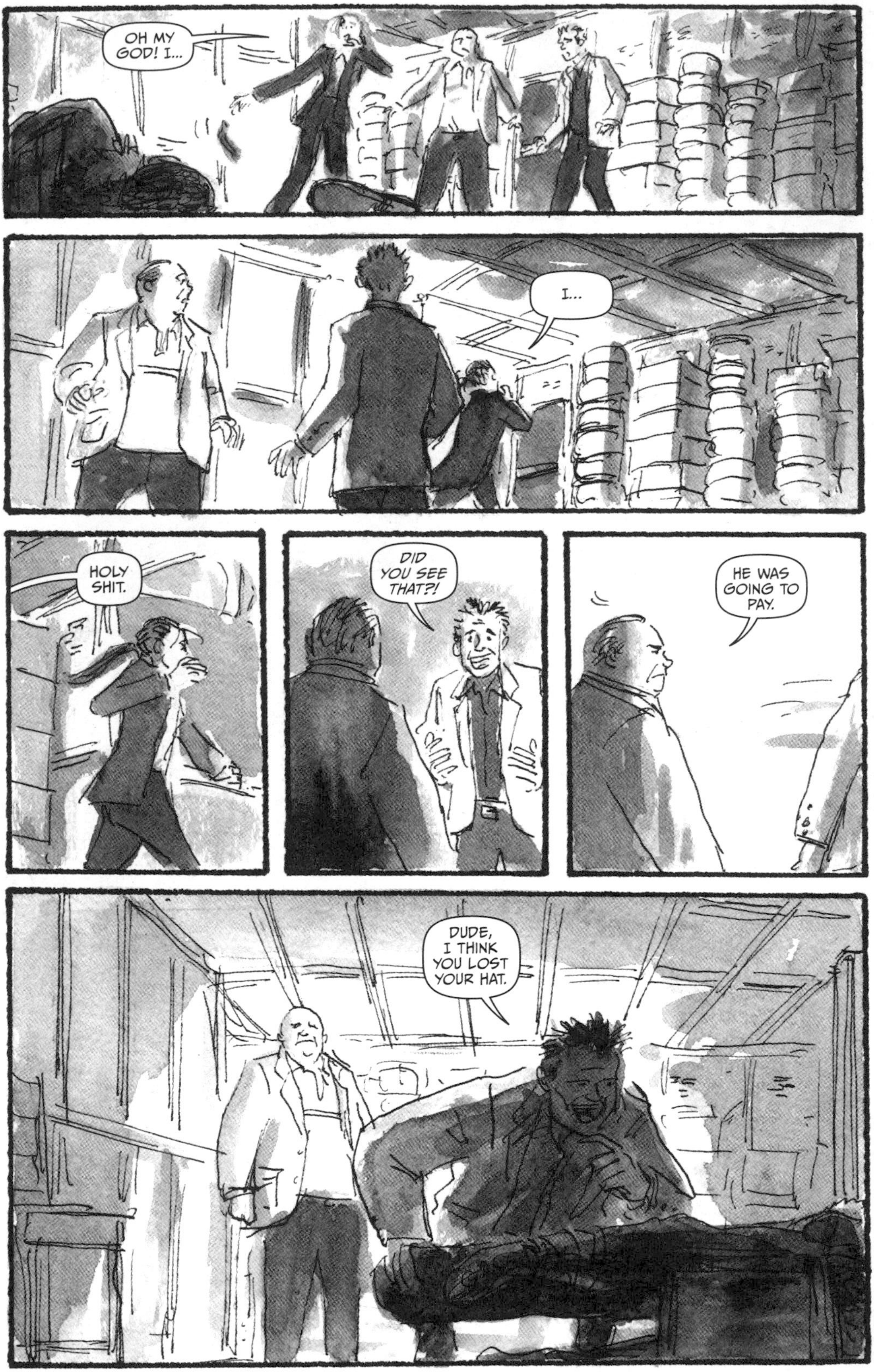
OH MY GOD! I...
I...
HOLY SHIT.
DID YOU SEE THAT?!
HE WAS GOING TO PAY.
DUDE, I THINK YOU LOST YOUR HAT.

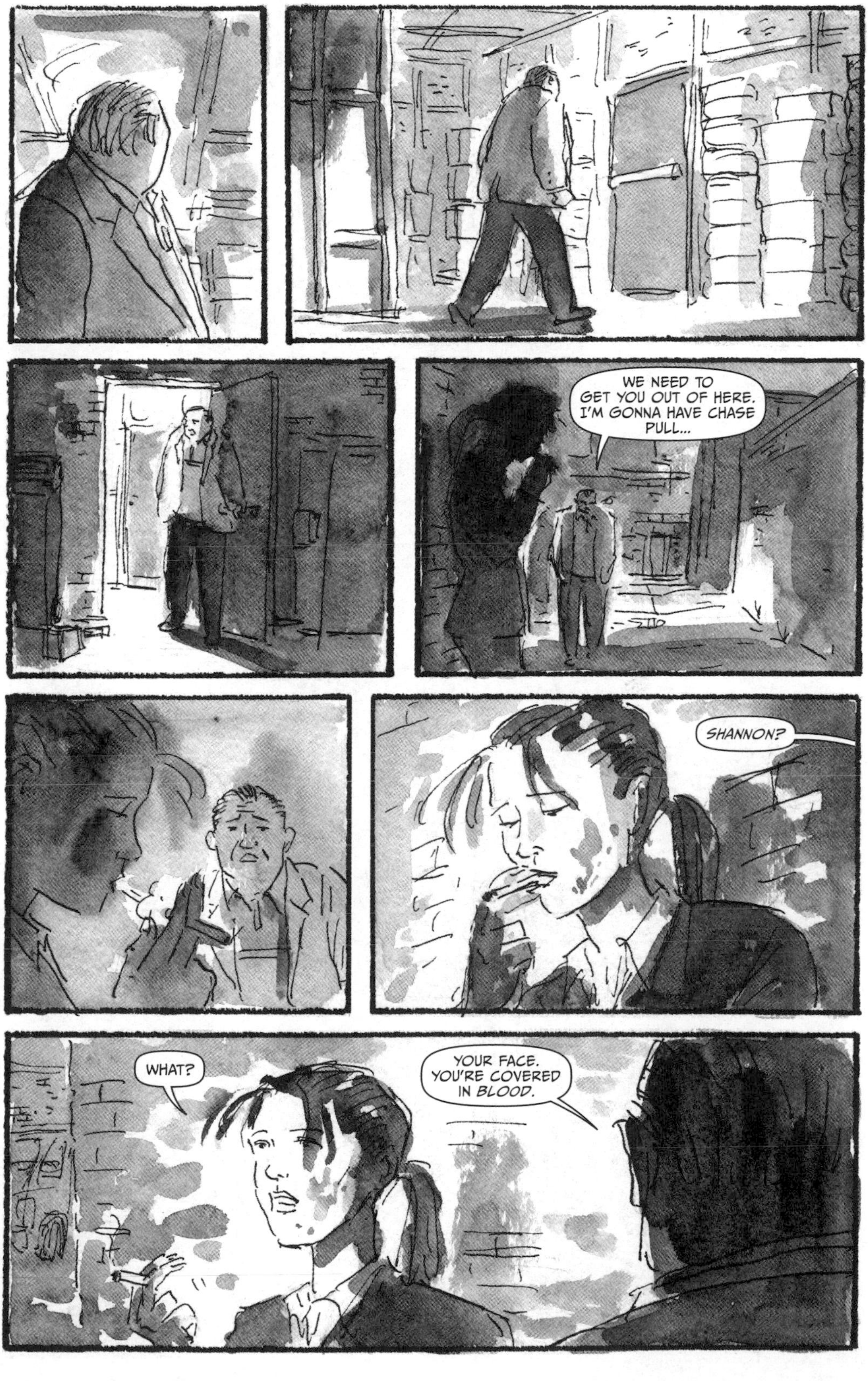
WE NEED TO GET YOU OUT OF HERE. I'M GONNA HAVE CHASE PULL...
SHANNON?
WHAT?
YOUR FACE. YOU'RE COVERED IN *BLOOD*.

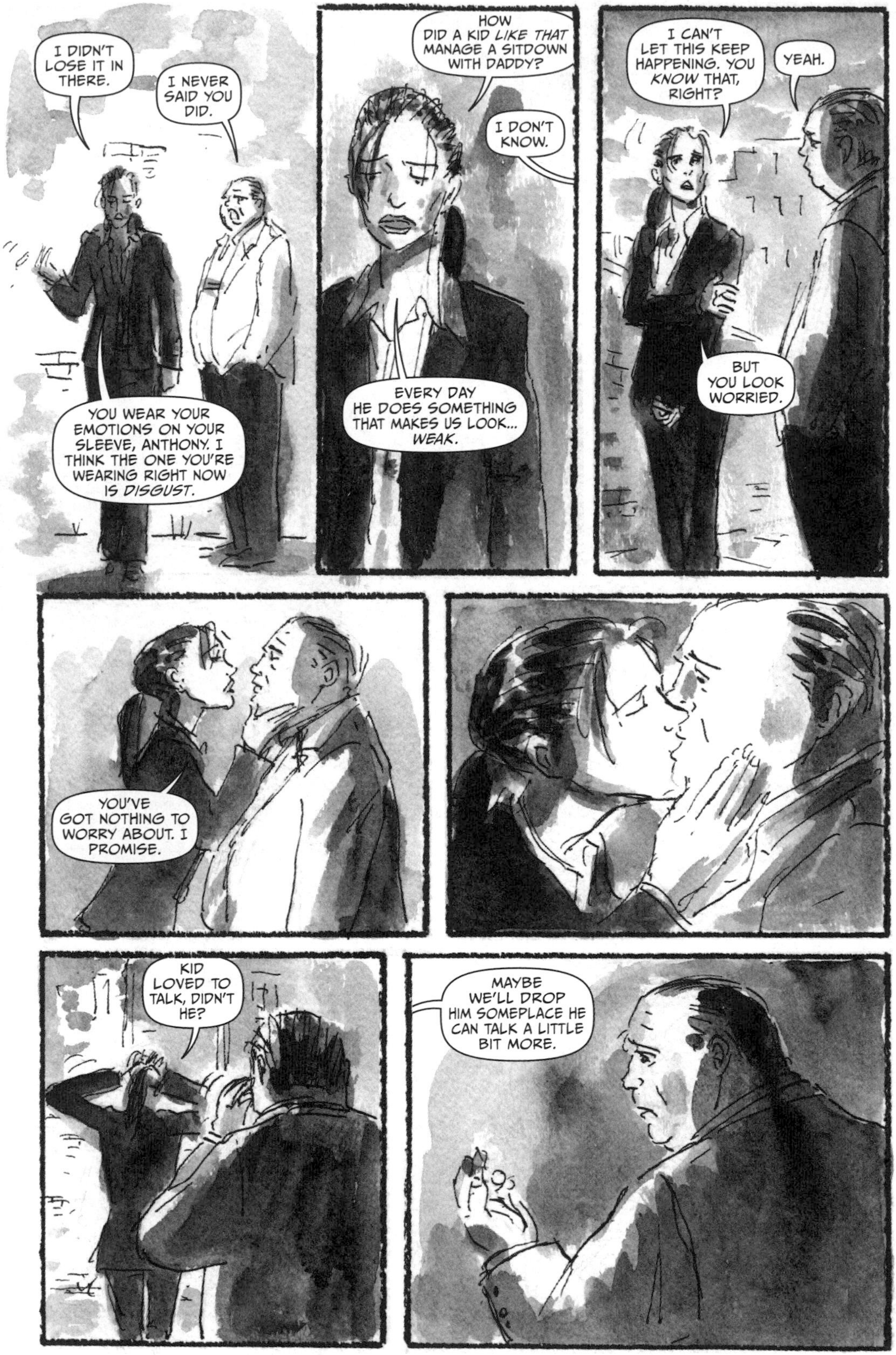
I DIDN'T LOSE IT IN THERE.
I NEVER SAID YOU DID.
YOU WEAR YOUR EMOTIONS ON YOUR SLEEVE, ANTHONY. I THINK THE ONE YOU'RE WEARING RIGHT NOW IS *DISGUST*.
HOW DID A KID *LIKE THAT* MANAGE A SITDOWN WITH DADDY?
I DON'T KNOW.
EVERY DAY HE DOES SOMETHING THAT MAKES US LOOK... *WEAK*.
I CAN'T LET THIS KEEP HAPPENING. YOU *KNOW* THAT, RIGHT?
YEAH.
BUT YOU LOOK WORRIED.
YOU'VE GOT NOTHING TO WORRY ABOUT. I PROMISE.
KID LOVED TO TALK, DIDN'T HE?
MAYBE WE'LL DROP HIM SOMEPLACE HE CAN TALK A LITTLE BIT MORE.

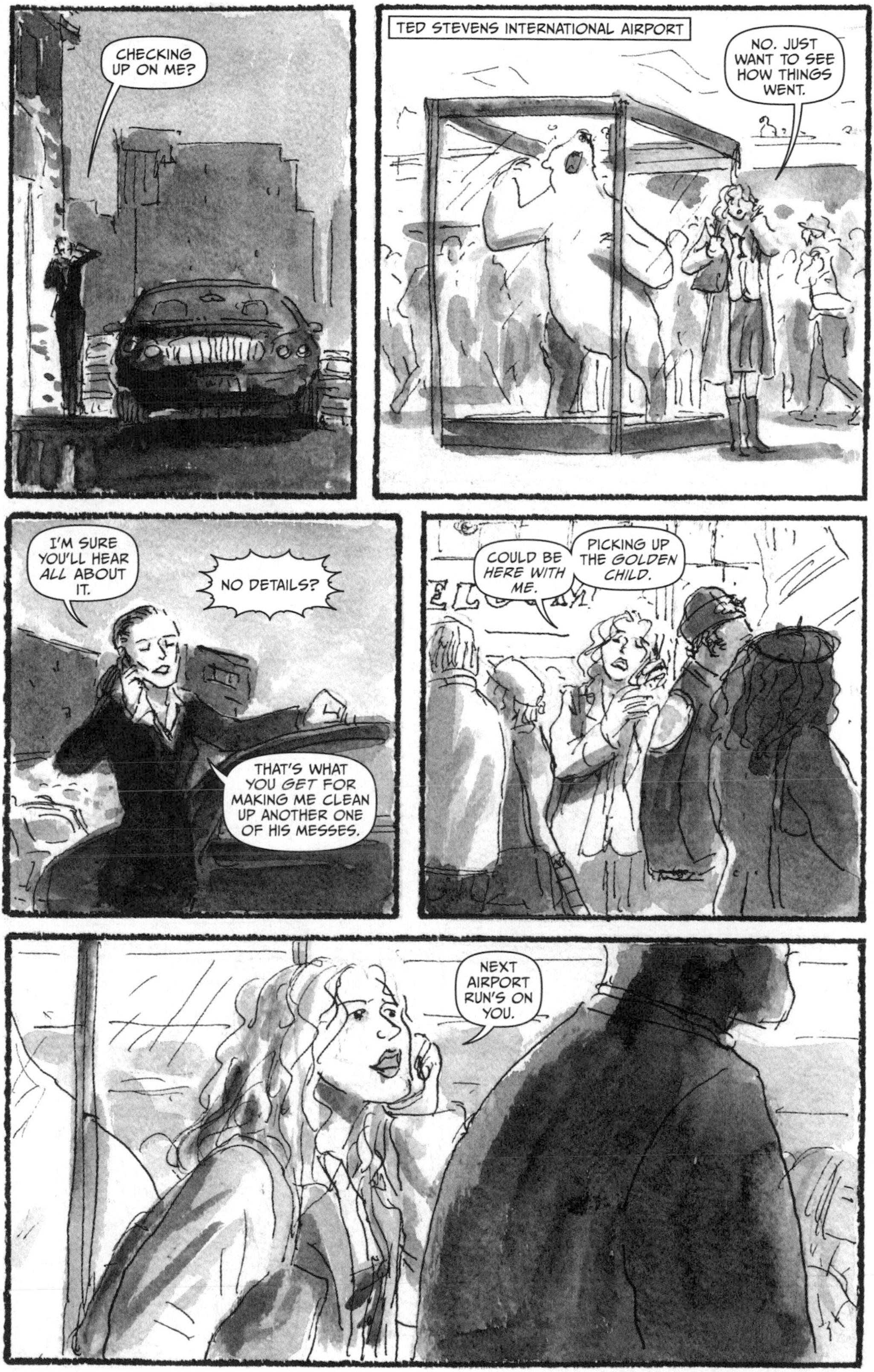
CHECKING UP ON ME?
TED STEVENS INTERNATIONAL AIRPORT
NO. JUST WANT TO SEE HOW THINGS WENT.
I'M SURE YOU'LL HEAR ALL ABOUT IT.
NO DETAILS?
THAT'S WHAT YOU GET FOR MAKING ME CLEAN UP ANOTHER ONE OF HIS MESSES.
PICKING UP THE GOLDEN CHILD.
COULD BE HERE WITH ME.
NEXT AIRPORT RUN'S ON YOU.

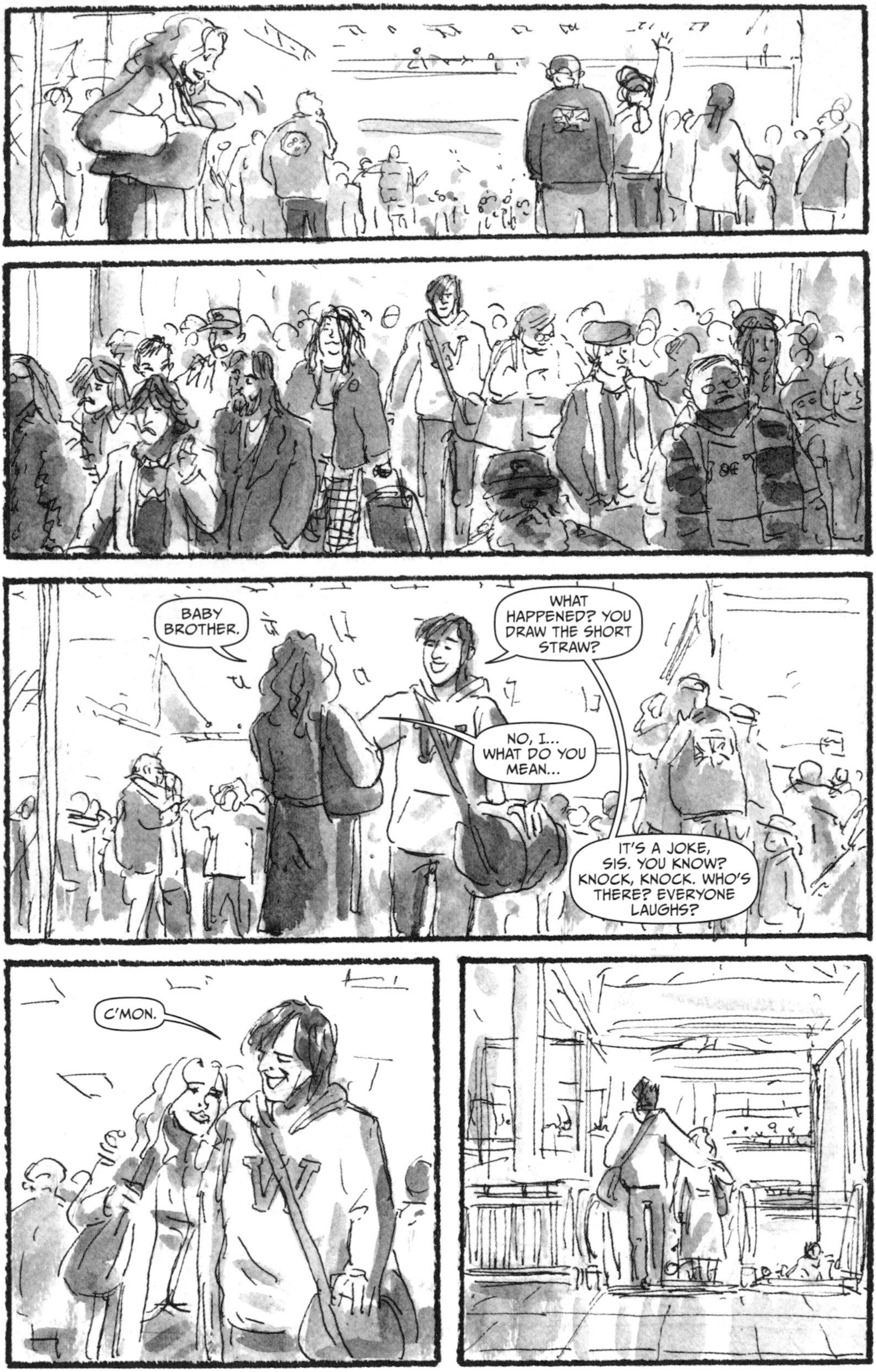
BABY BROTHER.
WHAT HAPPENED? YOU DRAW THE SHORT STRAW?
NO, I... WHAT DO YOU MEAN...
IT'S A JOKE, SIS. YOU KNOW? KNOCK, KNOCK. WHO'S THERE? EVERYONE LAUGHS?
C'MON.

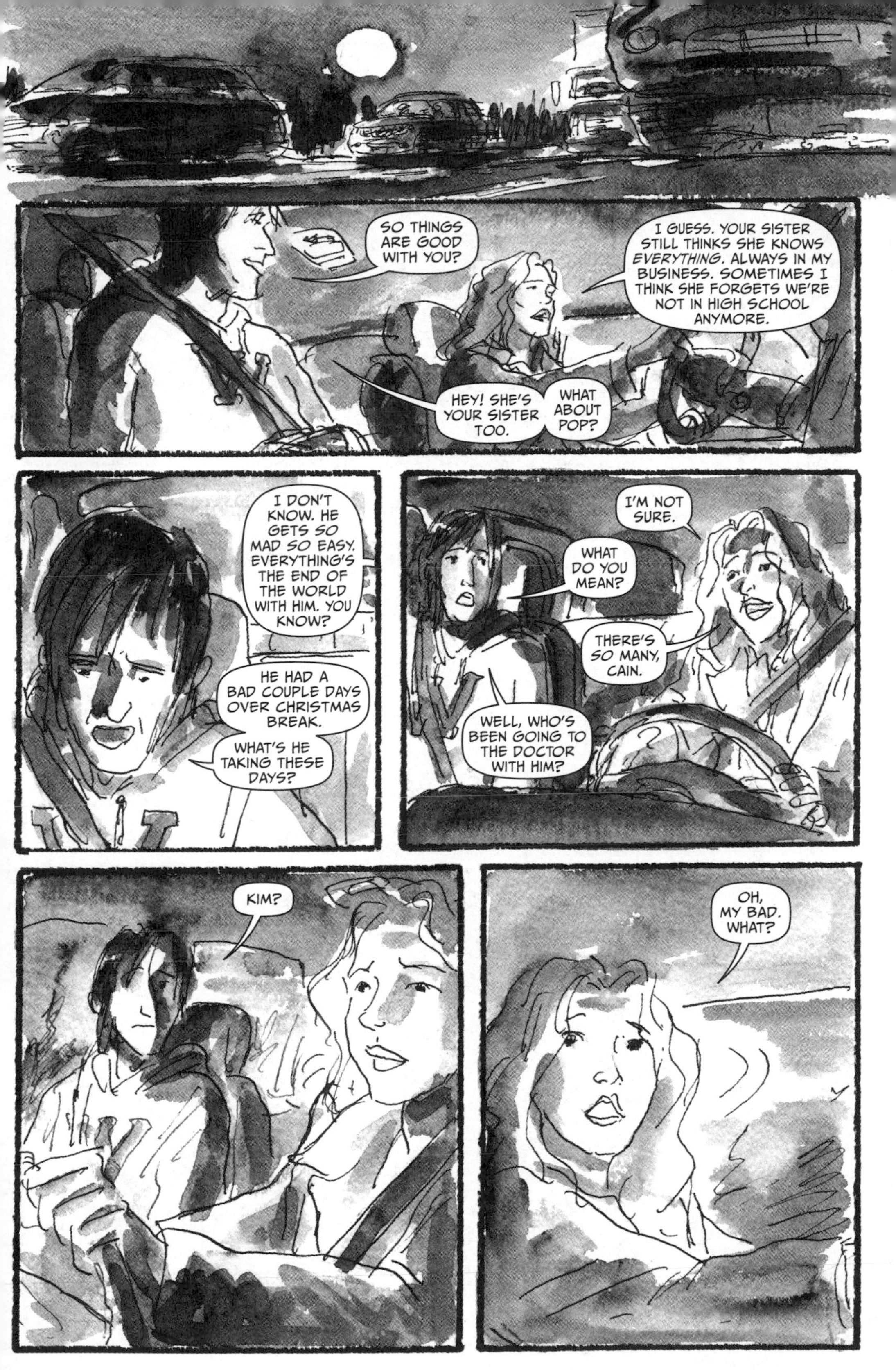
SO THINGS ARE GOOD WITH YOU?
I GUESS. YOUR SISTER STILL THINKS SHE KNOWS *EVERYTHING*. ALWAYS IN MY BUSINESS. SOMETIMES I THINK SHE FORGETS WE'RE NOT IN HIGH SCHOOL ANYMORE.
HEY! SHE'S YOUR SISTER TOO.
WHAT ABOUT POP?
I DON'T KNOW. HE GETS SO MAD *SO* EASY. EVERYTHING'S THE END OF THE WORLD WITH HIM. YOU KNOW?
HE HAD A BAD COUPLE DAYS OVER CHRISTMAS BREAK.
WHAT'S HE TAKING THESE DAYS?
I'M NOT SURE.
WHAT DO YOU MEAN?
THERE'S SO MANY, CAIN.
WELL, WHO'S BEEN GOING TO THE DOCTOR WITH HIM?
KIM?
OH, MY BAD. WHAT?

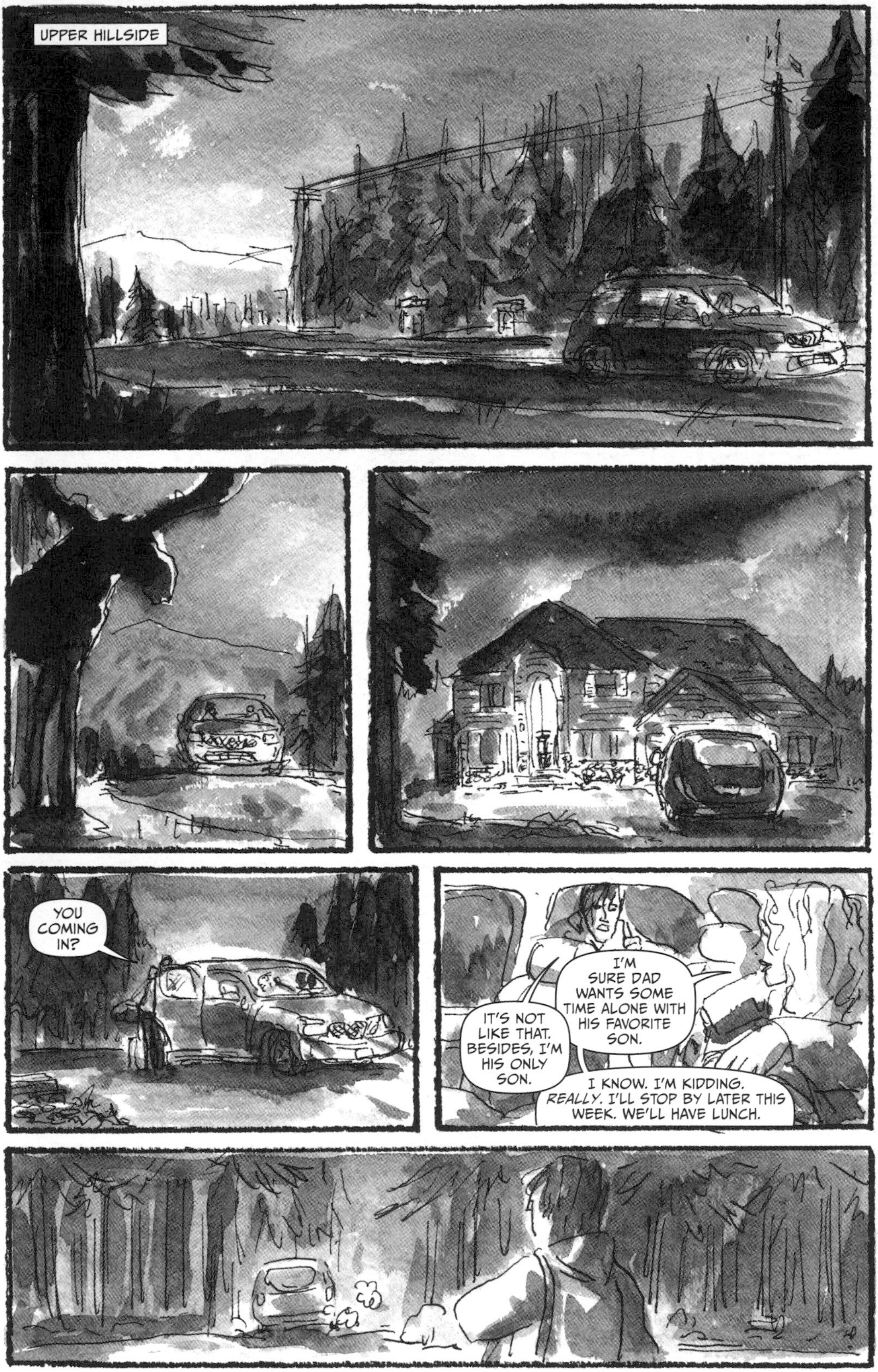
UPPER HILLSIDE
YOU COMING IN?
I'M SURE DAD WANTS SOME TIME ALONE WITH HIS FAVORITE SON.
IT'S NOT LIKE THAT. BESIDES, I'M HIS ONLY SON.
I KNOW. I'M KIDDING. *REALLY.* I'LL STOP BY LATER THIS WEEK. WE'LL HAVE LUNCH.

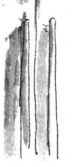

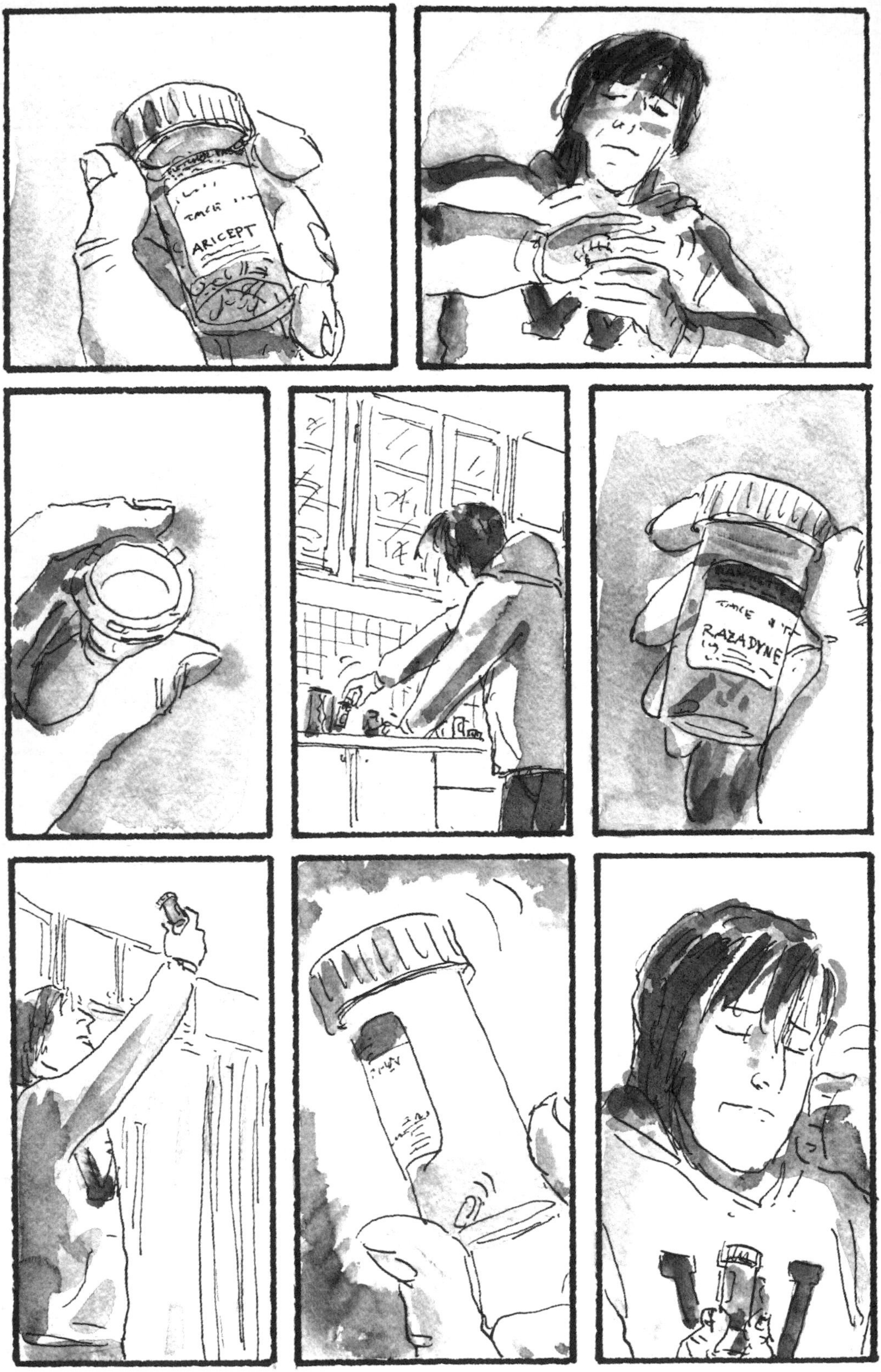
ARICEPT
RAZADYNE

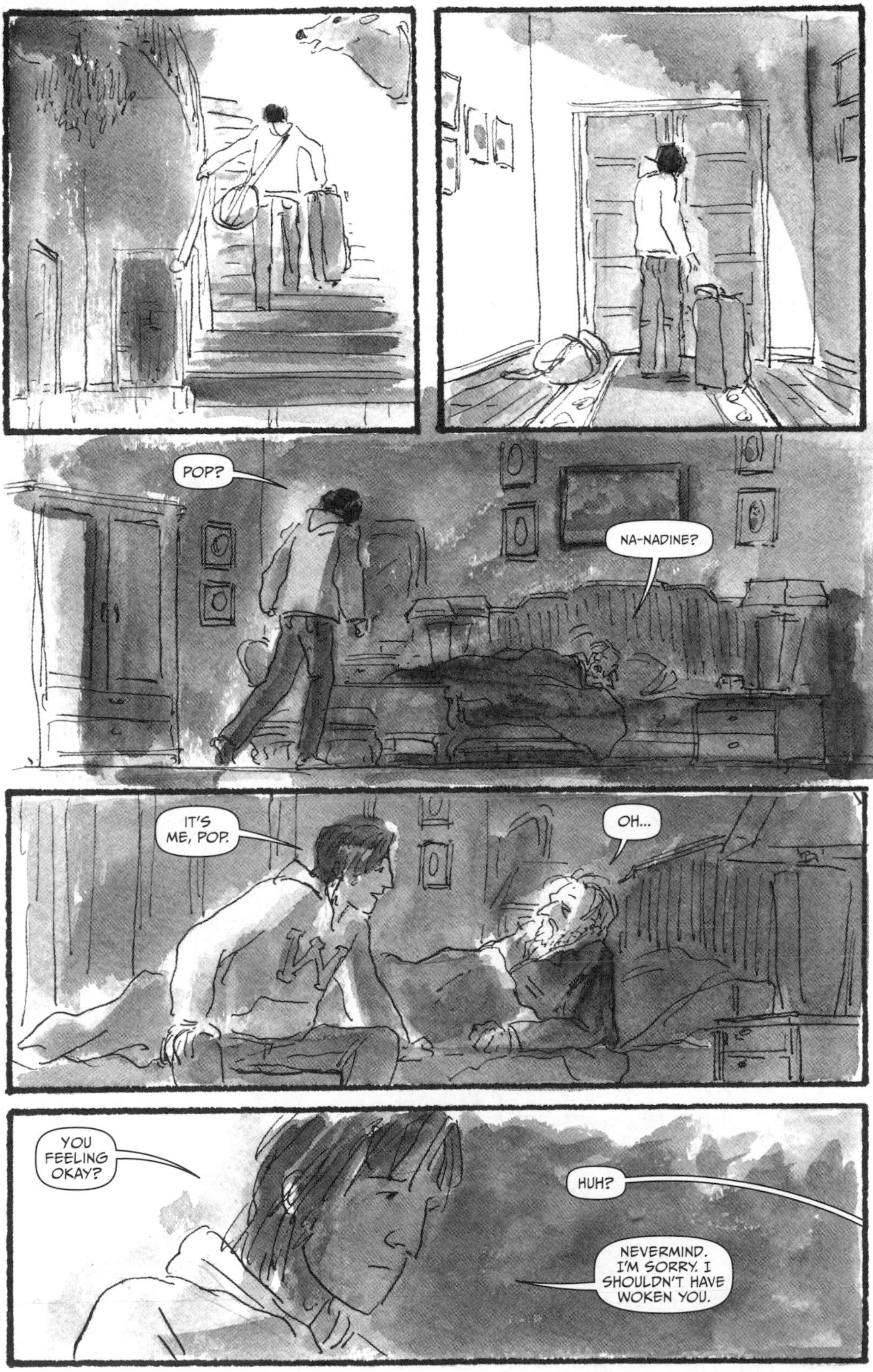
POP?
NA-NADINE?
IT'S ME, POP.
OH...
YOU FEELING OKAY?
HUH?
NEVERMIND. I'M SORRY. I SHOULDN'T HAVE WOKEN YOU.

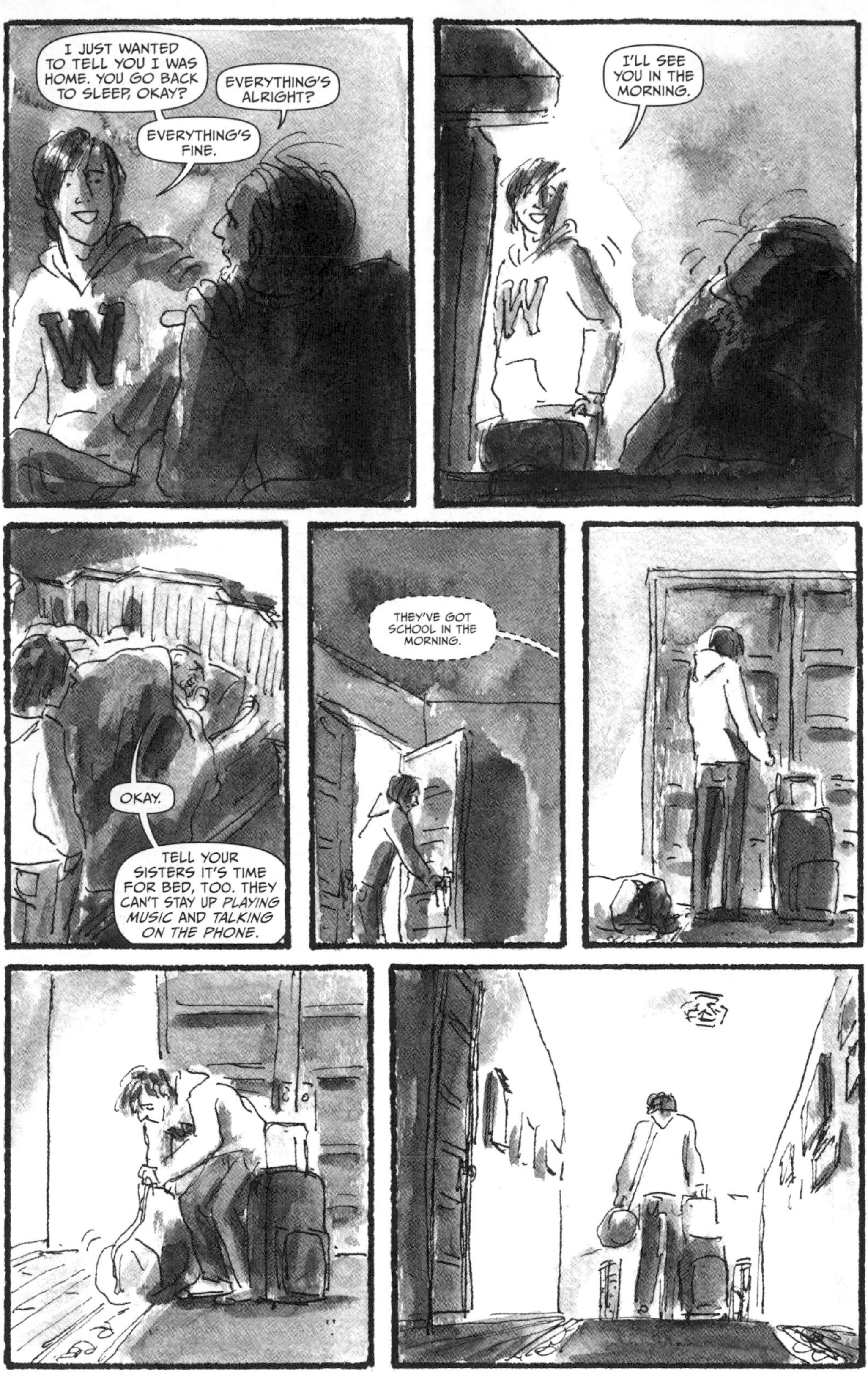
I JUST WANTED TO TELL YOU I WAS HOME. YOU GO BACK TO SLEEP, OKAY?
EVERYTHING'S ALRIGHT?
EVERYTHING'S FINE.
I'LL SEE YOU IN THE MORNING.
OKAY.
TELL YOUR SISTERS IT'S TIME FOR BED, TOO. THEY CAN'T STAY UP *PLAYING MUSIC* AND *TALKING ON THE PHONE.*
THEY'VE GOT SCHOOL IN THE MORNING.

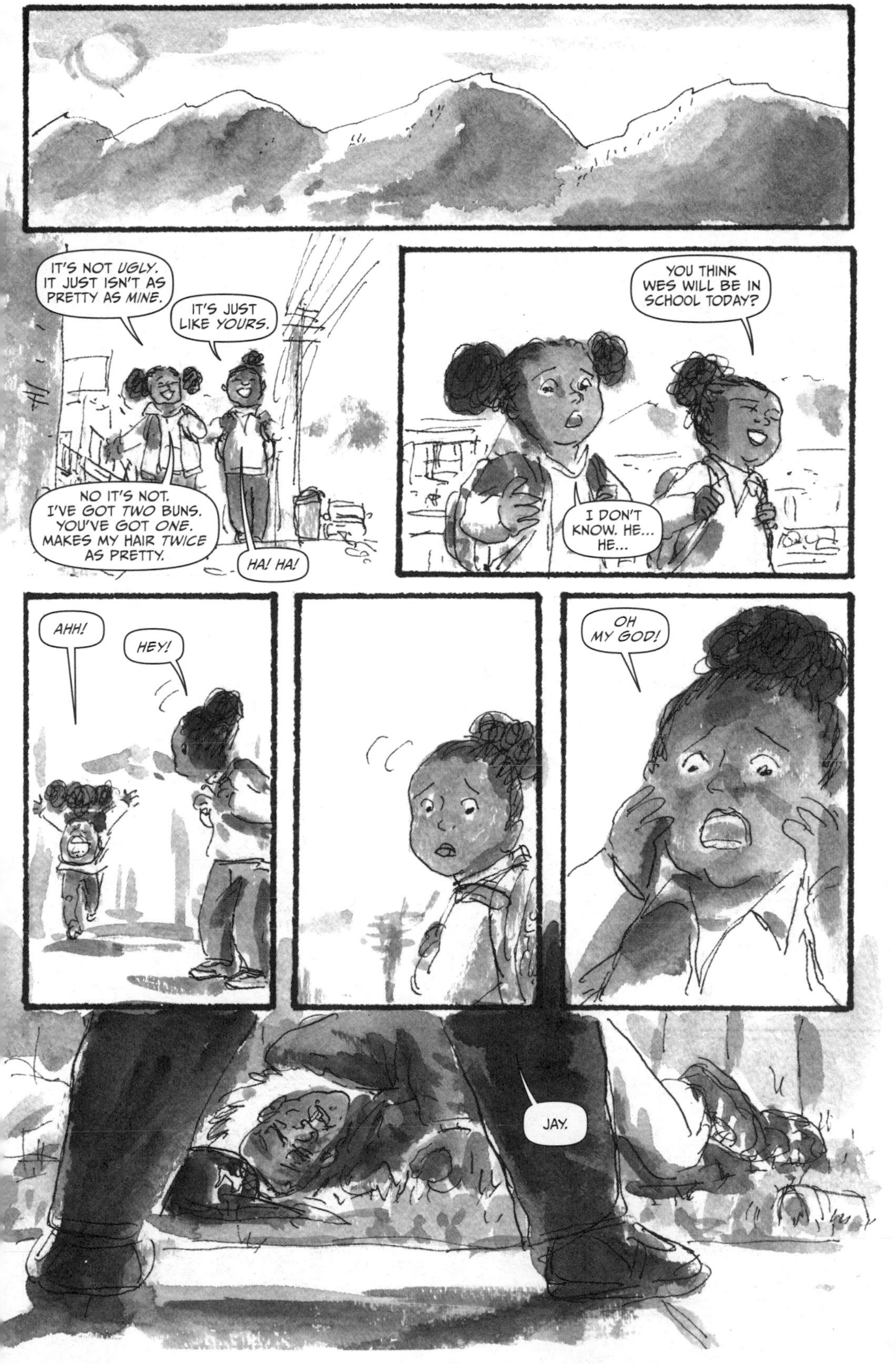
IT'S NOT UGLY. IT JUST ISN'T AS PRETTY AS MINE.
IT'S JUST LIKE YOURS.
NO IT'S NOT. I'VE GOT TWO BUNS. YOU'VE GOT ONE. MAKES MY HAIR TWICE AS PRETTY.
HA! HA!
YOU THINK WES WILL BE IN SCHOOL TODAY?
I DON'T KNOW. HE... HE...
AHH!
HEY!
OH MY GOD!
JAY.

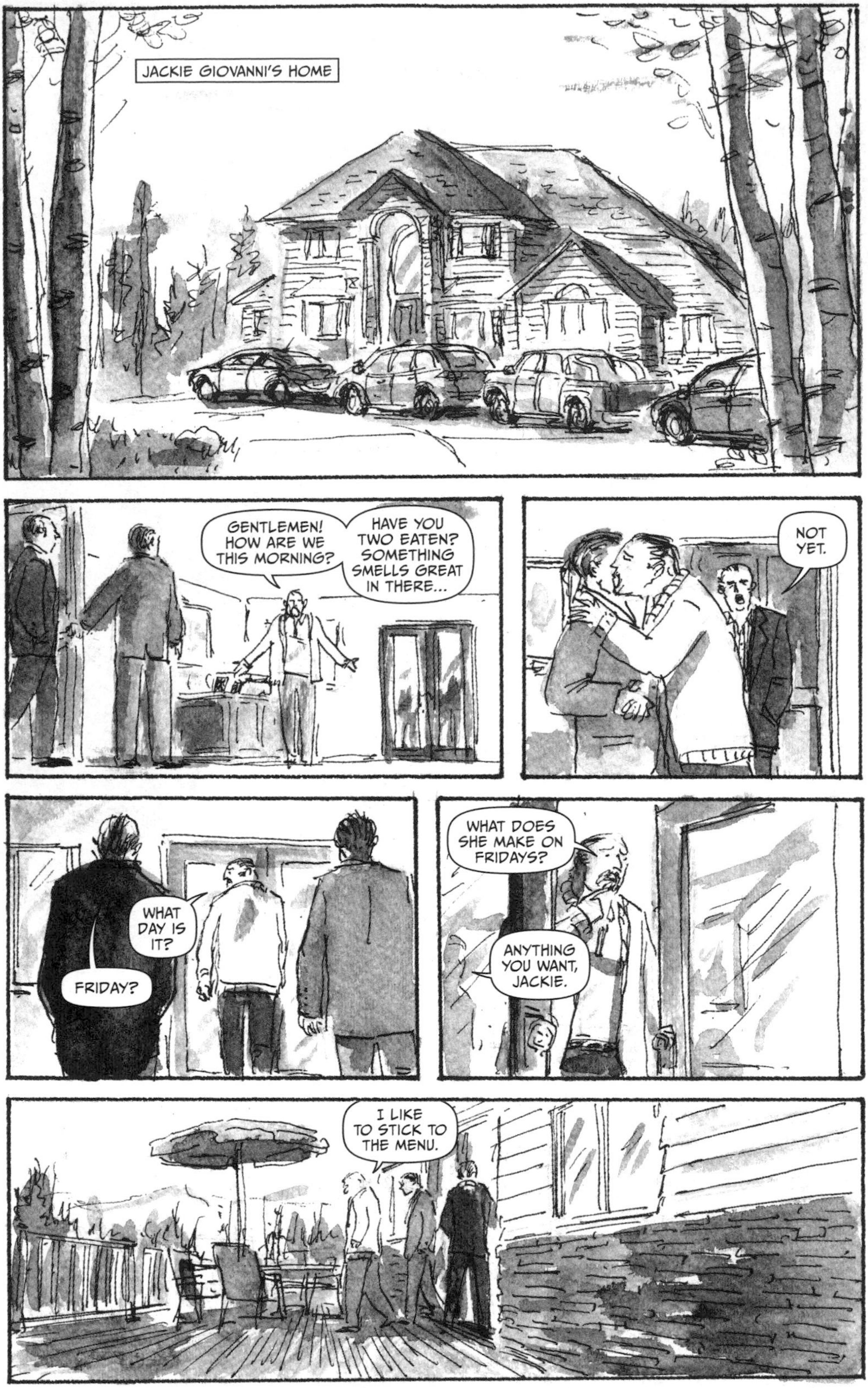
JACKIE GIOVANNI'S HOME
GENTLEMEN! HOW ARE WE THIS MORNING?
HAVE YOU TWO EATEN? SOMETHING SMELLS GREAT IN THERE...
NOT YET.
WHAT DAY IS IT?
FRIDAY?
WHAT DOES SHE MAKE ON FRIDAYS?
ANYTHING YOU WANT, JACKIE.
I LIKE TO STICK TO THE MENU.

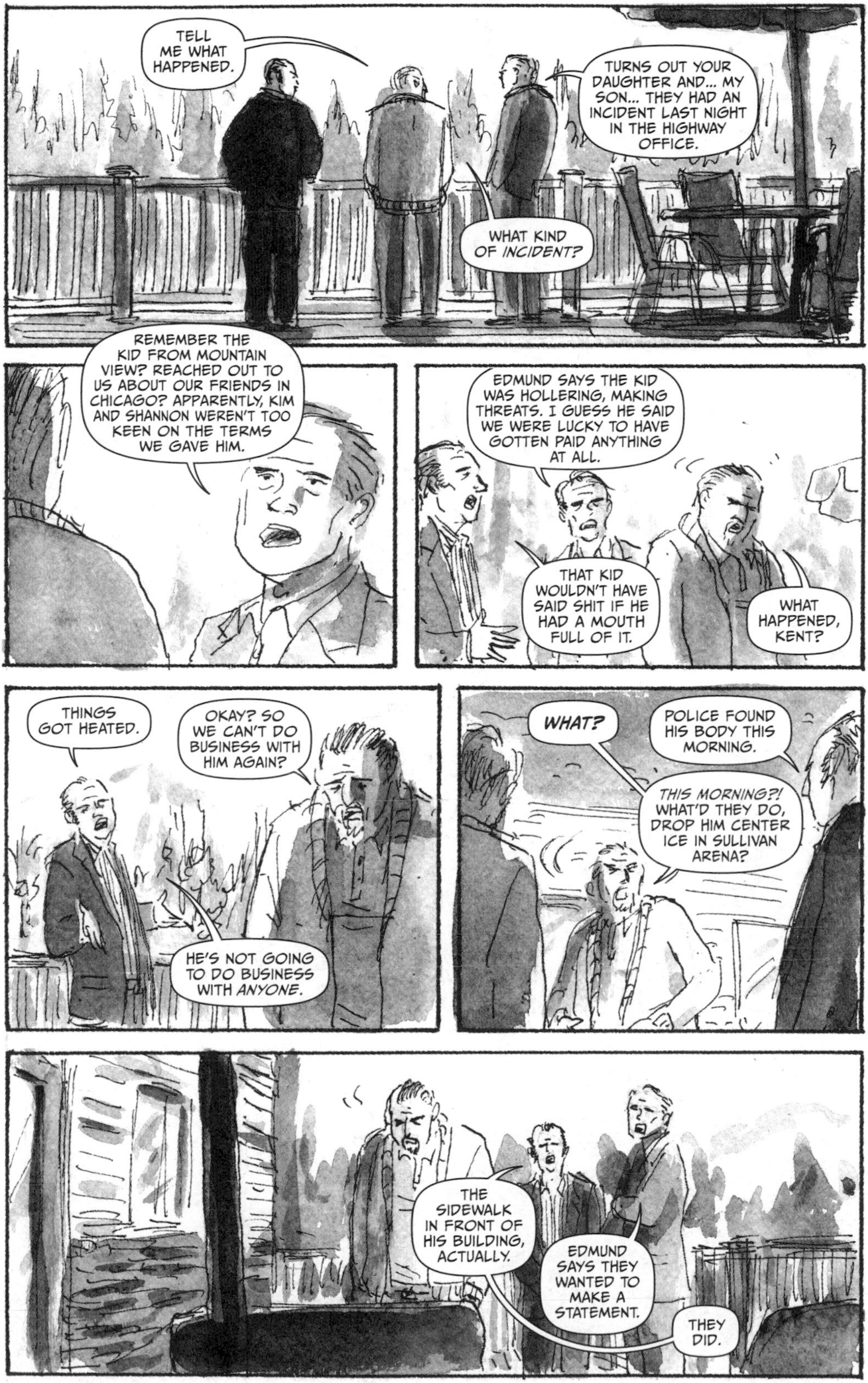
TELL ME WHAT HAPPENED.
TURNS OUT YOUR DAUGHTER AND... MY SON... THEY HAD AN INCIDENT LAST NIGHT IN THE HIGHWAY OFFICE.
WHAT KIND OF *INCIDENT?*
REMEMBER THE KID FROM MOUNTAIN VIEW? REACHED OUT TO US ABOUT OUR FRIENDS IN CHICAGO? APPARENTLY, KIM AND SHANNON WEREN'T TOO KEEN ON THE TERMS WE GAVE HIM.
EDMUND SAYS THE KID WAS HOLLERING, MAKING THREATS. I GUESS HE SAID WE WERE LUCKY TO HAVE GOTTEN PAID ANYTHING AT ALL.
THAT KID WOULDN'T HAVE SAID SHIT IF HE HAD A MOUTH FULL OF IT.
WHAT HAPPENED, KENT?
THINGS GOT HEATED.
OKAY? SO WE CAN'T DO BUSINESS WITH HIM AGAIN?
HE'S NOT GOING TO DO BUSINESS WITH *ANYONE*.
WHAT?
POLICE FOUND HIS BODY THIS MORNING.
THIS MORNING?! WHAT'D THEY DO, DROP HIM CENTER ICE IN SULLIVAN ARENA?
THE SIDEWALK IN FRONT OF HIS BUILDING, ACTUALLY.
EDMUND SAYS THEY WANTED TO MAKE A STATEMENT.
THEY DID.

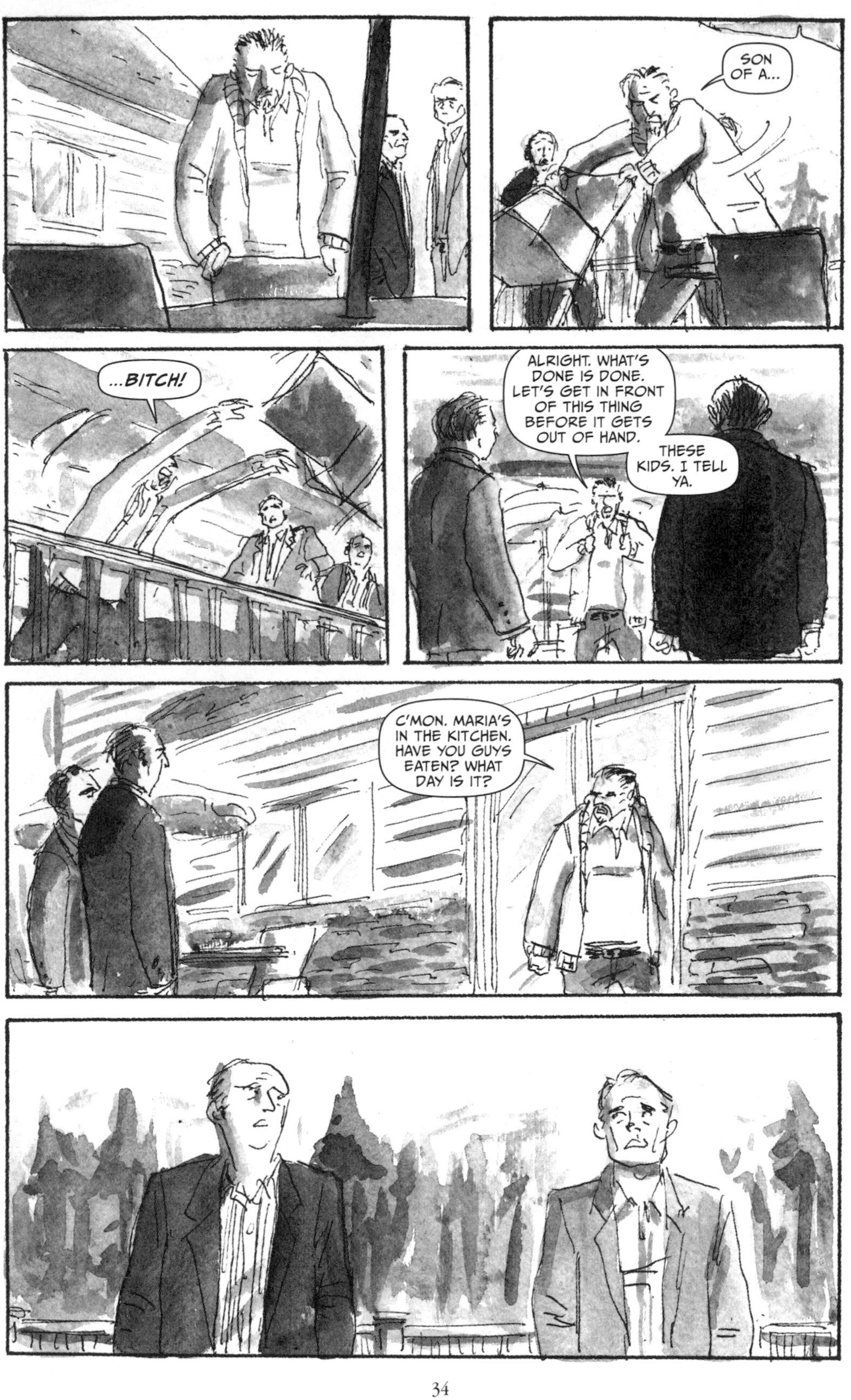
SON OF A...
...BITCH!
ALRIGHT. WHAT'S DONE IS DONE. LET'S GET IN FRONT OF THIS THING BEFORE IT GETS OUT OF HAND.
THESE KIDS. I TELL YA.
C'MON. MARIA'S IN THE KITCHEN. HAVE YOU GUYS EATEN? WHAT DAY IS IT?

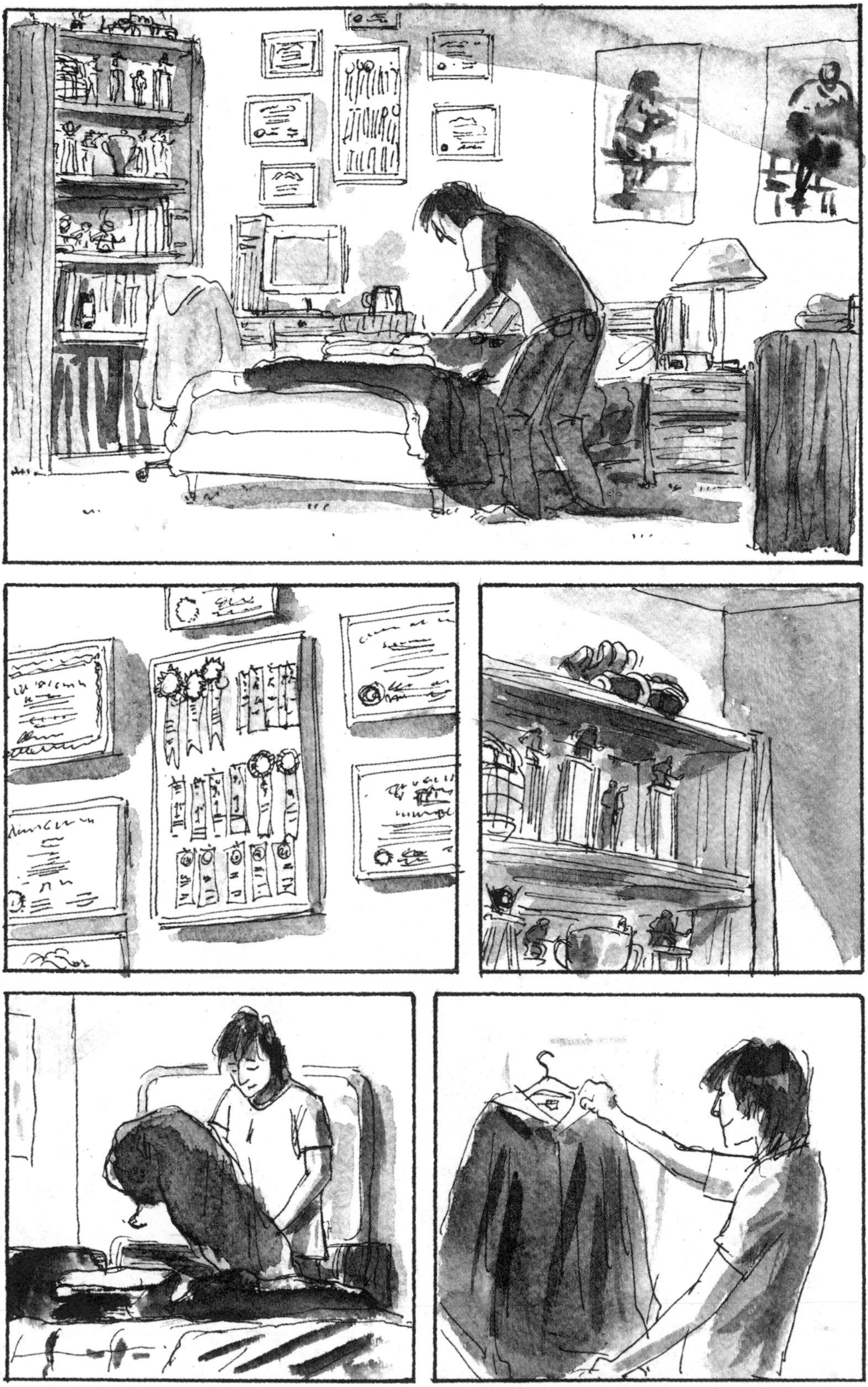

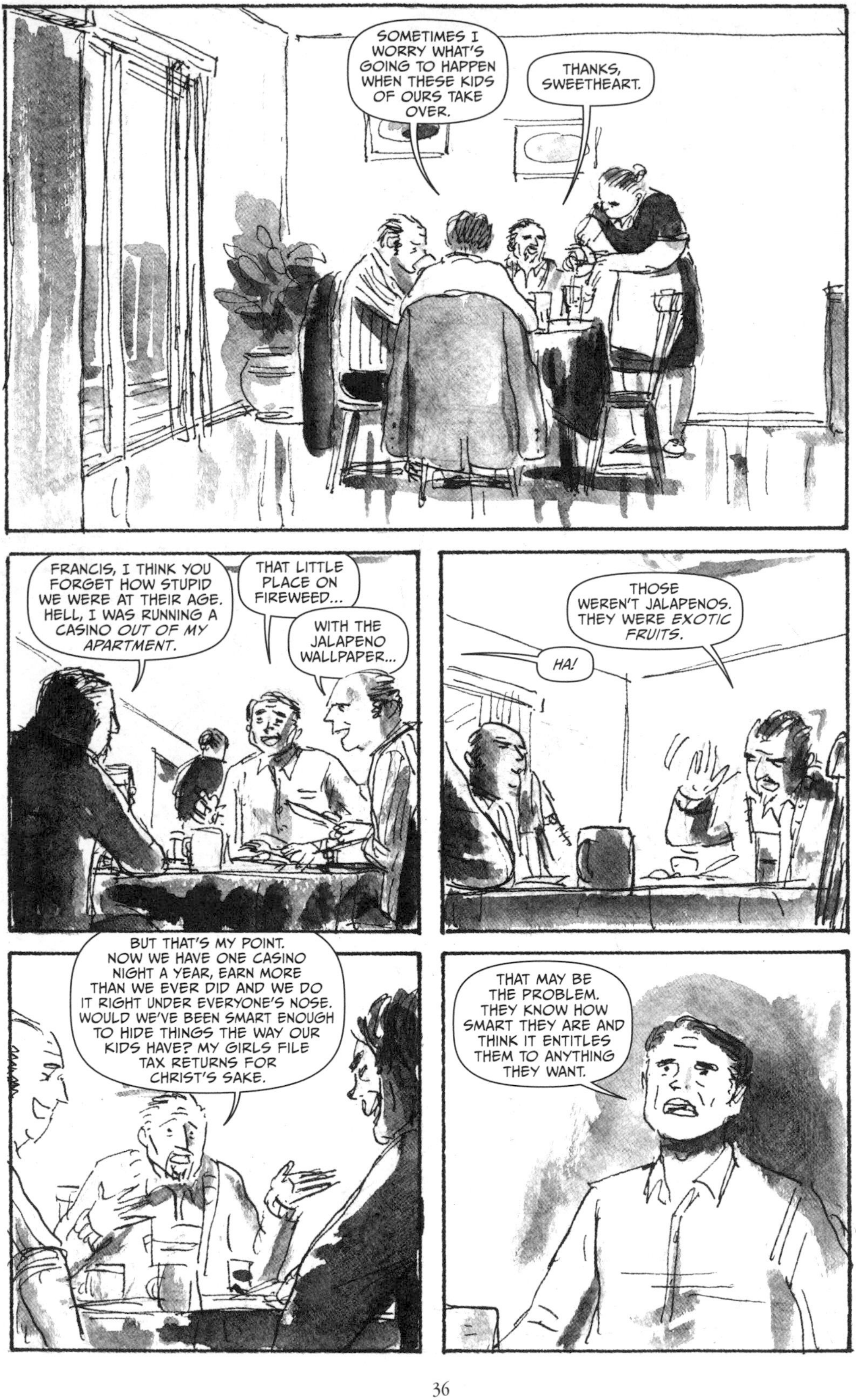
SOMETIMES I WORRY WHAT'S GOING TO HAPPEN WHEN THESE KIDS OF OURS TAKE OVER.
THANKS, SWEETHEART.
FRANCIS, I THINK YOU FORGET HOW STUPID WE WERE AT THEIR AGE. HELL, I WAS RUNNING A CASINO *OUT OF MY APARTMENT*.
THAT LITTLE PLACE ON FIREWEED...
WITH THE JALAPENO WALLPAPER...
THOSE WEREN'T JALAPENOS. THEY WERE *EXOTIC FRUITS*.
HA!
BUT THAT'S MY POINT. NOW WE HAVE ONE CASINO NIGHT A YEAR, EARN MORE THAN WE EVER DID AND WE DO IT RIGHT UNDER EVERYONE'S NOSE. WOULD WE'VE BEEN SMART ENOUGH TO HIDE THINGS THE WAY OUR KIDS HAVE? MY GIRLS FILE TAX RETURNS FOR CHRIST'S SAKE.
THAT MAY BE THE PROBLEM. THEY KNOW HOW SMART THEY ARE AND THINK IT ENTITLES THEM TO ANYTHING THEY WANT.

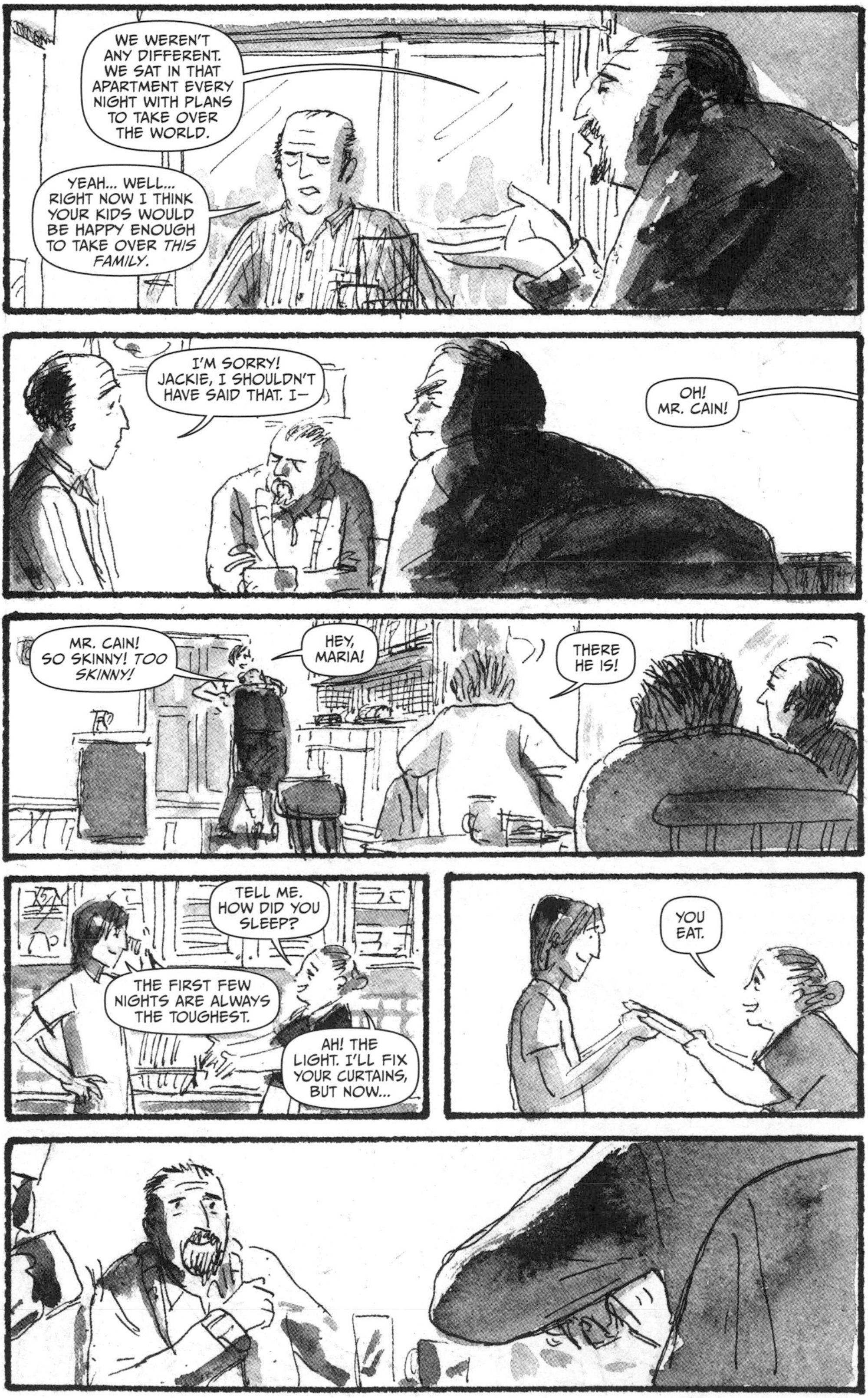
WE WEREN'T ANY DIFFERENT. WE SAT IN THAT APARTMENT EVERY NIGHT WITH PLANS TO TAKE OVER THE WORLD.
YEAH... WELL... RIGHT NOW I THINK YOUR KIDS WOULD BE HAPPY ENOUGH TO TAKE OVER *THIS FAMILY*.
I'M SORRY! JACKIE, I SHOULDN'T HAVE SAID THAT. I—
OH! MR. CAIN!
MR. CAIN! SO SKINNY! *TOO SKINNY!*
HEY, MARIA!
THERE HE IS!
TELL ME. HOW DID YOU SLEEP?
THE FIRST FEW NIGHTS ARE ALWAYS THE TOUGHEST.
AH! THE LIGHT. I'LL FIX YOUR CURTAINS, BUT NOW...
YOU EAT.

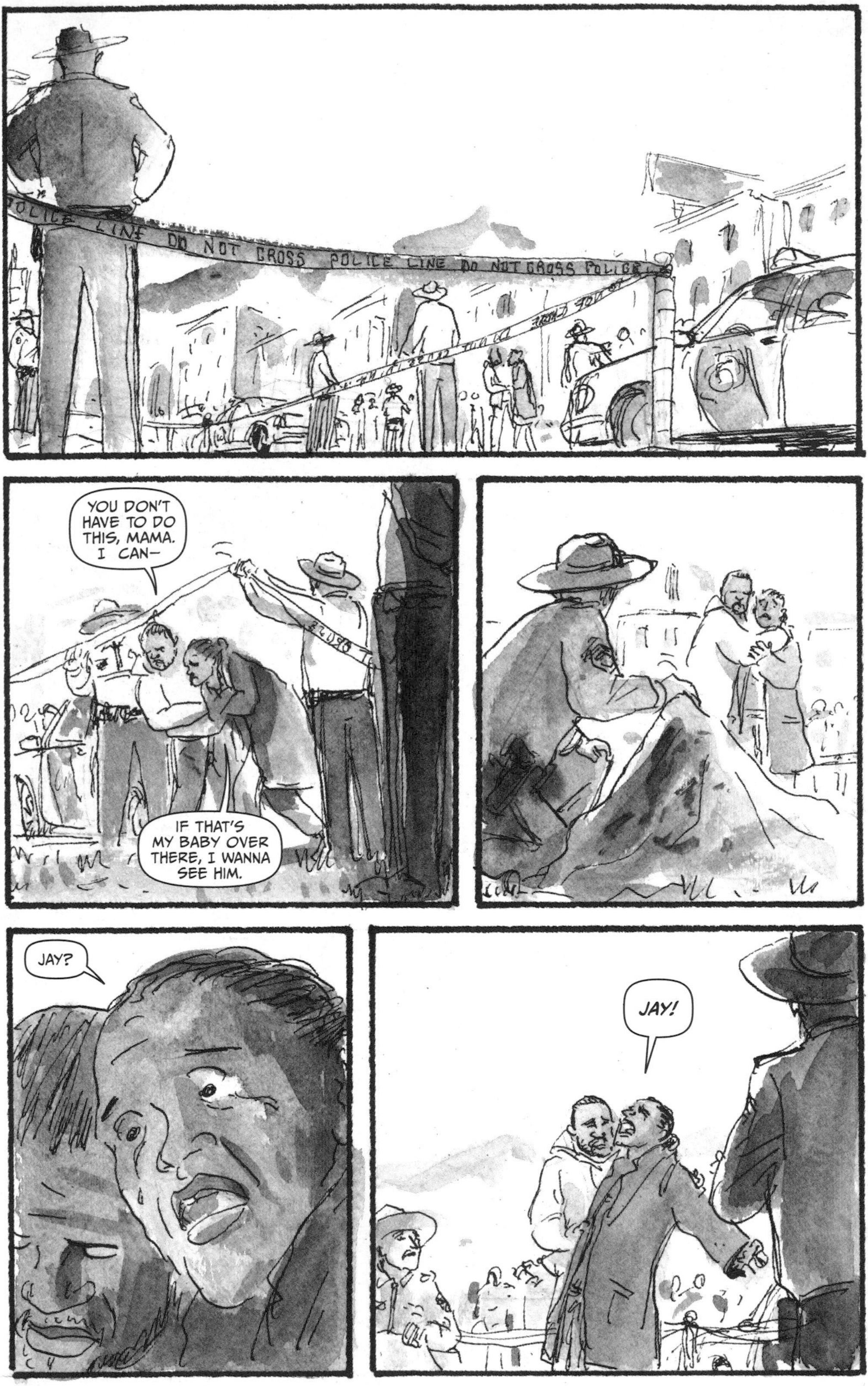
POLICE LINE DO NOT CROSS POLICE LINE DO NOT CROSS POLICE
YOU DON'T HAVE TO DO THIS, MAMA. I CAN—
IF THAT'S MY BABY OVER THERE, I WANNA SEE HIM.
JAY?
JAY!

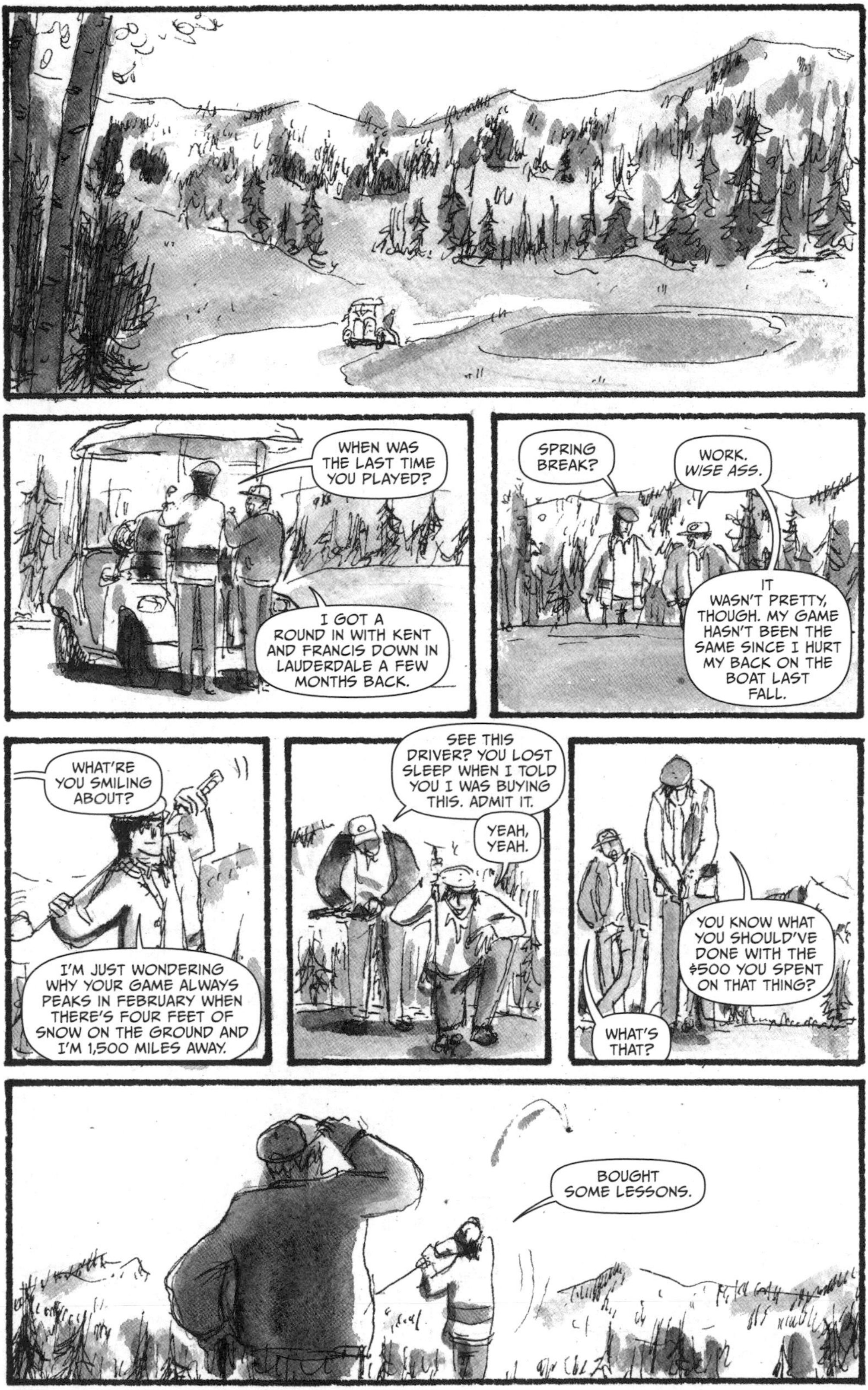
WHEN WAS THE LAST TIME YOU PLAYED?
I GOT A ROUND IN WITH KENT AND FRANCIS DOWN IN LAUDERDALE A FEW MONTHS BACK.
SPRING BREAK?
WORK. WISE ASS.
IT WASN'T PRETTY, THOUGH. MY GAME HASN'T BEEN THE SAME SINCE I HURT MY BACK ON THE BOAT LAST FALL.
WHAT'RE YOU SMILING ABOUT?
I'M JUST WONDERING WHY YOUR GAME ALWAYS PEAKS IN FEBRUARY WHEN THERE'S FOUR FEET OF SNOW ON THE GROUND AND I'M 1,500 MILES AWAY.
SEE THIS DRIVER? YOU LOST SLEEP WHEN I TOLD YOU I WAS BUYING THIS. ADMIT IT.
YEAH, YEAH.
YOU KNOW WHAT YOU SHOULD'VE DONE WITH THE $500 YOU SPENT ON THAT THING?
WHAT'S THAT?
BOUGHT SOME LESSONS.

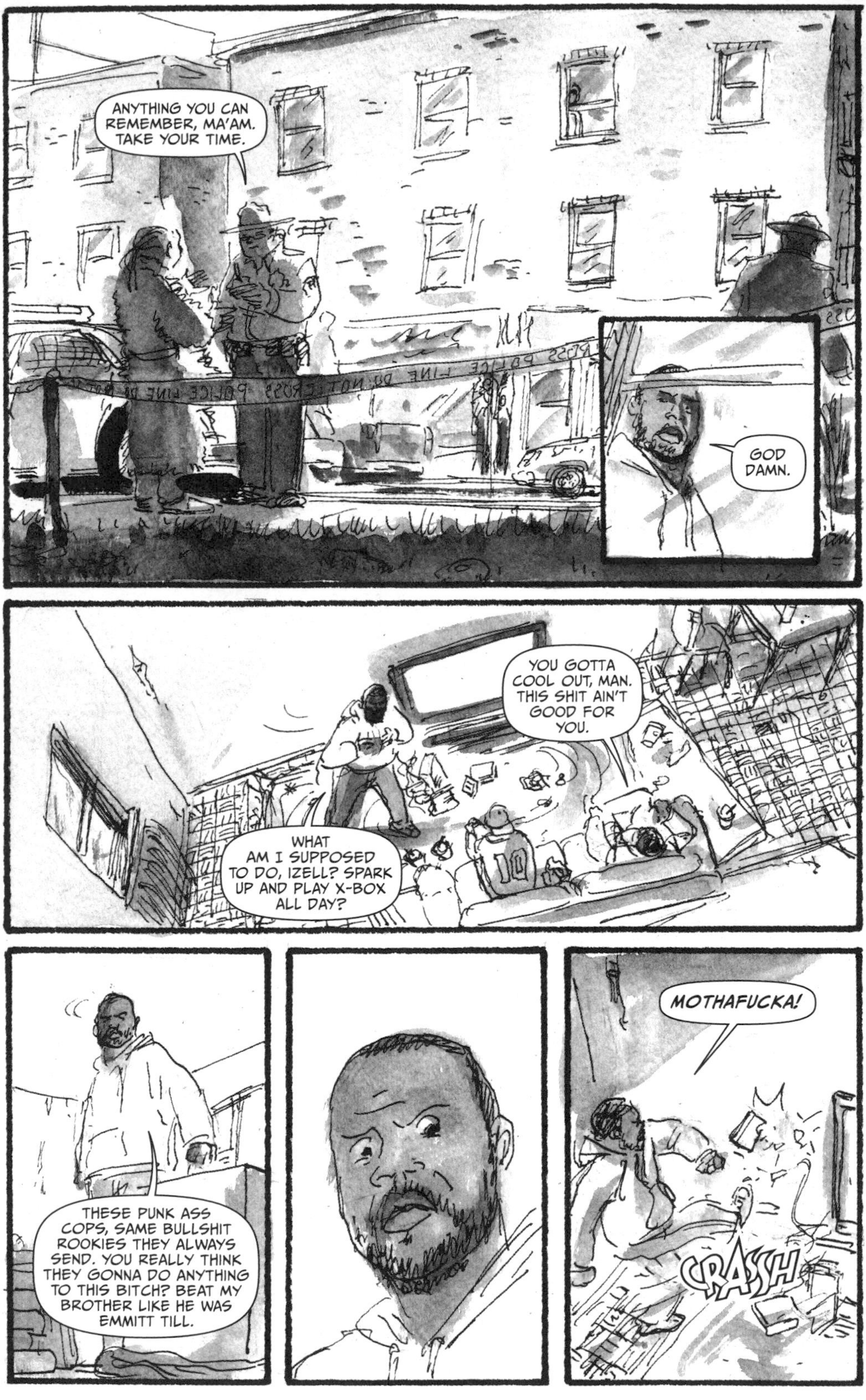
ANYTHING YOU CAN REMEMBER, MA'AM. TAKE YOUR TIME.
GOD DAMN.
YOU GOTTA COOL OUT, MAN. THIS SHIT AIN'T GOOD FOR YOU.
WHAT AM I SUPPOSED TO DO, IZELL? SPARK UP AND PLAY X-BOX ALL DAY?
THESE PUNK ASS COPS, SAME BULLSHIT ROOKIES THEY ALWAYS SEND. YOU REALLY THINK THEY GONNA DO ANYTHING TO THIS BITCH? BEAT MY BROTHER LIKE HE WAS EMMITT TILL.
MOTHAFUCKA!
CRASH

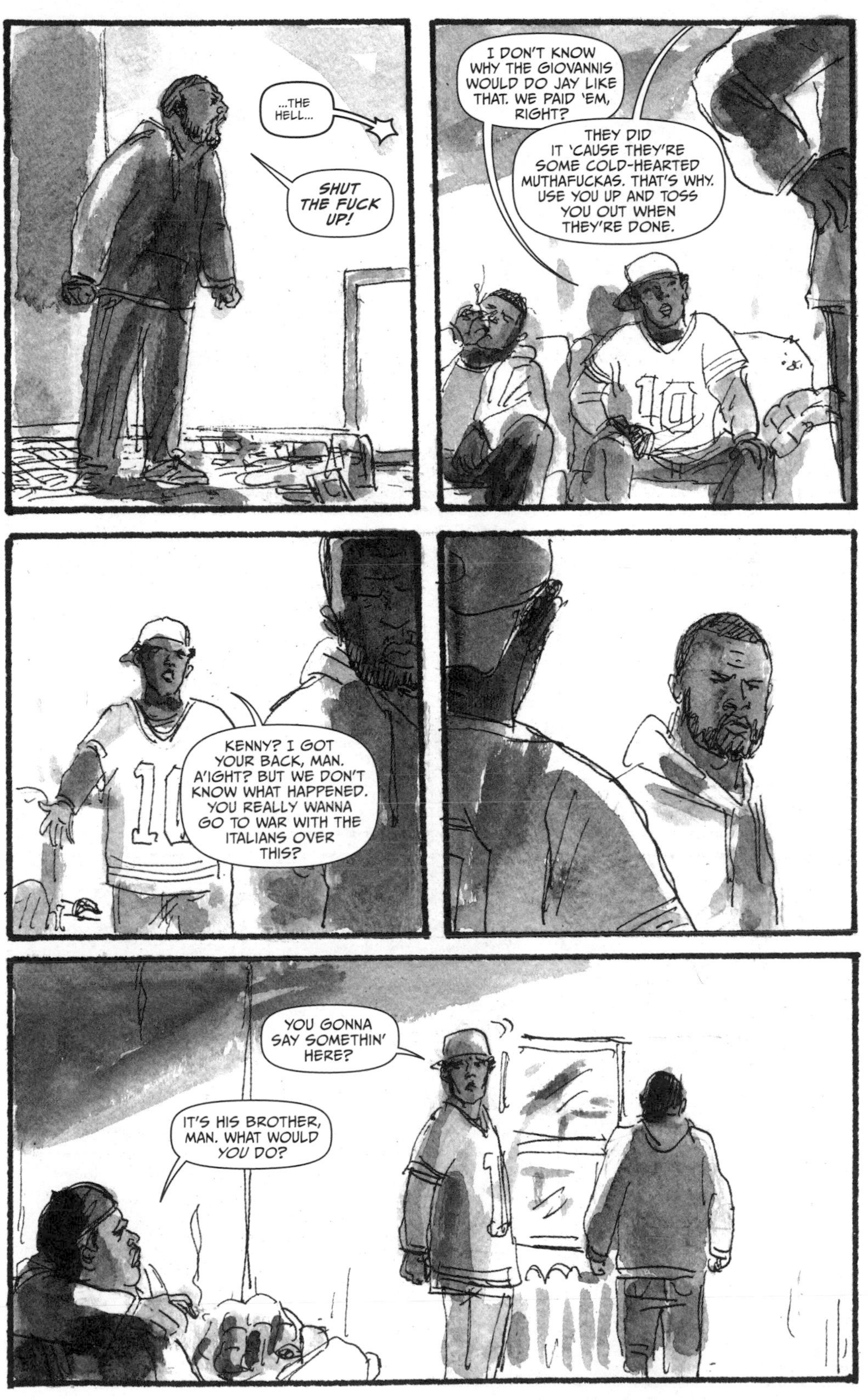

...THE HELL...
SHUT THE FUCK UP!
I DON'T KNOW WHY THE GIOVANNIS WOULD DO JAY LIKE THAT. WE PAID 'EM, RIGHT?
THEY DID IT 'CAUSE THEY'RE SOME COLD-HEARTED MUTHAFUCKAS. THAT'S WHY. USE YOU UP AND TOSS YOU OUT WHEN THEY'RE DONE.
KENNY? I GOT YOUR BACK, MAN. A'IGHT? BUT WE DON'T KNOW WHAT HAPPENED. YOU REALLY WANNA GO TO WAR WITH THE ITALIANS OVER THIS?
YOU GONNA SAY SOMETHIN' HERE?
IT'S HIS BROTHER, MAN. WHAT WOULD YOU DO?

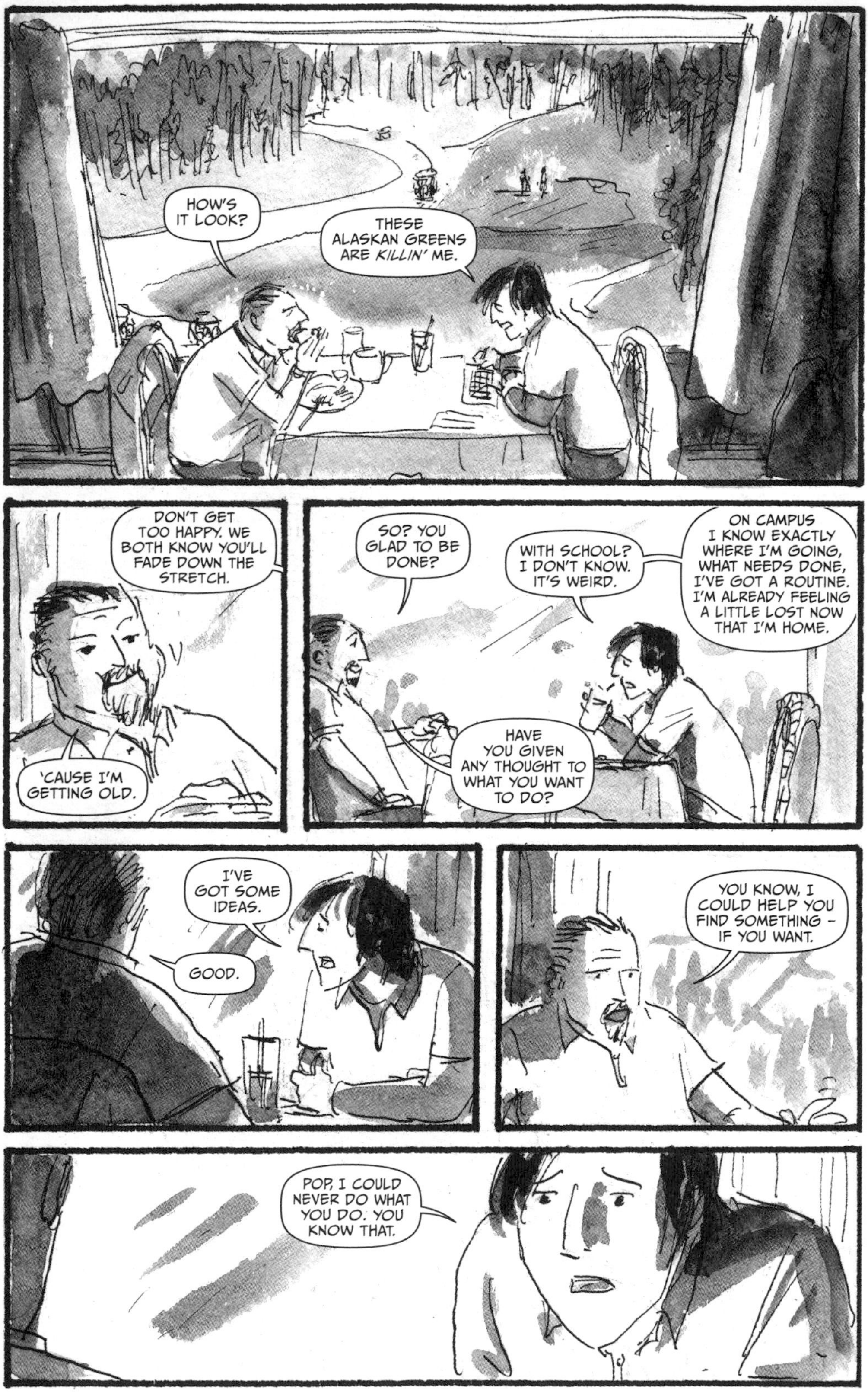
HOW'S IT LOOK?
THESE ALASKAN GREENS ARE *KILLIN'* ME.
DON'T GET TOO HAPPY. WE BOTH KNOW YOU'LL FADE DOWN THE STRETCH.
'CAUSE I'M GETTING OLD.
SO? YOU GLAD TO BE DONE?
WITH SCHOOL? I DON'T KNOW. IT'S WEIRD.
ON CAMPUS I KNOW EXACTLY WHERE I'M GOING, WHAT NEEDS DONE, I'VE GOT A ROUTINE. I'M ALREADY FEELING A LITTLE LOST NOW THAT I'M HOME.
HAVE YOU GIVEN ANY THOUGHT TO WHAT YOU WANT TO DO?
I'VE GOT SOME IDEAS.
GOOD.
YOU KNOW, I COULD HELP YOU FIND SOMETHING – IF YOU WANT.
POP, I COULD NEVER DO WHAT YOU DO. YOU KNOW THAT.

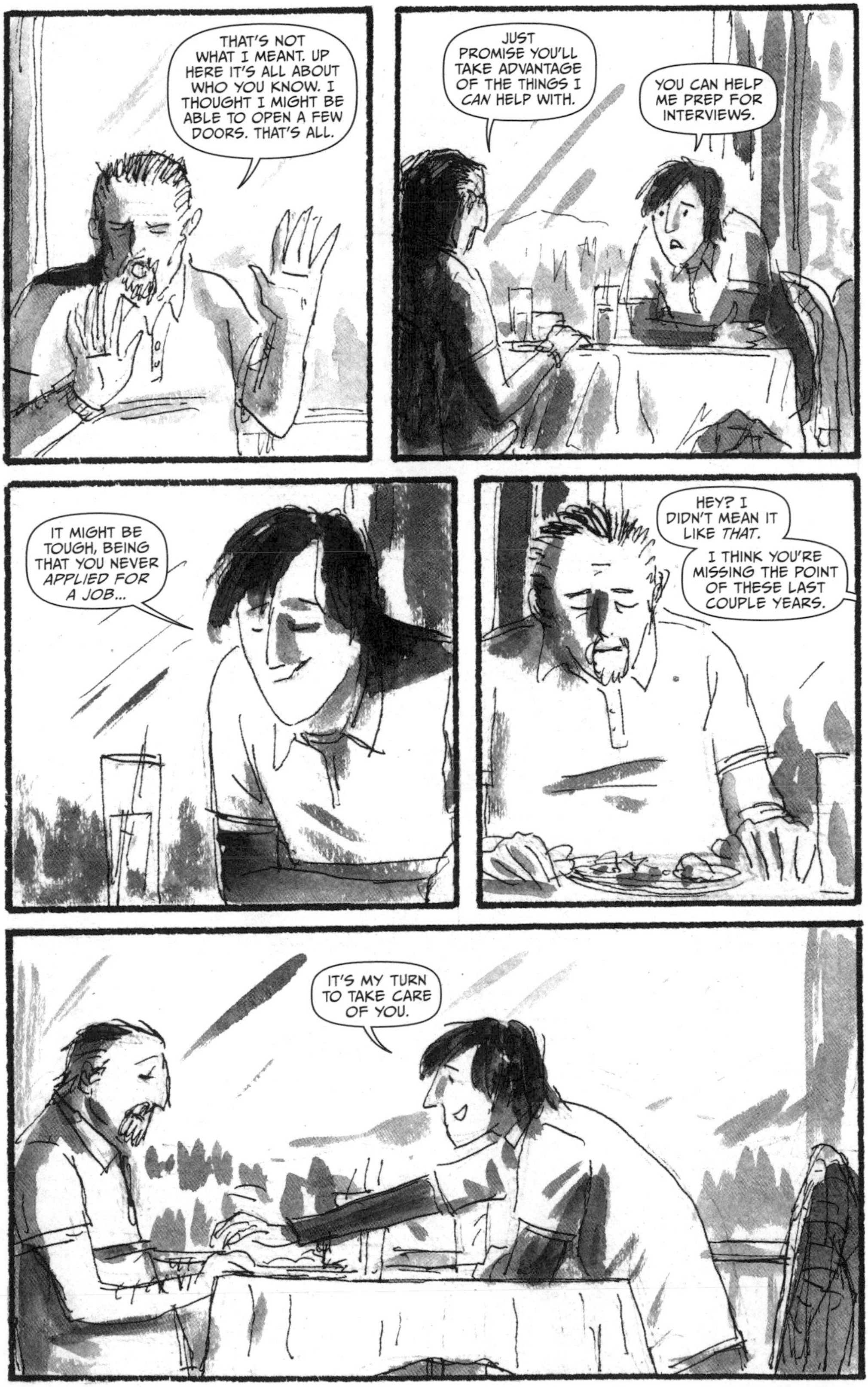
THAT'S NOT WHAT I MEANT. UP HERE IT'S ALL ABOUT WHO YOU KNOW. I THOUGHT I MIGHT BE ABLE TO OPEN A FEW DOORS. THAT'S ALL.
JUST PROMISE YOU'LL TAKE ADVANTAGE OF THE THINGS I *CAN* HELP WITH.
YOU CAN HELP ME PREP FOR INTERVIEWS.
IT MIGHT BE TOUGH, BEING THAT YOU NEVER *APPLIED FOR A JOB*...
HEY? I DIDN'T MEAN IT LIKE *THAT*.
I THINK YOU'RE MISSING THE POINT OF THESE LAST COUPLE YEARS.
IT'S MY TURN TO TAKE CARE OF YOU.

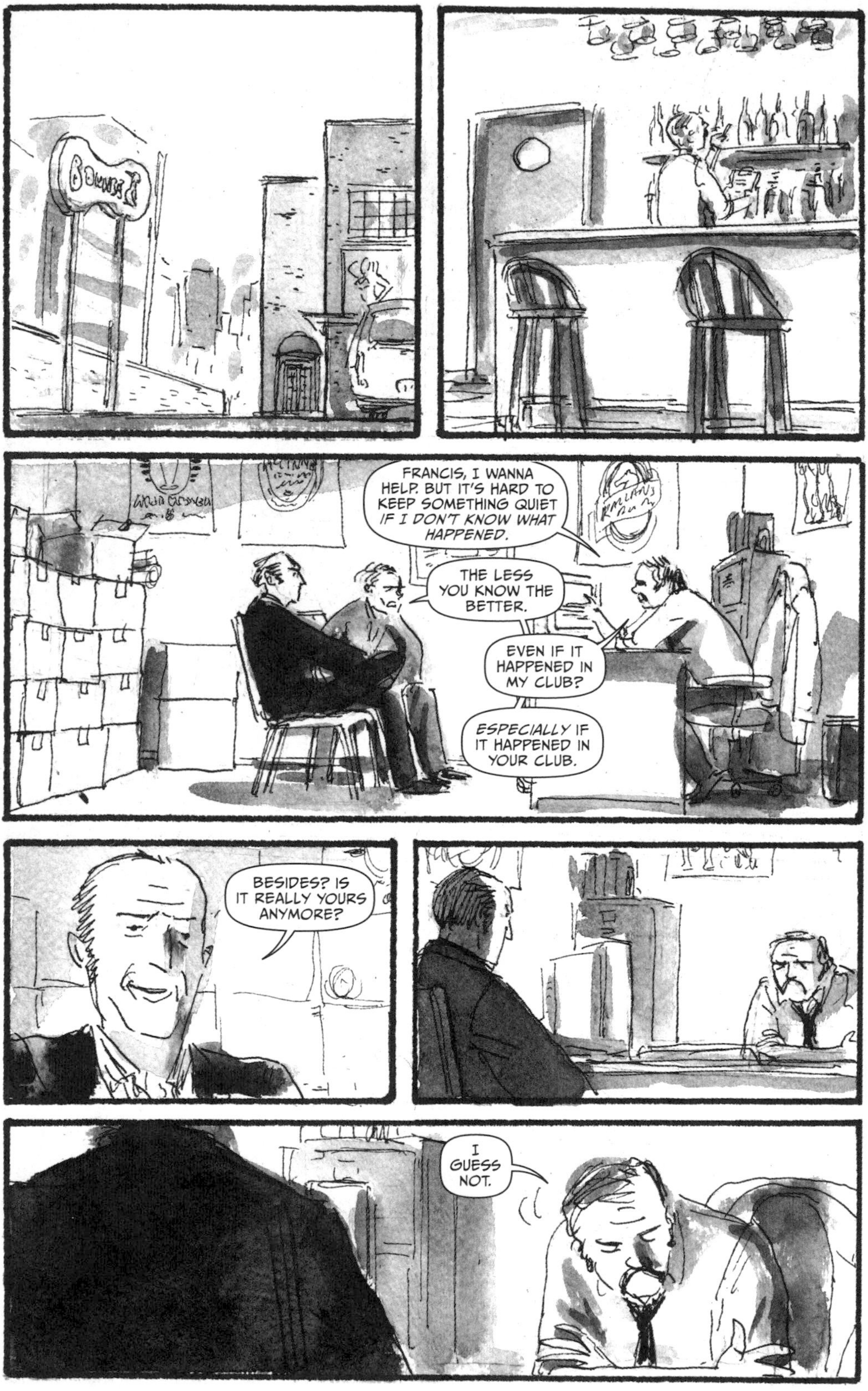
FRANCIS, I WANNA HELP. BUT IT'S HARD TO KEEP SOMETHING QUIET IF I DON'T KNOW WHAT HAPPENED.
THE LESS YOU KNOW THE BETTER.
EVEN IF IT HAPPENED IN MY CLUB?
ESPECIALLY IF IT HAPPENED IN YOUR CLUB.
BESIDES? IS IT REALLY YOURS ANYMORE?
I GUESS NOT.

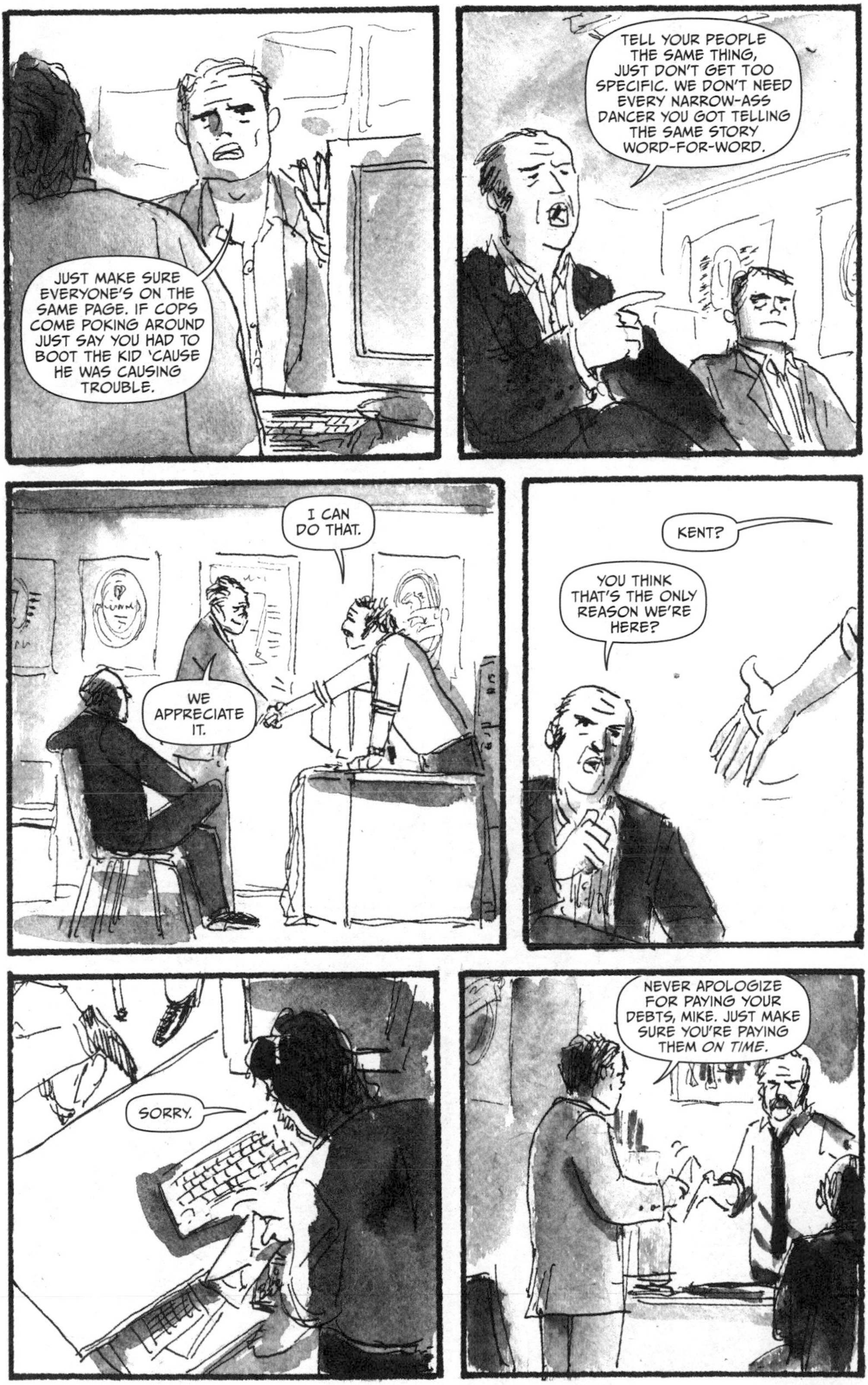
JUST MAKE SURE EVERYONE'S ON THE SAME PAGE. IF COPS COME POKING AROUND JUST SAY YOU HAD TO BOOT THE KID 'CAUSE HE WAS CAUSING TROUBLE.
TELL YOUR PEOPLE THE SAME THING, JUST DON'T GET TOO SPECIFIC. WE DON'T NEED EVERY NARROW-ASS DANCER YOU GOT TELLING THE SAME STORY WORD-FOR-WORD.
I CAN DO THAT.
WE APPRECIATE IT.
KENT?
YOU THINK THAT'S THE ONLY REASON WE'RE HERE?
SORRY.
NEVER APOLOGIZE FOR PAYING YOUR DEBTS, MIKE. JUST MAKE SURE YOU'RE PAYING THEM *ON TIME*.

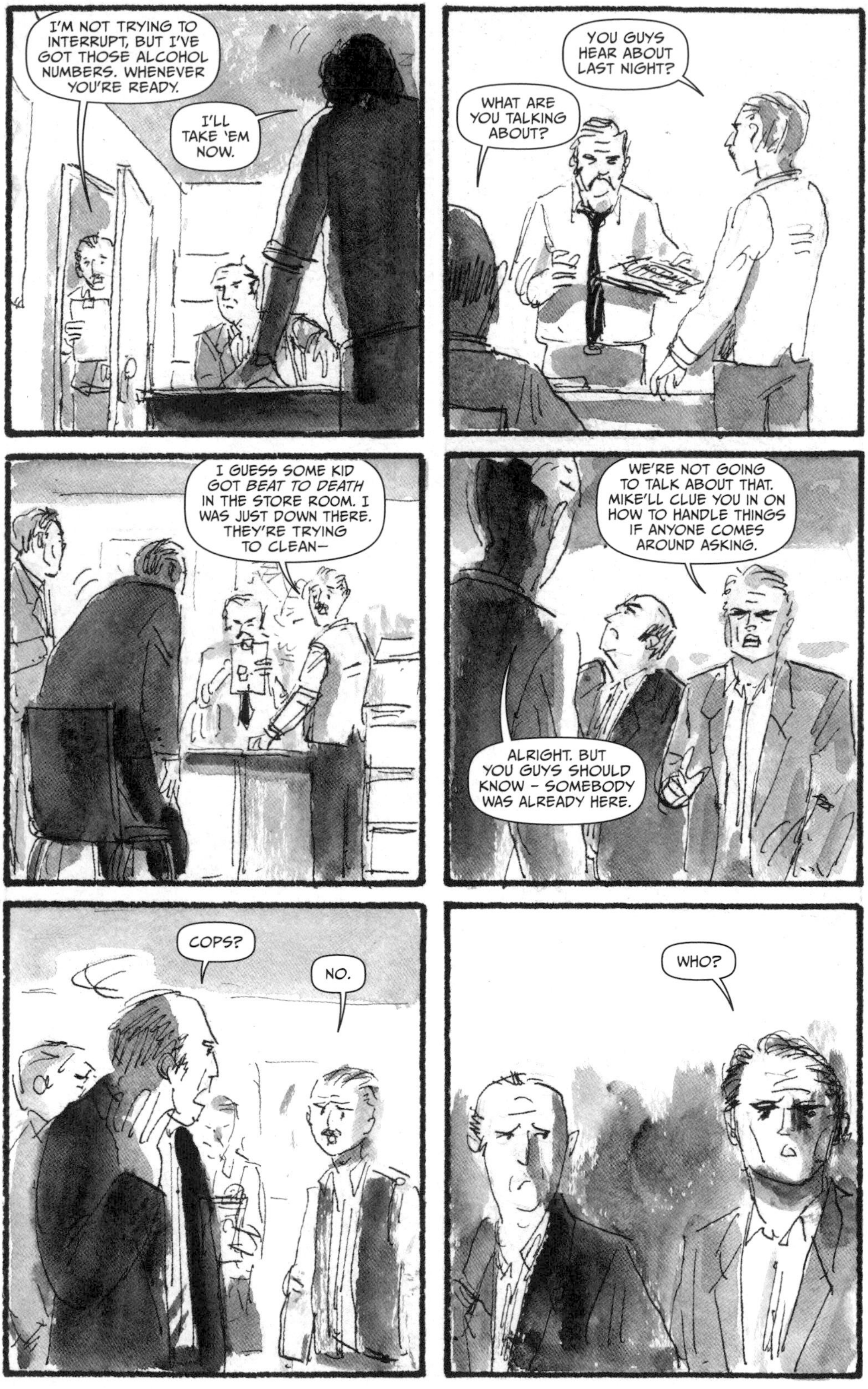

I'M NOT TRYING TO INTERRUPT, BUT I'VE GOT THOSE ALCOHOL NUMBERS. WHENEVER YOU'RE READY.
I'LL TAKE 'EM NOW.
YOU GUYS HEAR ABOUT LAST NIGHT?
WHAT ARE YOU TALKING ABOUT?
I GUESS SOME KID GOT *BEAT TO DEATH* IN THE STORE ROOM. I WAS JUST DOWN THERE. THEY'RE TRYING TO CLEAN—
WE'RE NOT GOING TO TALK ABOUT THAT. MIKE'LL CLUE YOU IN ON HOW TO HANDLE THINGS IF ANYONE COMES AROUND ASKING.
ALRIGHT. BUT YOU GUYS SHOULD KNOW - SOMEBODY WAS ALREADY HERE.
COPS?
NO.
WHO?

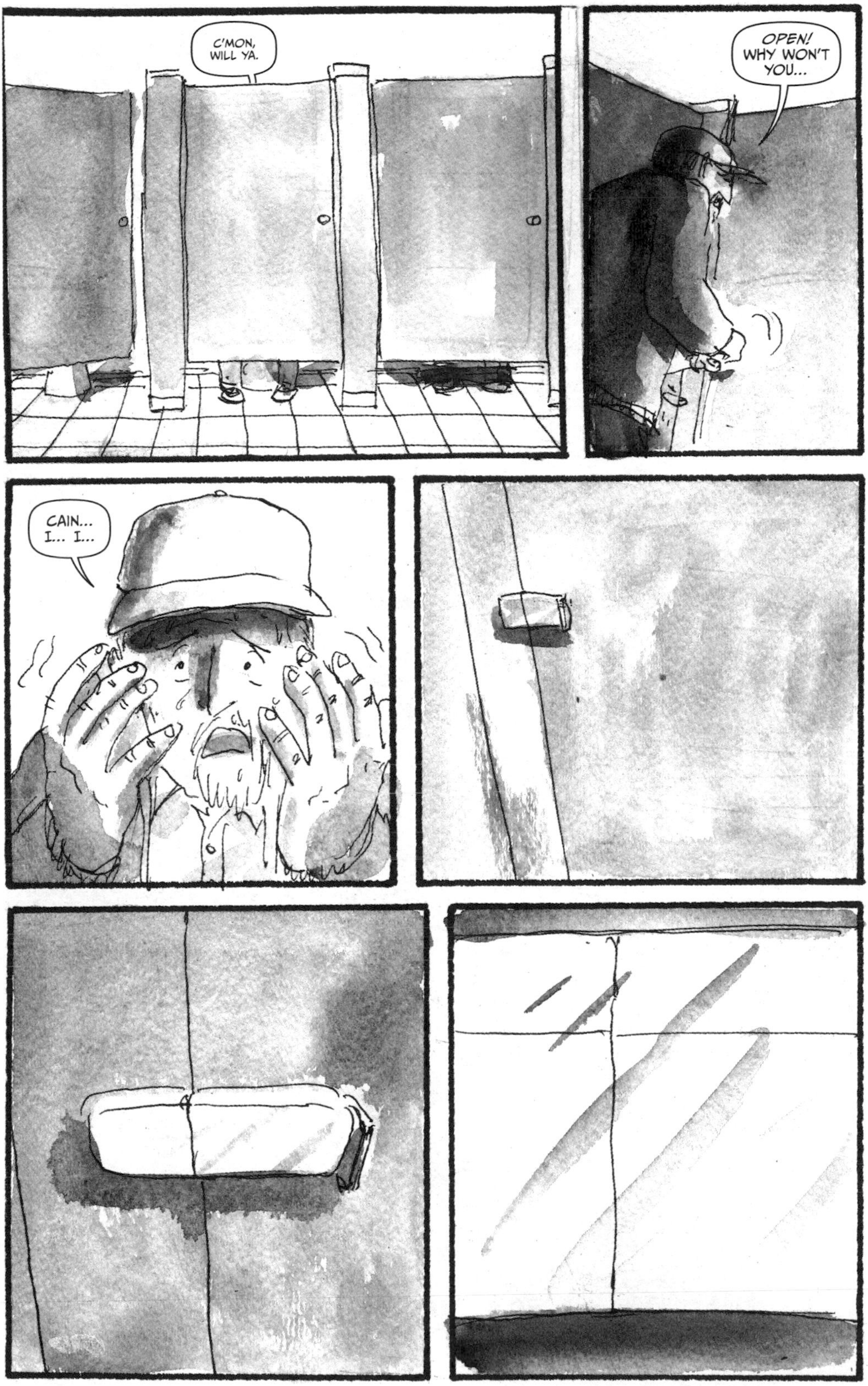
C'MON, WILL YA.
OPEN! WHY WON'T YOU...
CAIN... I... I...

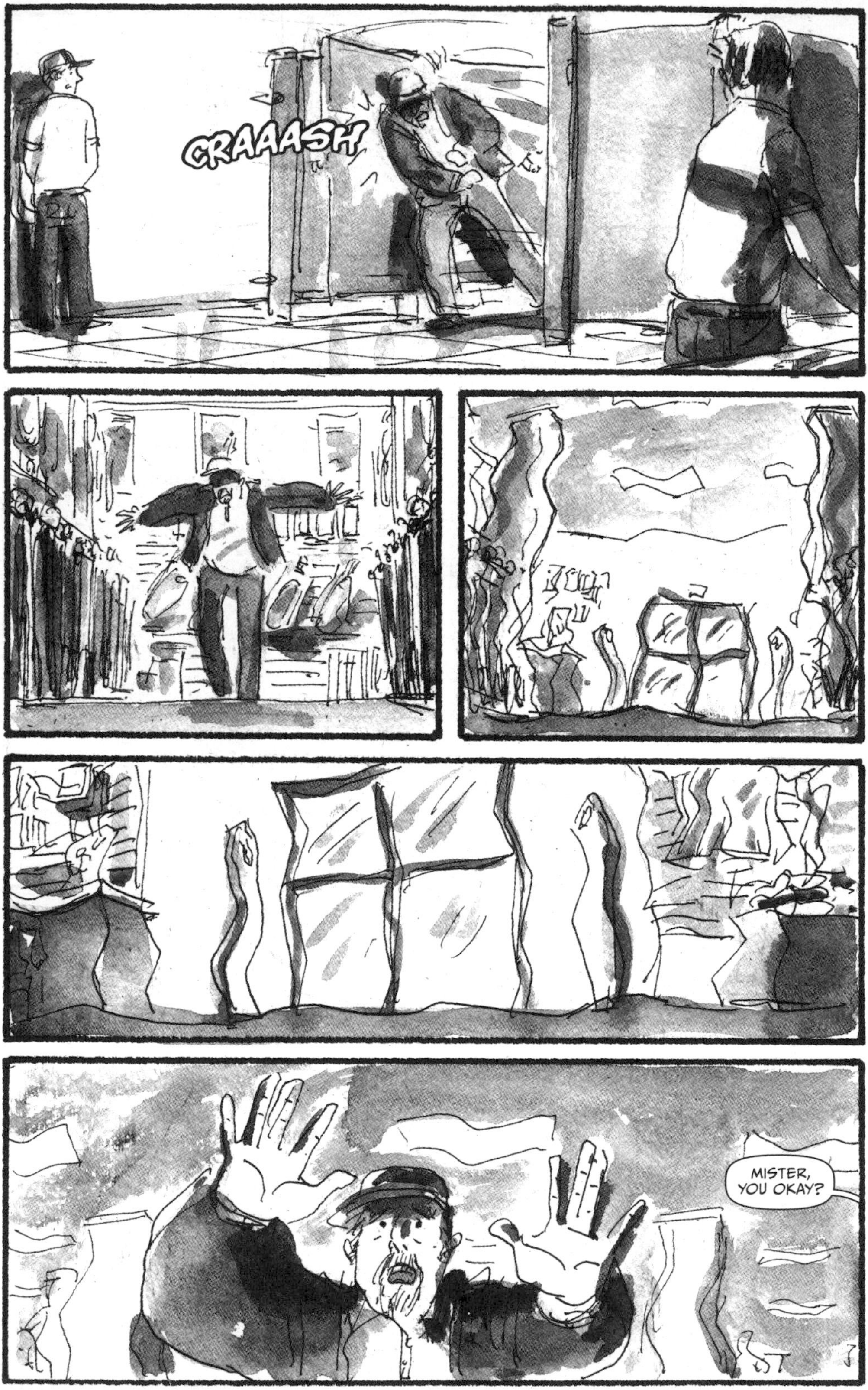
CRAAASH
MISTER, YOU OKAY?

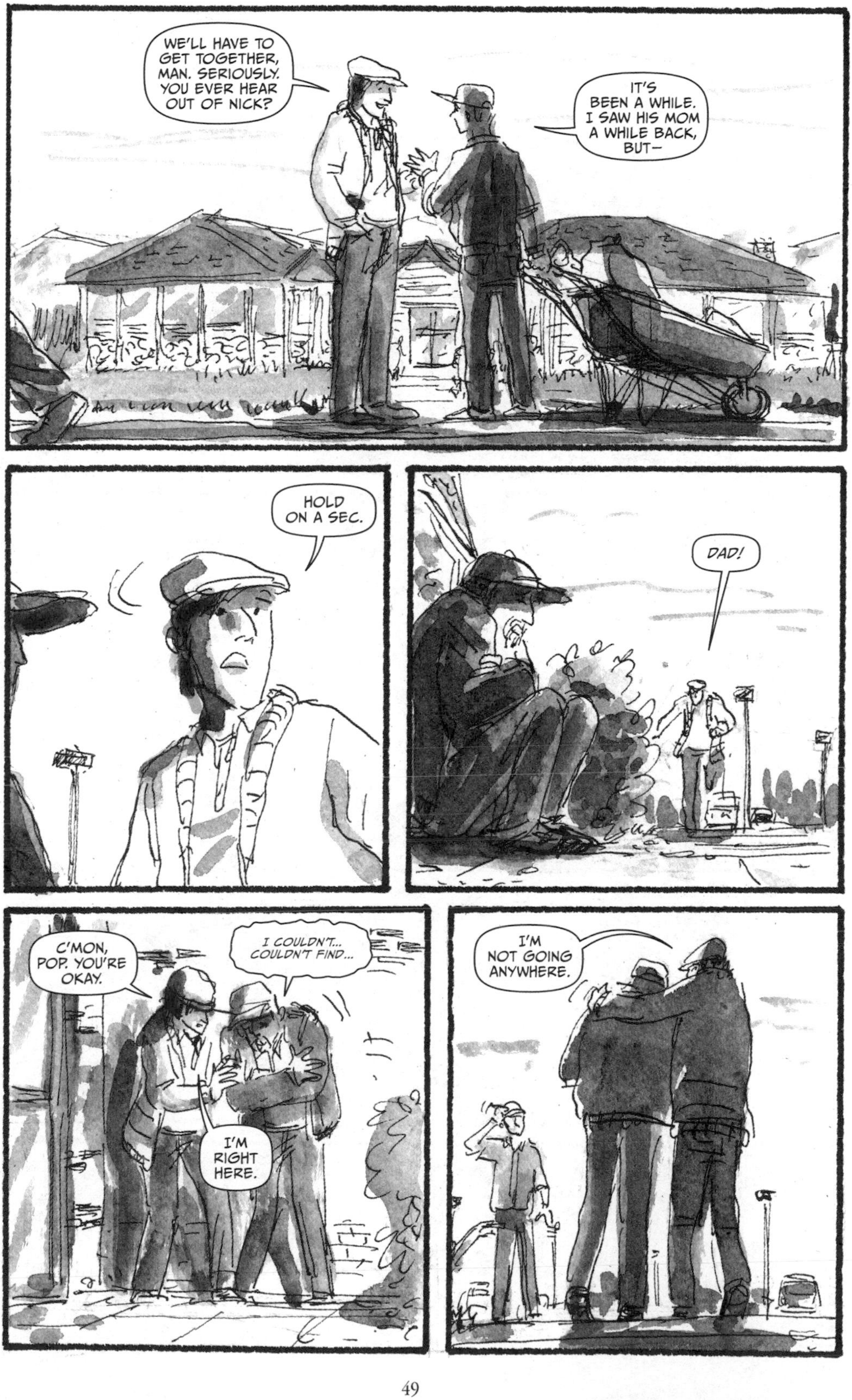
WE'LL HAVE TO GET TOGETHER, MAN. SERIOUSLY. YOU EVER HEAR OUT OF NICK?
IT'S BEEN A WHILE. I SAW HIS MOM A WHILE BACK, BUT–
HOLD ON A SEC.
DAD!
C'MON, POP. YOU'RE OKAY.
I COULDN'T... COULDN'T FIND...
I'M RIGHT HERE.
I'M NOT GOING ANYWHERE.

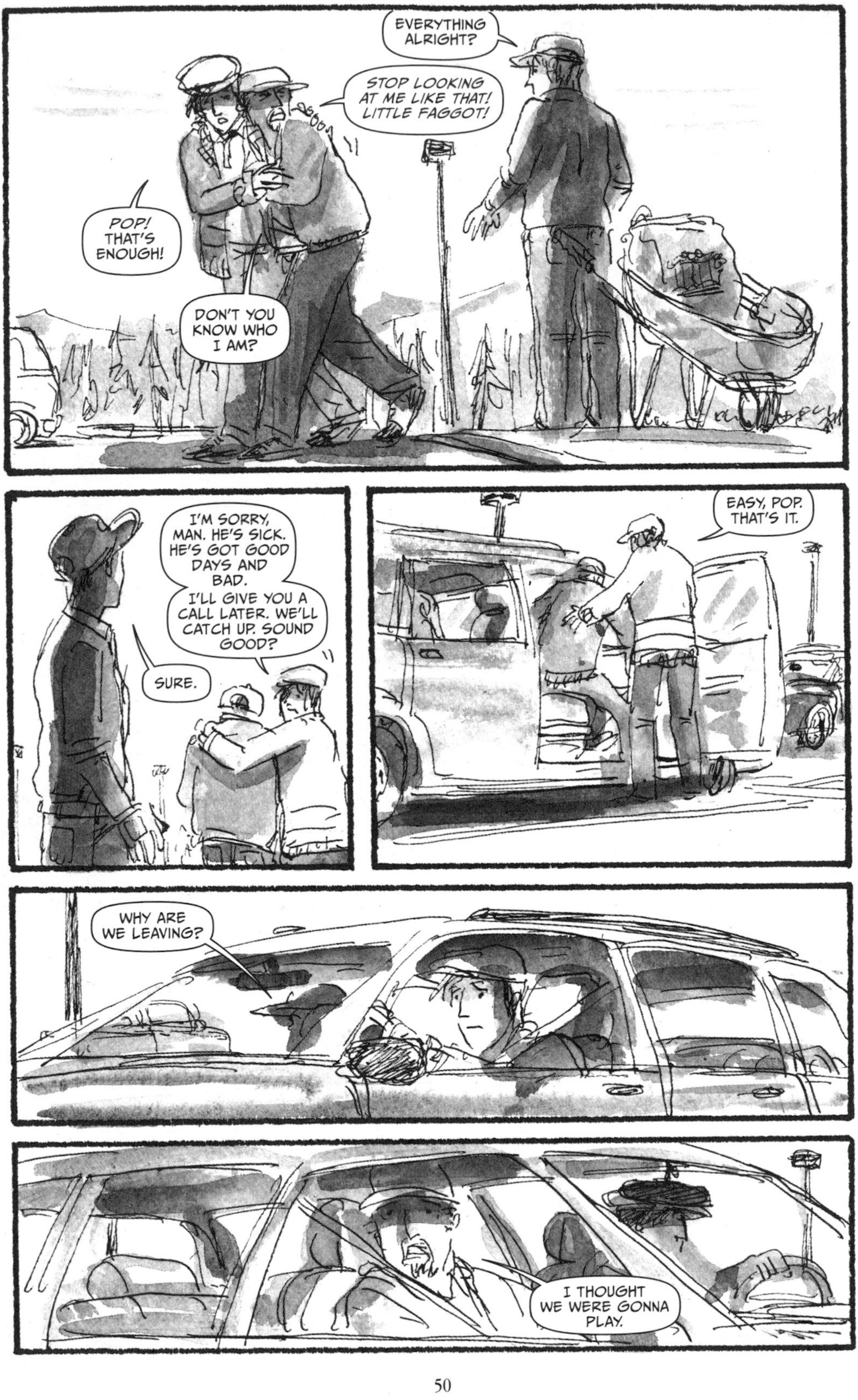
EVERYTHING ALRIGHT?
STOP LOOKING AT ME LIKE THAT! LITTLE FAGGOT!
POP! THAT'S ENOUGH!
DON'T YOU KNOW WHO I AM?
I'M SORRY, MAN. HE'S SICK. HE'S GOT GOOD DAYS AND BAD.
I'LL GIVE YOU A CALL LATER. WE'LL CATCH UP. SOUND GOOD?
SURE.
EASY, POP. THAT'S IT.
WHY ARE WE LEAVING?
I THOUGHT WE WERE GONNA PLAY.

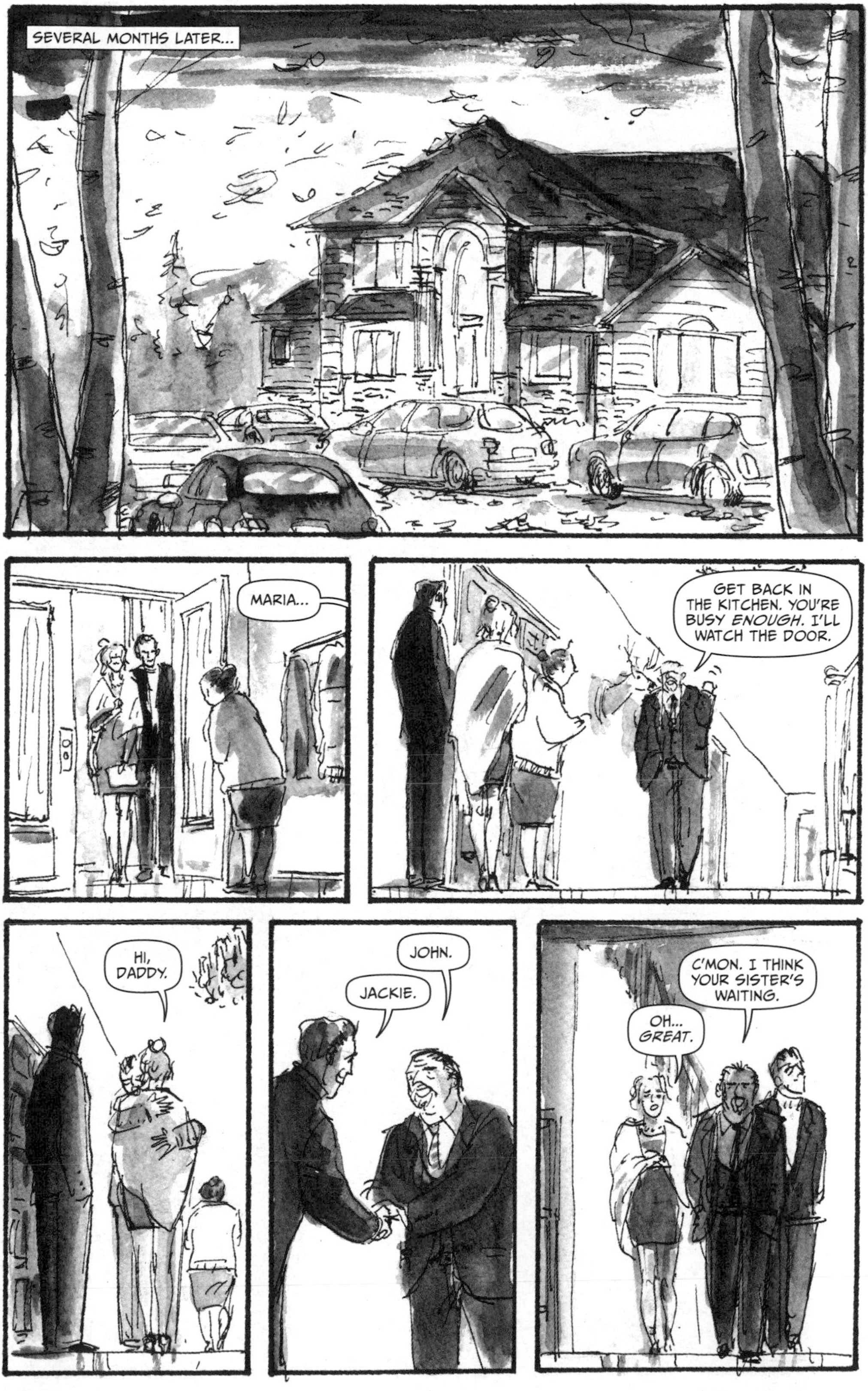
SEVERAL MONTHS LATER...
MARIA...
GET BACK IN THE KITCHEN. YOU'RE BUSY *ENOUGH*. I'LL WATCH THE DOOR.
HI, DADDY.
JACKIE.
JOHN.
C'MON. I THINK YOUR SISTER'S WAITING.
OH... GREAT.

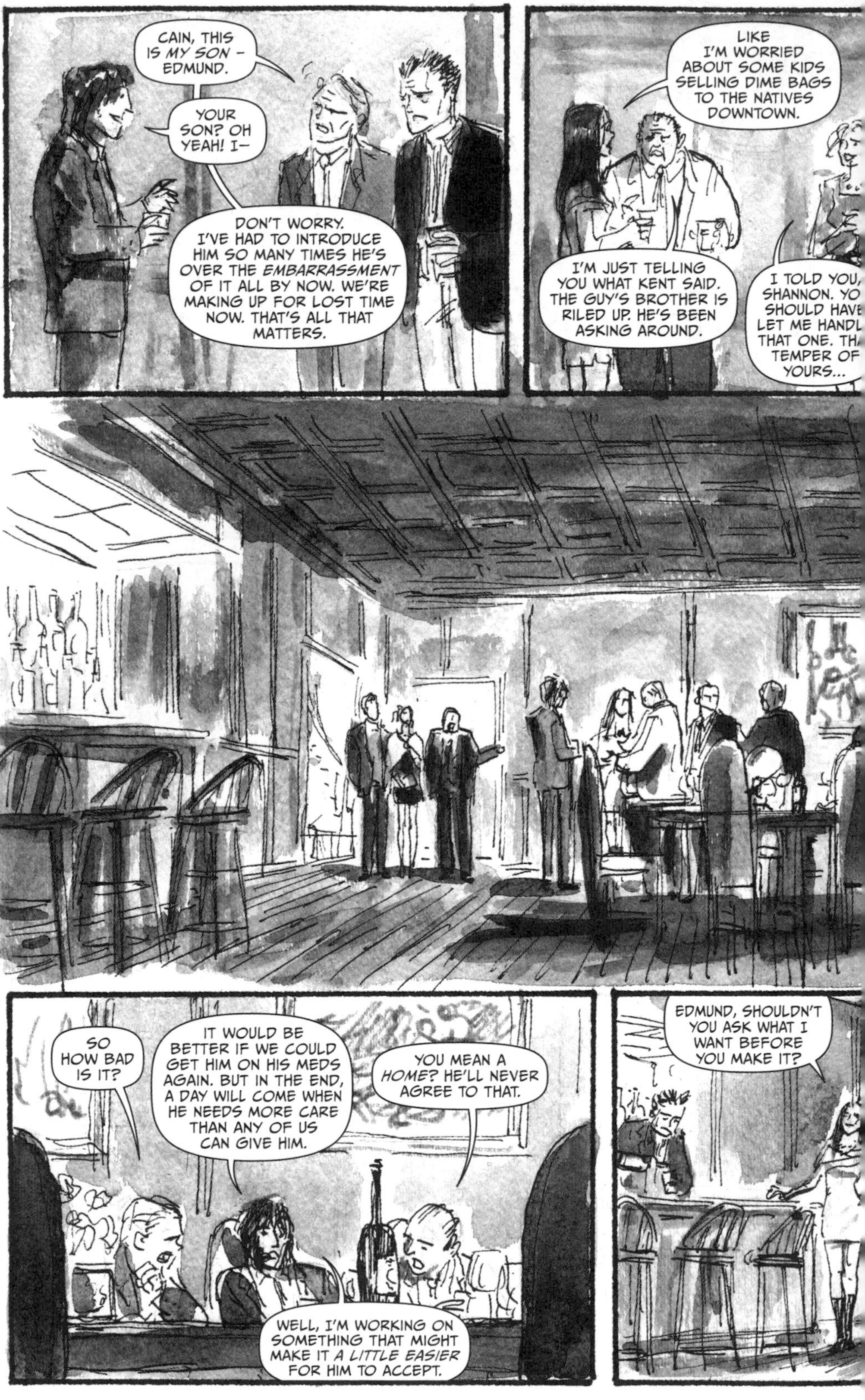
CAIN, THIS IS MY SON – EDMUND.
YOUR SON? OH YEAH! I–
DON'T WORRY. I'VE HAD TO INTRODUCE HIM SO MANY TIMES HE'S OVER THE EMBARRASSMENT OF IT ALL BY NOW. WE'RE MAKING UP FOR LOST TIME NOW. THAT'S ALL THAT MATTERS.
LIKE I'M WORRIED ABOUT SOME KIDS SELLING DIME BAGS TO THE NATIVES DOWNTOWN.
I'M JUST TELLING YOU WHAT KENT SAID. THE GUY'S BROTHER IS RILED UP. HE'S BEEN ASKING AROUND.
I TOLD YOU, SHANNON. YO SHOULD HAVE LET ME HANDL THAT ONE. THA TEMPER OF YOURS...
SO HOW BAD IS IT?
IT WOULD BE BETTER IF WE COULD GET HIM ON HIS MEDS AGAIN. BUT IN THE END, A DAY WILL COME WHEN HE NEEDS MORE CARE THAN ANY OF US CAN GIVE HIM.
YOU MEAN A HOME? HE'LL NEVER AGREE TO THAT.
WELL, I'M WORKING ON SOMETHING THAT MIGHT MAKE IT A LITTLE EASIER FOR HIM TO ACCEPT.
EDMUND, SHOULDN'T YOU ASK WHAT I WANT BEFORE YOU MAKE IT?

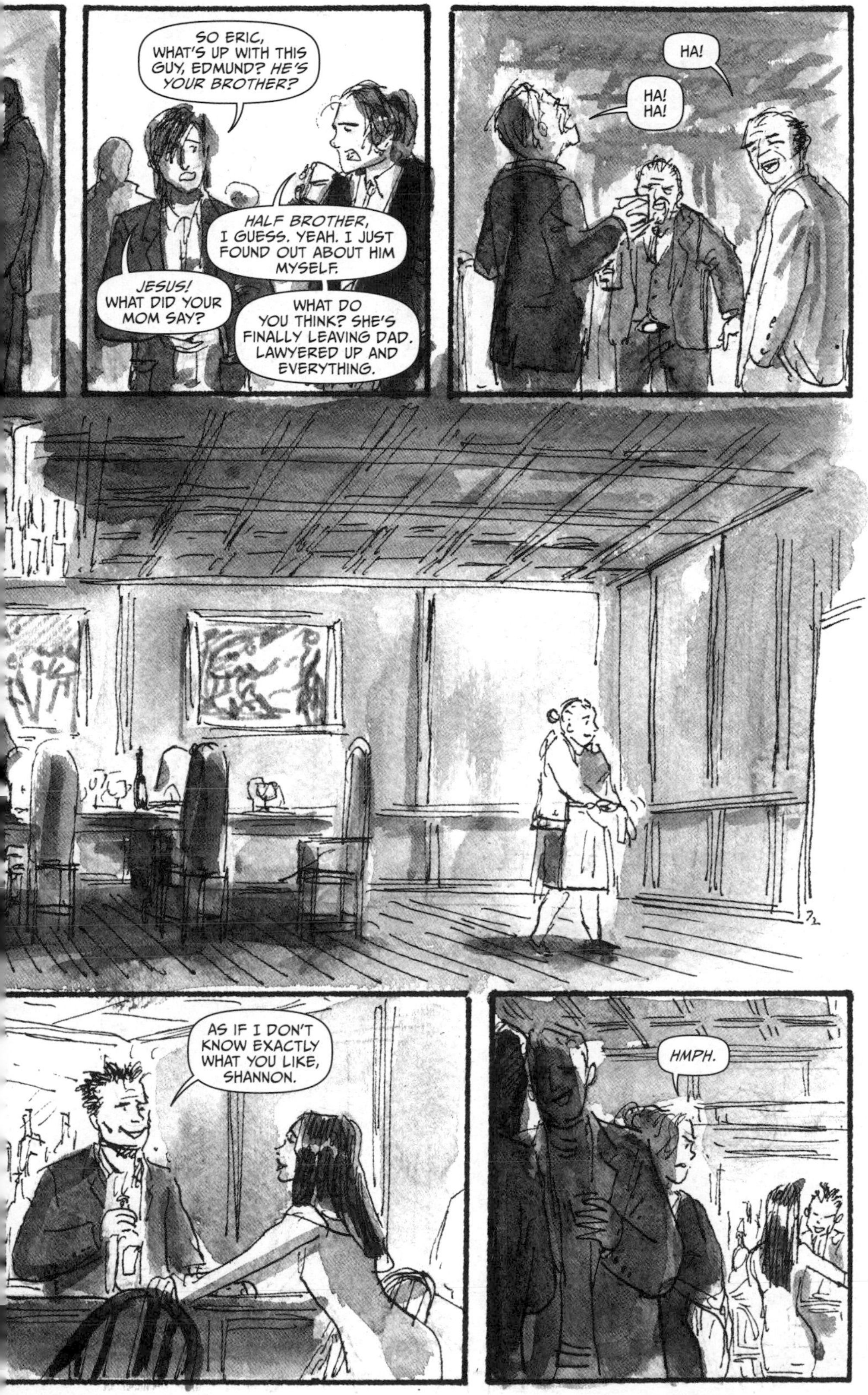
SO ERIC, WHAT'S UP WITH THIS GUY, EDMUND? HE'S YOUR BROTHER?
HALF BROTHER, I GUESS. YEAH. I JUST FOUND OUT ABOUT HIM MYSELF.
JESUS! WHAT DID YOUR MOM SAY?
WHAT DO YOU THINK? SHE'S FINALLY LEAVING DAD. LAWYERED UP AND EVERYTHING.
HA!
HA! HA!
AS IF I DON'T KNOW EXACTLY WHAT YOU LIKE, SHANNON.
HMPH.

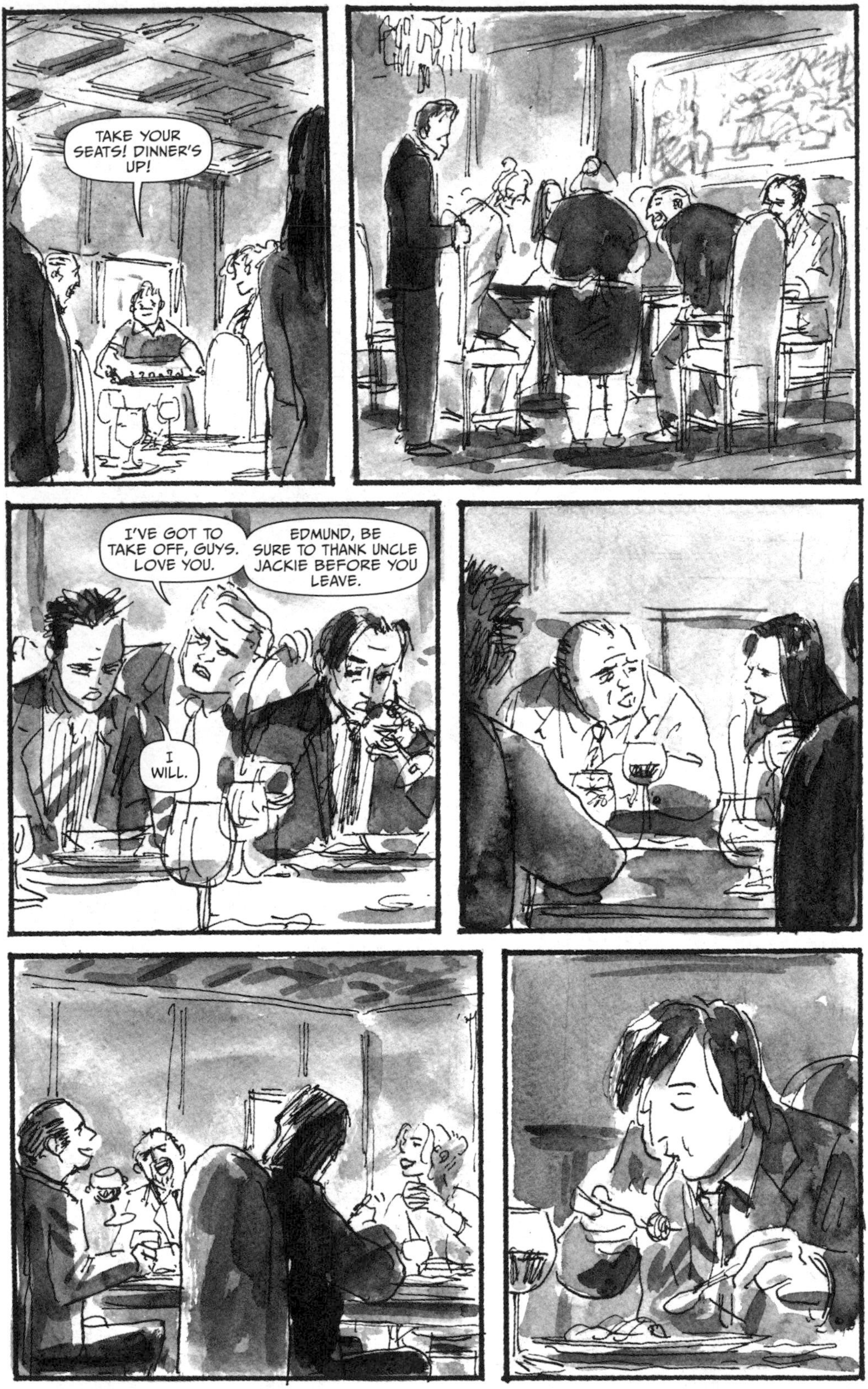
TAKE YOUR SEATS! DINNER'S UP!
I'VE GOT TO TAKE OFF, GUYS. LOVE YOU.
EDMUND, BE SURE TO THANK UNCLE JACKIE BEFORE YOU LEAVE.
I WILL.

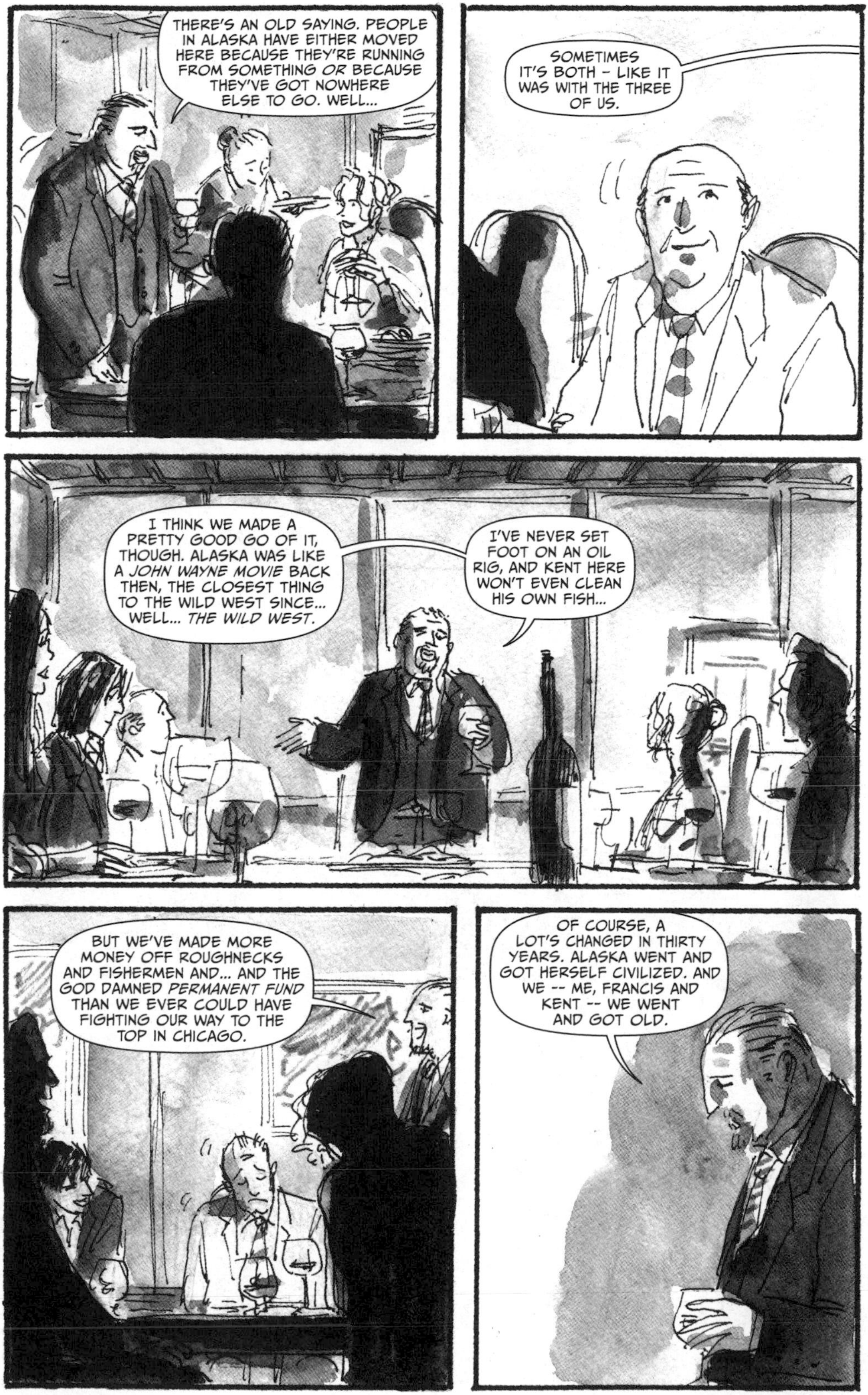
THERE'S AN OLD SAYING. PEOPLE IN ALASKA HAVE EITHER MOVED HERE BECAUSE THEY'RE RUNNING FROM SOMETHING OR BECAUSE THEY'VE GOT NOWHERE ELSE TO GO. WELL...
SOMETIMES IT'S BOTH – LIKE IT WAS WITH THE THREE OF US.
I THINK WE MADE A PRETTY GOOD GO OF IT, THOUGH. ALASKA WAS LIKE A JOHN WAYNE MOVIE BACK THEN, THE CLOSEST THING TO THE WILD WEST SINCE... WELL... THE WILD WEST.
I'VE NEVER SET FOOT ON AN OIL RIG, AND KENT HERE WON'T EVEN CLEAN HIS OWN FISH...
BUT WE'VE MADE MORE MONEY OFF ROUGHNECKS AND FISHERMEN AND... AND THE GOD DAMNED PERMANENT FUND THAN WE EVER COULD HAVE FIGHTING OUR WAY TO THE TOP IN CHICAGO.
OF COURSE, A LOT'S CHANGED IN THIRTY YEARS. ALASKA WENT AND GOT HERSELF CIVILIZED. AND WE -- ME, FRANCIS AND KENT -- WE WENT AND GOT OLD.

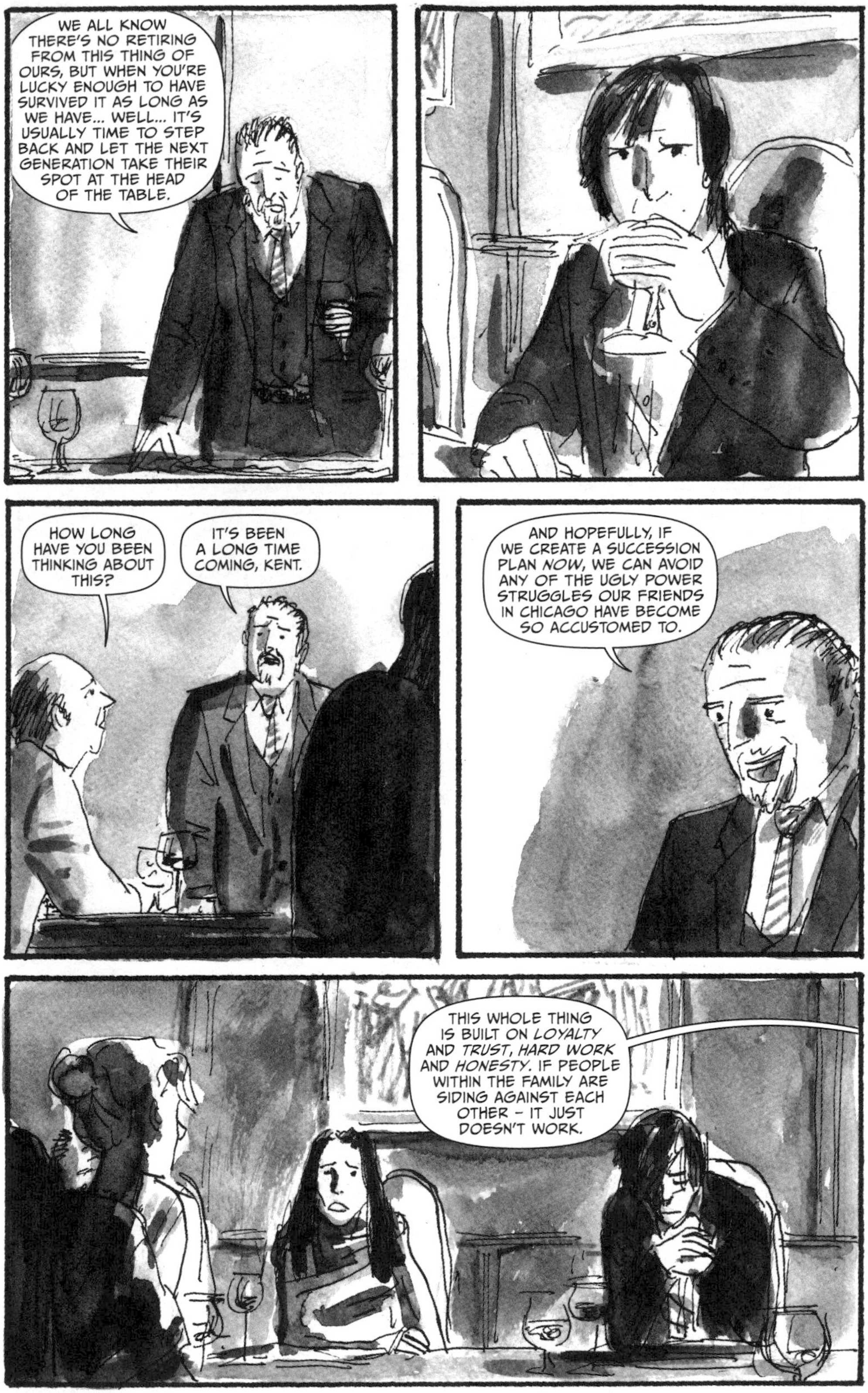
WE ALL KNOW THERE'S NO RETIRING FROM THIS THING OF OURS, BUT WHEN YOU'RE LUCKY ENOUGH TO HAVE SURVIVED IT AS LONG AS WE HAVE... WELL... IT'S USUALLY TIME TO STEP BACK AND LET THE NEXT GENERATION TAKE THEIR SPOT AT THE HEAD OF THE TABLE.
HOW LONG HAVE YOU BEEN THINKING ABOUT THIS?
IT'S BEEN A LONG TIME COMING, KENT.
AND HOPEFULLY, IF WE CREATE A SUCCESSION PLAN NOW, WE CAN AVOID ANY OF THE UGLY POWER STRUGGLES OUR FRIENDS IN CHICAGO HAVE BECOME SO ACCUSTOMED TO.
THIS WHOLE THING IS BUILT ON LOYALTY AND TRUST, HARD WORK AND HONESTY. IF PEOPLE WITHIN THE FAMILY ARE SIDING AGAINST EACH OTHER – IT JUST DOESN'T WORK.

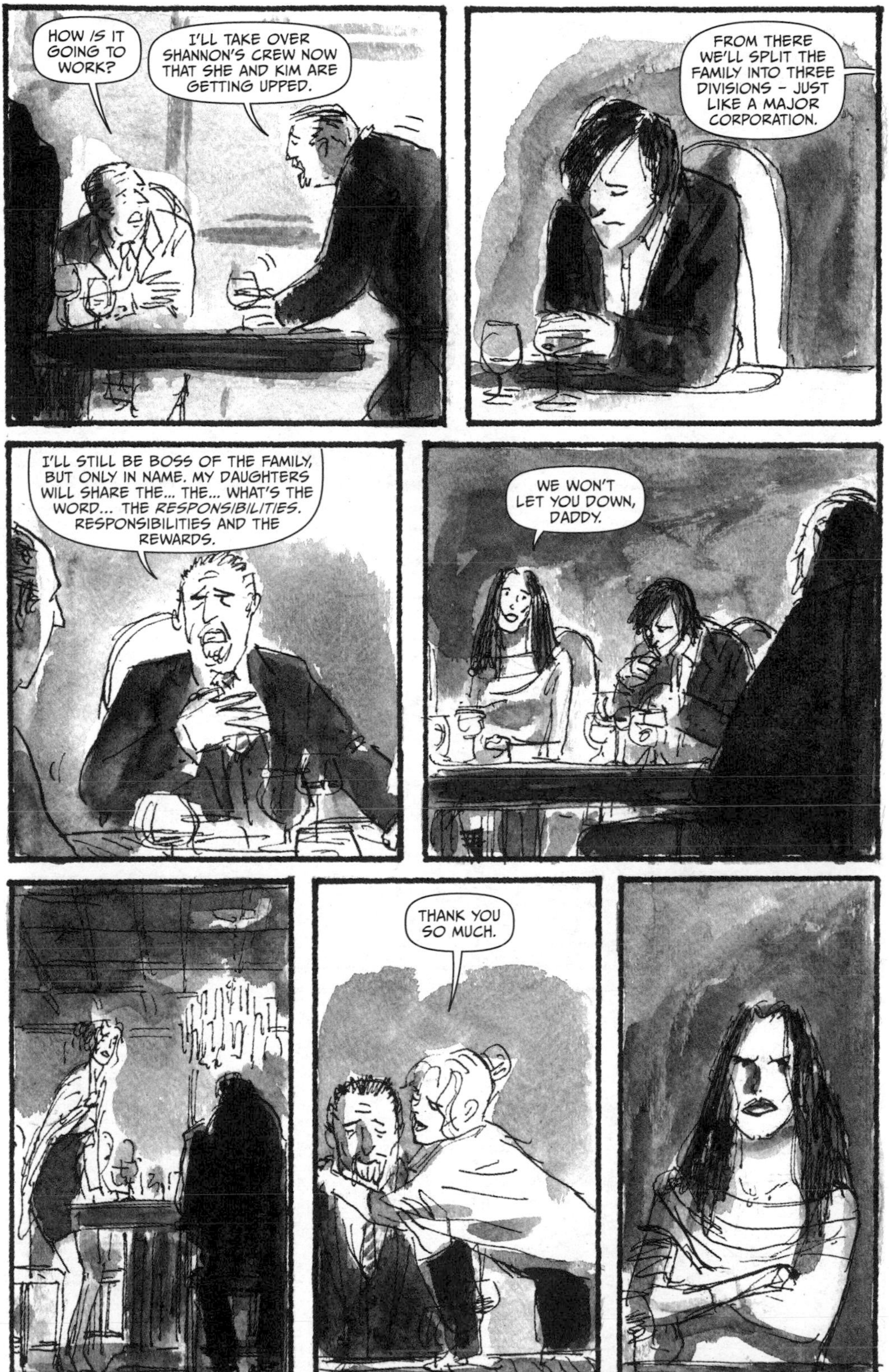
HOW IS IT GOING TO WORK?
I'LL TAKE OVER SHANNON'S CREW NOW THAT SHE AND KIM ARE GETTING UPPED.
FROM THERE WE'LL SPLIT THE FAMILY INTO THREE DIVISIONS – JUST LIKE A MAJOR CORPORATION.
I'LL STILL BE BOSS OF THE FAMILY, BUT ONLY IN NAME. MY DAUGHTERS WILL SHARE THE... THE... WHAT'S THE WORD... THE *RESPONSIBILITIES*. RESPONSIBILITIES AND THE REWARDS.
WE WON'T LET YOU DOWN, DADDY.
THANK YOU SO MUCH.

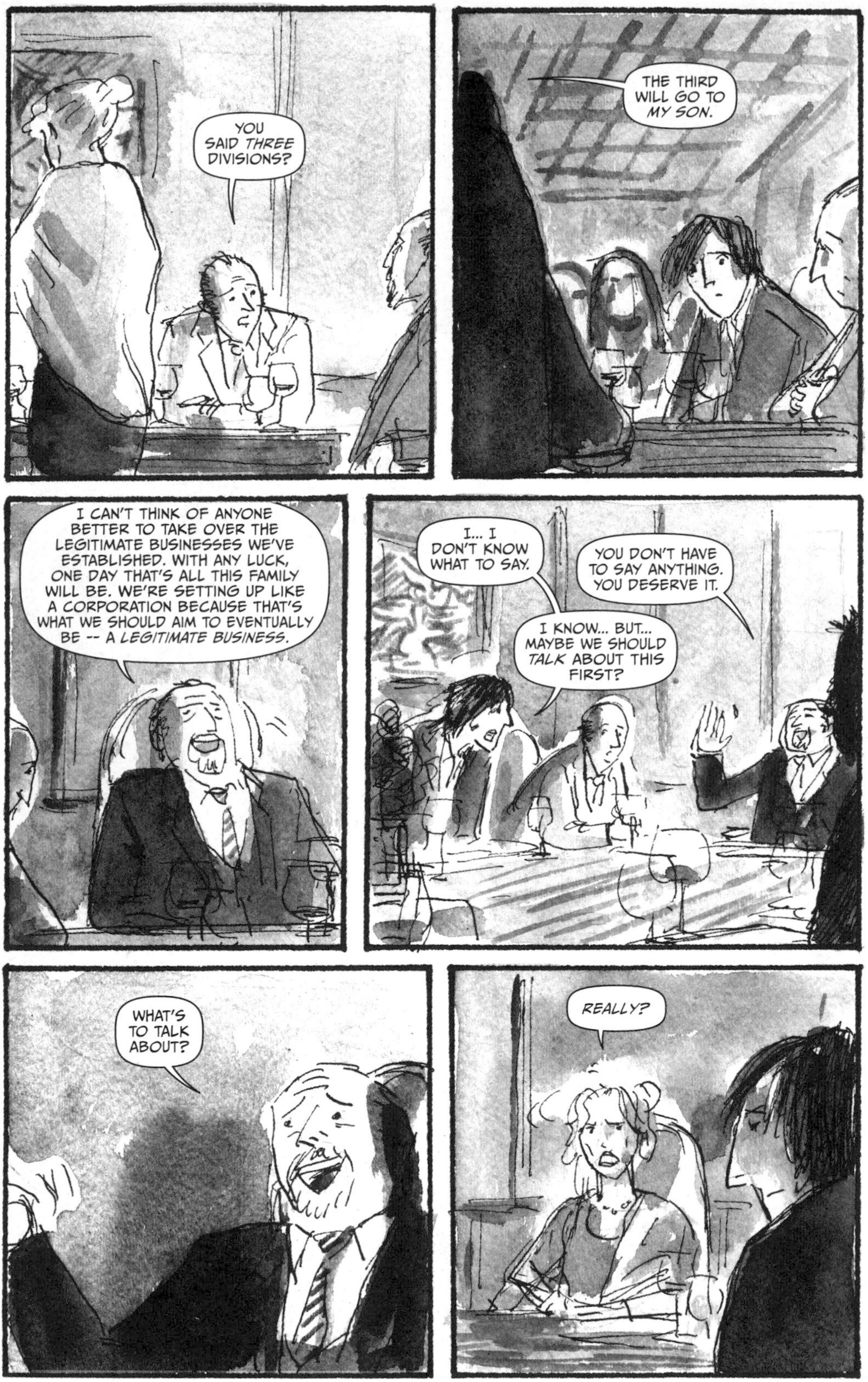
YOU SAID *THREE* DIVISIONS?
THE THIRD WILL GO TO *MY SON.*
I CAN'T THINK OF ANYONE BETTER TO TAKE OVER THE LEGITIMATE BUSINESSES WE'VE ESTABLISHED. WITH ANY LUCK, ONE DAY THAT'S ALL THIS FAMILY WILL BE. WE'RE SETTING UP LIKE A CORPORATION BECAUSE THAT'S WHAT WE SHOULD AIM TO EVENTUALLY BE -- A *LEGITIMATE BUSINESS.*
I... I DON'T KNOW WHAT TO SAY.
YOU DON'T HAVE TO SAY ANYTHING. YOU DESERVE IT.
I KNOW... BUT... MAYBE WE SHOULD *TALK* ABOUT THIS FIRST?
WHAT'S TO TALK ABOUT?
REALLY?

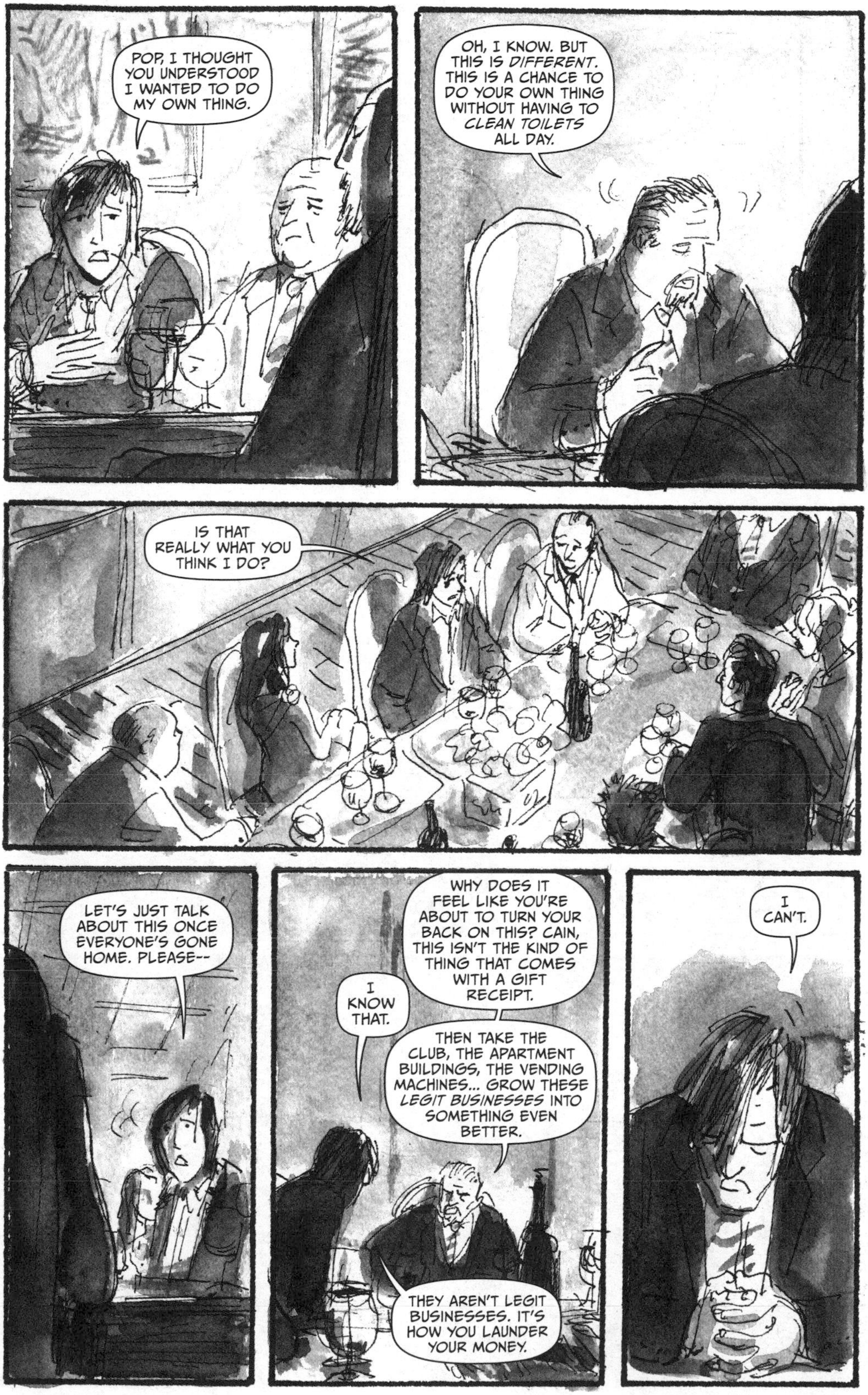

POP, I THOUGHT YOU UNDERSTOOD I WANTED TO DO MY OWN THING.
OH, I KNOW. BUT THIS IS *DIFFERENT*. THIS IS A CHANCE TO DO YOUR OWN THING WITHOUT HAVING TO *CLEAN TOILETS* ALL DAY.
IS THAT REALLY WHAT YOU THINK I DO?
LET'S JUST TALK ABOUT THIS ONCE EVERYONE'S GONE HOME. PLEASE--
WHY DOES IT FEEL LIKE YOU'RE ABOUT TO TURN YOUR BACK ON THIS? CAIN, THIS ISN'T THE KIND OF THING THAT COMES WITH A GIFT RECEIPT.
I KNOW THAT.
THEN TAKE THE CLUB, THE APARTMENT BUILDINGS, THE VENDING MACHINES... GROW THESE *LEGIT BUSINESSES* INTO SOMETHING EVEN BETTER.
THEY AREN'T LEGIT BUSINESSES. IT'S HOW YOU LAUNDER YOUR MONEY.
I CAN'T.

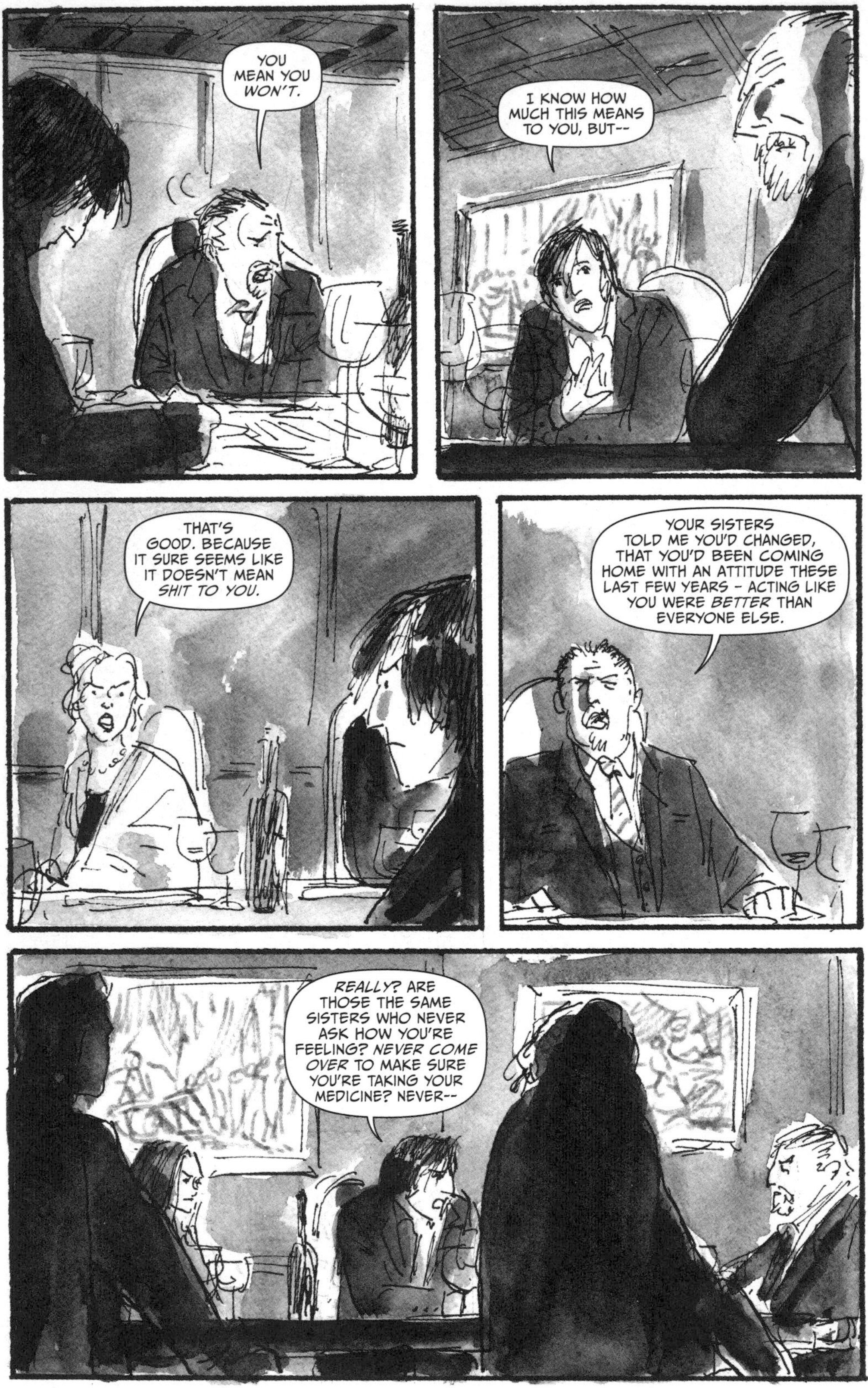
YOU MEAN YOU *WON'T.*
I KNOW HOW MUCH THIS MEANS TO YOU, BUT--
THAT'S GOOD. BECAUSE IT SURE SEEMS LIKE IT DOESN'T MEAN *SHIT TO YOU.*
YOUR SISTERS TOLD ME YOU'D CHANGED, THAT YOU'D BEEN COMING HOME WITH AN ATTITUDE THESE LAST FEW YEARS – ACTING LIKE YOU WERE *BETTER* THAN EVERYONE ELSE.
REALLY? ARE THOSE THE SAME SISTERS WHO NEVER ASK HOW YOU'RE FEELING? *NEVER COME OVER* TO MAKE SURE YOU'RE TAKING YOUR MEDICINE? NEVER--

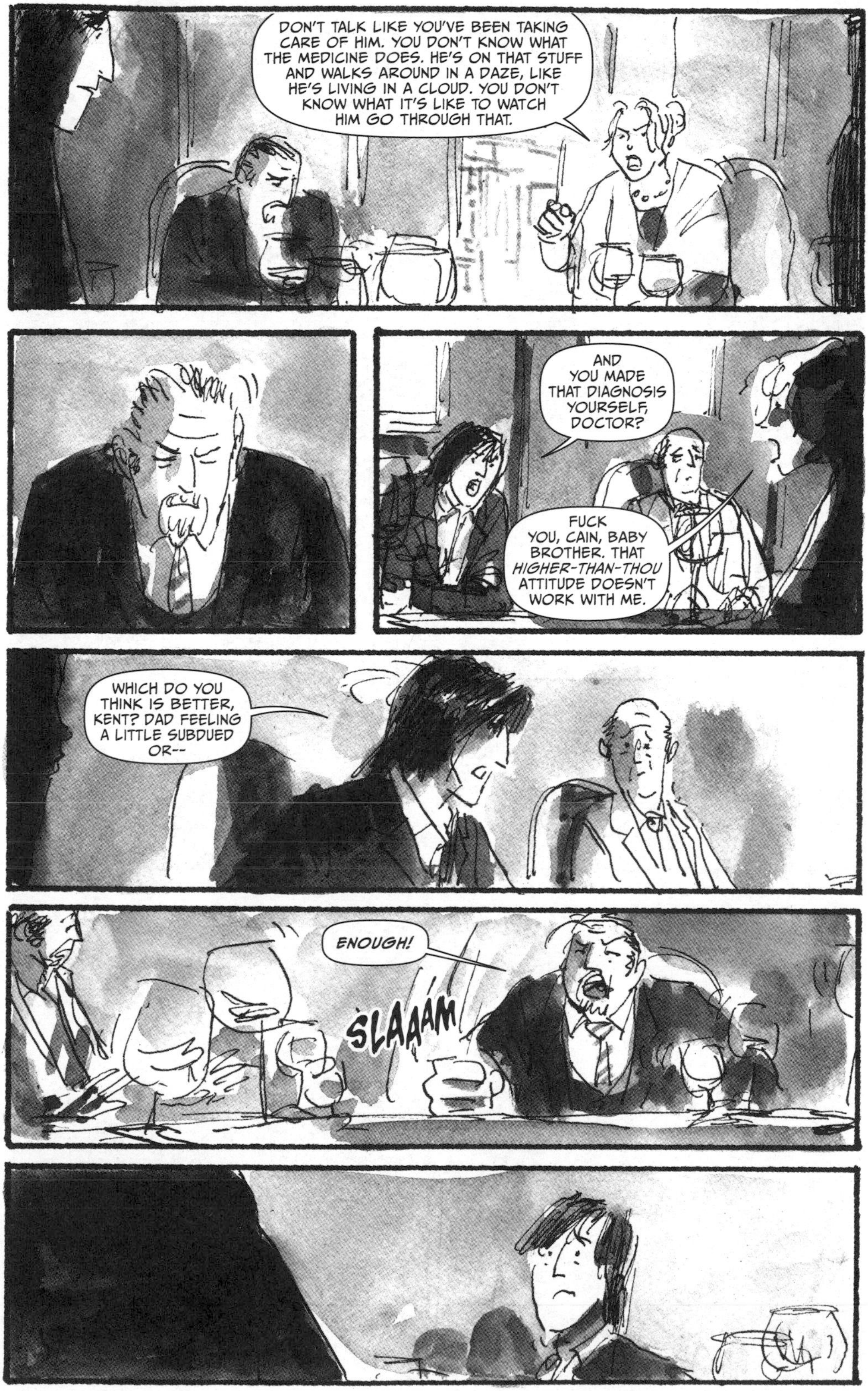

DON'T TALK LIKE YOU'VE BEEN TAKING CARE OF HIM. YOU DON'T KNOW WHAT THE MEDICINE DOES. HE'S ON THAT STUFF AND WALKS AROUND IN A DAZE, LIKE HE'S LIVING IN A CLOUD. YOU DON'T KNOW WHAT IT'S LIKE TO WATCH HIM GO THROUGH THAT.
AND YOU MADE THAT DIAGNOSIS YOURSELF, DOCTOR?
FUCK YOU, CAIN, BABY BROTHER. THAT *HIGHER-THAN-THOU* ATTITUDE DOESN'T WORK WITH ME.
WHICH DO YOU THINK IS BETTER, KENT? DAD FEELING A LITTLE SUBDUED OR--
ENOUGH!
SLAAAM

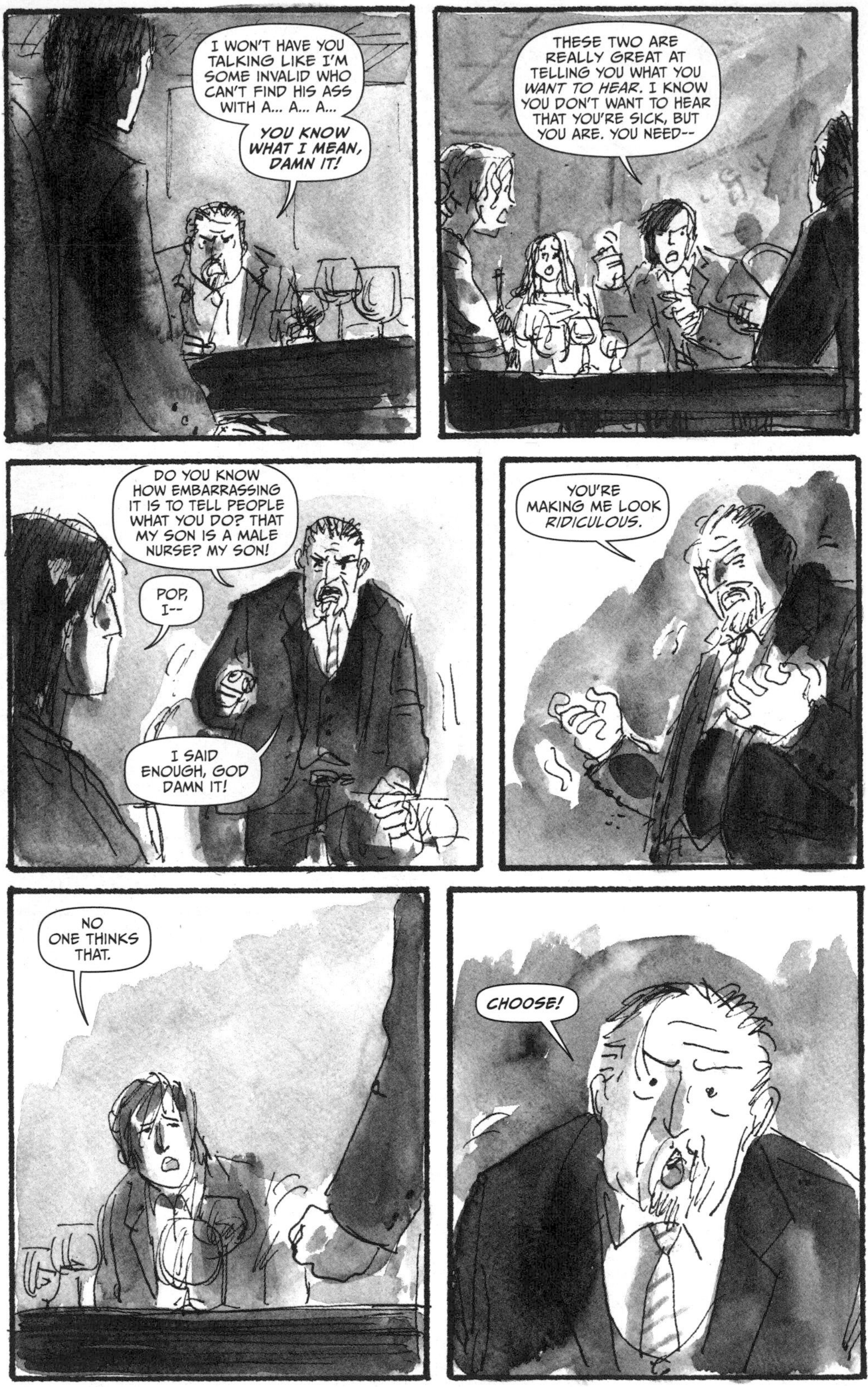
I WON'T HAVE YOU TALKING LIKE I'M SOME INVALID WHO CAN'T FIND HIS ASS WITH A... A... A...
YOU KNOW WHAT I MEAN, DAMN IT!
THESE TWO ARE REALLY GREAT AT TELLING YOU WHAT YOU WANT TO HEAR. I KNOW YOU DON'T WANT TO HEAR THAT YOU'RE SICK, BUT YOU ARE. YOU NEED--
DO YOU KNOW HOW EMBARRASSING IT IS TO TELL PEOPLE WHAT YOU DO? THAT MY SON IS A MALE NURSE? MY SON!
POP, I--
I SAID ENOUGH, GOD DAMN IT!
YOU'RE MAKING ME LOOK RIDICULOUS.
NO ONE THINKS THAT.
CHOOSE!

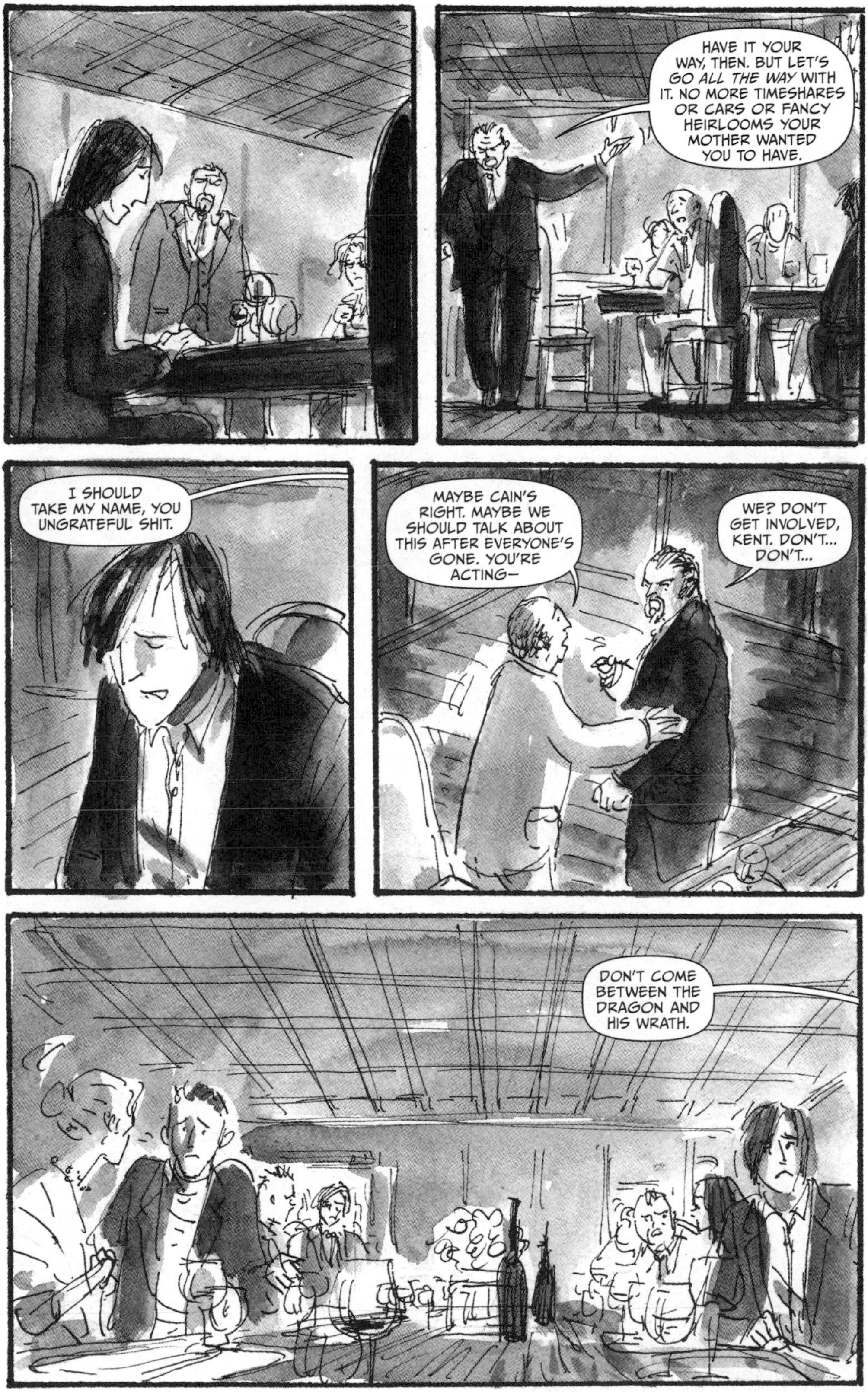
HAVE IT YOUR WAY, THEN. BUT LET'S GO *ALL THE WAY* WITH IT. NO MORE TIMESHARES OR CARS OR FANCY HEIRLOOMS YOUR MOTHER WANTED YOU TO HAVE.
I SHOULD TAKE MY NAME, YOU UNGRATEFUL SHIT.
MAYBE CAIN'S RIGHT. MAYBE WE SHOULD TALK ABOUT THIS AFTER EVERYONE'S GONE. YOU'RE ACTING–
WE? DON'T GET INVOLVED, KENT. DON'T... DON'T...
DON'T COME BETWEEN THE DRAGON AND HIS WRATH.

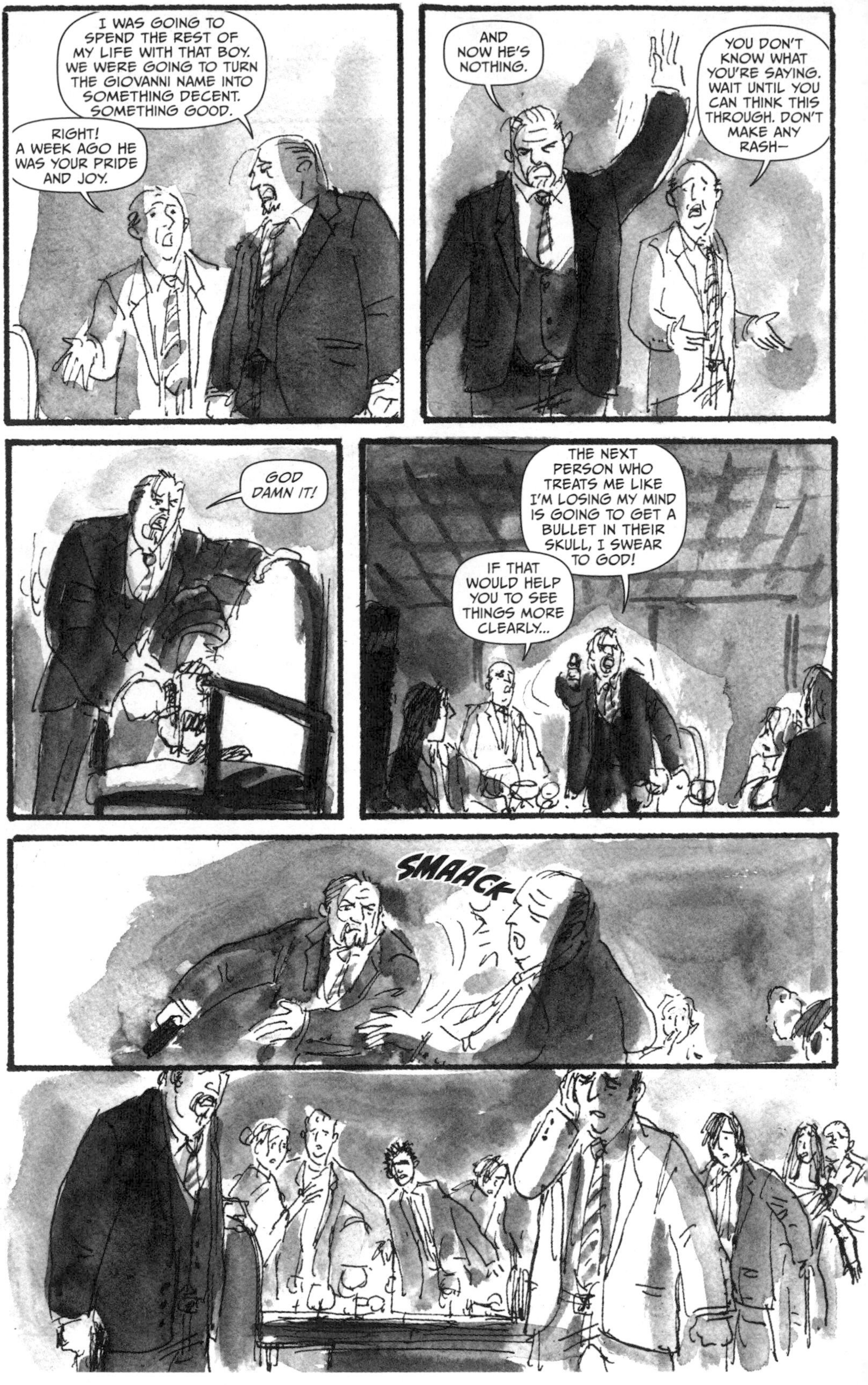
I WAS GOING TO SPEND THE REST OF MY LIFE WITH THAT BOY. WE WERE GOING TO TURN THE GIOVANNI NAME INTO SOMETHING DECENT. SOMETHING GOOD.
RIGHT! A WEEK AGO HE WAS YOUR PRIDE AND JOY.
AND NOW HE'S NOTHING.
YOU DON'T KNOW WHAT YOU'RE SAYING. WAIT UNTIL YOU CAN THINK THIS THROUGH. DON'T MAKE ANY RASH—
GOD DAMN IT!
THE NEXT PERSON WHO TREATS ME LIKE I'M LOSING MY MIND IS GOING TO GET A BULLET IN THEIR SKULL, I SWEAR TO GOD!
IF THAT WOULD HELP YOU TO SEE THINGS MORE CLEARLY...
SMAACK

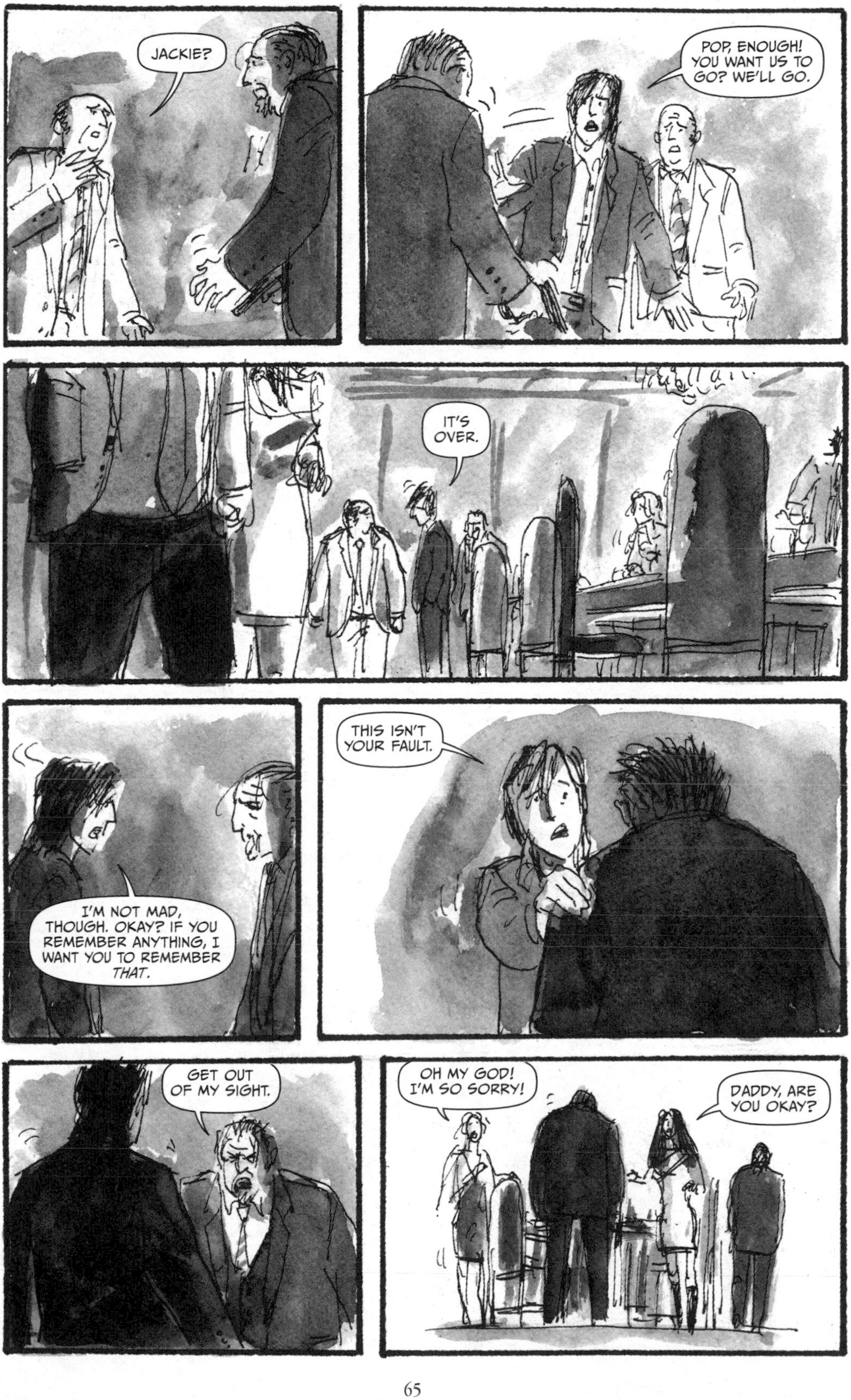
JACKIE?
POP, ENOUGH! YOU WANT US TO GO? WE'LL GO.
IT'S OVER.
I'M NOT MAD, THOUGH. OKAY? IF YOU REMEMBER ANYTHING, I WANT YOU TO REMEMBER THAT.
THIS ISN'T YOUR FAULT.
GET OUT OF MY SIGHT.
OH MY GOD! I'M SO SORRY!
DADDY, ARE YOU OKAY?

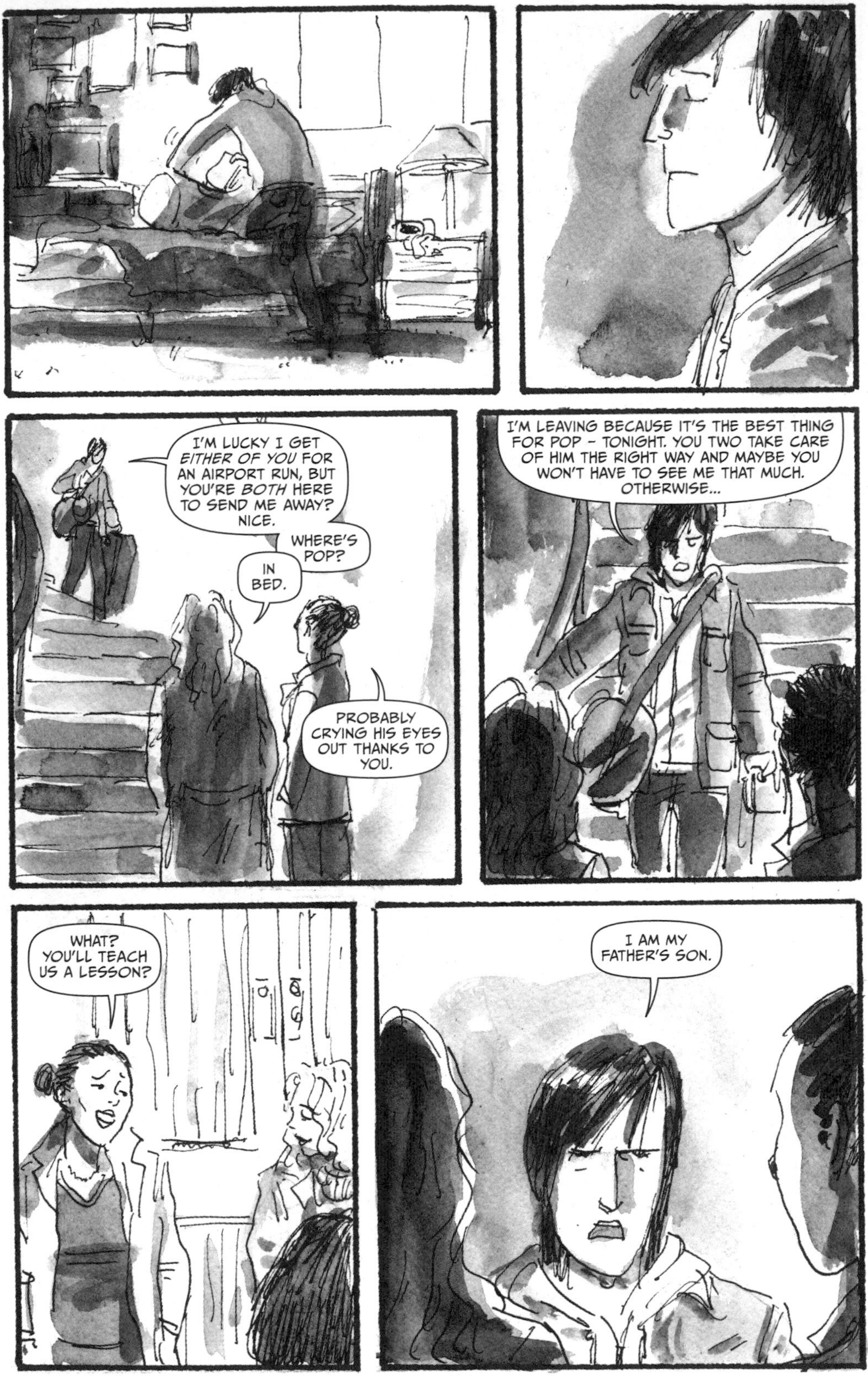
I'M LUCKY I GET *EITHER OF YOU* FOR AN AIRPORT RUN, BUT YOU'RE *BOTH* HERE TO SEND ME AWAY? NICE.
WHERE'S POP?
IN BED.
PROBABLY CRYING HIS EYES OUT THANKS TO YOU.
I'M LEAVING BECAUSE IT'S THE BEST THING FOR POP – TONIGHT. YOU TWO TAKE CARE OF HIM THE RIGHT WAY AND MAYBE YOU WON'T HAVE TO SEE ME THAT MUCH. OTHERWISE...
WHAT? YOU'LL TEACH US A LESSON?
I AM MY FATHER'S SON.

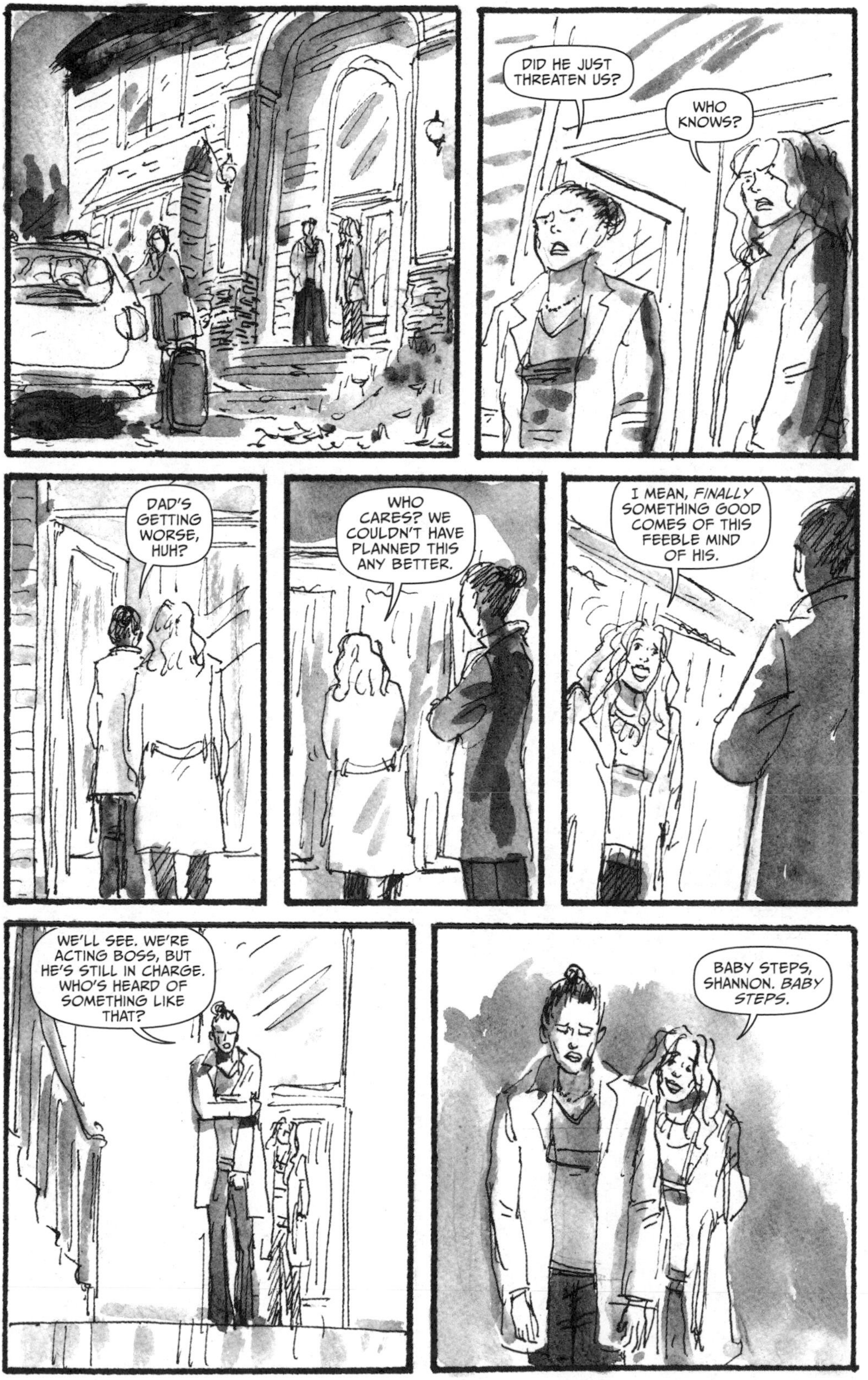
DID HE JUST THREATEN US?
WHO KNOWS?
DAD'S GETTING WORSE, HUH?
WHO CARES? WE COULDN'T HAVE PLANNED THIS ANY BETTER.
I MEAN, *FINALLY* SOMETHING GOOD COMES OF THIS FEEBLE MIND OF HIS.
WE'LL SEE. WE'RE ACTING BOSS, BUT HE'S STILL IN CHARGE. WHO'S HEARD OF SOMETHING LIKE THAT?
BABY STEPS, SHANNON. *BABY STEPS.*

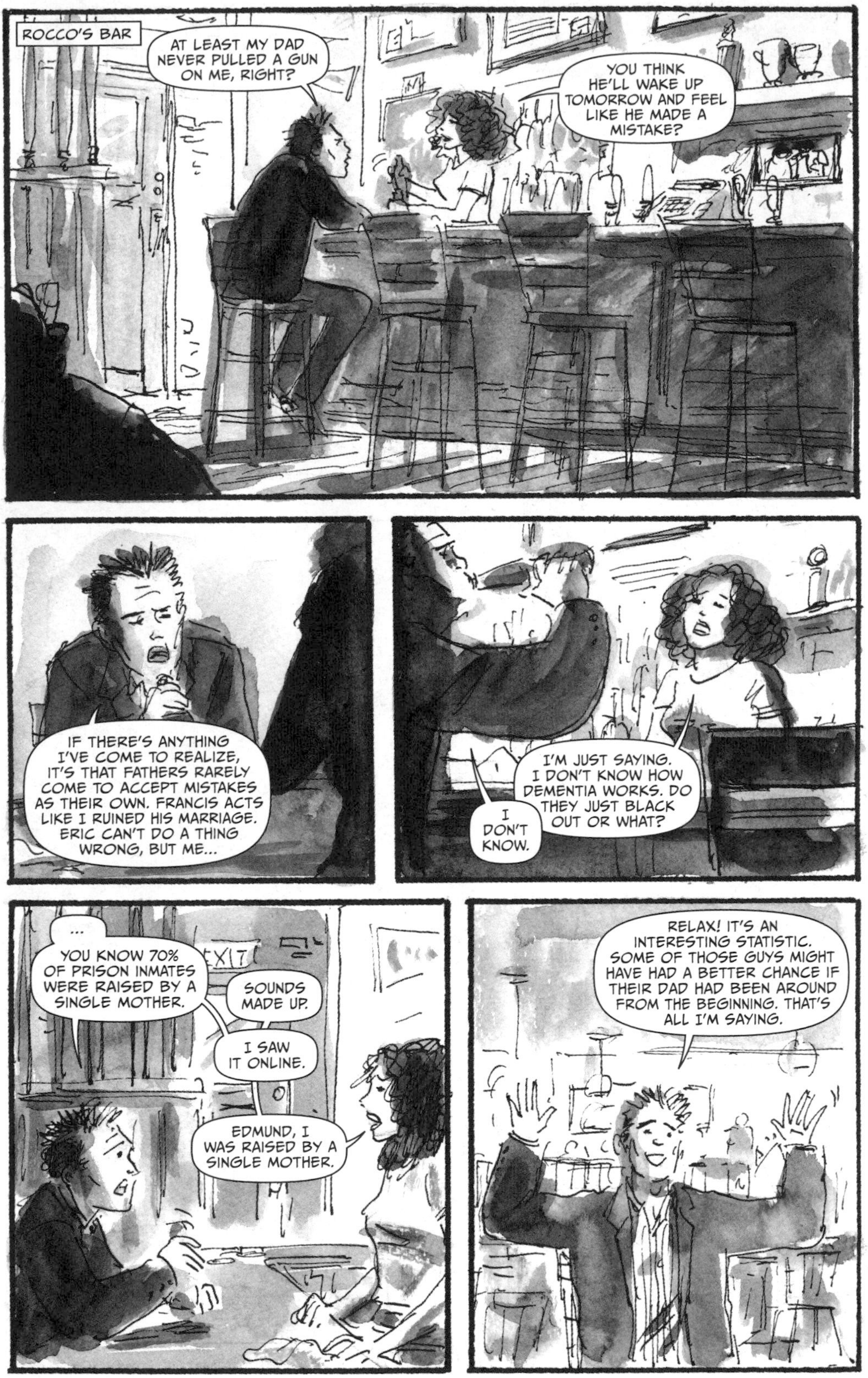
ROCCO'S BAR
AT LEAST MY DAD NEVER PULLED A GUN ON ME, RIGHT?
YOU THINK HE'LL WAKE UP TOMORROW AND FEEL LIKE HE MADE A MISTAKE?
IF THERE'S ANYTHING I'VE COME TO REALIZE, IT'S THAT FATHERS RARELY COME TO ACCEPT MISTAKES AS THEIR OWN. FRANCIS ACTS LIKE I RUINED HIS MARRIAGE. ERIC CAN'T DO A THING WRONG, BUT ME...
I'M JUST SAYING. I DON'T KNOW HOW DEMENTIA WORKS. DO THEY JUST BLACK OUT OR WHAT?
I DON'T KNOW.
...
YOU KNOW 70% OF PRISON INMATES WERE RAISED BY A SINGLE MOTHER.
SOUNDS MADE UP.
I SAW IT ONLINE.
EDMUND, I WAS RAISED BY A SINGLE MOTHER.
EXIT
RELAX! IT'S AN INTERESTING STATISTIC. SOME OF THOSE GUYS MIGHT HAVE HAD A BETTER CHANCE IF THEIR DAD HAD BEEN AROUND FROM THE BEGINNING. THAT'S ALL I'M SAYING.

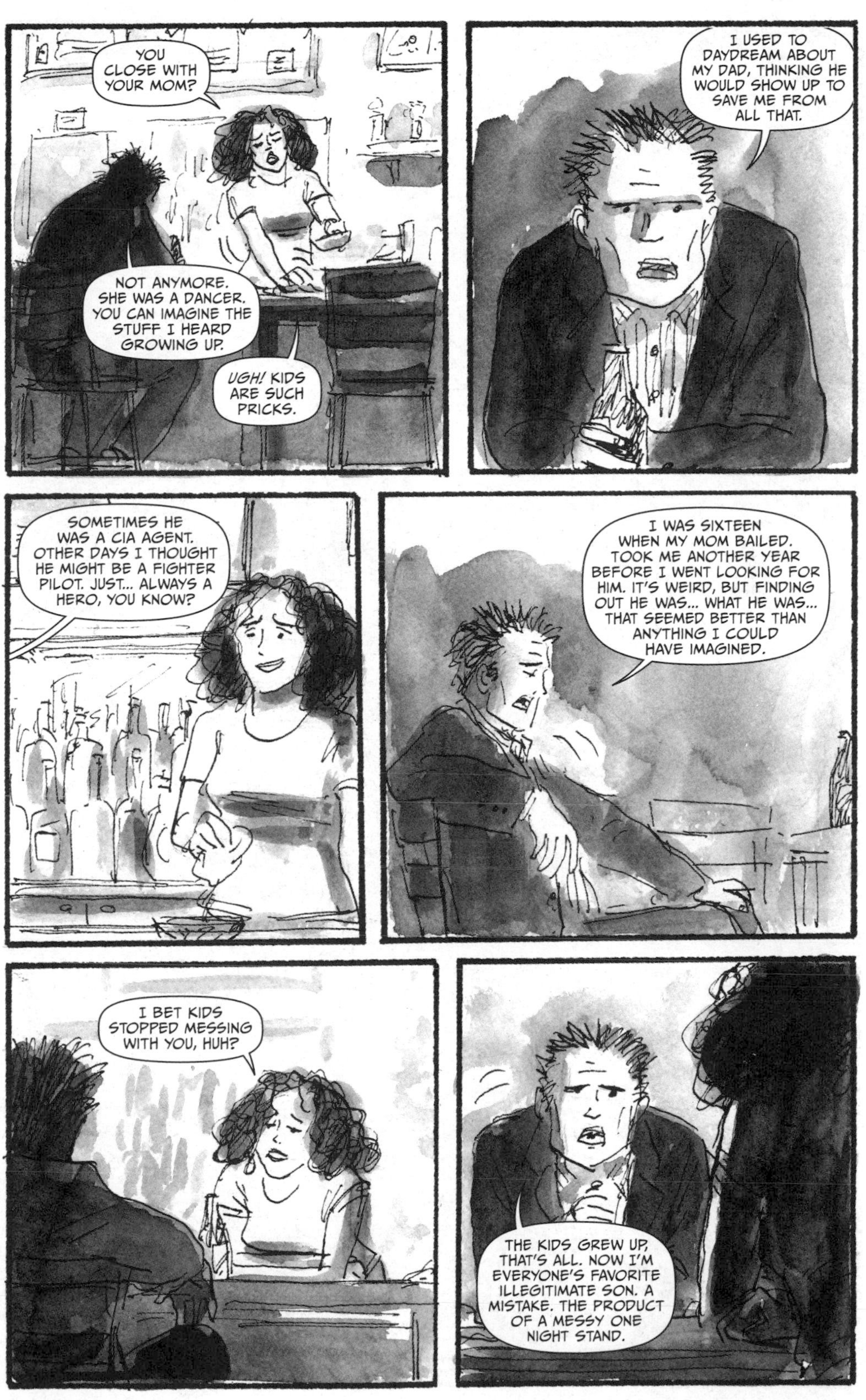
YOU CLOSE WITH YOUR MOM?
NOT ANYMORE. SHE WAS A DANCER. YOU CAN IMAGINE THE STUFF I HEARD GROWING UP.
UGH! KIDS ARE SUCH PRICKS.
I USED TO DAYDREAM ABOUT MY DAD, THINKING HE WOULD SHOW UP TO SAVE ME FROM ALL THAT.
SOMETIMES HE WAS A CIA AGENT. OTHER DAYS I THOUGHT HE MIGHT BE A FIGHTER PILOT. JUST... ALWAYS A HERO, YOU KNOW?
I WAS SIXTEEN WHEN MY MOM BAILED. TOOK ME ANOTHER YEAR BEFORE I WENT LOOKING FOR HIM. IT'S WEIRD, BUT FINDING OUT HE WAS... WHAT HE WAS... THAT SEEMED BETTER THAN ANYTHING I COULD HAVE IMAGINED.
I BET KIDS STOPPED MESSING WITH YOU, HUH?
THE KIDS GREW UP, THAT'S ALL. NOW I'M EVERYONE'S FAVORITE ILLEGITIMATE SON. A MISTAKE. THE PRODUCT OF A MESSY ONE NIGHT STAND.

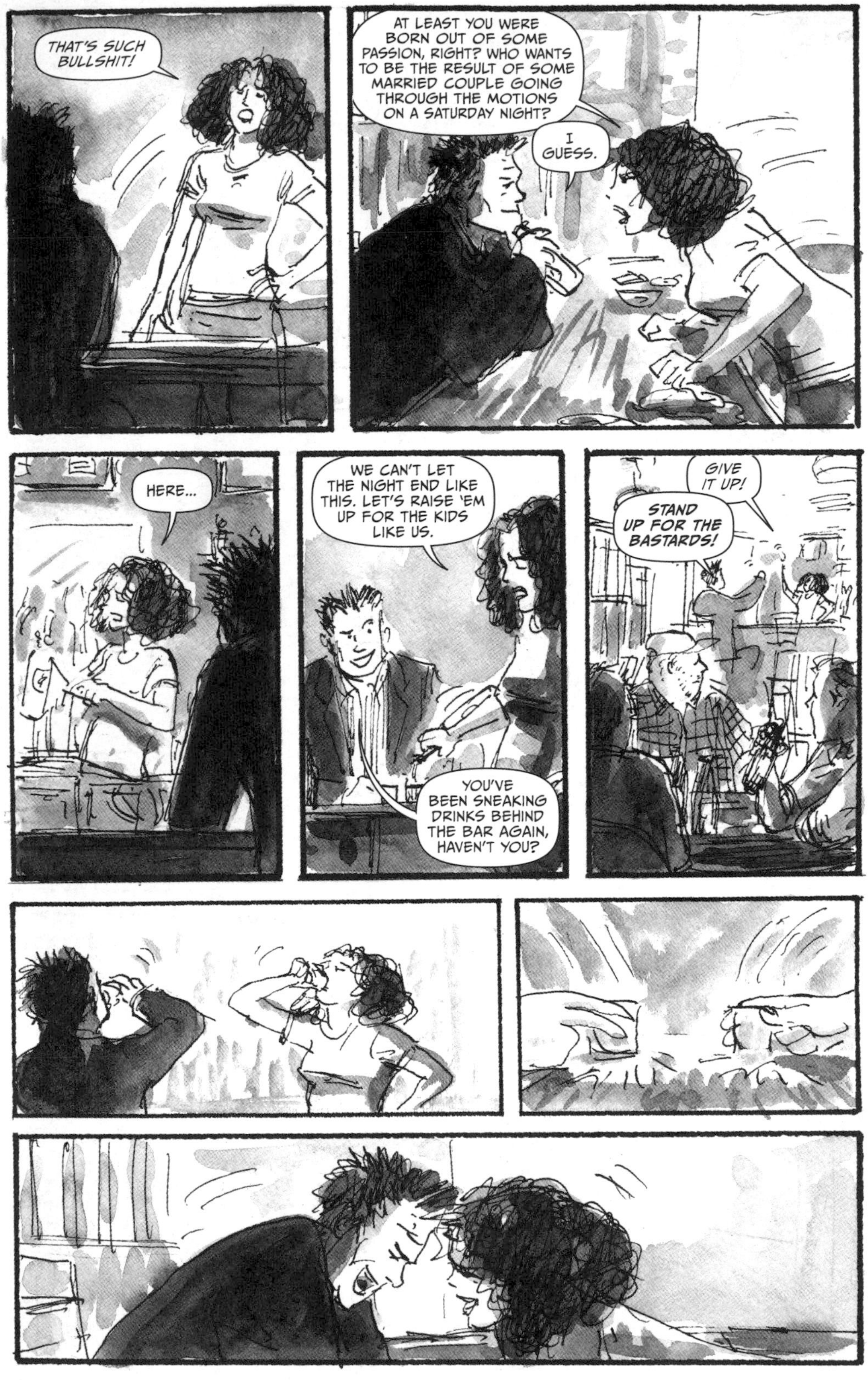
THAT'S SUCH BULLSHIT!
AT LEAST YOU WERE BORN OUT OF SOME PASSION, RIGHT? WHO WANTS TO BE THE RESULT OF SOME MARRIED COUPLE GOING THROUGH THE MOTIONS ON A SATURDAY NIGHT?
I GUESS.
HERE...
WE CAN'T LET THE NIGHT END LIKE THIS. LET'S RAISE 'EM UP FOR THE KIDS LIKE US.
YOU'VE BEEN SNEAKING DRINKS BEHIND THE BAR AGAIN, HAVEN'T YOU?
GIVE IT UP!
STAND UP FOR THE BASTARDS!

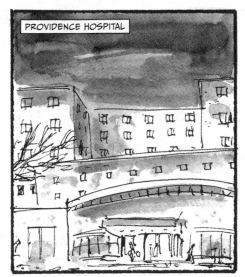

PROVIDENCE HOSPITAL

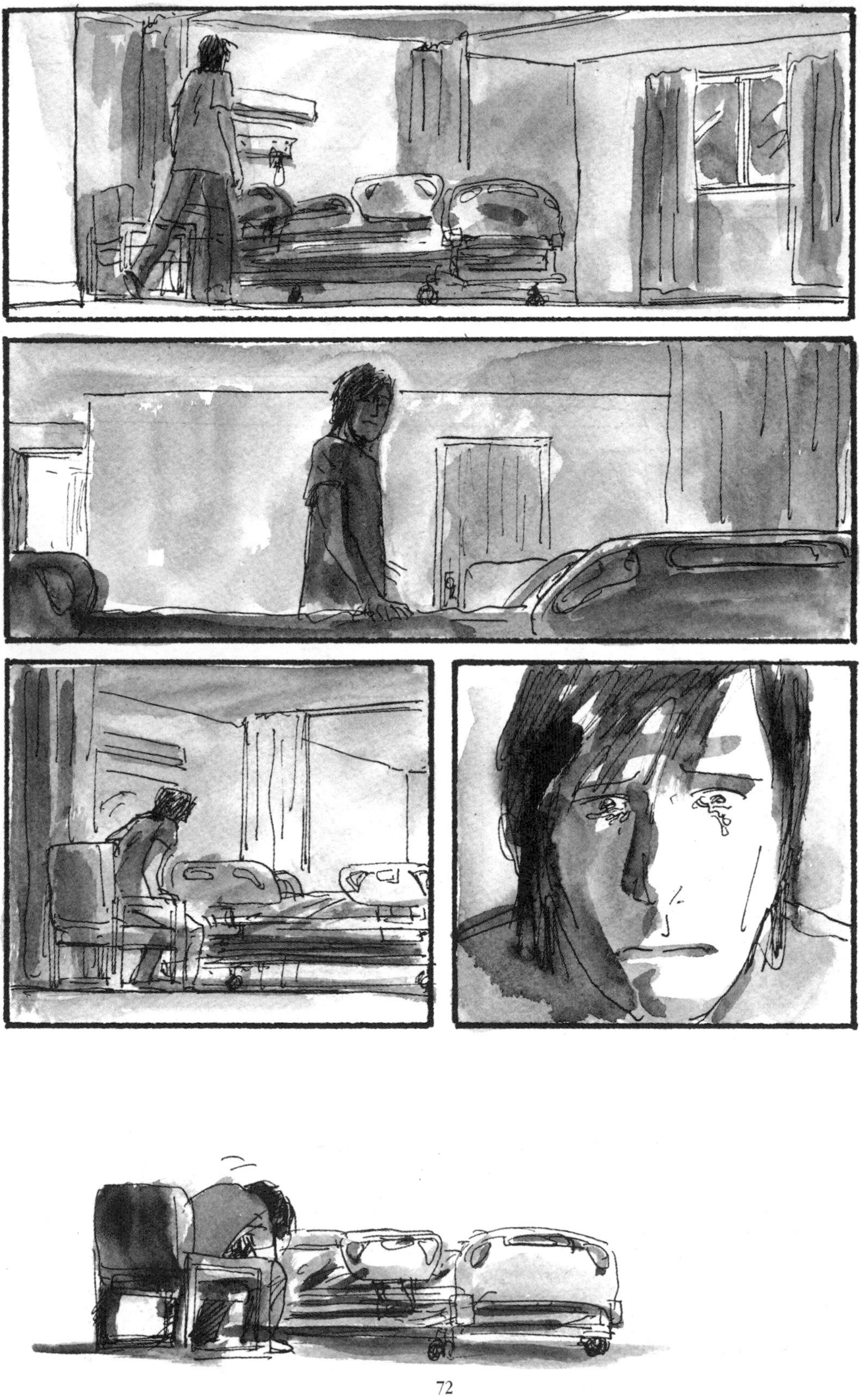

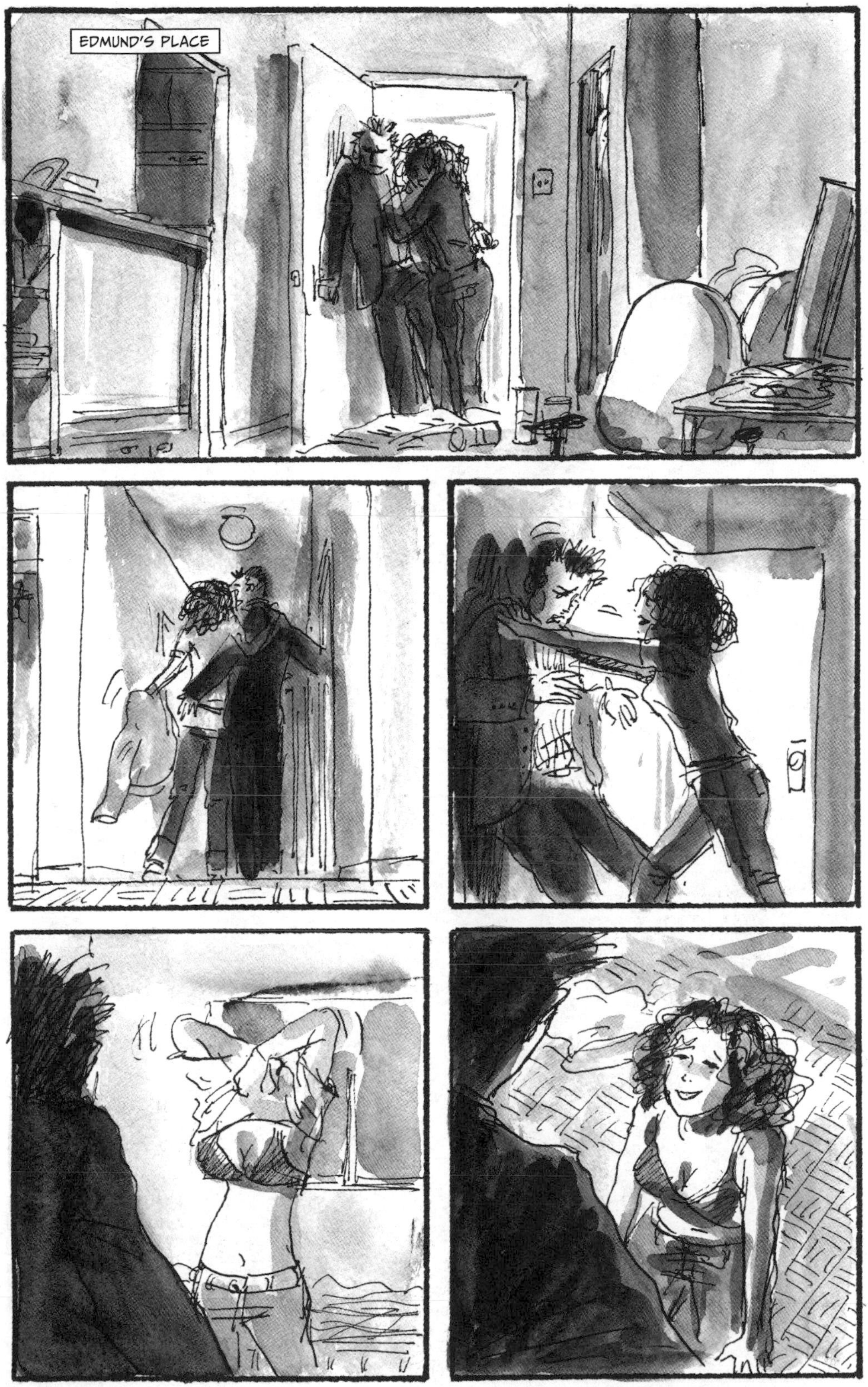
EDMUND'S PLACE

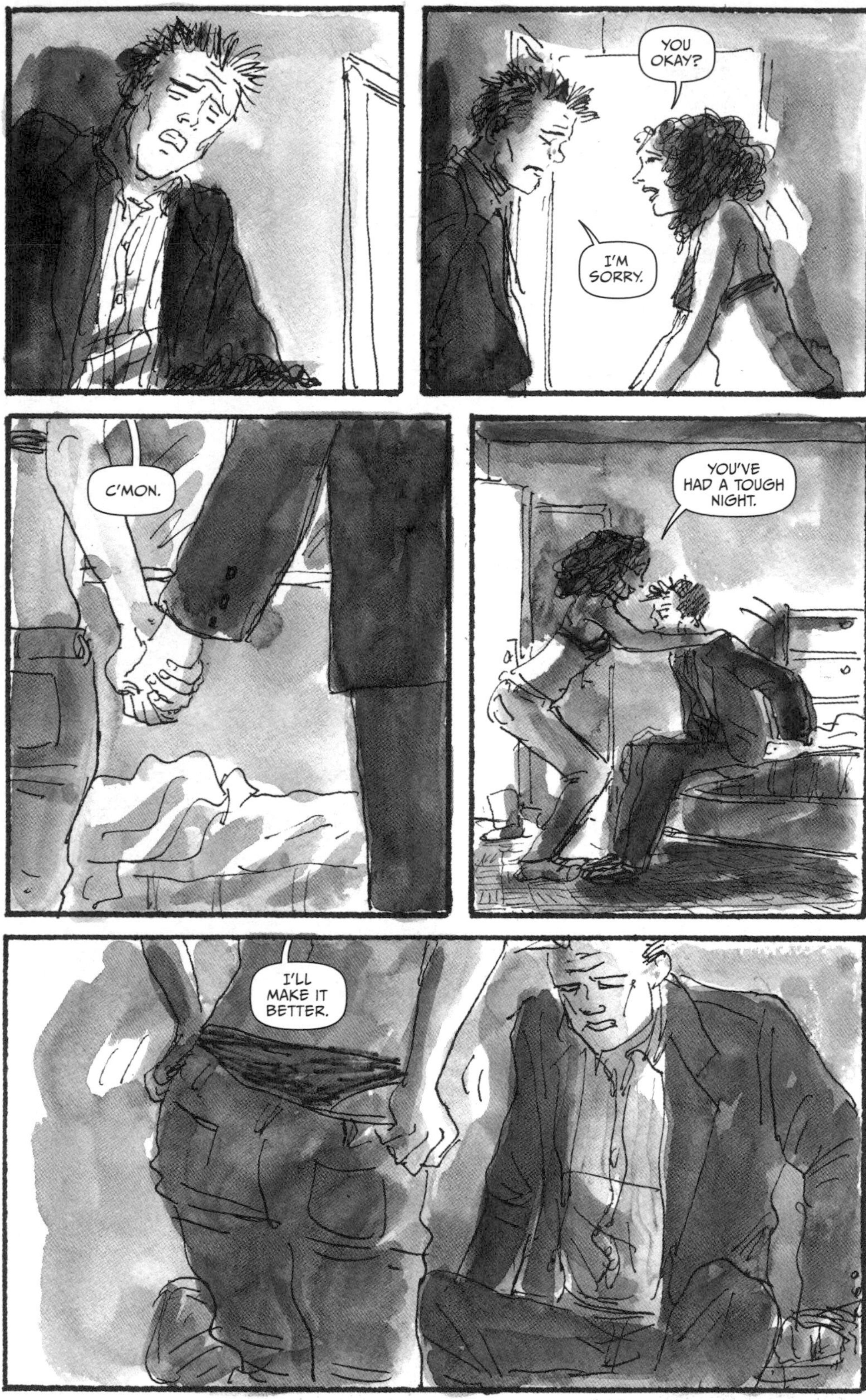
YOU OKAY?
I'M SORRY.
C'MON.
YOU'VE HAD A TOUGH NIGHT.
I'LL MAKE IT BETTER.

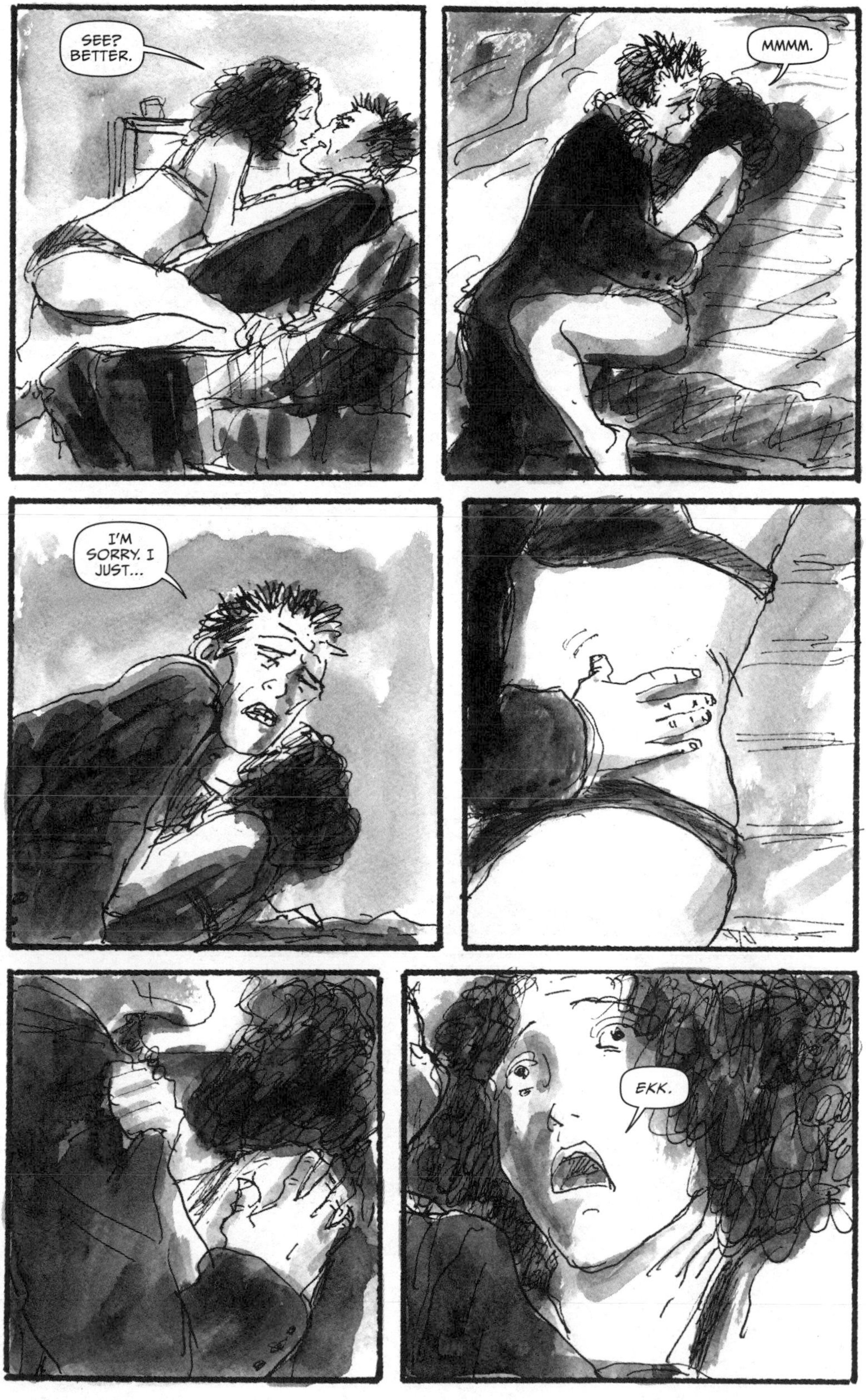
SEE? BETTER.
MMMM.
I'M SORRY. I JUST...
EKK.

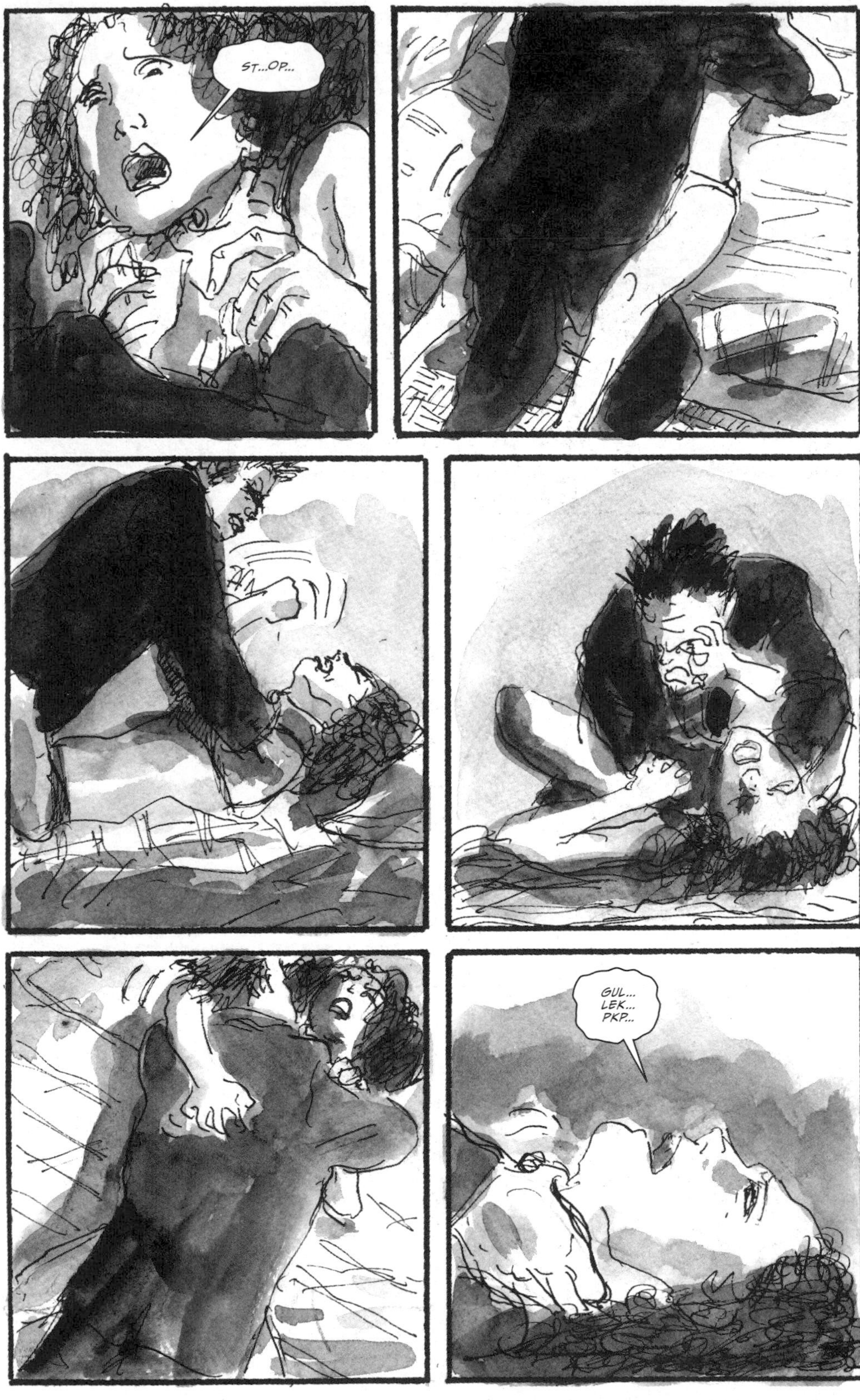
ST...OP...
GUL... LEK... PKP...

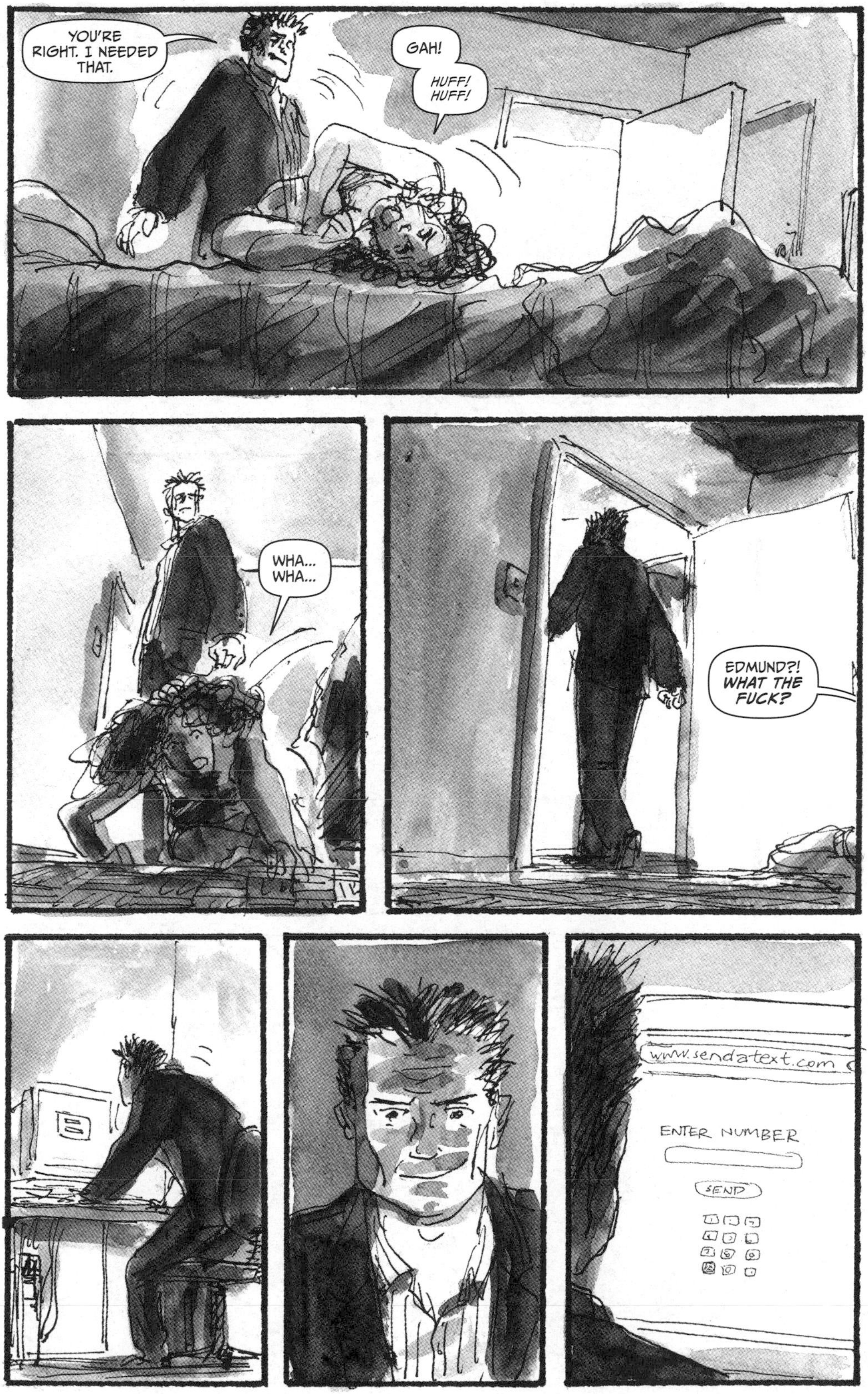
YOU'RE RIGHT. I NEEDED THAT.
GAH!
HUFF! HUFF!
WHA... WHA...
EDMUND?! WHAT THE FUCK?
www.sendatext.com
ENTER NUMBER
SEND

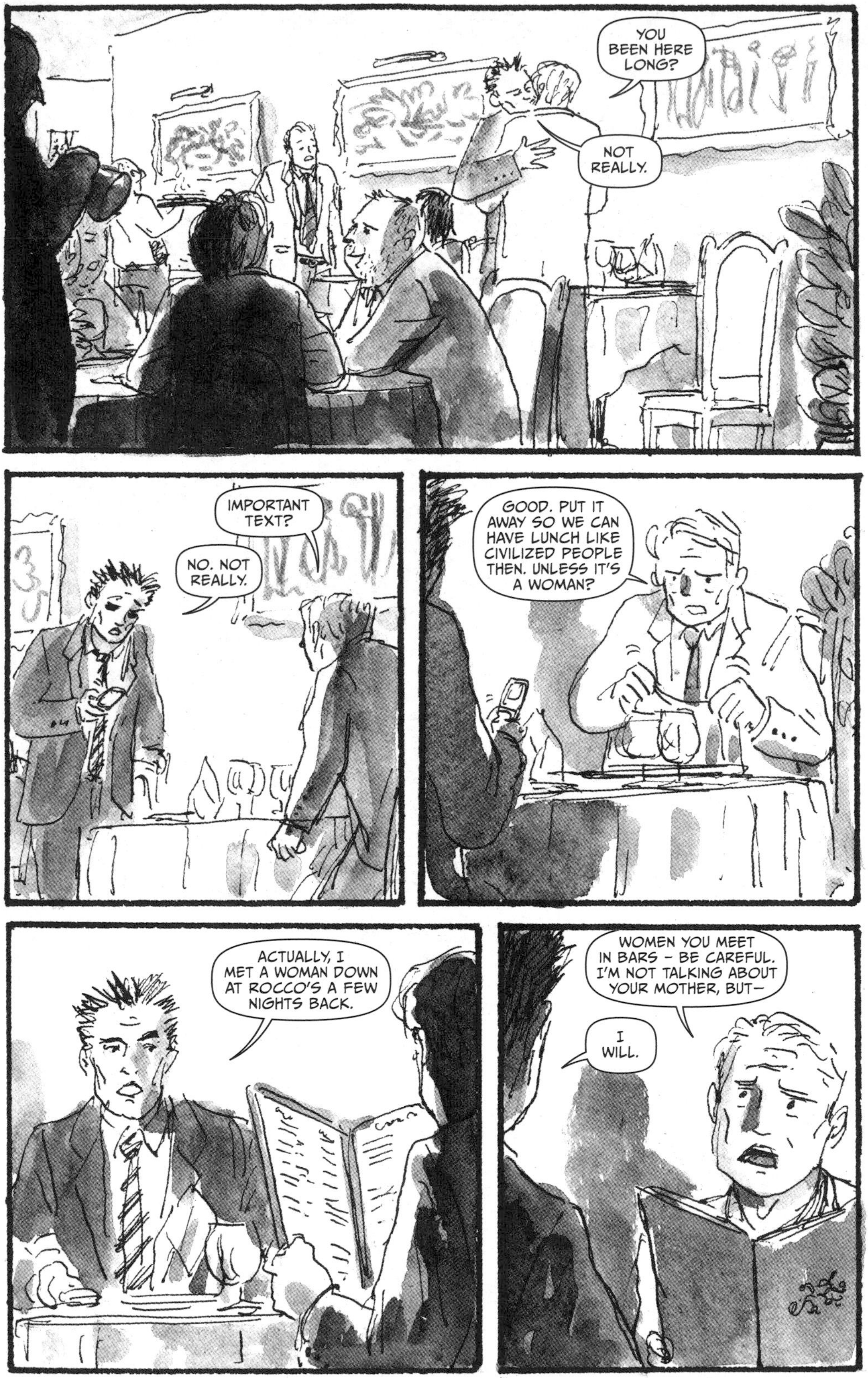
YOU BEEN HERE LONG?
NOT REALLY.
IMPORTANT TEXT?
NO. NOT REALLY.
GOOD. PUT IT AWAY SO WE CAN HAVE LUNCH LIKE CIVILIZED PEOPLE THEN. UNLESS IT'S A WOMAN?
ACTUALLY, I MET A WOMAN DOWN AT ROCCO'S A FEW NIGHTS BACK.
WOMEN YOU MEET IN BARS – BE CAREFUL. I'M NOT TALKING ABOUT YOUR MOTHER, BUT—
I WILL.

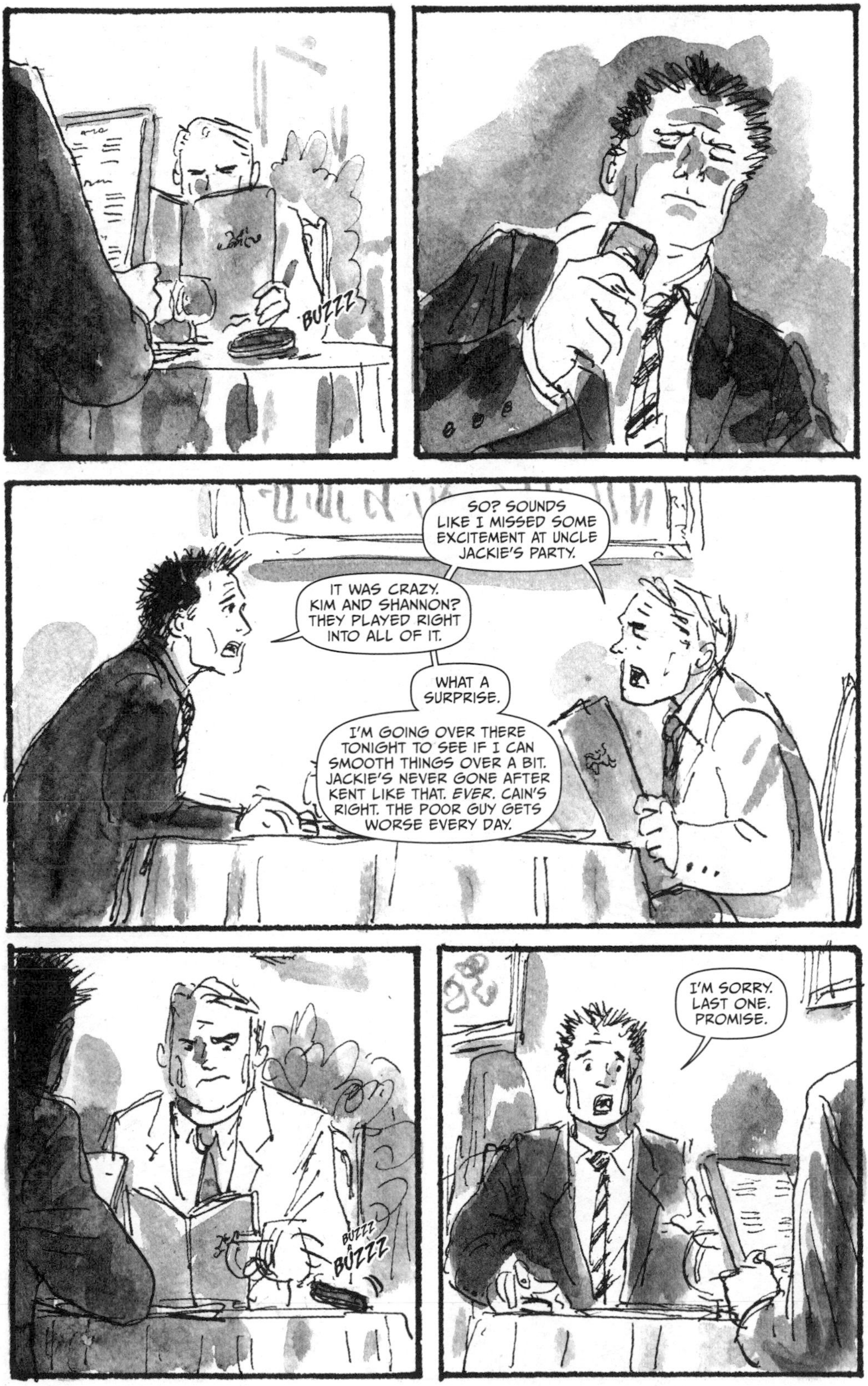
BUZZZ
SO? SOUNDS LIKE I MISSED SOME EXCITEMENT AT UNCLE JACKIE'S PARTY.
IT WAS CRAZY. KIM AND SHANNON? THEY PLAYED RIGHT INTO ALL OF IT.
WHAT A SURPRISE.
I'M GOING OVER THERE TONIGHT TO SEE IF I CAN SMOOTH THINGS OVER A BIT. JACKIE'S NEVER GONE AFTER KENT LIKE THAT. *EVER*. CAIN'S RIGHT. THE POOR GUY GETS WORSE EVERY DAY.
BUZZZ BUZZZ
I'M SORRY. LAST ONE. PROMISE.

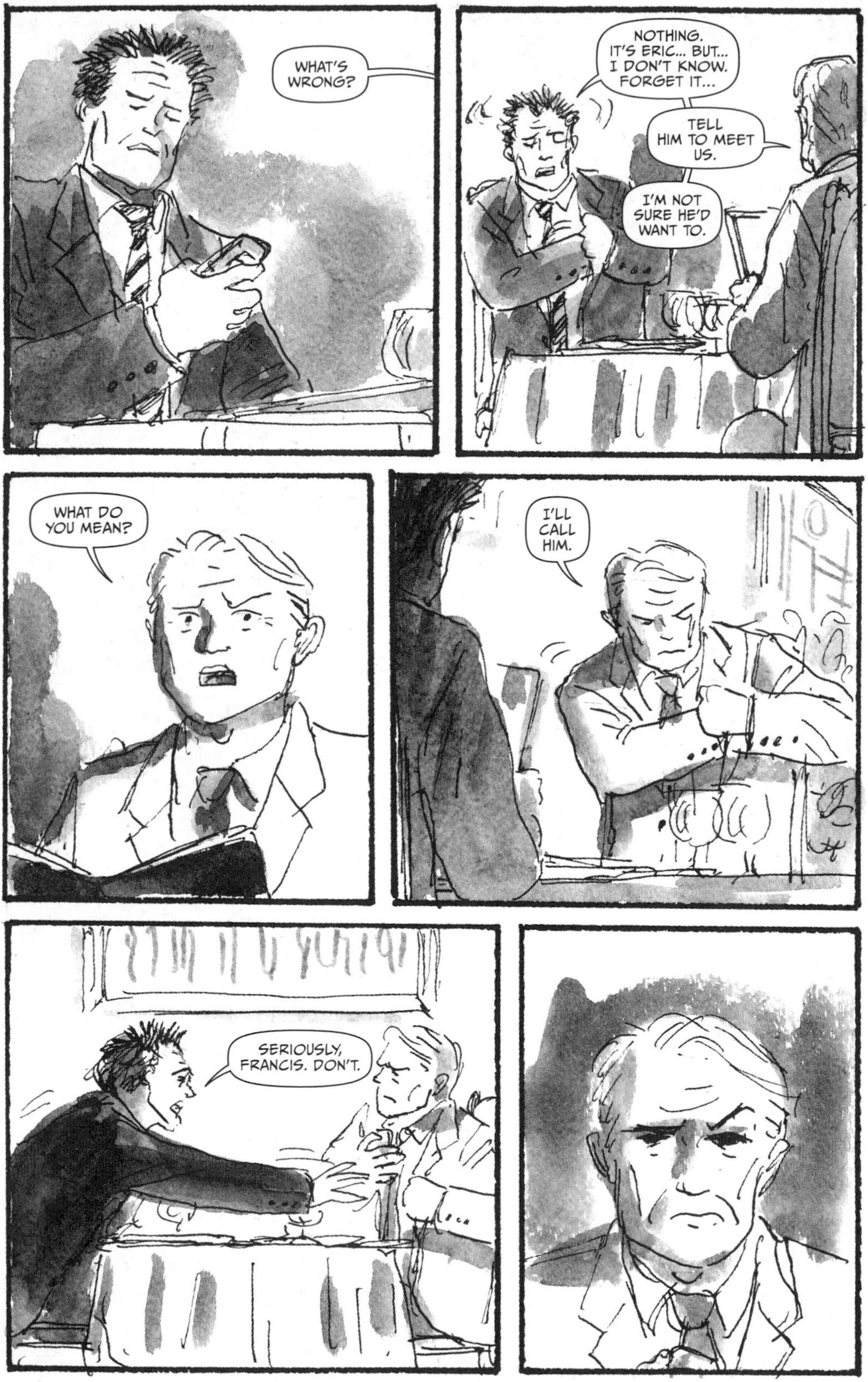
WHAT'S WRONG?
NOTHING. IT'S ERIC... BUT... I DON'T KNOW. FORGET IT...
TELL HIM TO MEET US.
I'M NOT SURE HE'D WANT TO.
WHAT DO YOU MEAN?
I'LL CALL HIM.
SERIOUSLY, FRANCIS. DON'T.

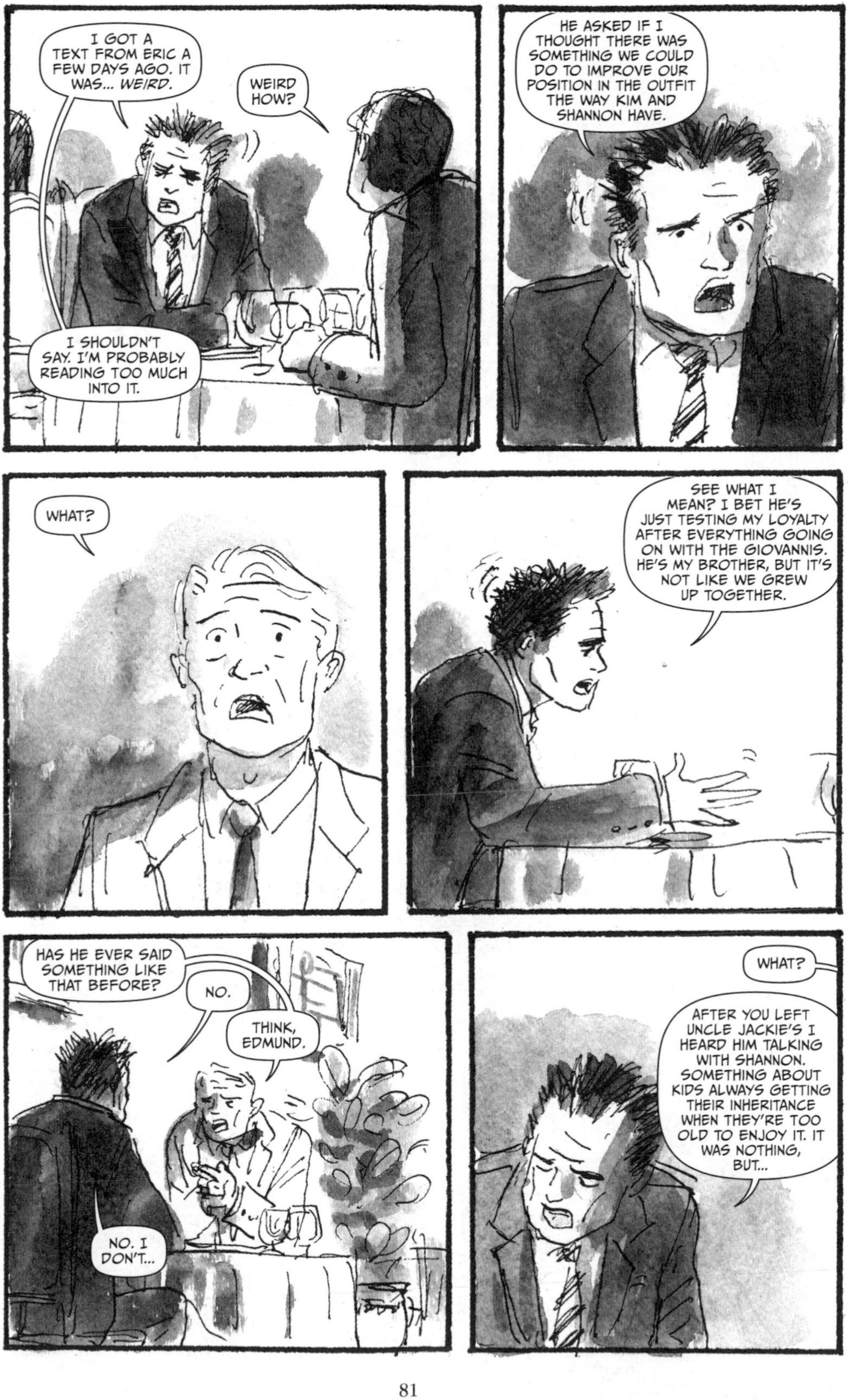
I GOT A TEXT FROM ERIC A FEW DAYS AGO. IT WAS... *WEIRD*.
WEIRD HOW?
I SHOULDN'T SAY. I'M PROBABLY READING TOO MUCH INTO IT.
HE ASKED IF I THOUGHT THERE WAS SOMETHING WE COULD DO TO IMPROVE OUR POSITION IN THE OUTFIT THE WAY KIM AND SHANNON HAVE.
WHAT?
SEE WHAT I MEAN? I BET HE'S JUST TESTING MY LOYALTY AFTER EVERYTHING GOING ON WITH THE GIOVANNIS. HE'S MY BROTHER, BUT IT'S NOT LIKE WE GREW UP TOGETHER.
HAS HE EVER SAID SOMETHING LIKE THAT BEFORE?
NO.
THINK, EDMUND.
NO. I DON'T...
WHAT?
AFTER YOU LEFT UNCLE JACKIE'S I HEARD HIM TALKING WITH SHANNON. SOMETHING ABOUT KIDS ALWAYS GETTING THEIR INHERITANCE WHEN THEY'RE TOO OLD TO ENJOY IT. IT WAS NOTHING, BUT...

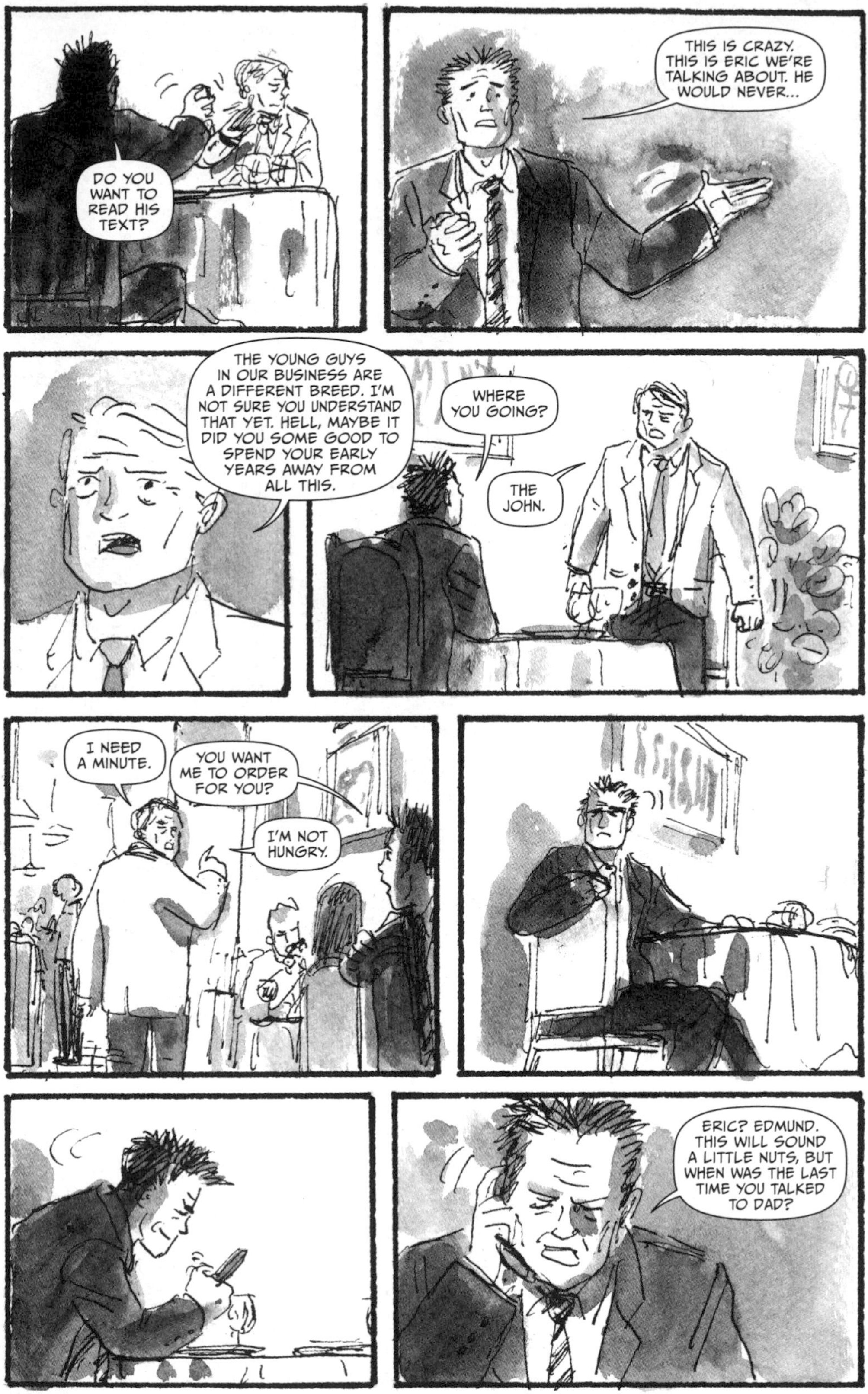
DO YOU WANT TO READ HIS TEXT?
THIS IS CRAZY. THIS IS ERIC WE'RE TALKING ABOUT. HE WOULD NEVER...
THE YOUNG GUYS IN OUR BUSINESS ARE A DIFFERENT BREED. I'M NOT SURE YOU UNDERSTAND THAT YET. HELL, MAYBE IT DID YOU SOME GOOD TO SPEND YOUR EARLY YEARS AWAY FROM ALL THIS.
WHERE YOU GOING?
THE JOHN.
I NEED A MINUTE.
YOU WANT ME TO ORDER FOR YOU?
I'M NOT HUNGRY.
ERIC? EDMUND. THIS WILL SOUND A LITTLE NUTS, BUT WHEN WAS THE LAST TIME YOU TALKED TO DAD?

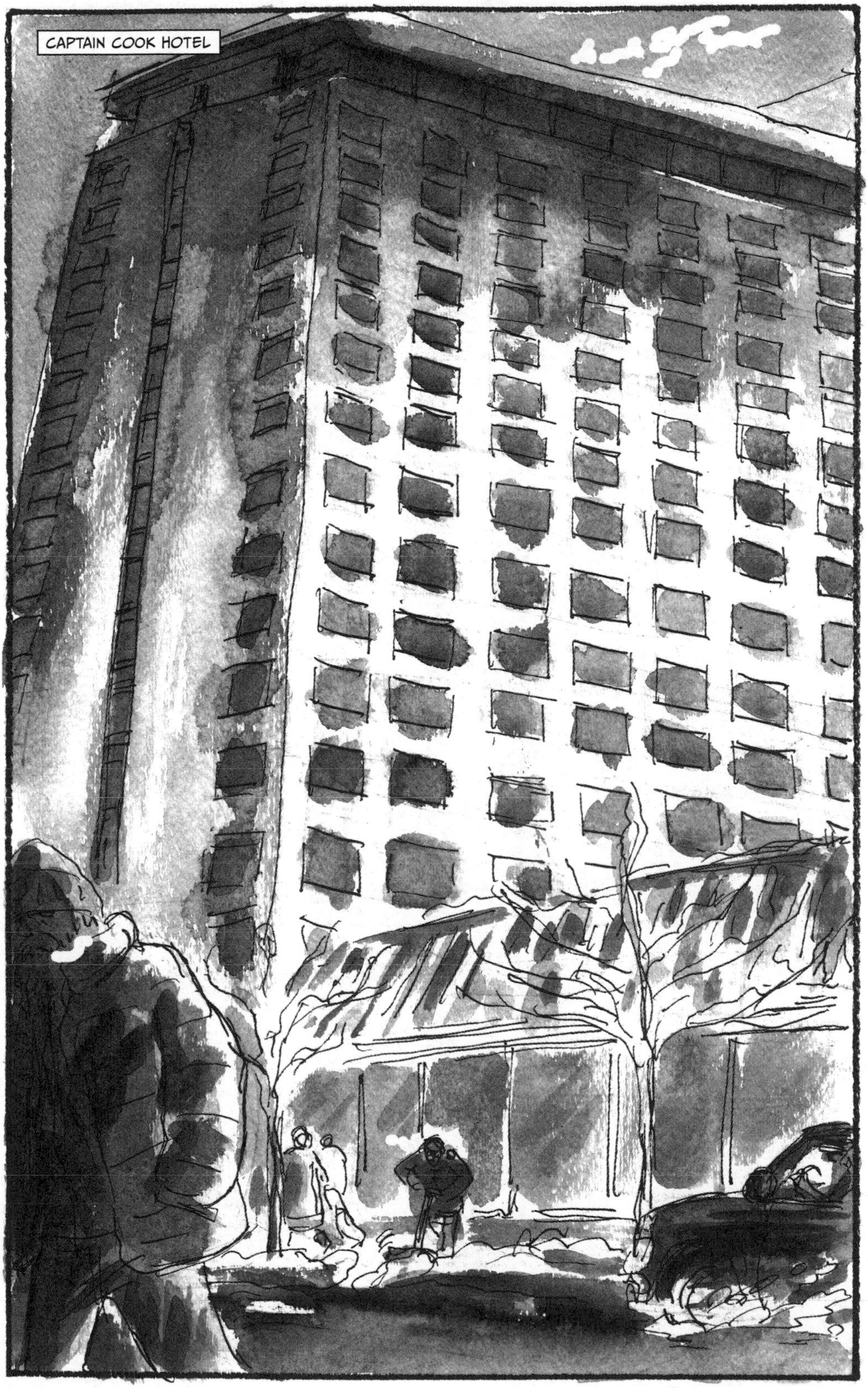
CAPTAIN COOK HOTEL

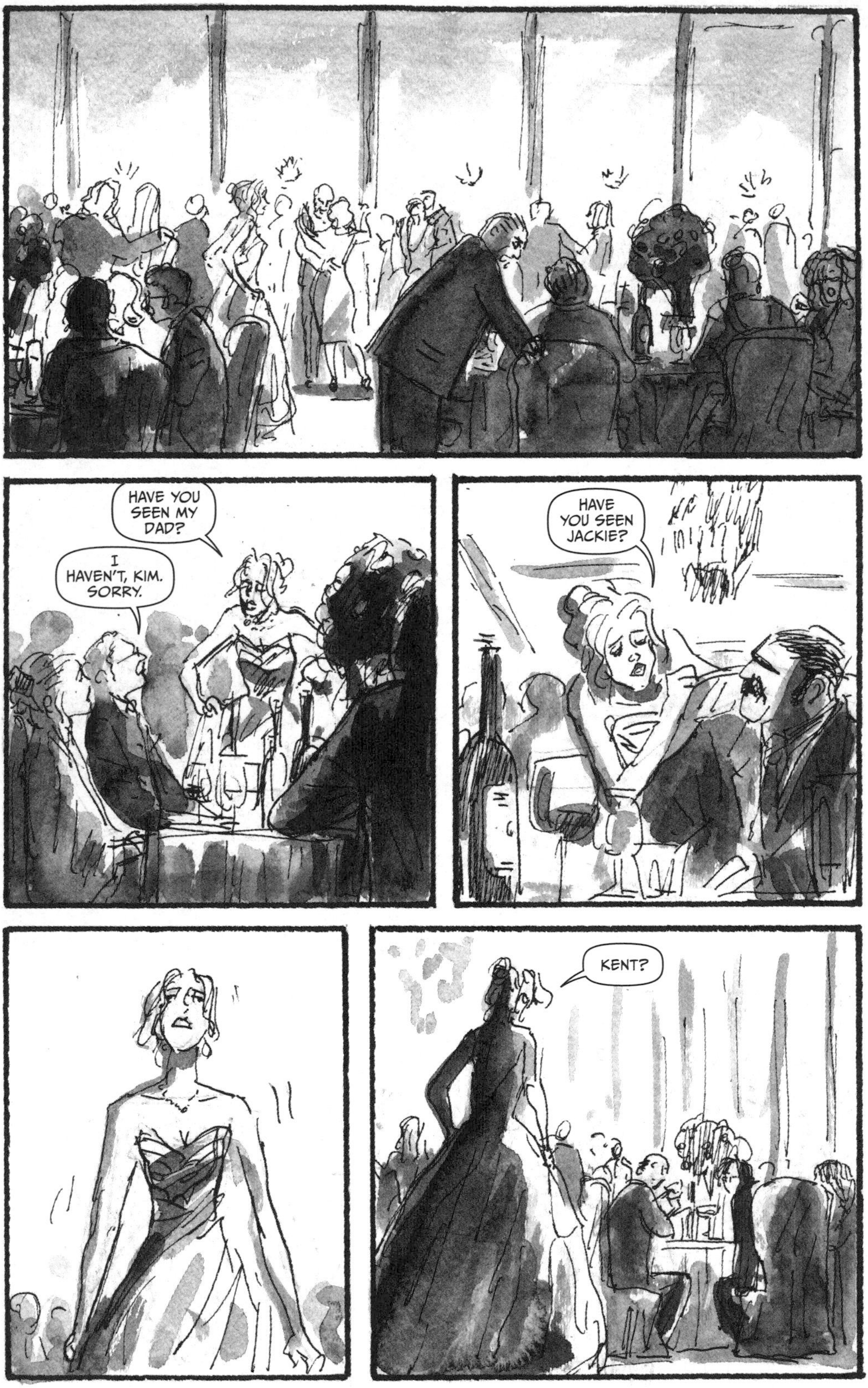
HAVE YOU SEEN MY DAD?
I HAVEN'T, KIM. SORRY.
HAVE YOU SEEN JACKIE?
KENT?

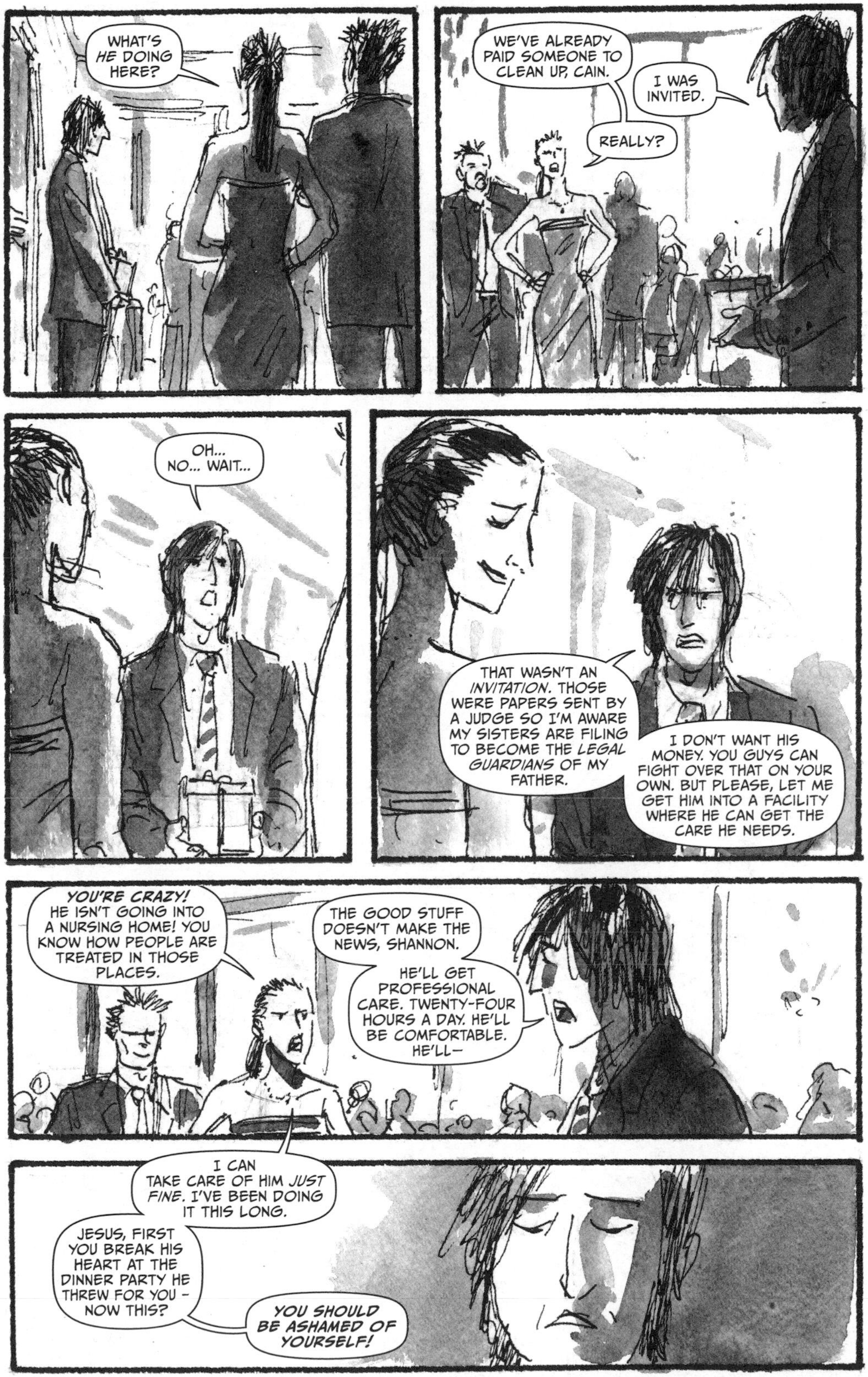
WHAT'S HE DOING HERE?
WE'VE ALREADY PAID SOMEONE TO CLEAN UP, CAIN.
I WAS INVITED.
REALLY?
OH... NO... WAIT...
THAT WASN'T AN INVITATION. THOSE WERE PAPERS SENT BY A JUDGE SO I'M AWARE MY SISTERS ARE FILING TO BECOME THE LEGAL GUARDIANS OF MY FATHER.
I DON'T WANT HIS MONEY. YOU GUYS CAN FIGHT OVER THAT ON YOUR OWN. BUT PLEASE, LET ME GET HIM INTO A FACILITY WHERE HE CAN GET THE CARE HE NEEDS.
YOU'RE CRAZY! HE ISN'T GOING INTO A NURSING HOME! YOU KNOW HOW PEOPLE ARE TREATED IN THOSE PLACES.
THE GOOD STUFF DOESN'T MAKE THE NEWS, SHANNON.
HE'LL GET PROFESSIONAL CARE. TWENTY-FOUR HOURS A DAY. HE'LL BE COMFORTABLE. HE'LL—
I CAN TAKE CARE OF HIM JUST FINE. I'VE BEEN DOING IT THIS LONG.
JESUS, FIRST YOU BREAK HIS HEART AT THE DINNER PARTY HE THREW FOR YOU - NOW THIS?
YOU SHOULD BE ASHAMED OF YOURSELF!

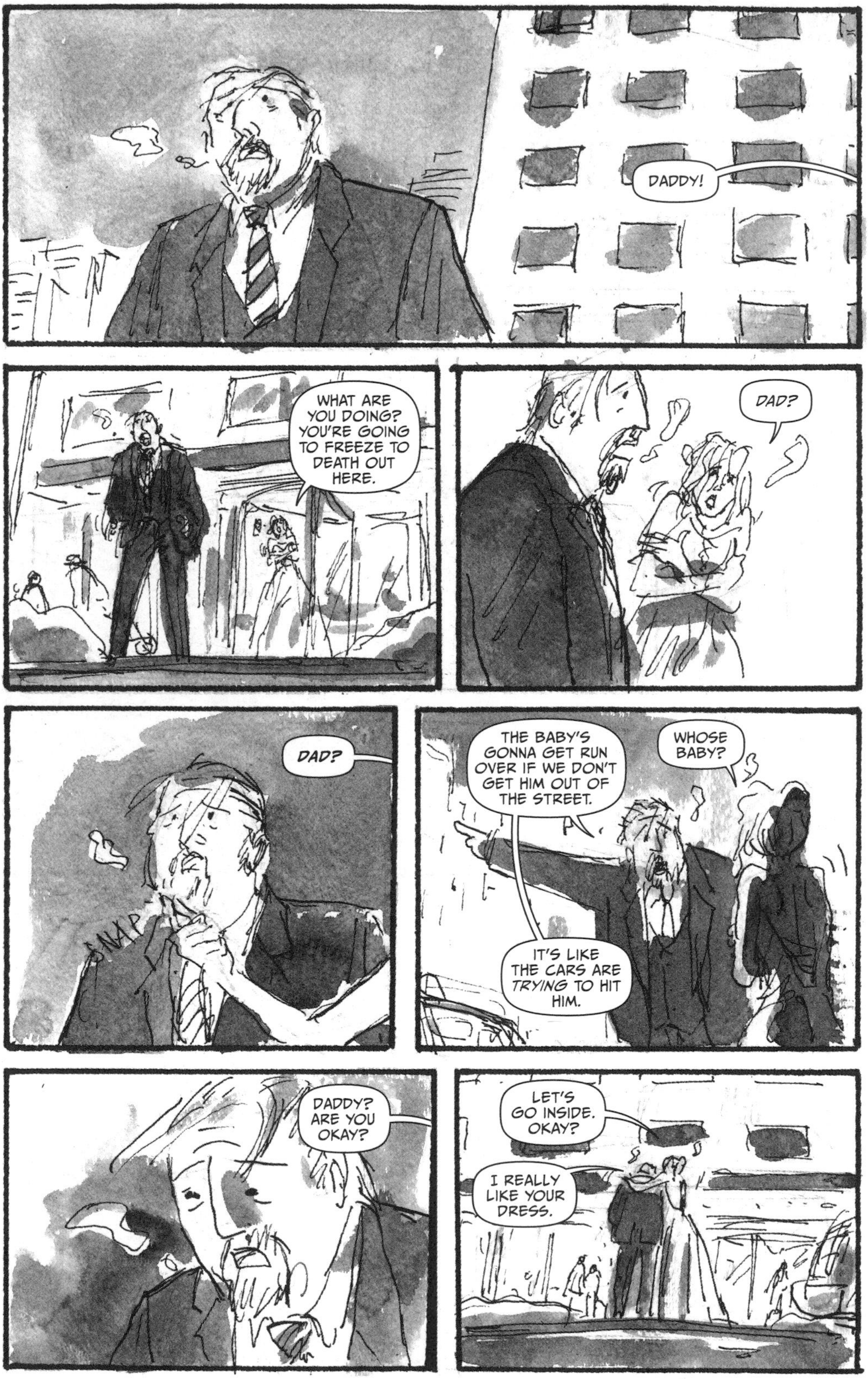
DADDY!
WHAT ARE YOU DOING? YOU'RE GOING TO FREEZE TO DEATH OUT HERE.
DAD?
DAD?
SNAP
THE BABY'S GONNA GET RUN OVER IF WE DON'T GET HIM OUT OF THE STREET.
WHOSE BABY?
IT'S LIKE THE CARS ARE *TRYING* TO HIT HIM.
DADDY? ARE YOU OKAY?
LET'S GO INSIDE. OKAY?
I REALLY LIKE YOUR DRESS.

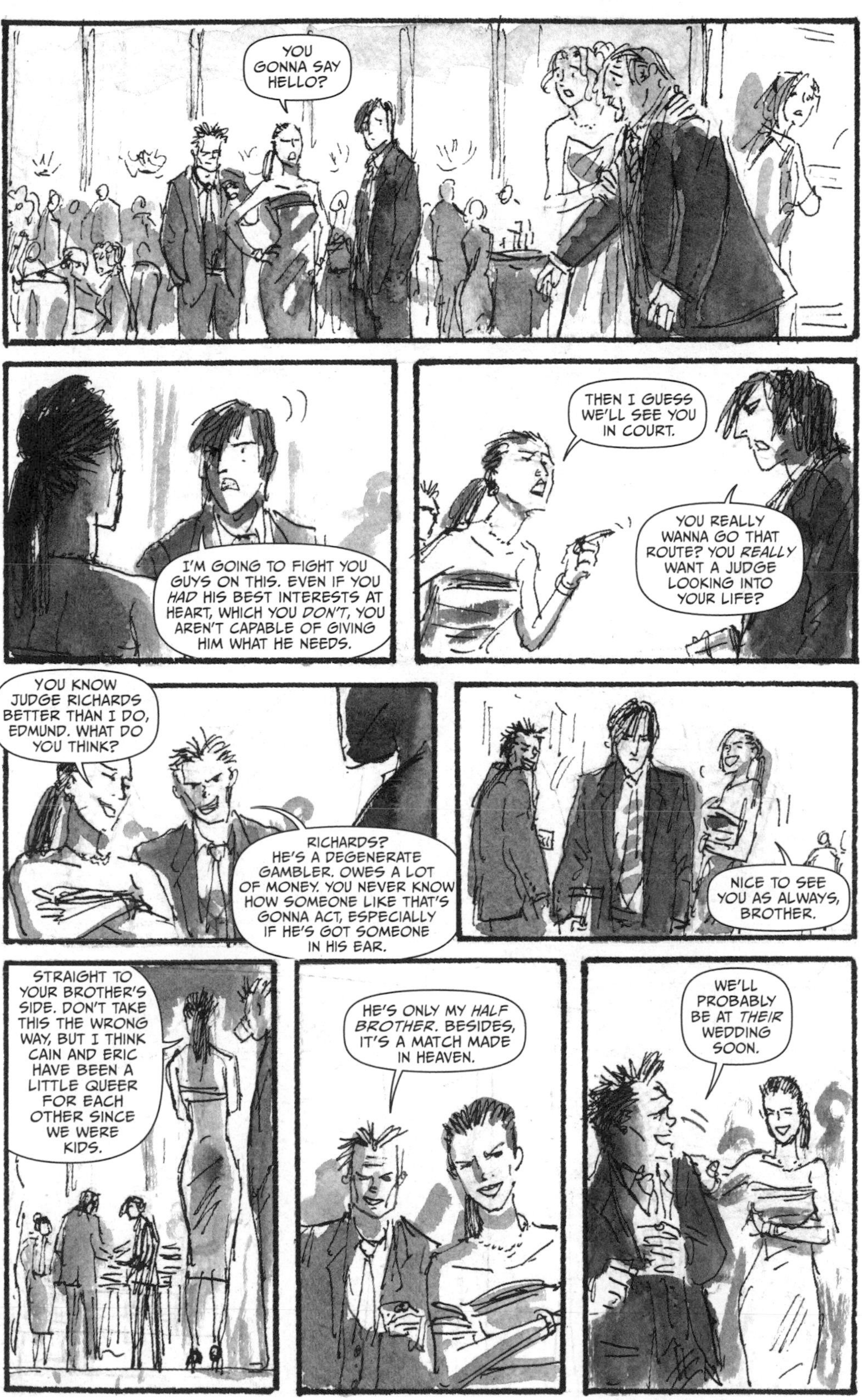
YOU GONNA SAY HELLO?
I'M GOING TO FIGHT YOU GUYS ON THIS. EVEN IF YOU *HAD* HIS BEST INTERESTS AT HEART, WHICH YOU *DON'T*, YOU AREN'T CAPABLE OF GIVING HIM WHAT HE NEEDS.
THEN I GUESS WE'LL SEE YOU IN COURT.
YOU REALLY WANNA GO THAT ROUTE? YOU *REALLY* WANT A JUDGE LOOKING INTO YOUR LIFE?
YOU KNOW JUDGE RICHARDS BETTER THAN I DO, EDMUND. WHAT DO YOU THINK?
RICHARDS? HE'S A DEGENERATE GAMBLER. OWES A LOT OF MONEY. YOU NEVER KNOW HOW SOMEONE LIKE THAT'S GONNA ACT, ESPECIALLY IF HE'S GOT SOMEONE IN HIS EAR.
NICE TO SEE YOU AS ALWAYS, BROTHER.
STRAIGHT TO YOUR BROTHER'S SIDE. DON'T TAKE THIS THE WRONG WAY, BUT I THINK CAIN AND ERIC HAVE BEEN A LITTLE QUEER FOR EACH OTHER SINCE WE WERE KIDS.
HE'S ONLY MY *HALF BROTHER*. BESIDES, IT'S A MATCH MADE IN HEAVEN.
WE'LL PROBABLY BE AT *THEIR* WEDDING SOON.

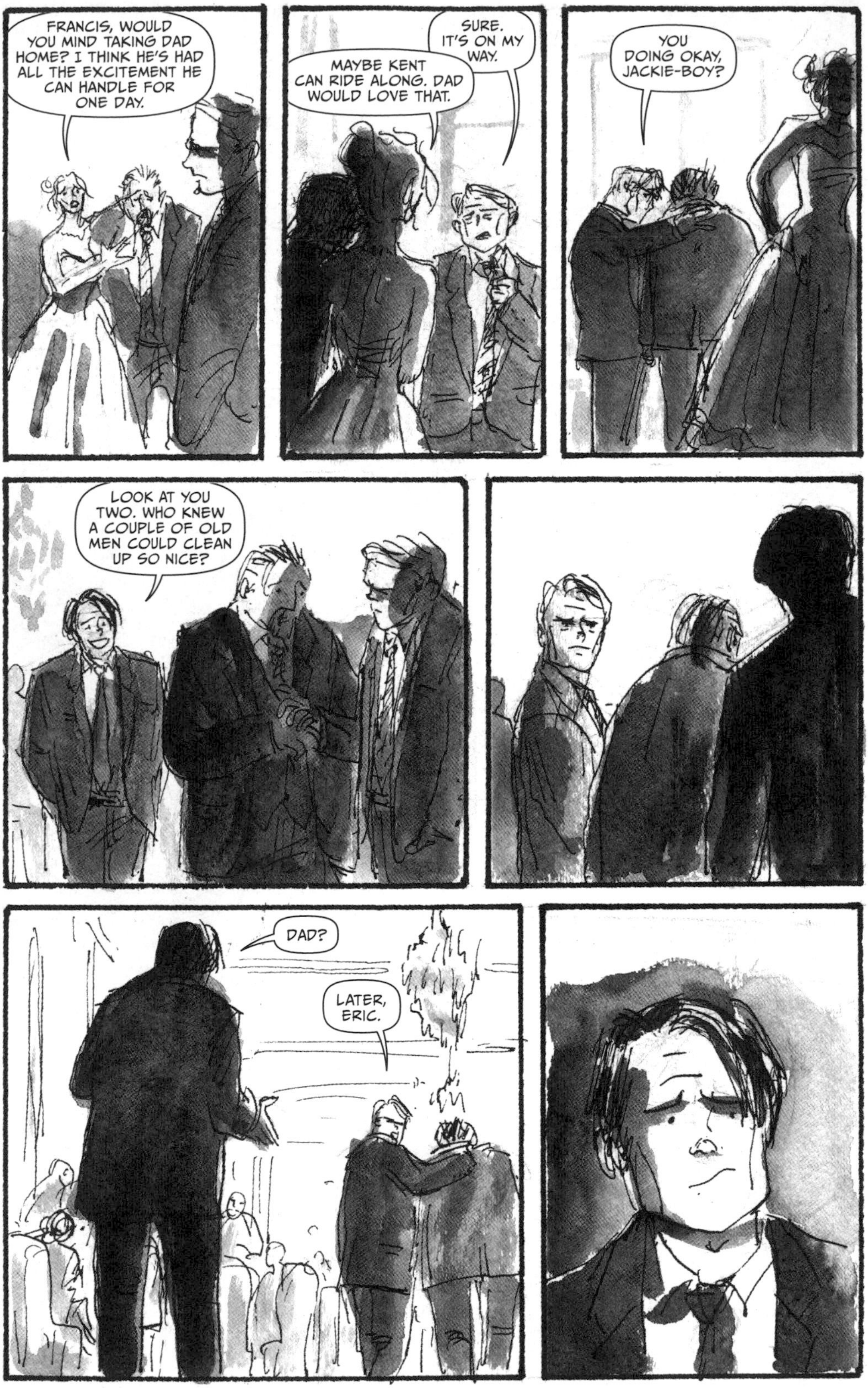
FRANCIS, WOULD YOU MIND TAKING DAD HOME? I THINK HE'S HAD ALL THE EXCITEMENT HE CAN HANDLE FOR ONE DAY.
MAYBE KENT CAN RIDE ALONG. DAD WOULD LOVE THAT.
SURE. IT'S ON MY WAY.
YOU DOING OKAY, JACKIE-BOY?
LOOK AT YOU TWO. WHO KNEW A COUPLE OF OLD MEN COULD CLEAN UP SO NICE?
DAD?
LATER, ERIC.

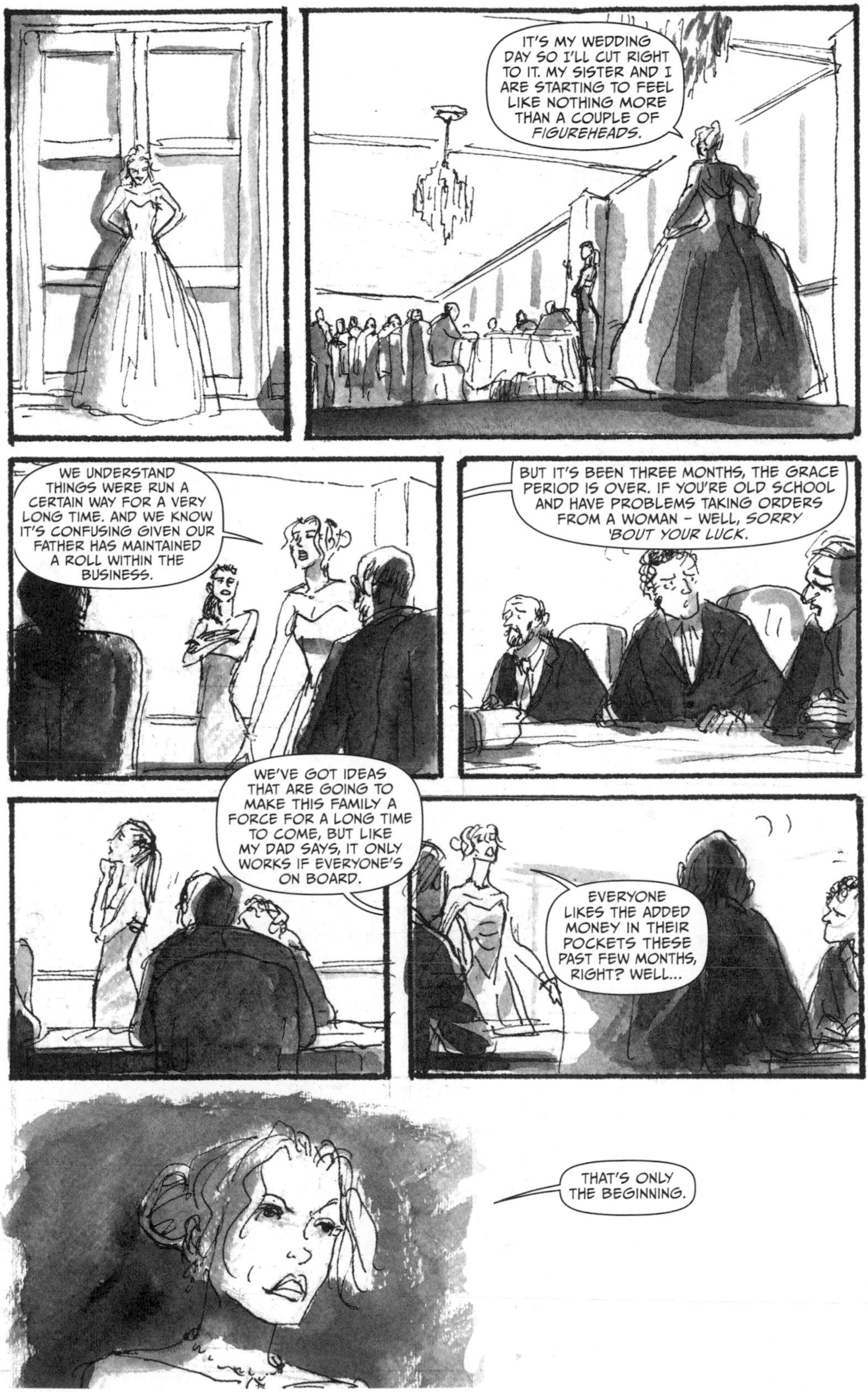

IT'S MY WEDDING DAY SO I'LL CUT RIGHT TO IT. MY SISTER AND I ARE STARTING TO FEEL LIKE NOTHING MORE THAN A COUPLE OF *FIGUREHEADS*.
WE UNDERSTAND THINGS WERE RUN A CERTAIN WAY FOR A VERY LONG TIME. AND WE KNOW IT'S CONFUSING GIVEN OUR FATHER HAS MAINTAINED A ROLL WITHIN THE BUSINESS.
BUT IT'S BEEN THREE MONTHS, THE GRACE PERIOD IS OVER. IF YOU'RE OLD SCHOOL AND HAVE PROBLEMS TAKING ORDERS FROM A WOMAN – WELL, *SORRY 'BOUT YOUR LUCK.*
WE'VE GOT IDEAS THAT ARE GOING TO MAKE THIS FAMILY A FORCE FOR A LONG TIME TO COME, BUT LIKE MY DAD SAYS, IT ONLY WORKS IF EVERYONE'S ON BOARD.
EVERYONE LIKES THE ADDED MONEY IN THEIR POCKETS THESE PAST FEW MONTHS, RIGHT? WELL...
THAT'S ONLY THE BEGINNING.

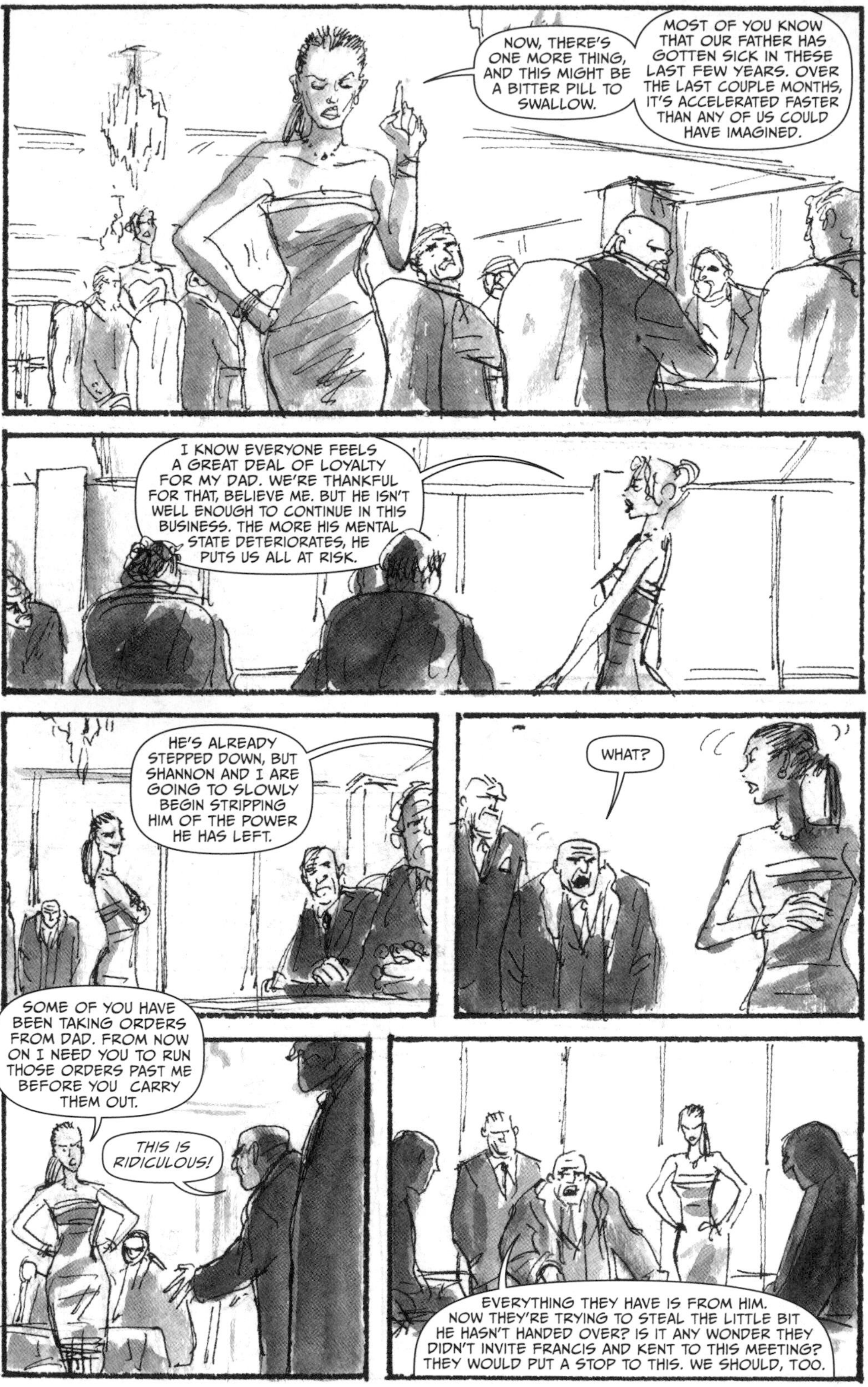

NOW, THERE'S ONE MORE THING, AND THIS MIGHT BE A BITTER PILL TO SWALLOW.
MOST OF YOU KNOW THAT OUR FATHER HAS GOTTEN SICK IN THESE LAST FEW YEARS. OVER THE LAST COUPLE MONTHS, IT'S ACCELERATED FASTER THAN ANY OF US COULD HAVE IMAGINED.
I KNOW EVERYONE FEELS A GREAT DEAL OF LOYALTY FOR MY DAD. WE'RE THANKFUL FOR THAT, BELIEVE ME. BUT HE ISN'T WELL ENOUGH TO CONTINUE IN THIS BUSINESS. THE MORE HIS MENTAL STATE DETERIORATES, HE PUTS US ALL AT RISK.
HE'S ALREADY STEPPED DOWN, BUT SHANNON AND I ARE GOING TO SLOWLY BEGIN STRIPPING HIM OF THE POWER HE HAS LEFT.
WHAT?
SOME OF YOU HAVE BEEN TAKING ORDERS FROM DAD. FROM NOW ON I NEED YOU TO RUN THOSE ORDERS PAST ME BEFORE YOU CARRY THEM OUT.
THIS IS RIDICULOUS!
EVERYTHING THEY HAVE IS FROM HIM. NOW THEY'RE TRYING TO STEAL THE LITTLE BIT HE HASN'T HANDED OVER? IS IT ANY WONDER THEY DIDN'T INVITE FRANCIS AND KENT TO THIS MEETING? THEY WOULD PUT A STOP TO THIS. WE SHOULD, TOO.

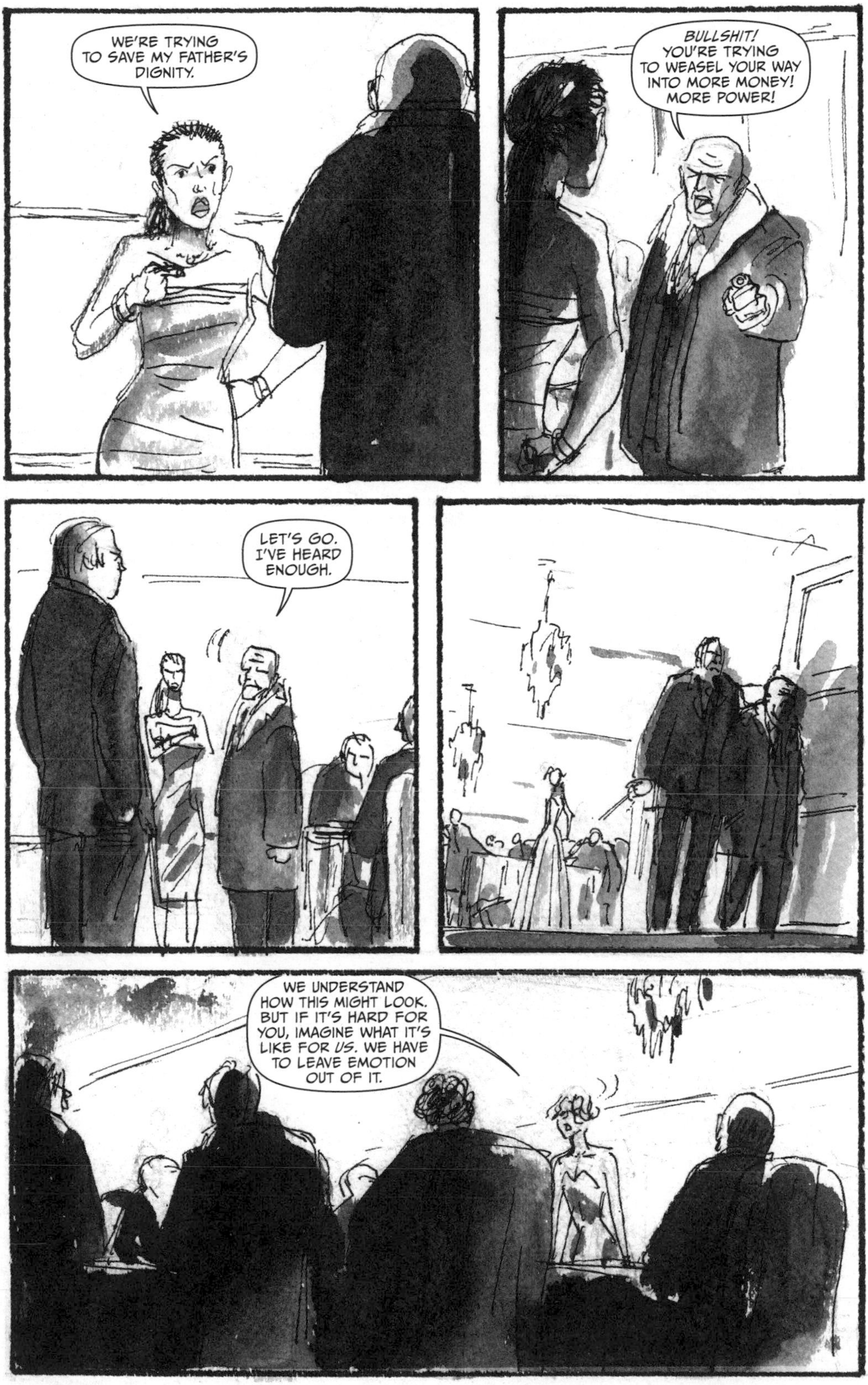
WE'RE TRYING TO SAVE MY FATHER'S DIGNITY.
BULLSHIT! YOU'RE TRYING TO WEASEL YOUR WAY INTO MORE MONEY! MORE POWER!
LET'S GO. I'VE HEARD ENOUGH.
WE UNDERSTAND HOW THIS MIGHT LOOK. BUT IF IT'S HARD FOR YOU, IMAGINE WHAT IT'S LIKE FOR *US*. WE HAVE TO LEAVE EMOTION OUT OF IT.

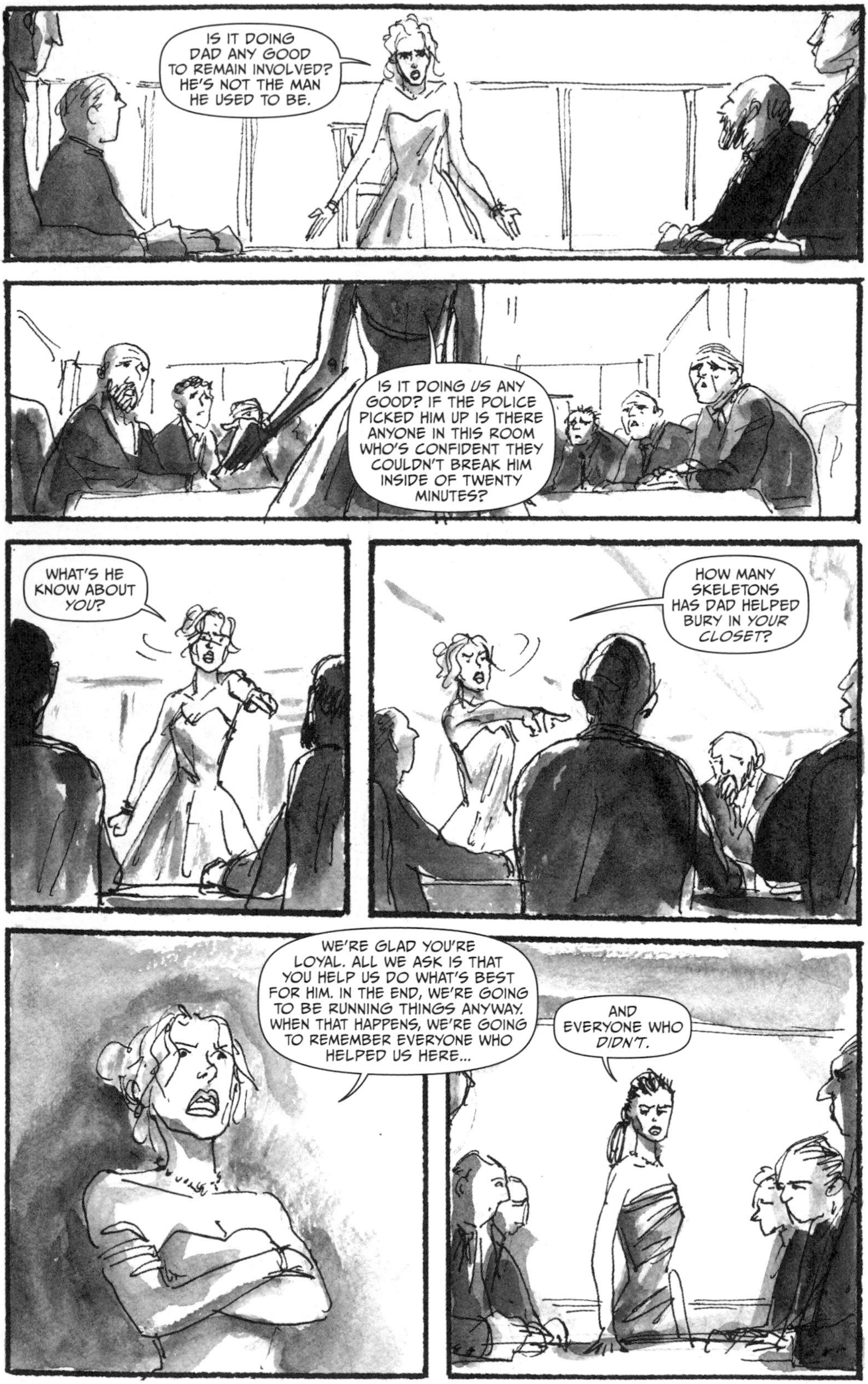
IS IT DOING DAD ANY GOOD TO REMAIN INVOLVED? HE'S NOT THE MAN HE USED TO BE.
IS IT DOING *US* ANY GOOD? IF THE POLICE PICKED HIM UP IS THERE ANYONE IN THIS ROOM WHO'S CONFIDENT THEY COULDN'T BREAK HIM INSIDE OF TWENTY MINUTES?
WHAT'S HE KNOW ABOUT *YOU*?
HOW MANY SKELETONS HAS DAD HELPED BURY IN *YOUR* CLOSET?
WE'RE GLAD YOU'RE LOYAL. ALL WE ASK IS THAT YOU HELP US DO WHAT'S BEST FOR HIM. IN THE END, WE'RE GOING TO BE RUNNING THINGS ANYWAY. WHEN THAT HAPPENS, WE'RE GOING TO REMEMBER EVERYONE WHO HELPED US HERE...
AND EVERYONE WHO *DIDN'T*.

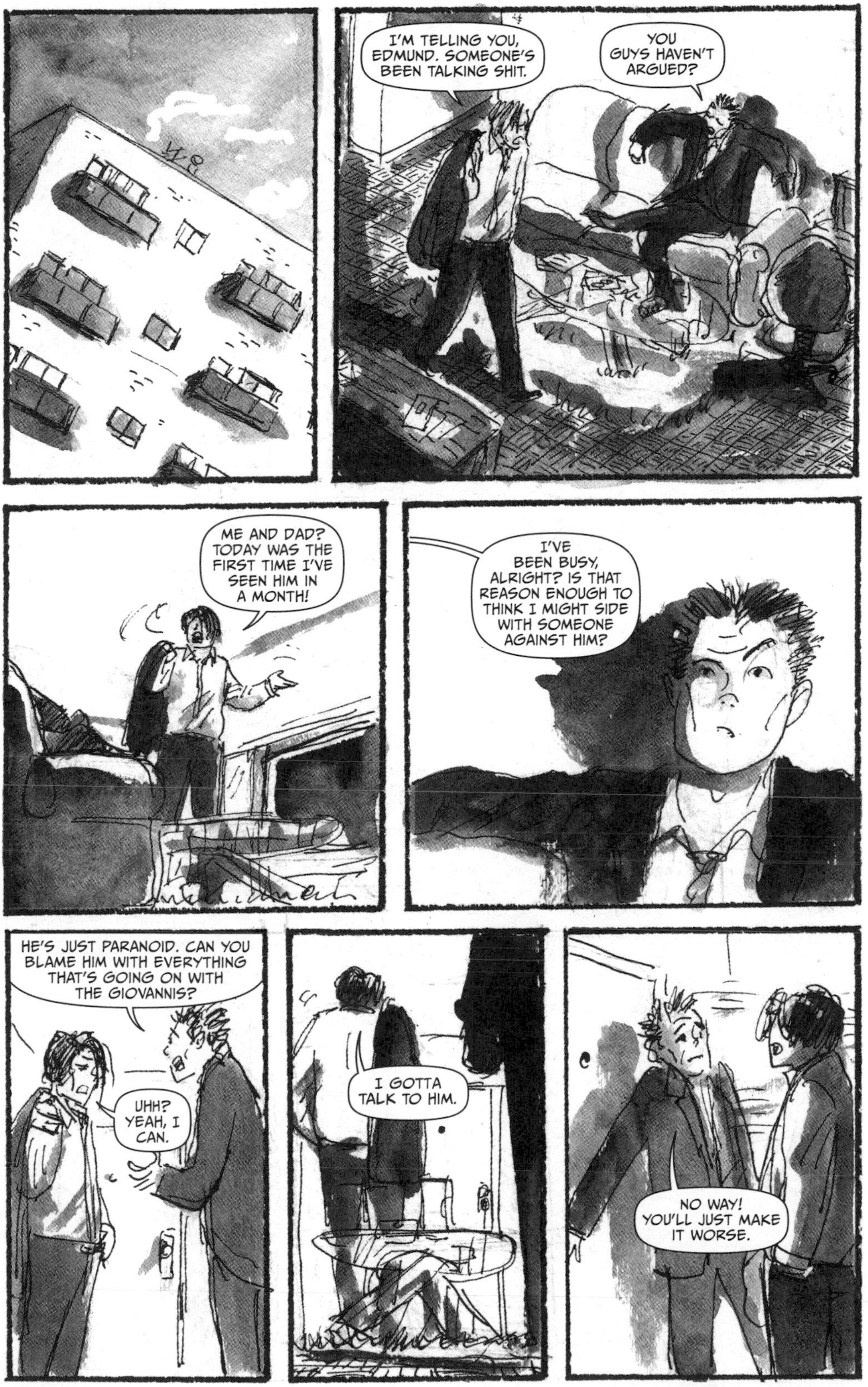
I'M TELLING YOU, EDMUND. SOMEONE'S BEEN TALKING SHIT.
YOU GUYS HAVEN'T ARGUED?
ME AND DAD? TODAY WAS THE FIRST TIME I'VE SEEN HIM IN A MONTH!
I'VE BEEN BUSY, ALRIGHT? IS THAT REASON ENOUGH TO THINK I MIGHT SIDE WITH SOMEONE AGAINST HIM?
HE'S JUST PARANOID. CAN YOU BLAME HIM WITH EVERYTHING THAT'S GOING ON WITH THE GIOVANNIS?
UHH? YEAH, I CAN.
I GOTTA TALK TO HIM.
NO WAY! YOU'LL JUST MAKE IT WORSE.

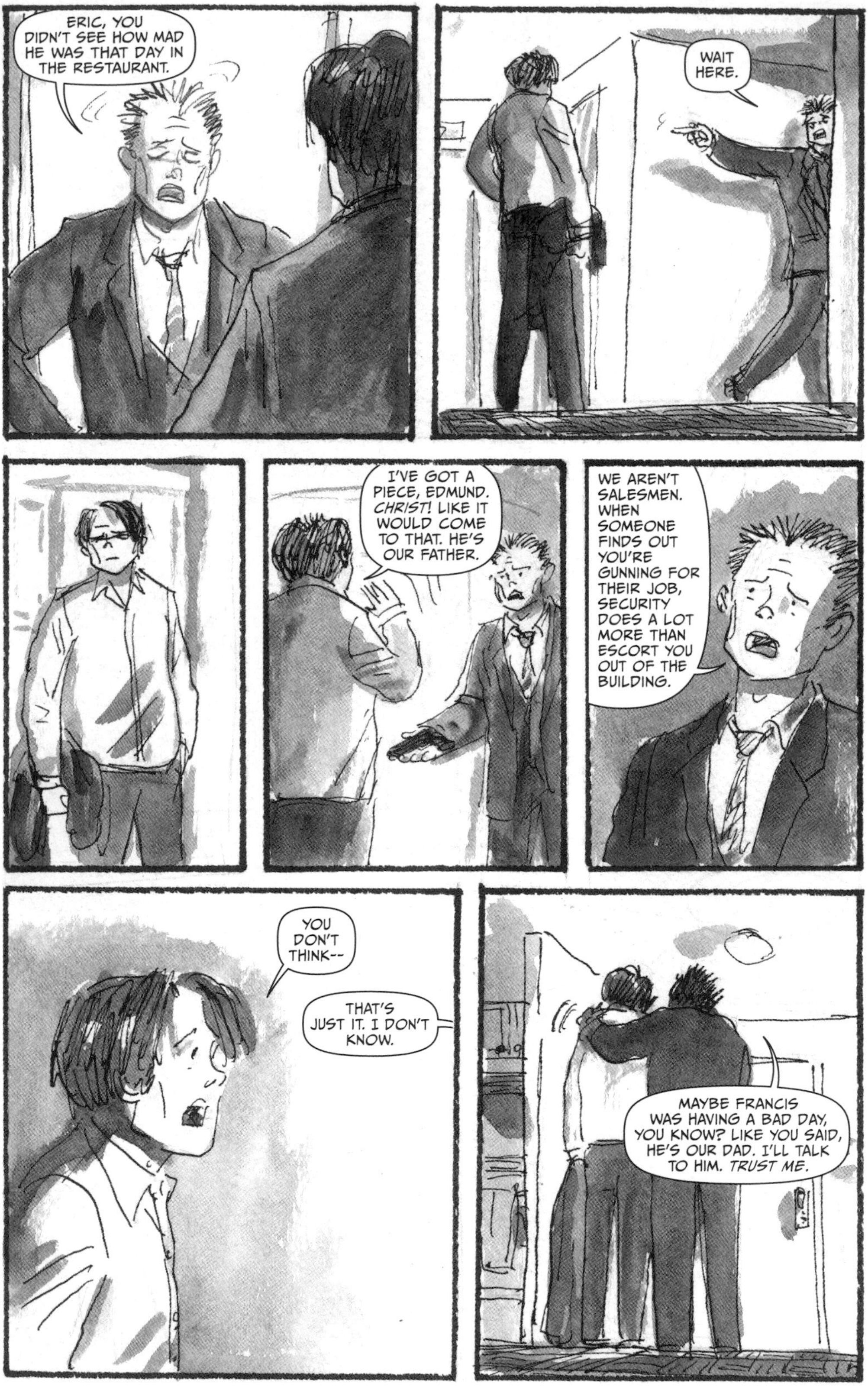
ERIC, YOU DIDN'T SEE HOW MAD HE WAS THAT DAY IN THE RESTAURANT.
WAIT HERE.
I'VE GOT A PIECE, EDMUND. *CHRIST!* LIKE IT WOULD COME TO THAT. HE'S OUR FATHER.
WE AREN'T SALESMEN. WHEN SOMEONE FINDS OUT YOU'RE GUNNING FOR THEIR JOB, SECURITY DOES A LOT MORE THAN ESCORT YOU OUT OF THE BUILDING.
YOU DON'T THINK--
THAT'S JUST IT. I DON'T KNOW.
MAYBE FRANCIS WAS HAVING A BAD DAY, YOU KNOW? LIKE YOU SAID, HE'S OUR DAD. I'LL TALK TO HIM. *TRUST ME.*

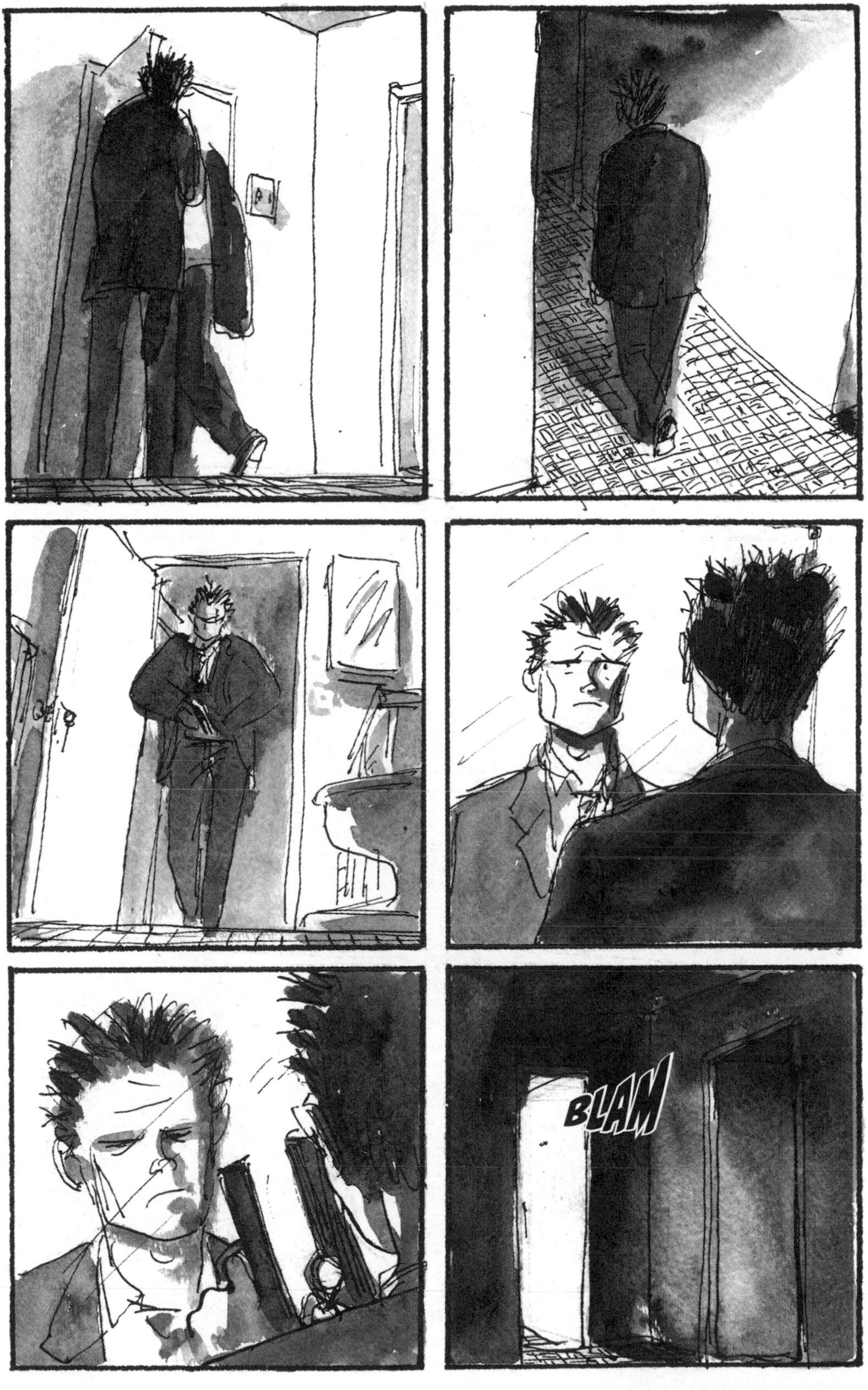
BLAM

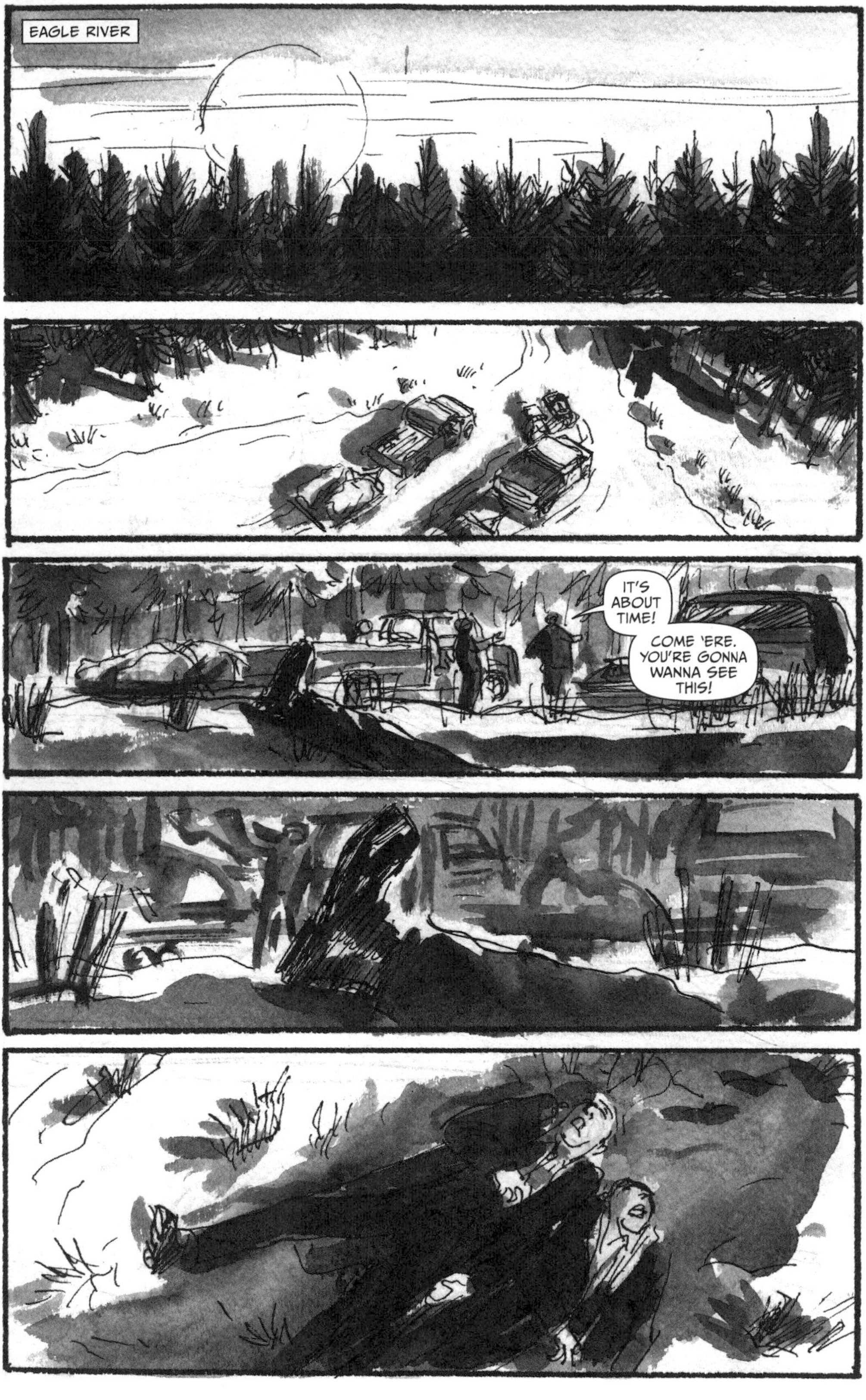
EAGLE RIVER
IT'S ABOUT TIME!
COME 'ERE. YOU'RE GONNA WANNA SEE THIS!

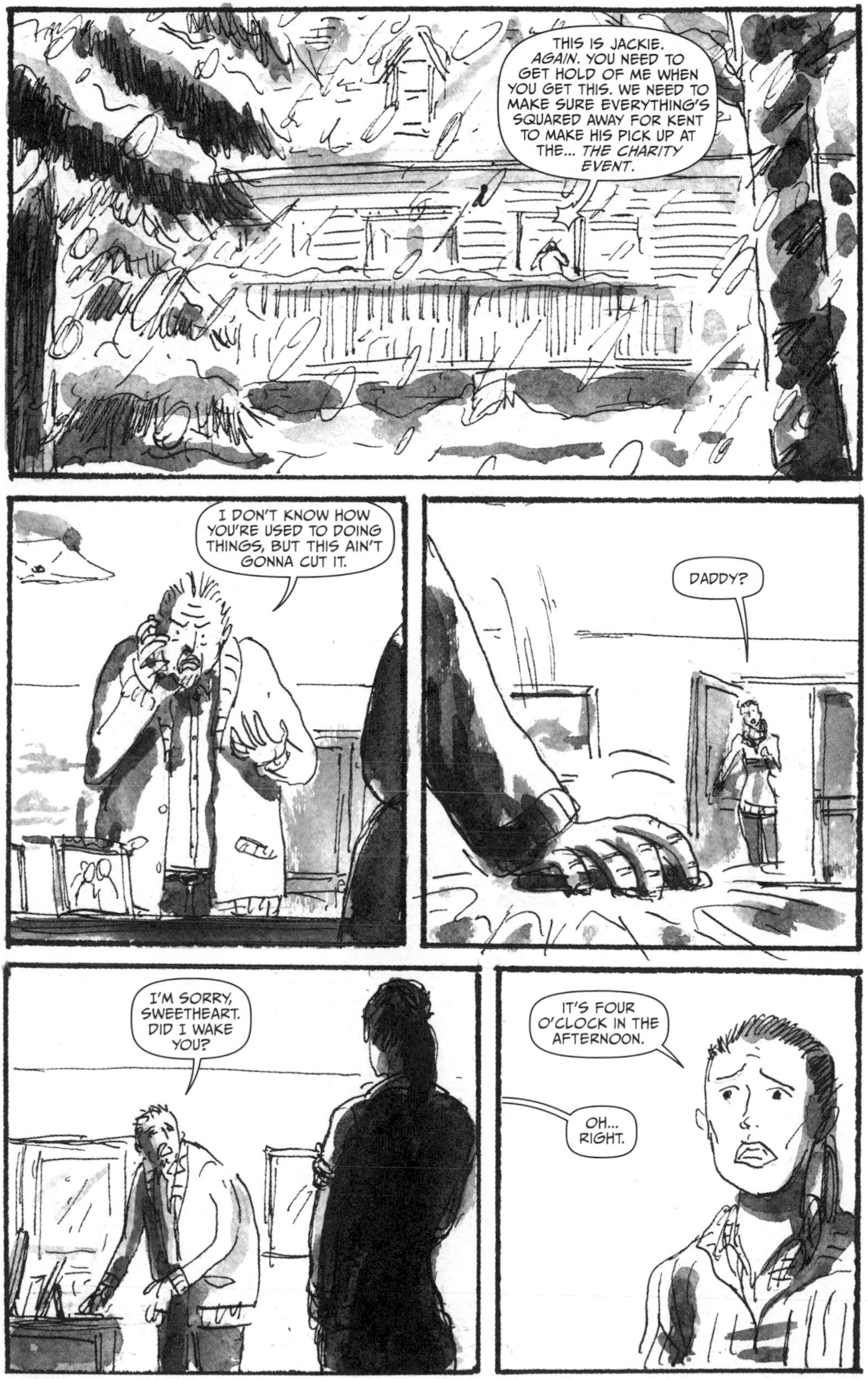
THIS IS JACKIE. AGAIN. YOU NEED TO GET HOLD OF ME WHEN YOU GET THIS. WE NEED TO MAKE SURE EVERYTHING'S SQUARED AWAY FOR KENT TO MAKE HIS PICK UP AT THE... THE CHARITY EVENT.
I DON'T KNOW HOW YOU'RE USED TO DOING THINGS, BUT THIS AIN'T GONNA CUT IT.
DADDY?
I'M SORRY, SWEETHEART. DID I WAKE YOU?
IT'S FOUR O'CLOCK IN THE AFTERNOON.
OH... RIGHT.

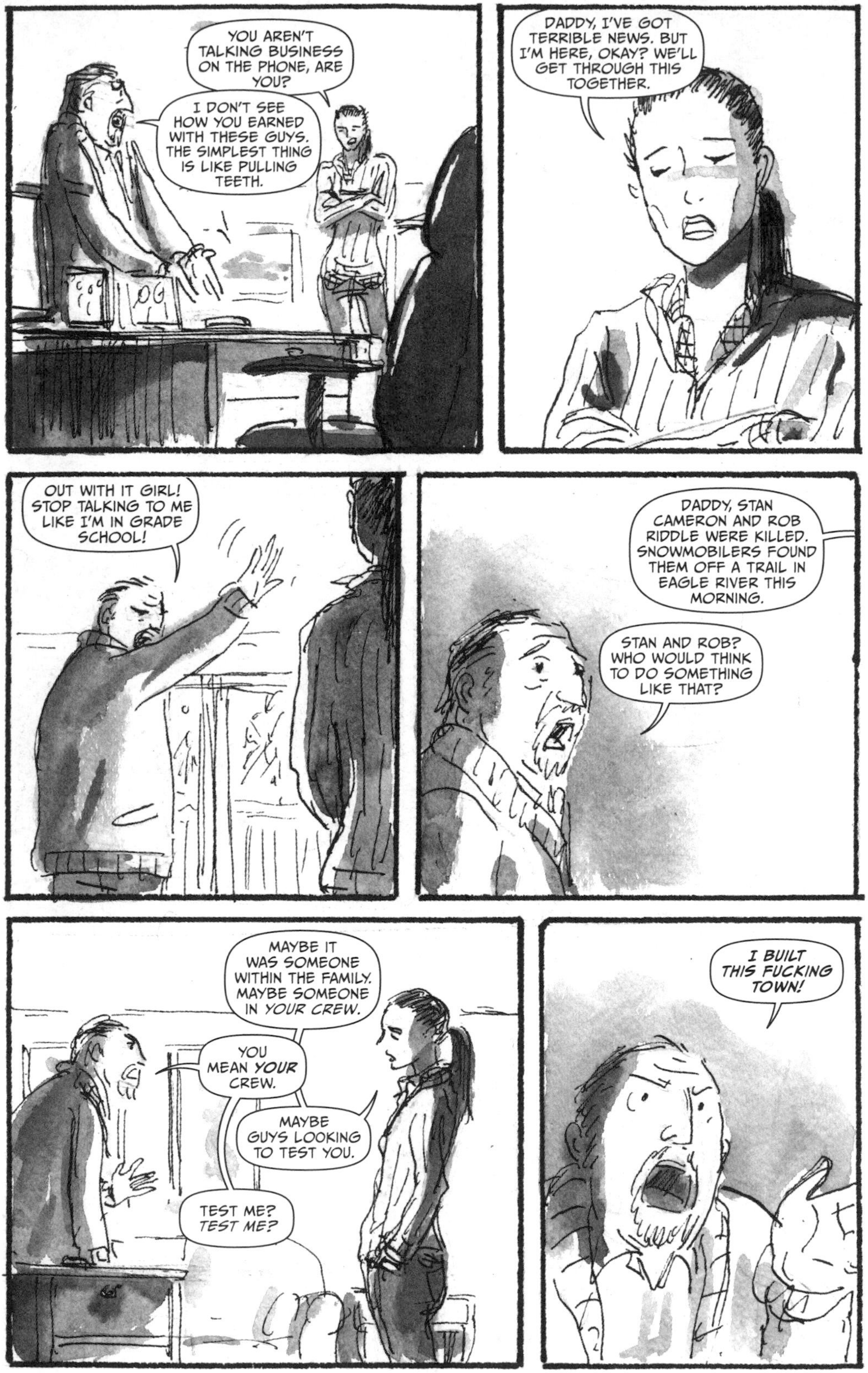
YOU AREN'T TALKING BUSINESS ON THE PHONE, ARE YOU?
I DON'T SEE HOW YOU EARNED WITH THESE GUYS. THE SIMPLEST THING IS LIKE PULLING TEETH.
DADDY, I'VE GOT TERRIBLE NEWS. BUT I'M HERE, OKAY? WE'LL GET THROUGH THIS TOGETHER.
OUT WITH IT GIRL! STOP TALKING TO ME LIKE I'M IN GRADE SCHOOL!
DADDY, STAN CAMERON AND ROB RIDDLE WERE KILLED. SNOWMOBILERS FOUND THEM OFF A TRAIL IN EAGLE RIVER THIS MORNING.
STAN AND ROB? WHO WOULD THINK TO DO SOMETHING LIKE THAT?
MAYBE IT WAS SOMEONE WITHIN THE FAMILY. MAYBE SOMEONE IN *YOUR CREW*.
YOU MEAN ***YOUR*** CREW.
MAYBE GUYS LOOKING TO TEST YOU.
TEST ME? *TEST ME?*
I BUILT THIS FUCKING TOWN!

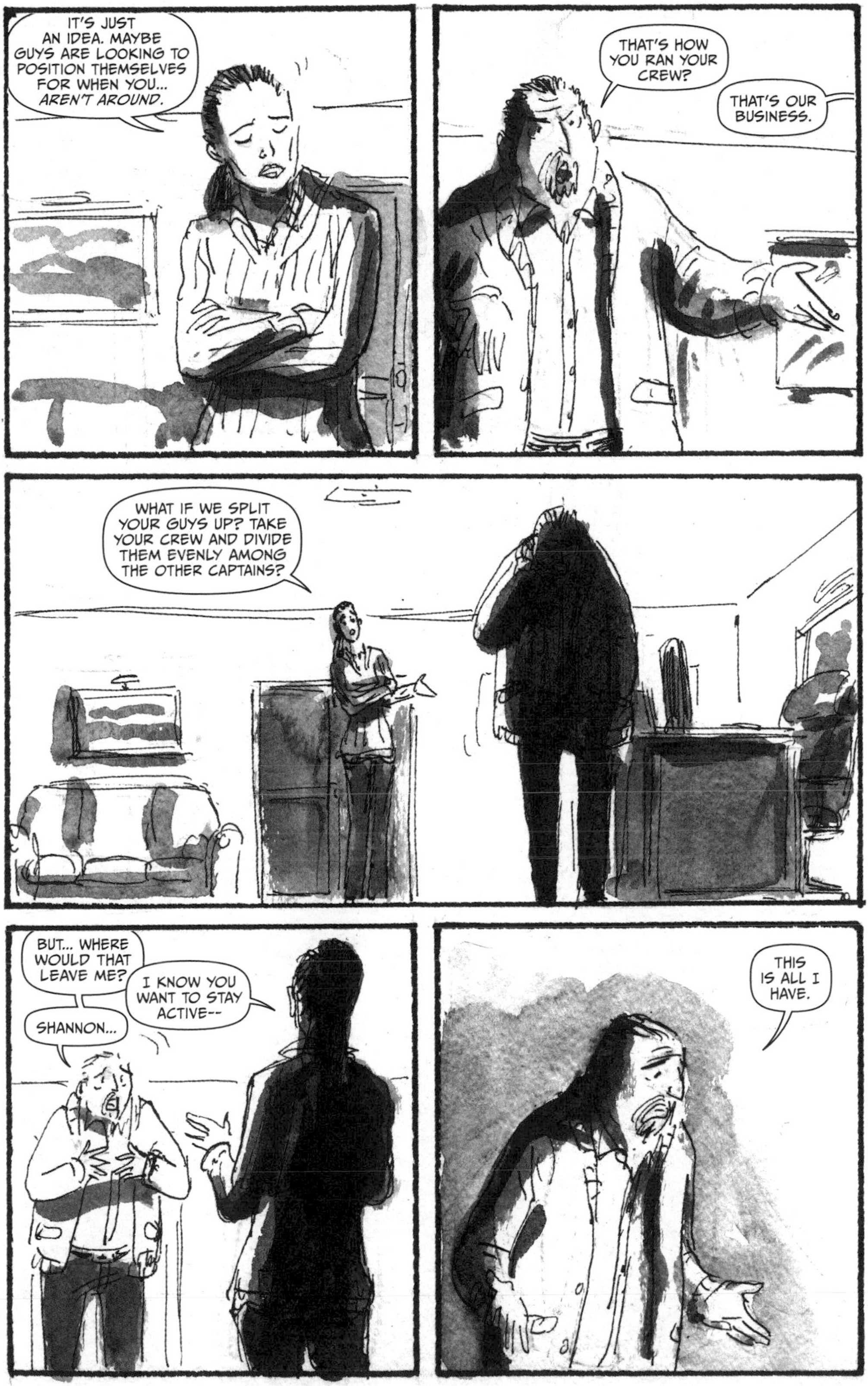
IT'S JUST AN IDEA. MAYBE GUYS ARE LOOKING TO POSITION THEMSELVES FOR WHEN YOU... *AREN'T AROUND.*
THAT'S HOW YOU RAN YOUR CREW?
THAT'S OUR BUSINESS.
WHAT IF WE SPLIT YOUR GUYS UP? TAKE YOUR CREW AND DIVIDE THEM EVENLY AMONG THE OTHER CAPTAINS?
BUT... WHERE WOULD THAT LEAVE ME?
I KNOW YOU WANT TO STAY ACTIVE--
SHANNON...
THIS IS ALL I HAVE.

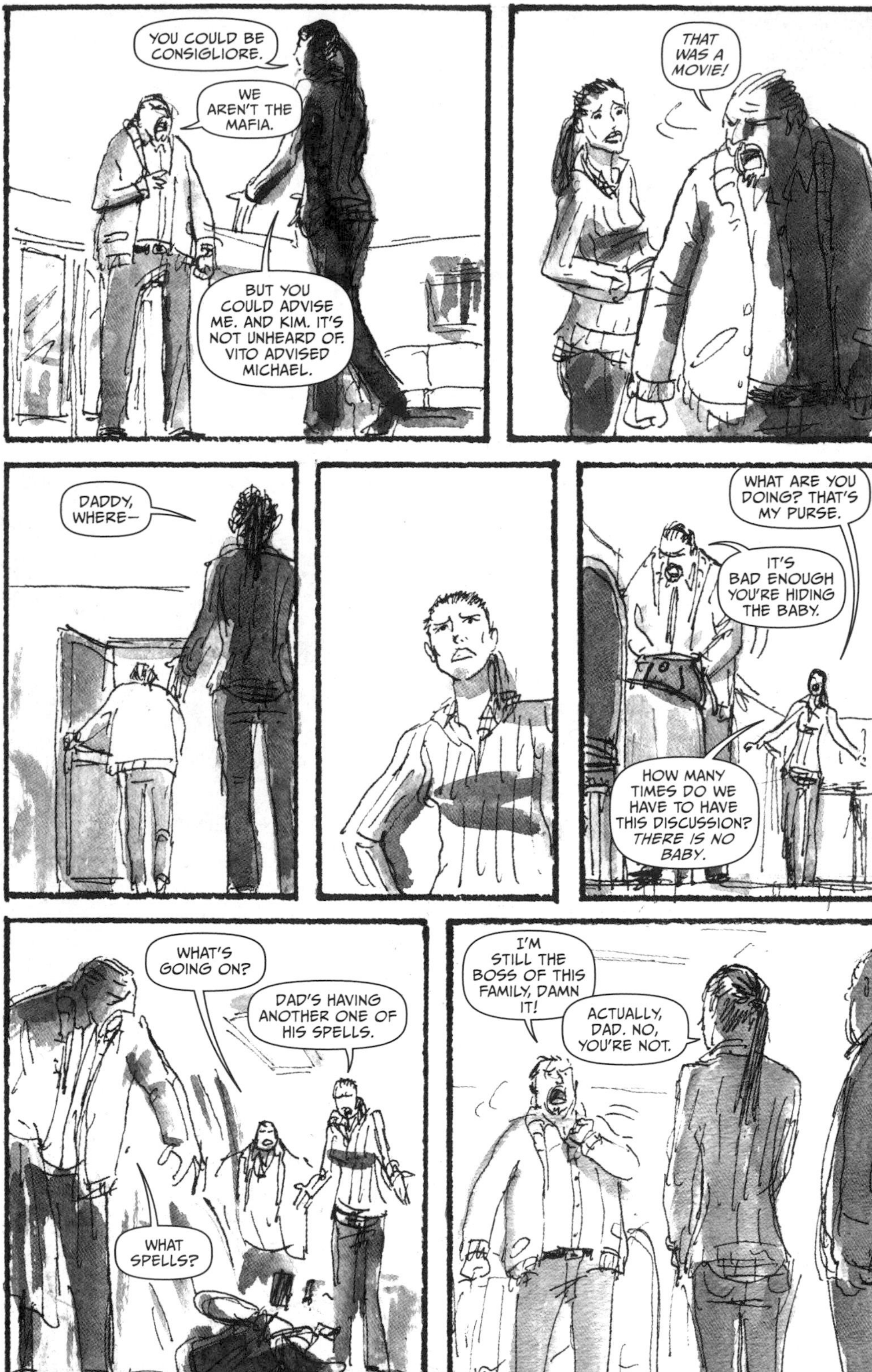
YOU COULD BE CONSIGLIORE.
WE AREN'T THE MAFIA.
BUT YOU COULD ADVISE ME. AND KIM. IT'S NOT UNHEARD OF. VITO ADVISED MICHAEL.
THAT WAS A MOVIE!
DADDY, WHERE–
WHAT ARE YOU DOING? THAT'S MY PURSE.
IT'S BAD ENOUGH YOU'RE HIDING THE BABY.
HOW MANY TIMES DO WE HAVE TO HAVE THIS DISCUSSION? THERE IS NO BABY.
WHAT'S GOING ON?
DAD'S HAVING ANOTHER ONE OF HIS SPELLS.
WHAT SPELLS?
I'M STILL THE BOSS OF THIS FAMILY, DAMN IT!
ACTUALLY, DAD. NO, YOU'RE NOT.

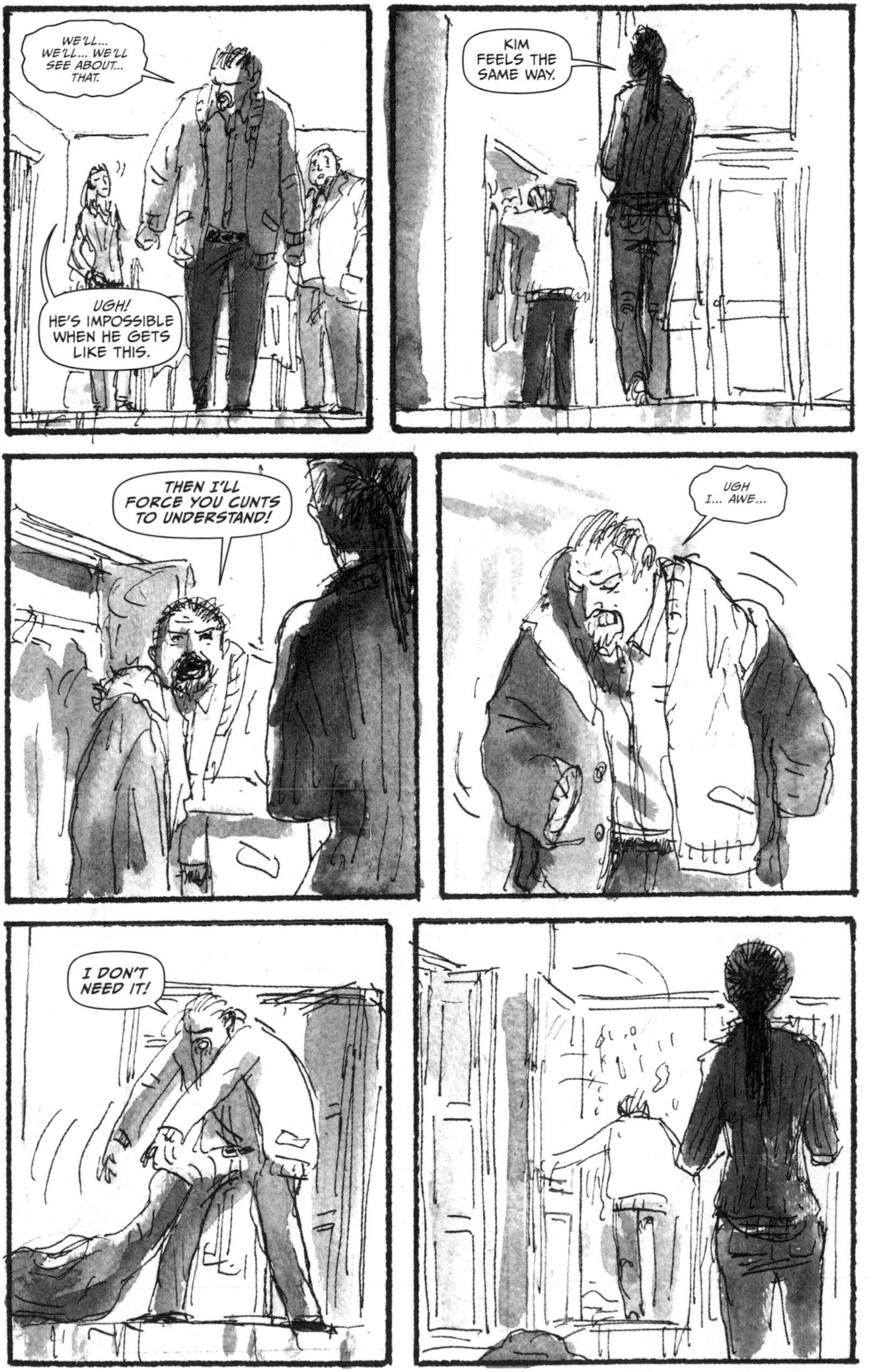
WE'LL... WE'LL... WE'LL SEE ABOUT... THAT.
UGH! HE'S IMPOSSIBLE WHEN HE GETS LIKE THIS.
KIM FEELS THE SAME WAY.
THEN I'LL FORCE YOU CUNTS TO UNDERSTAND!
UGH I... AWE...
I DON'T NEED IT!

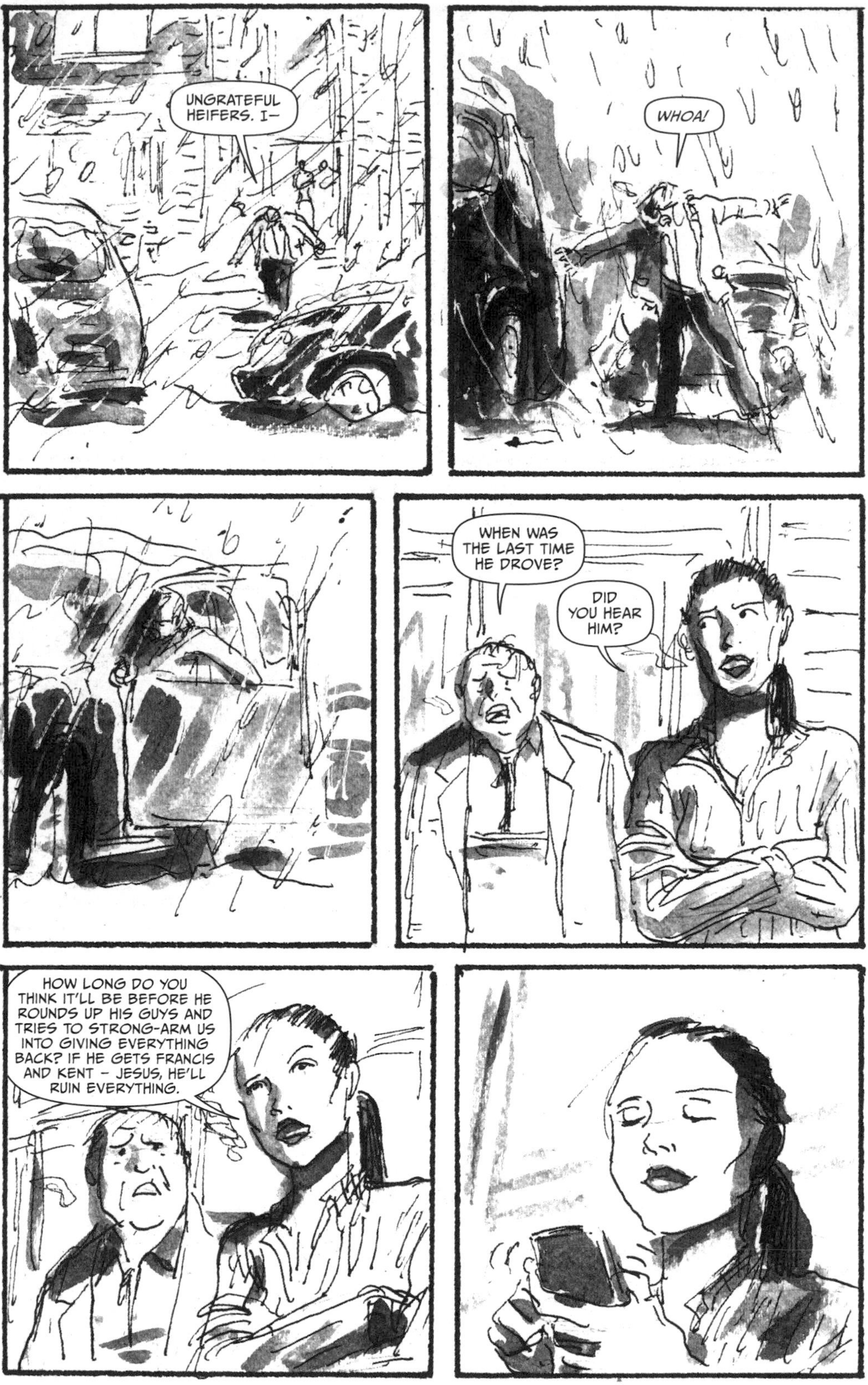
UNGRATEFUL HEIFERS. I—
WHOA!
WHEN WAS THE LAST TIME HE DROVE?
DID YOU HEAR HIM?
HOW LONG DO YOU THINK IT'LL BE BEFORE HE ROUNDS UP HIS GUYS AND TRIES TO STRONG-ARM US INTO GIVING EVERYTHING BACK? IF HE GETS FRANCIS AND KENT – JESUS, HE'LL RUIN EVERYTHING.

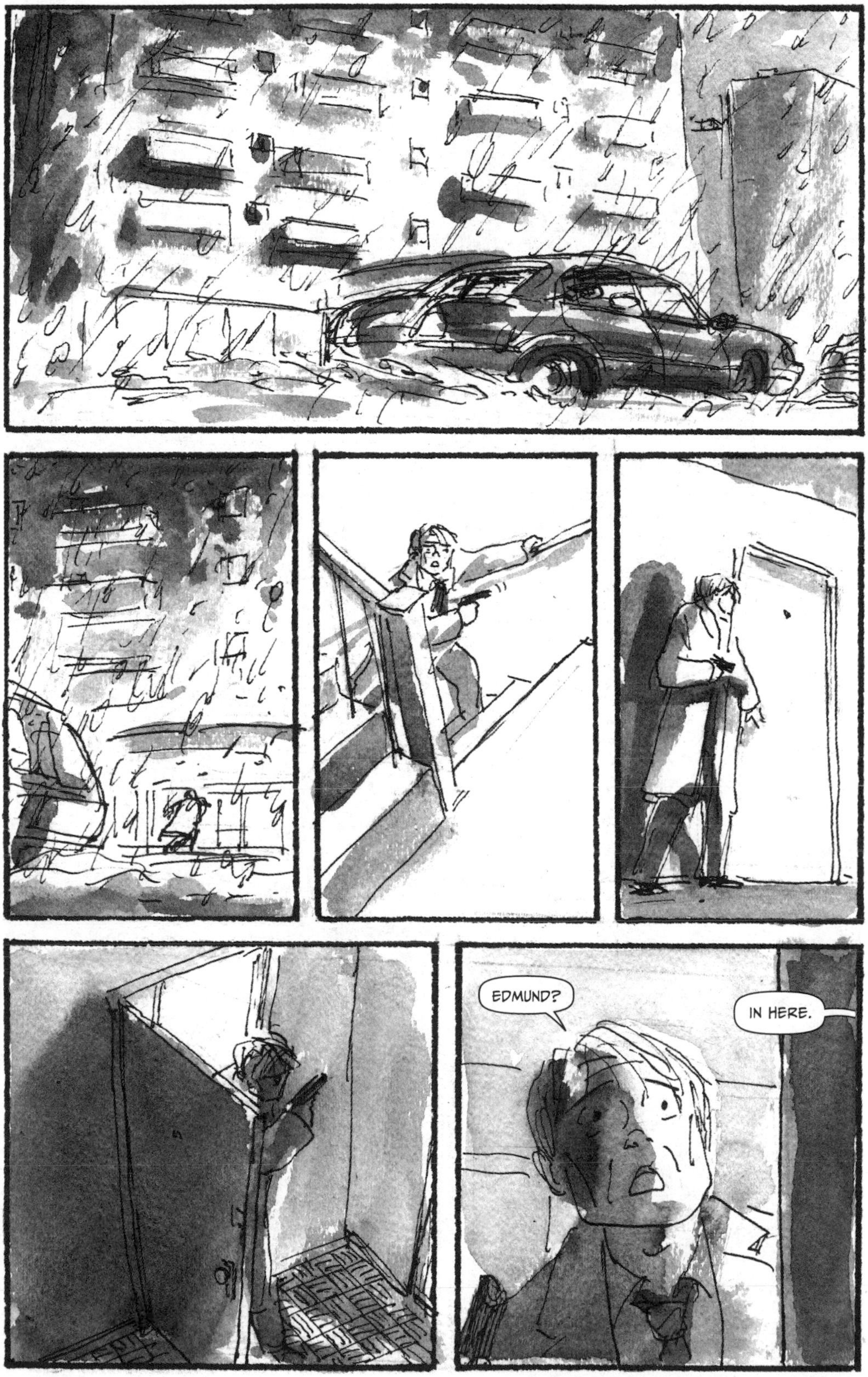
EDMUND?
IN HERE.

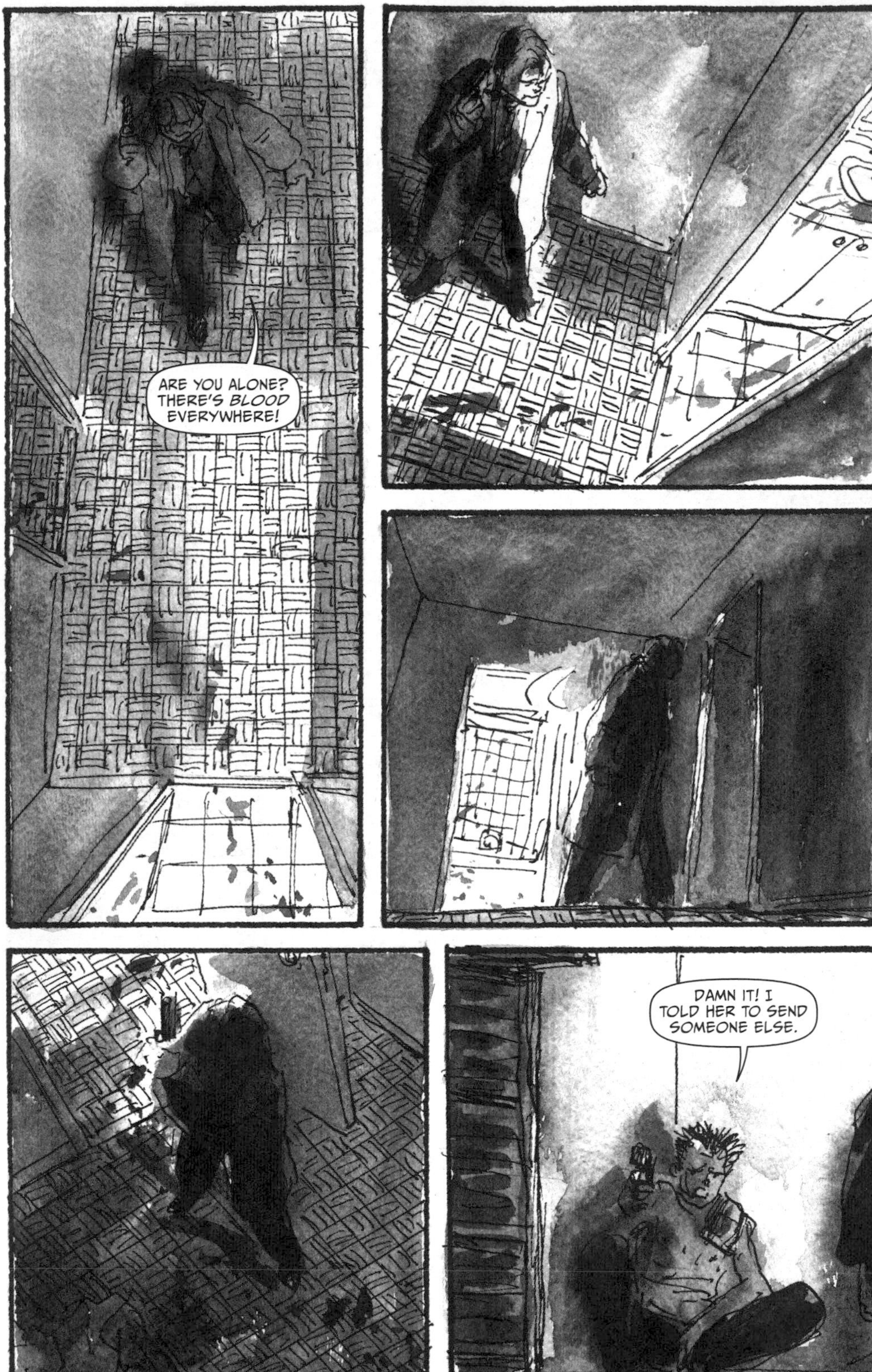
ARE YOU ALONE? THERE'S *BLOOD* EVERYWHERE!
DAMN IT! I TOLD HER TO SEND SOMEONE ELSE.

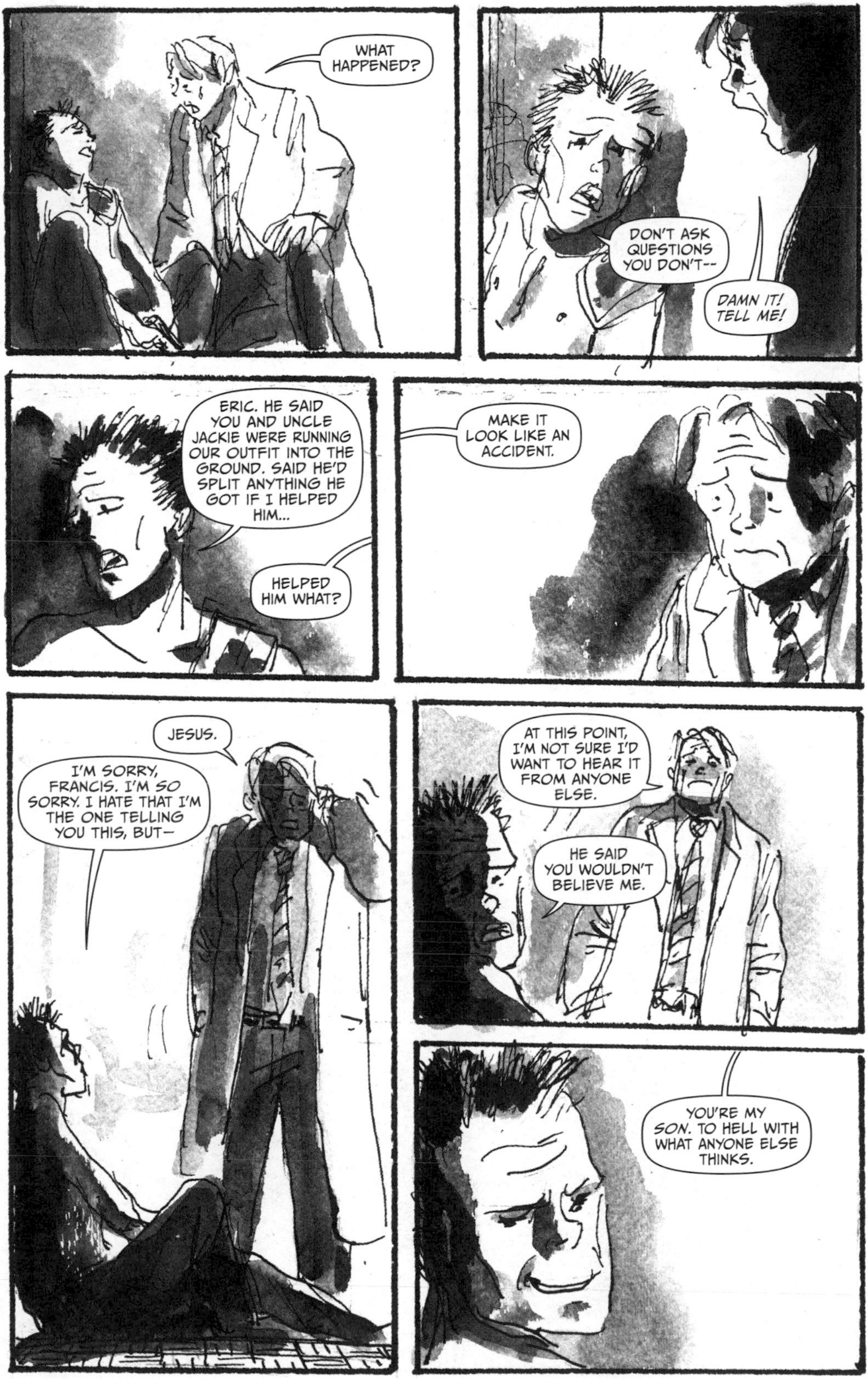
WHAT HAPPENED?
DON'T ASK QUESTIONS YOU DON'T--
DAMN IT! TELL ME!
ERIC. HE SAID YOU AND UNCLE JACKIE WERE RUNNING OUR OUTFIT INTO THE GROUND. SAID HE'D SPLIT ANYTHING HE GOT IF I HELPED HIM...
HELPED HIM WHAT?
MAKE IT LOOK LIKE AN ACCIDENT.
JESUS.
I'M SORRY, FRANCIS. I'M SO SORRY. I HATE THAT I'M THE ONE TELLING YOU THIS, BUT—
AT THIS POINT, I'M NOT SURE I'D WANT TO HEAR IT FROM ANYONE ELSE.
HE SAID YOU WOULDN'T BELIEVE ME.
YOU'RE MY SON. TO HELL WITH WHAT ANYONE ELSE THINKS.

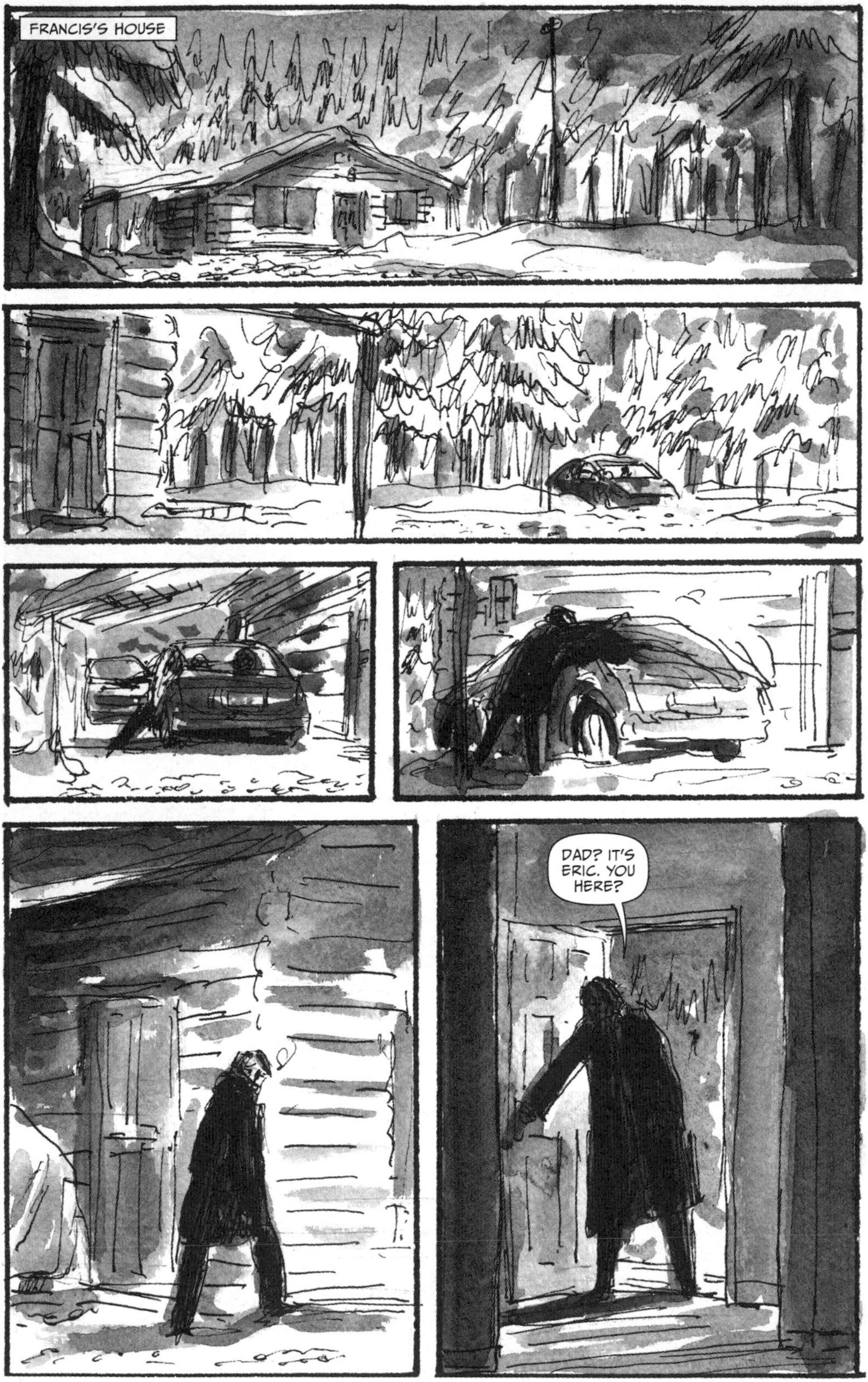
FRANCIS'S HOUSE
DAD? IT'S ERIC. YOU HERE?

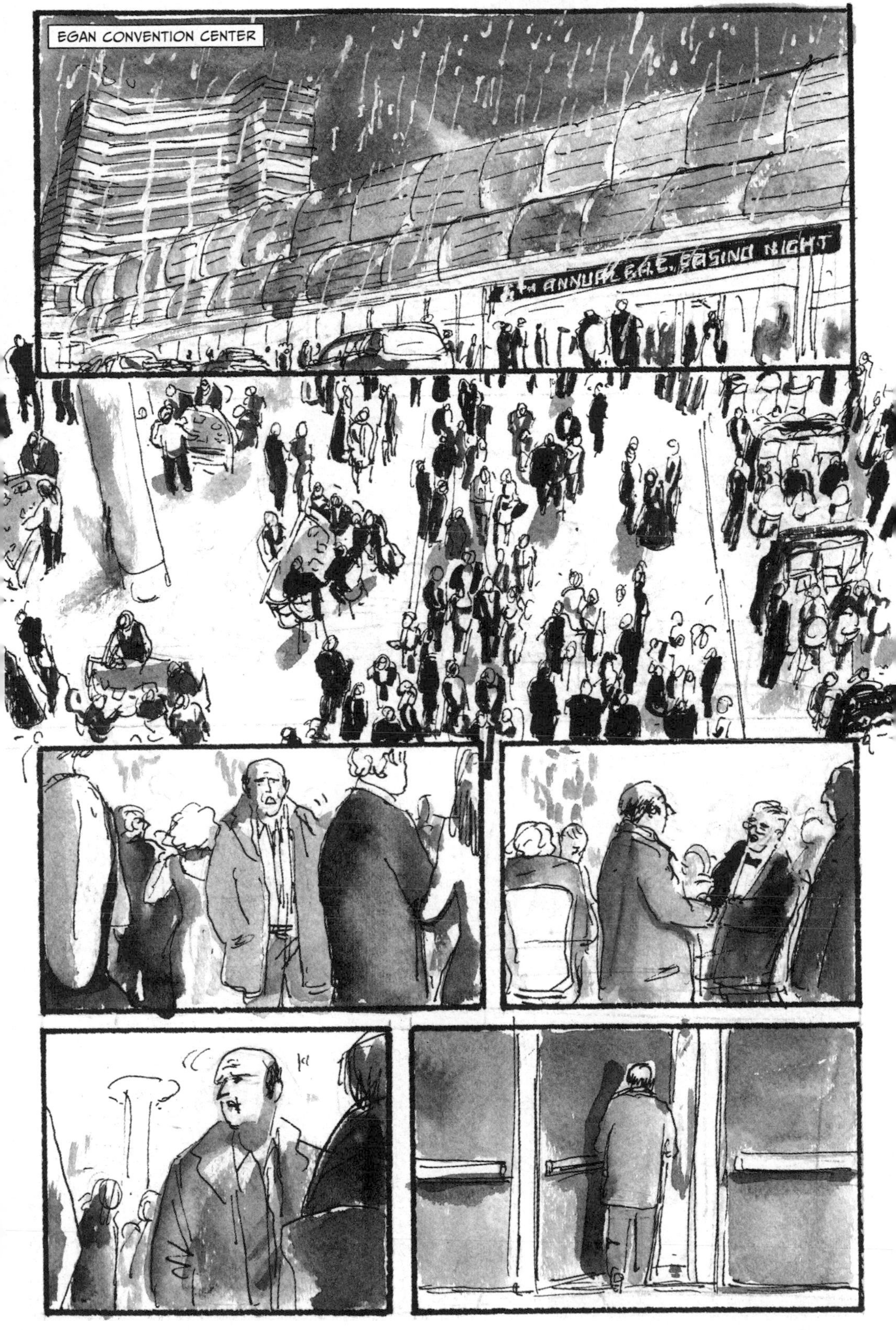
EGAN CONVENTION CENTER
ANNUAL CASINO NIGHT

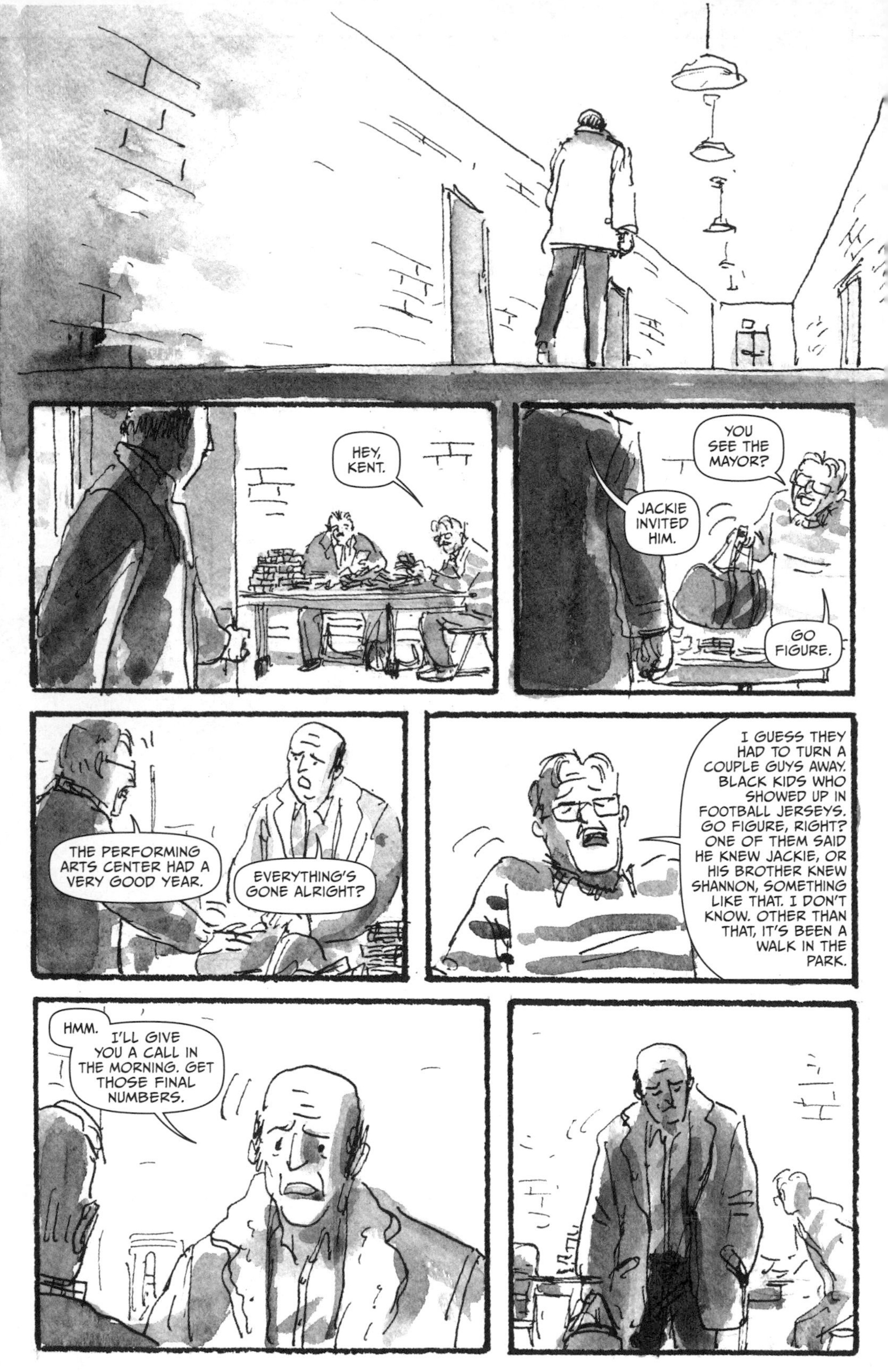
HEY, KENT.
YOU SEE THE MAYOR?
JACKIE INVITED HIM.
GO FIGURE.
THE PERFORMING ARTS CENTER HAD A VERY GOOD YEAR.
EVERYTHING'S GONE ALRIGHT?
I GUESS THEY HAD TO TURN A COUPLE GUYS AWAY. BLACK KIDS WHO SHOWED UP IN FOOTBALL JERSEYS. GO FIGURE, RIGHT? ONE OF THEM SAID HE KNEW JACKIE, OR HIS BROTHER KNEW SHANNON, SOMETHING LIKE THAT. I DON'T KNOW. OTHER THAN THAT, IT'S BEEN A WALK IN THE PARK.
HMM.
I'LL GIVE YOU A CALL IN THE MORNING. GET THOSE FINAL NUMBERS.

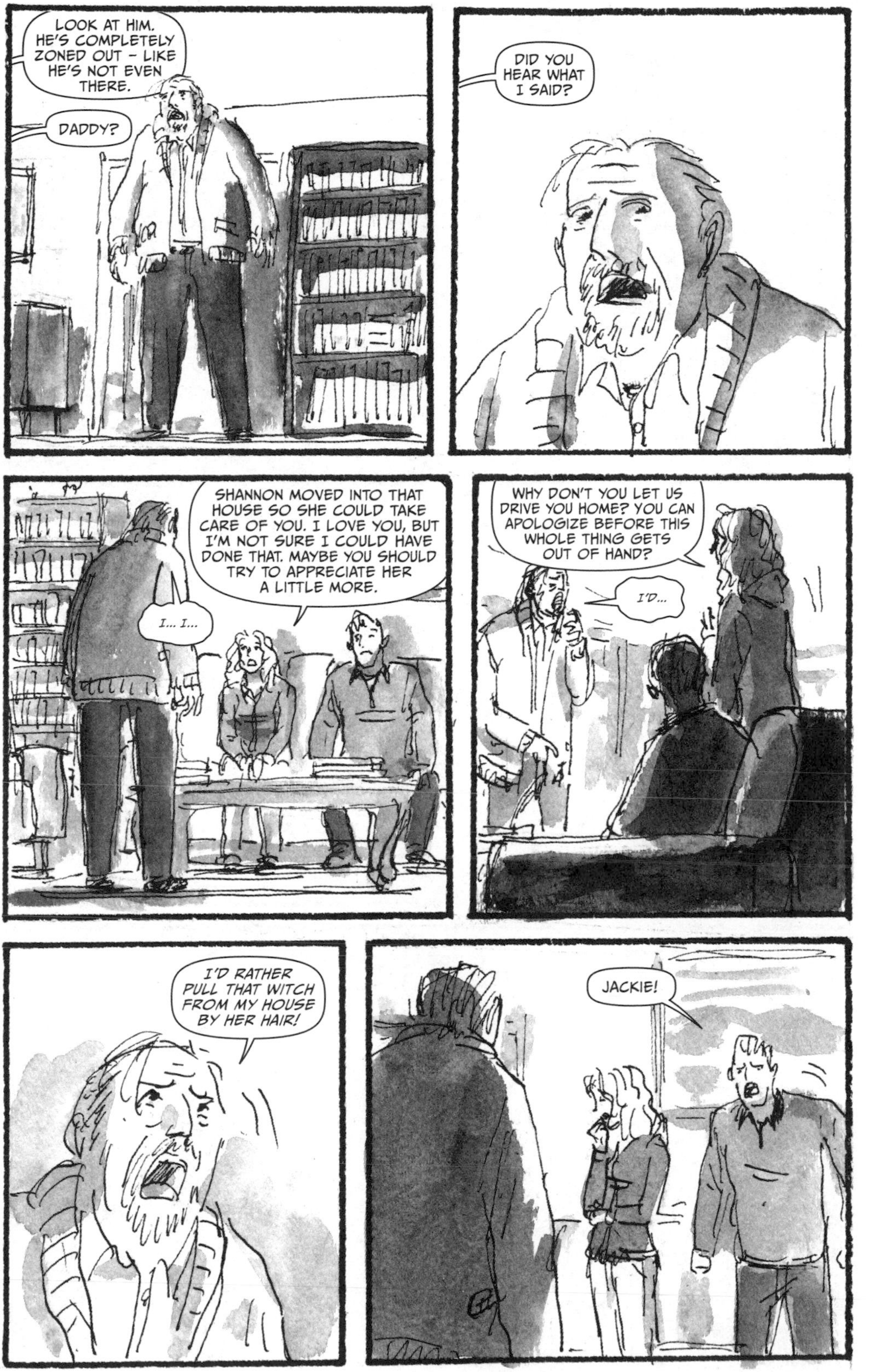
LOOK AT HIM. HE'S COMPLETELY ZONED OUT – LIKE HE'S NOT EVEN THERE.
DADDY?
DID YOU HEAR WHAT I SAID?
SHANNON MOVED INTO THAT HOUSE SO SHE COULD TAKE CARE OF YOU. I LOVE YOU, BUT I'M NOT SURE I COULD HAVE DONE THAT. MAYBE YOU SHOULD TRY TO APPRECIATE HER A LITTLE MORE.
I... I...
WHY DON'T YOU LET US DRIVE YOU HOME? YOU CAN APOLOGIZE BEFORE THIS WHOLE THING GETS OUT OF HAND?
I'D...
I'D RATHER PULL THAT WITCH FROM MY HOUSE BY HER HAIR!
JACKIE!

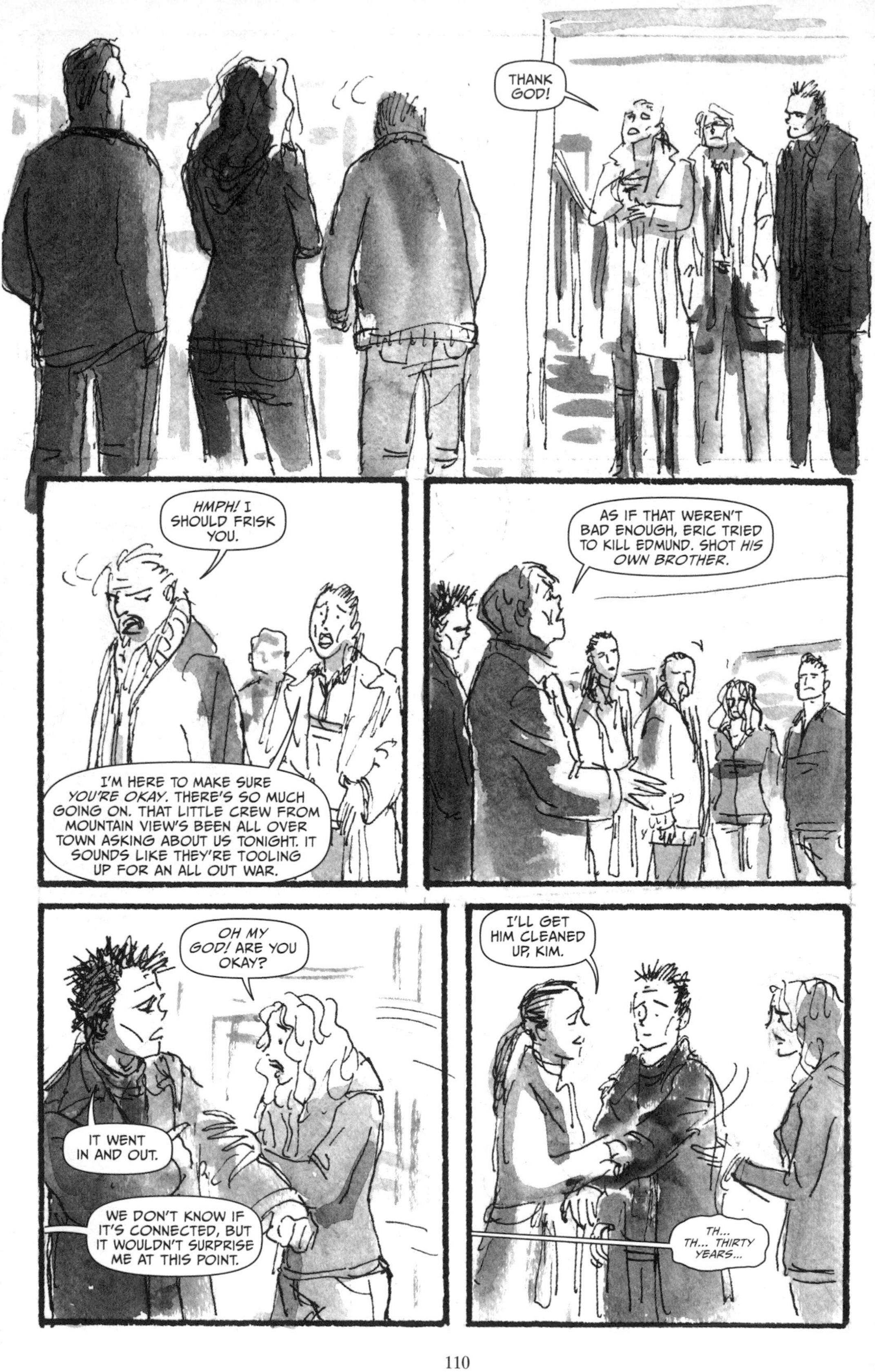
THANK GOD!
HMPH! I SHOULD FRISK YOU.
I'M HERE TO MAKE SURE YOU'RE OKAY. THERE'S SO MUCH GOING ON. THAT LITTLE CREW FROM MOUNTAIN VIEW'S BEEN ALL OVER TOWN ASKING ABOUT US TONIGHT. IT SOUNDS LIKE THEY'RE TOOLING UP FOR AN ALL OUT WAR.
AS IF THAT WEREN'T BAD ENOUGH, ERIC TRIED TO KILL EDMUND. SHOT HIS OWN BROTHER.
OH MY GOD! ARE YOU OKAY?
IT WENT IN AND OUT.
WE DON'T KNOW IF IT'S CONNECTED, BUT IT WOULDN'T SURPRISE ME AT THIS POINT.
I'LL GET HIM CLEANED UP, KIM.
TH... TH... THIRTY YEARS...

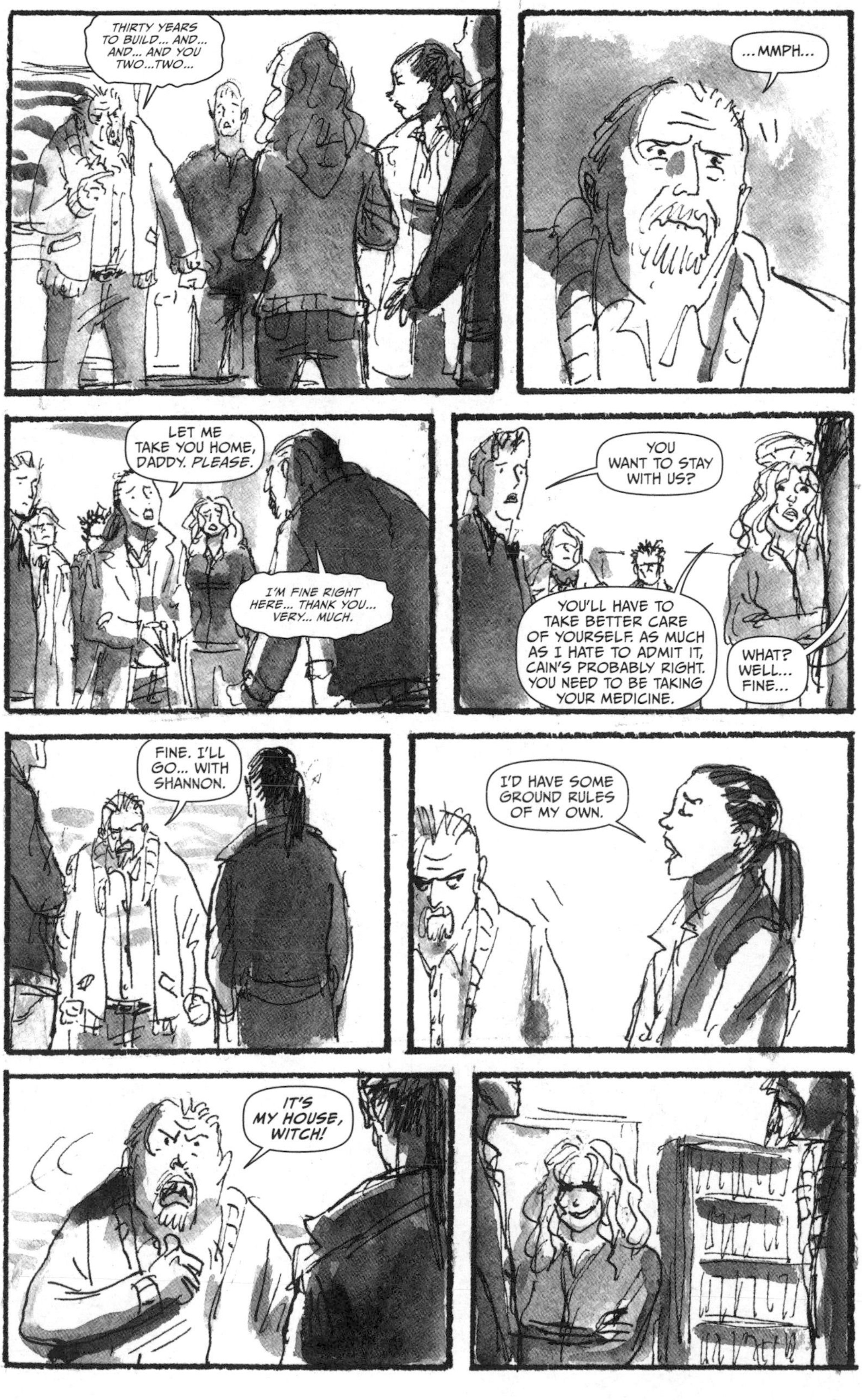
THIRTY YEARS TO BUILD... AND... AND... AND YOU TWO...TWO...
...MMPH...
LET ME TAKE YOU HOME, DADDY. PLEASE.
I'M FINE RIGHT HERE... THANK YOU... VERY... MUCH.
YOU WANT TO STAY WITH US?
YOU'LL HAVE TO TAKE BETTER CARE OF YOURSELF. AS MUCH AS I HATE TO ADMIT IT, CAIN'S PROBABLY RIGHT. YOU NEED TO BE TAKING YOUR MEDICINE.
WHAT? WELL... FINE...
FINE. I'LL GO... WITH SHANNON.
I'D HAVE SOME GROUND RULES OF MY OWN.
IT'S MY HOUSE, WITCH!

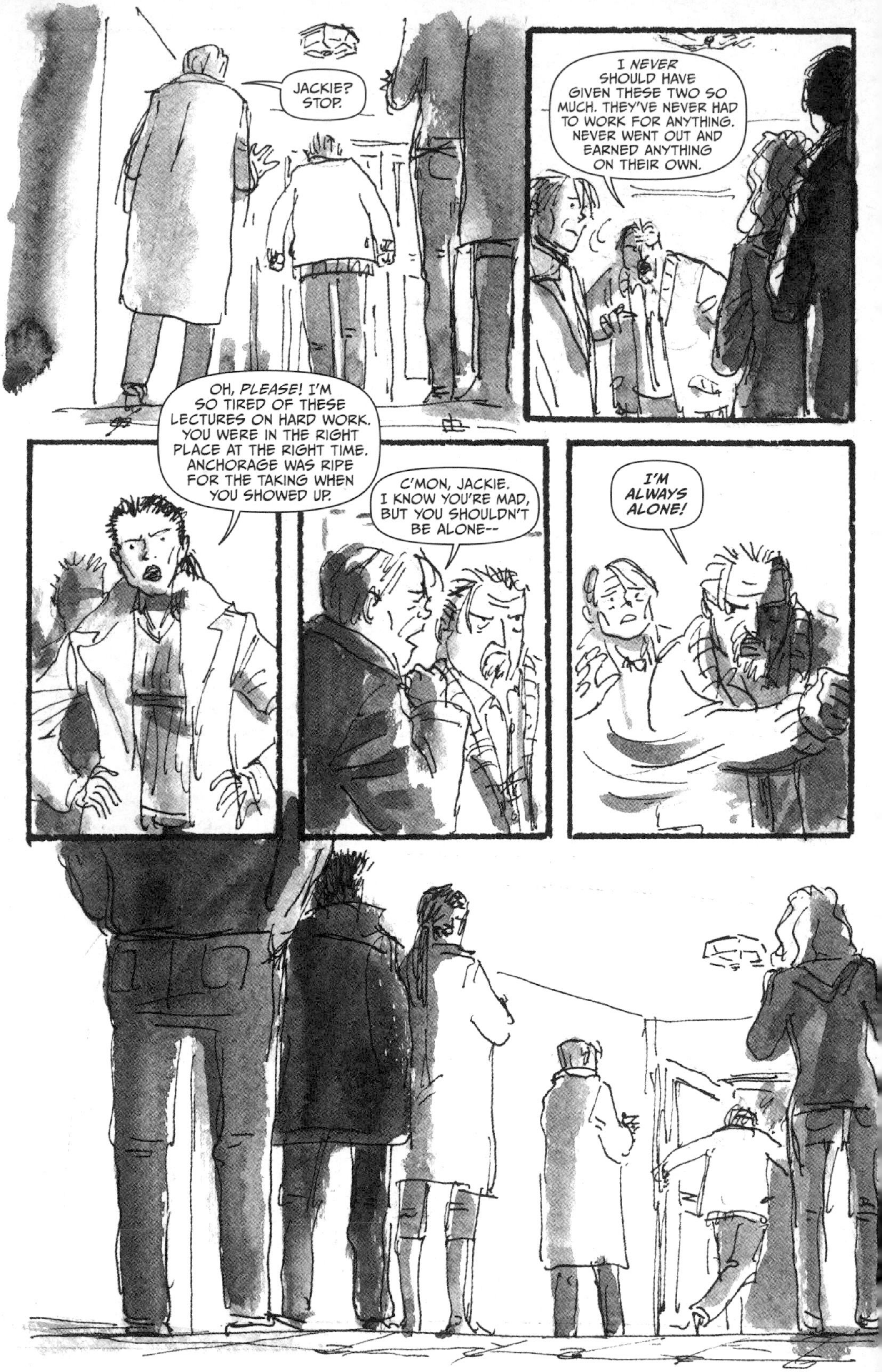
JACKIE? STOP.
I NEVER SHOULD HAVE GIVEN THESE TWO SO MUCH. THEY'VE NEVER HAD TO WORK FOR ANYTHING. NEVER WENT OUT AND EARNED ANYTHING ON THEIR OWN.
OH, PLEASE! I'M SO TIRED OF THESE LECTURES ON HARD WORK. YOU WERE IN THE RIGHT PLACE AT THE RIGHT TIME. ANCHORAGE WAS RIPE FOR THE TAKING WHEN YOU SHOWED UP.
C'MON, JACKIE. I KNOW YOU'RE MAD, BUT YOU SHOULDN'T BE ALONE--
I'M ALWAYS ALONE!

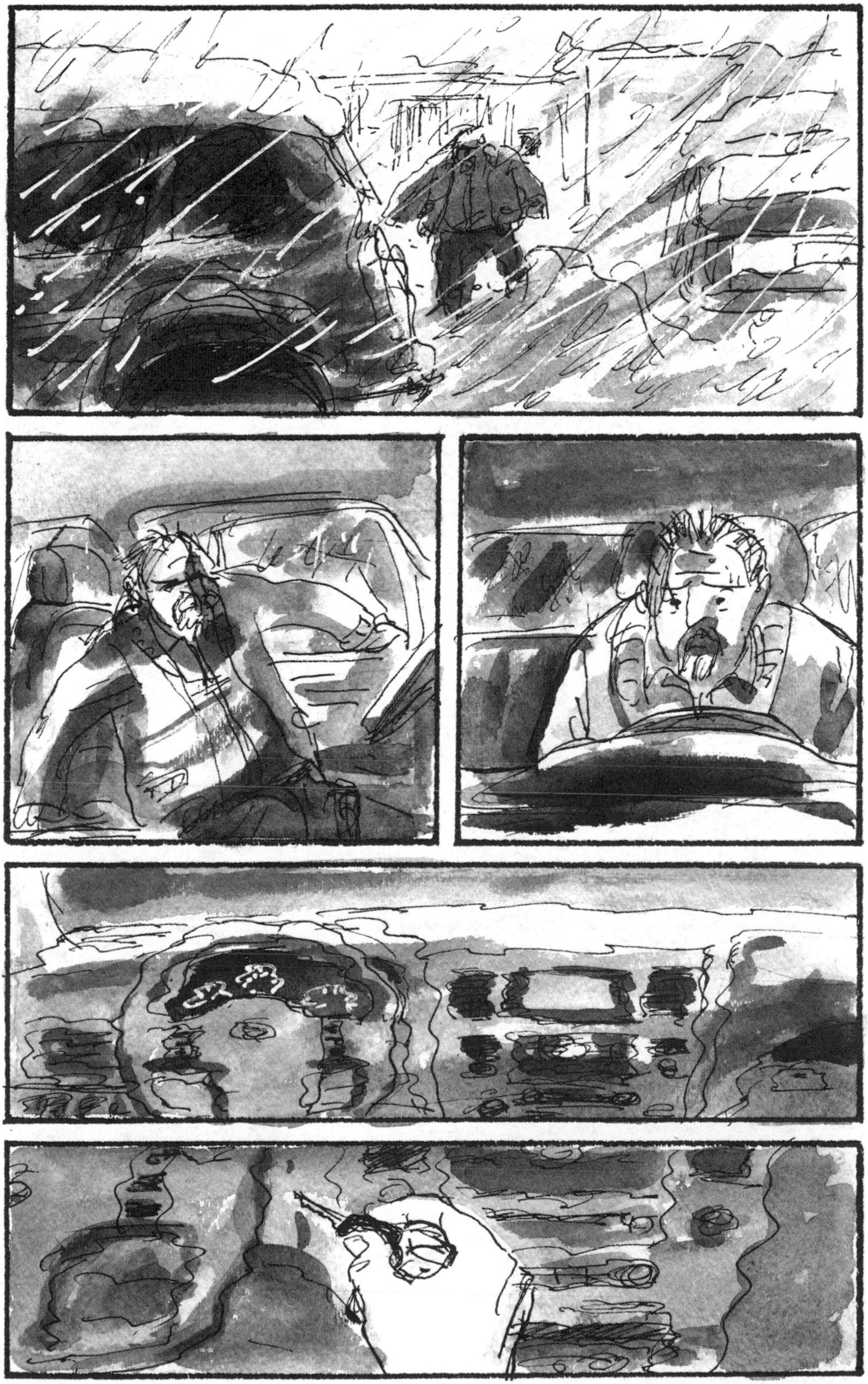

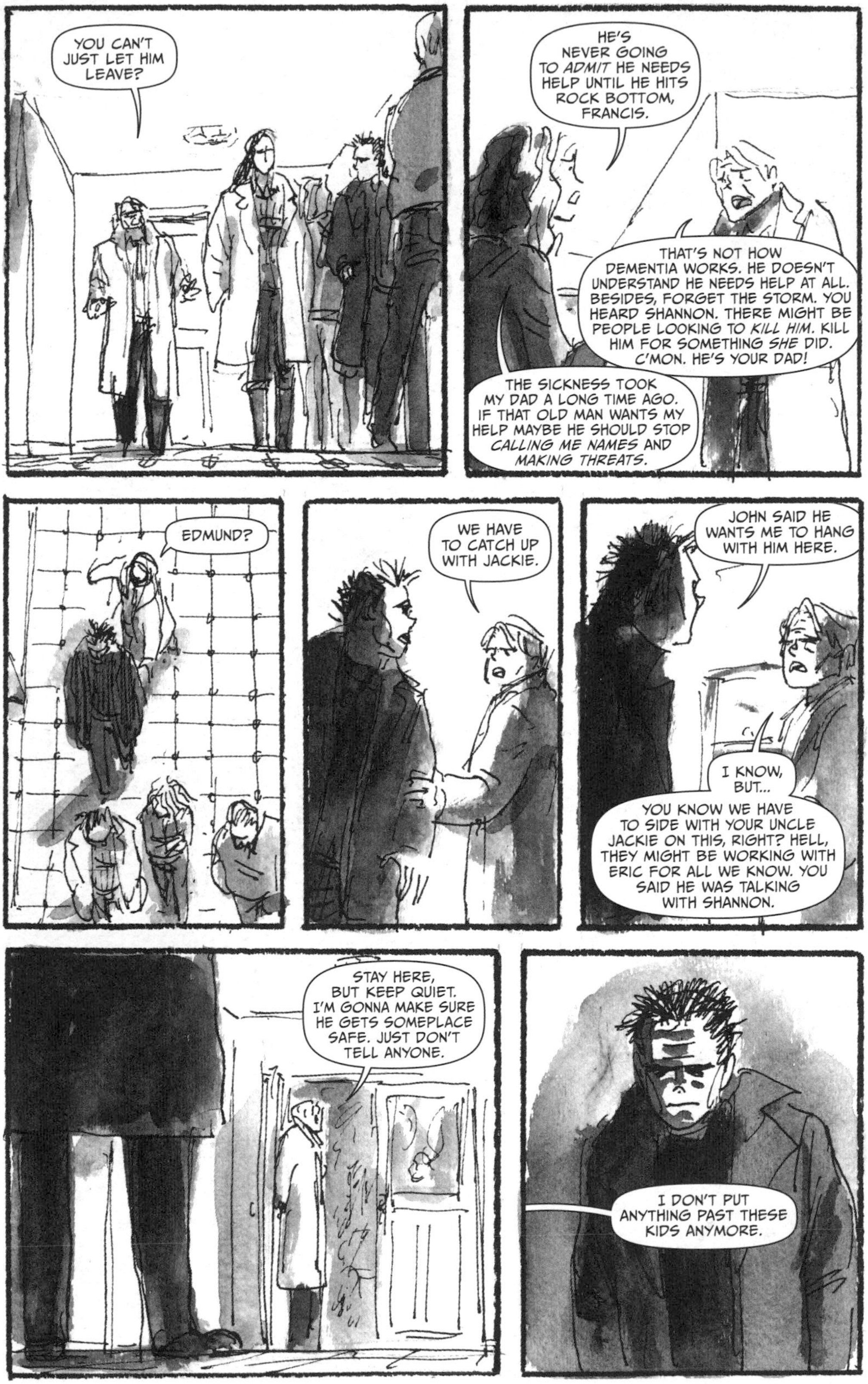
YOU CAN'T JUST LET HIM LEAVE?
HE'S NEVER GOING TO *ADMIT* HE NEEDS HELP UNTIL HE HITS ROCK BOTTOM, FRANCIS.
THAT'S NOT HOW DEMENTIA WORKS. HE DOESN'T UNDERSTAND HE NEEDS HELP AT ALL. BESIDES, FORGET THE STORM. YOU HEARD SHANNON. THERE MIGHT BE PEOPLE LOOKING TO *KILL HIM*. KILL HIM FOR SOMETHING *SHE* DID. C'MON. HE'S YOUR DAD!
THE SICKNESS TOOK MY DAD A LONG TIME AGO. IF THAT OLD MAN WANTS MY HELP MAYBE HE SHOULD STOP *CALLING ME NAMES* AND *MAKING THREATS*.
EDMUND?
WE HAVE TO CATCH UP WITH JACKIE.
JOHN SAID HE WANTS ME TO HANG WITH HIM HERE.
I KNOW, BUT...
YOU KNOW WE HAVE TO SIDE WITH YOUR UNCLE JACKIE ON THIS, RIGHT? HELL, THEY MIGHT BE WORKING WITH ERIC FOR ALL WE KNOW. YOU SAID HE WAS TALKING WITH SHANNON.
STAY HERE, BUT KEEP QUIET. I'M GONNA MAKE SURE HE GETS SOMEPLACE SAFE. JUST DON'T TELL ANYONE.
I DON'T PUT ANYTHING PAST THESE KIDS ANYMORE.

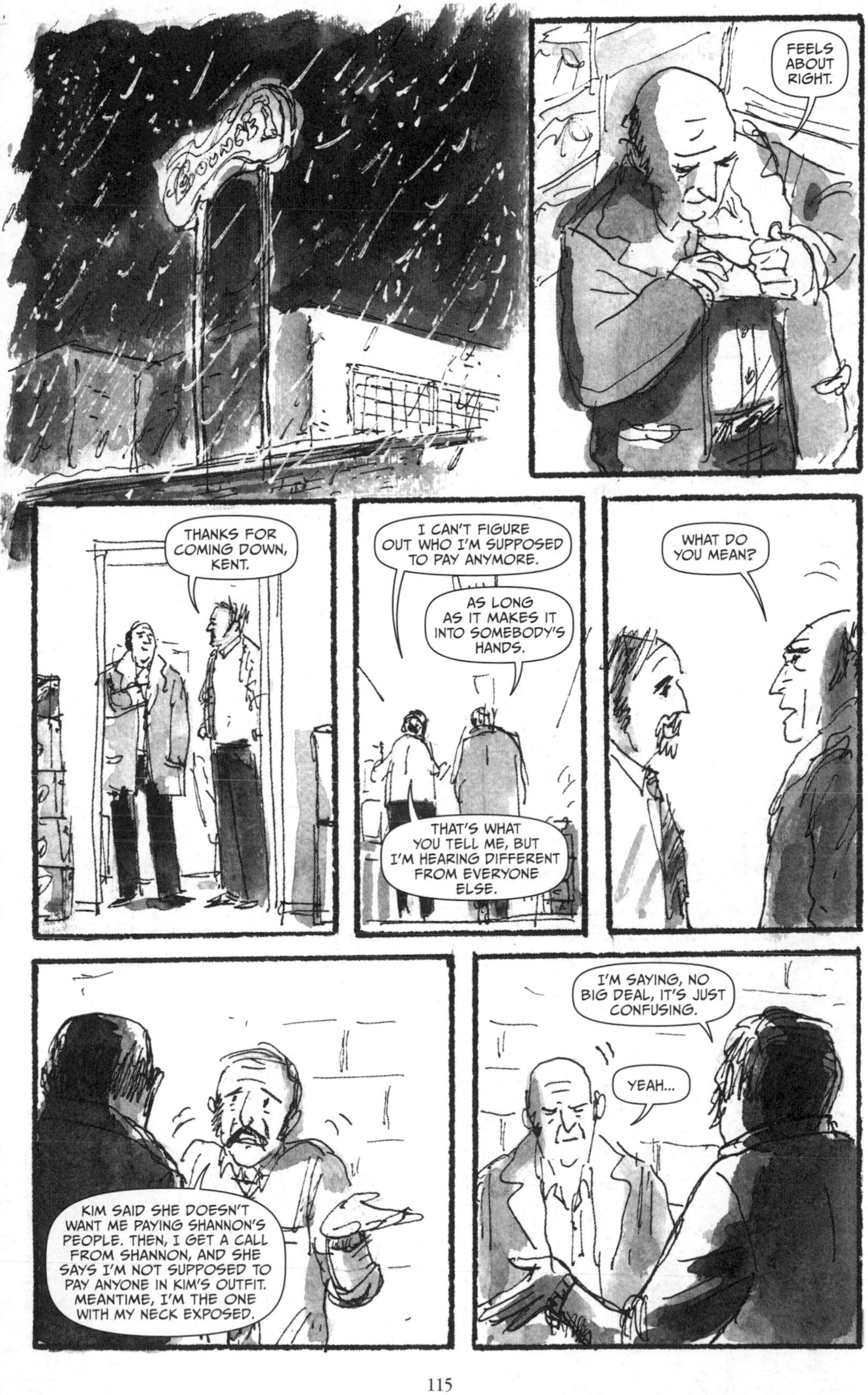
FEELS ABOUT RIGHT.
THANKS FOR COMING DOWN, KENT.
I CAN'T FIGURE OUT WHO I'M SUPPOSED TO PAY ANYMORE.
AS LONG AS IT MAKES IT INTO SOMEBODY'S HANDS.
THAT'S WHAT YOU TELL ME, BUT I'M HEARING DIFFERENT FROM EVERYONE ELSE.
WHAT DO YOU MEAN?
KIM SAID SHE DOESN'T WANT ME PAYING SHANNON'S PEOPLE. THEN, I GET A CALL FROM SHANNON, AND SHE SAYS I'M NOT SUPPOSED TO PAY ANYONE IN KIM'S OUTFIT. MEANTIME, I'M THE ONE WITH MY NECK EXPOSED.
I'M SAYING, NO BIG DEAL, IT'S JUST CONFUSING.
YEAH...

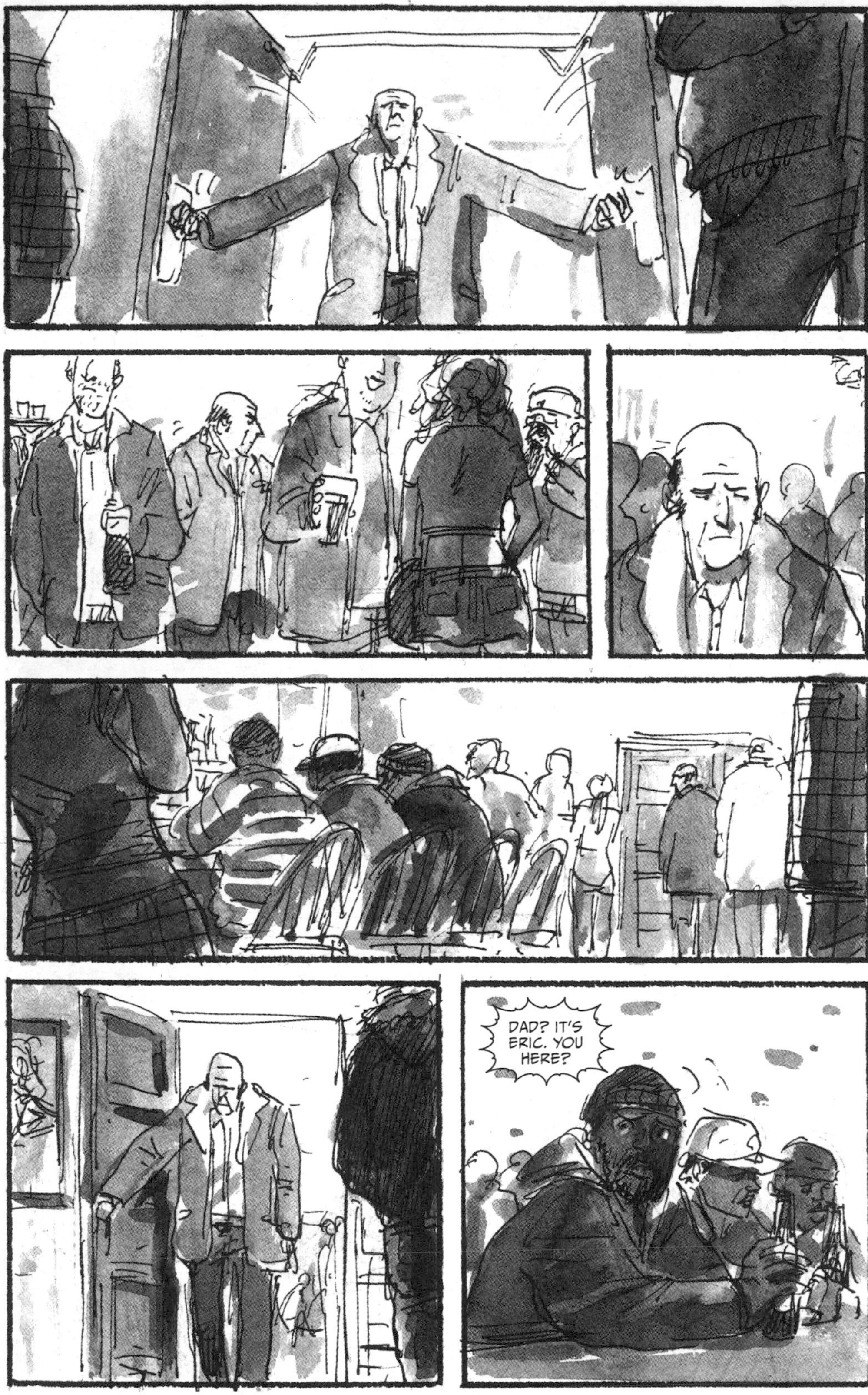
DAD? IT'S ERIC. YOU HERE?

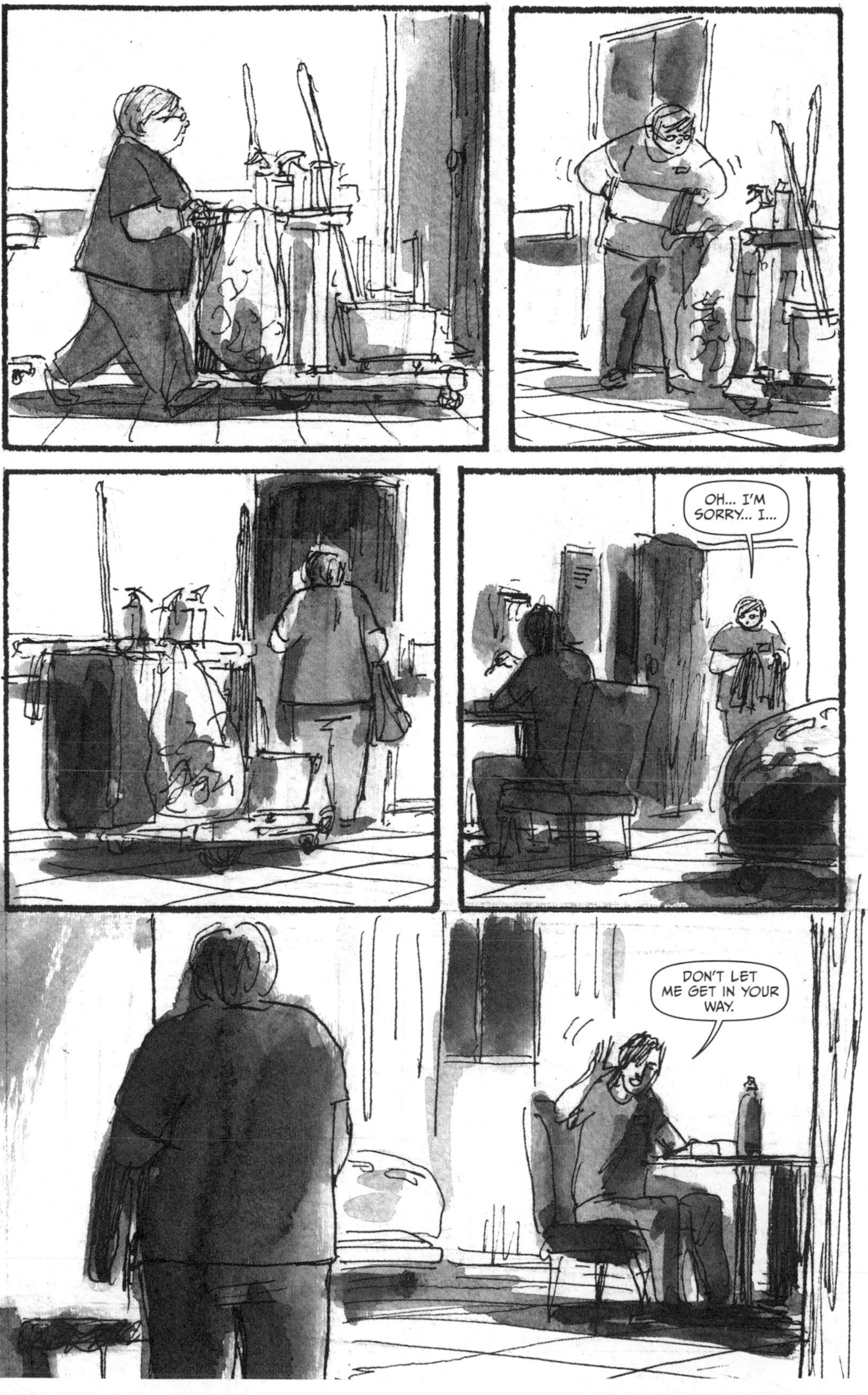
OH... I'M SORRY... I...
DON'T LET ME GET IN YOUR WAY.

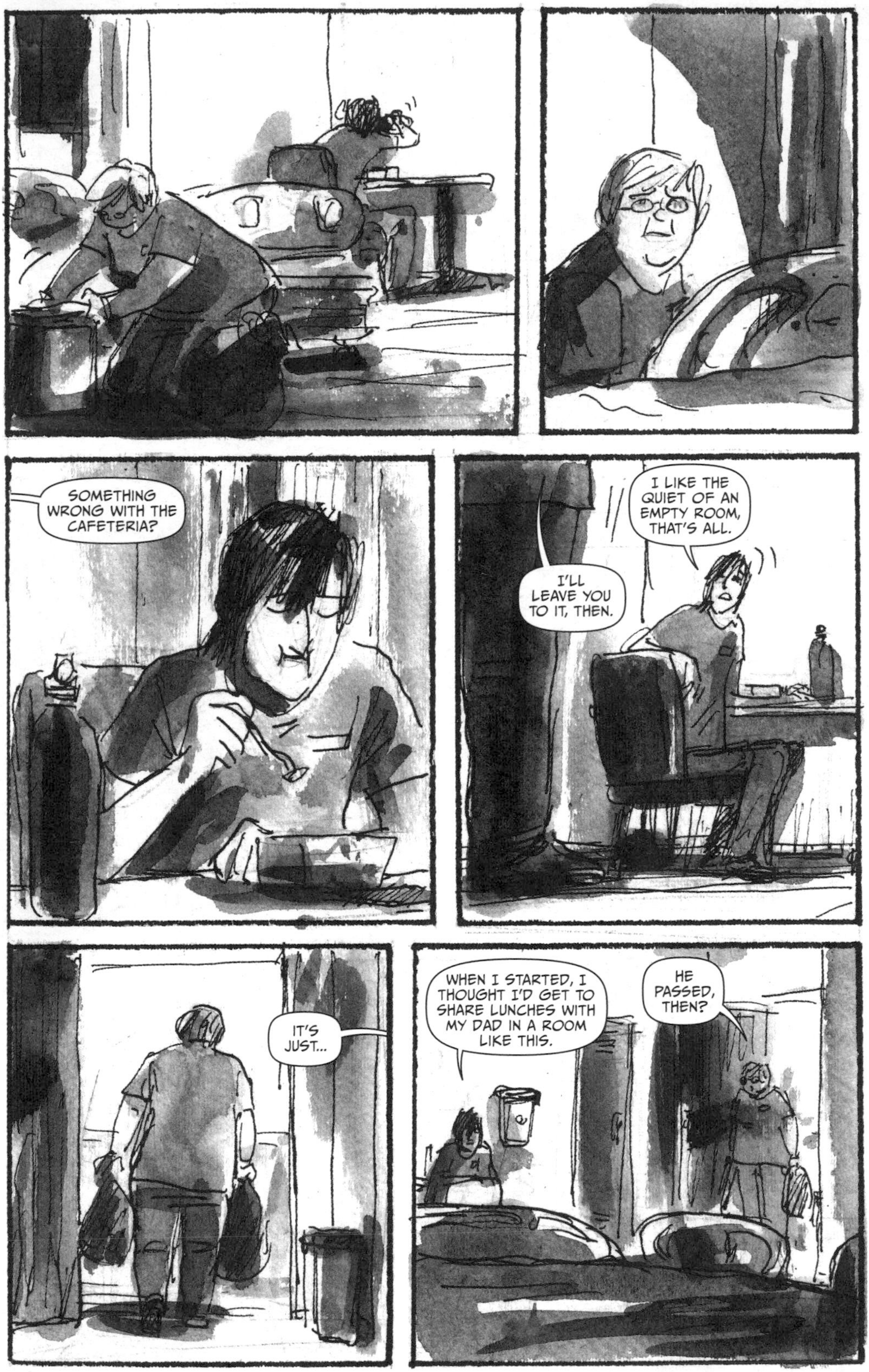
SOMETHING WRONG WITH THE CAFETERIA?
I LIKE THE QUIET OF AN EMPTY ROOM, THAT'S ALL.
I'LL LEAVE YOU TO IT, THEN.
IT'S JUST...
WHEN I STARTED, I THOUGHT I'D GET TO SHARE LUNCHES WITH MY DAD IN A ROOM LIKE THIS.
HE PASSED, THEN?

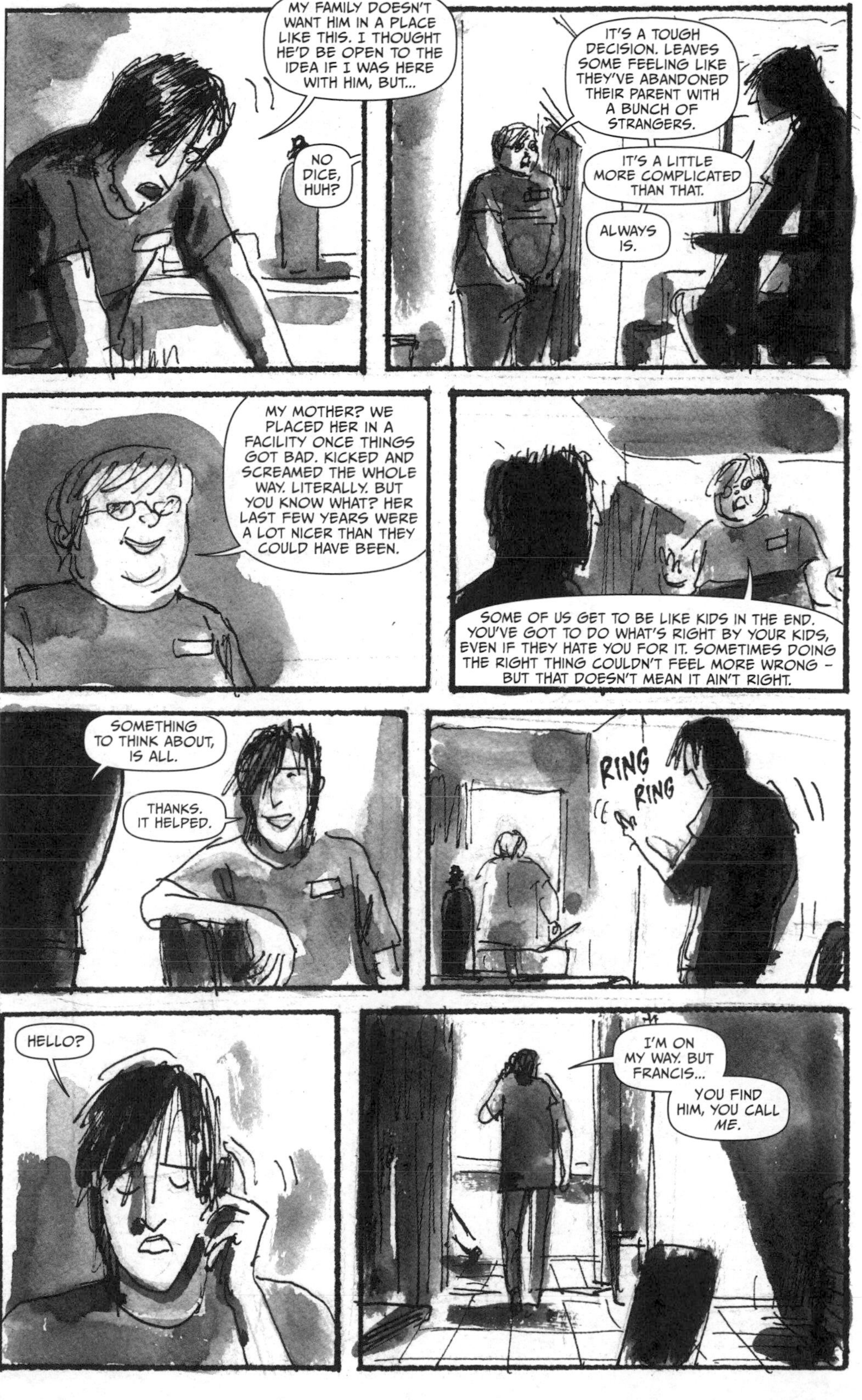
MY FAMILY DOESN'T WANT HIM IN A PLACE LIKE THIS. I THOUGHT HE'D BE OPEN TO THE IDEA IF I WAS HERE WITH HIM, BUT...
NO DICE, HUH?
IT'S A TOUGH DECISION. LEAVES SOME FEELING LIKE THEY'VE ABANDONED THEIR PARENT WITH A BUNCH OF STRANGERS.
IT'S A LITTLE MORE COMPLICATED THAN THAT.
ALWAYS IS.
MY MOTHER? WE PLACED HER IN A FACILITY ONCE THINGS GOT BAD. KICKED AND SCREAMED THE WHOLE WAY. LITERALLY. BUT YOU KNOW WHAT? HER LAST FEW YEARS WERE A LOT NICER THAN THEY COULD HAVE BEEN.
SOME OF US GET TO BE LIKE KIDS IN THE END. YOU'VE GOT TO DO WHAT'S RIGHT BY YOUR KIDS, EVEN IF THEY HATE YOU FOR IT. SOMETIMES DOING THE RIGHT THING COULDN'T FEEL MORE WRONG – BUT THAT DOESN'T MEAN IT AIN'T RIGHT.
SOMETHING TO THINK ABOUT, IS ALL.
THANKS. IT HELPED.
RING RING
HELLO?
I'M ON MY WAY. BUT FRANCIS...
YOU FIND HIM, YOU CALL ME.

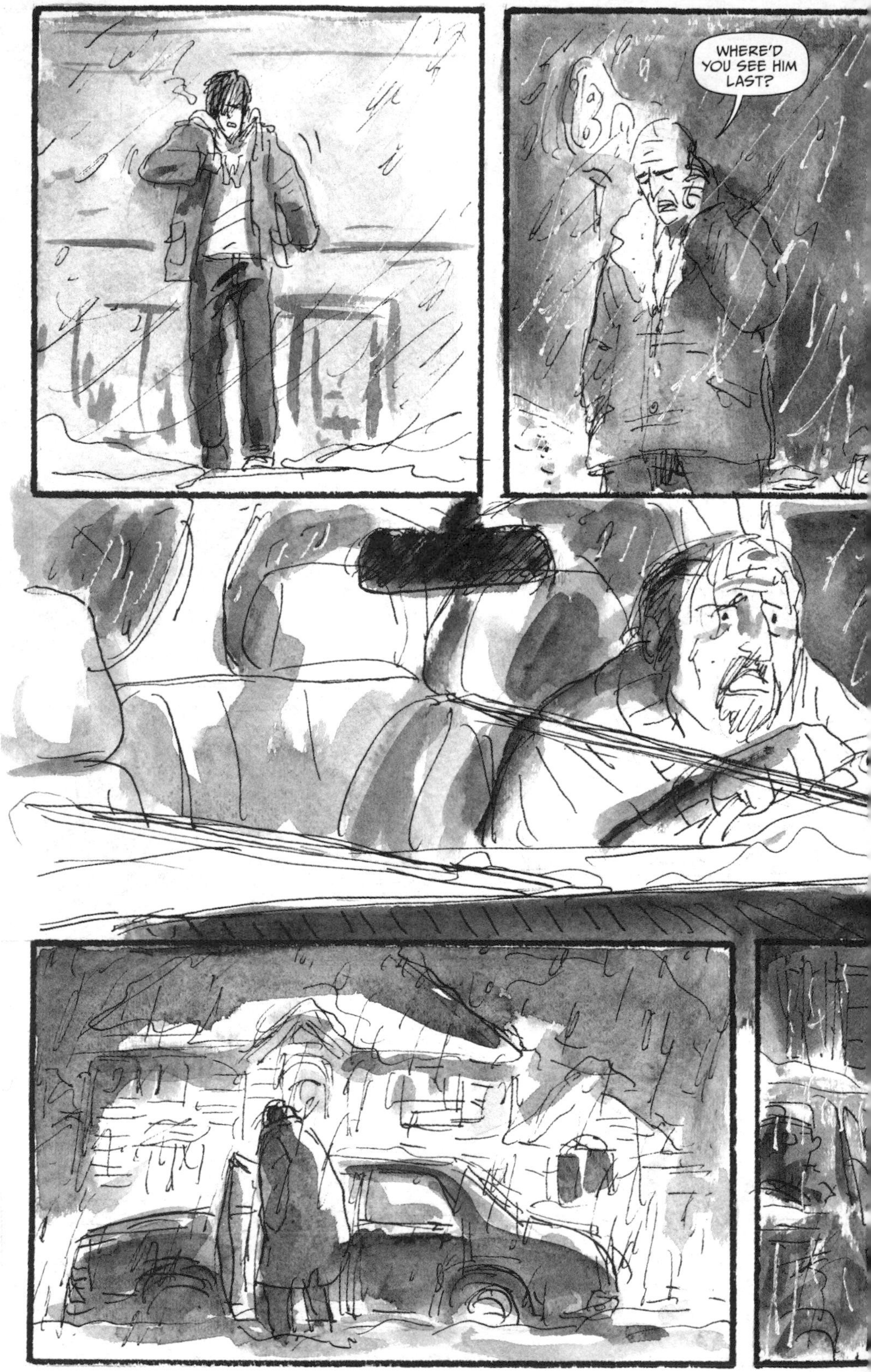
WHERE'D YOU SEE HIM LAST?

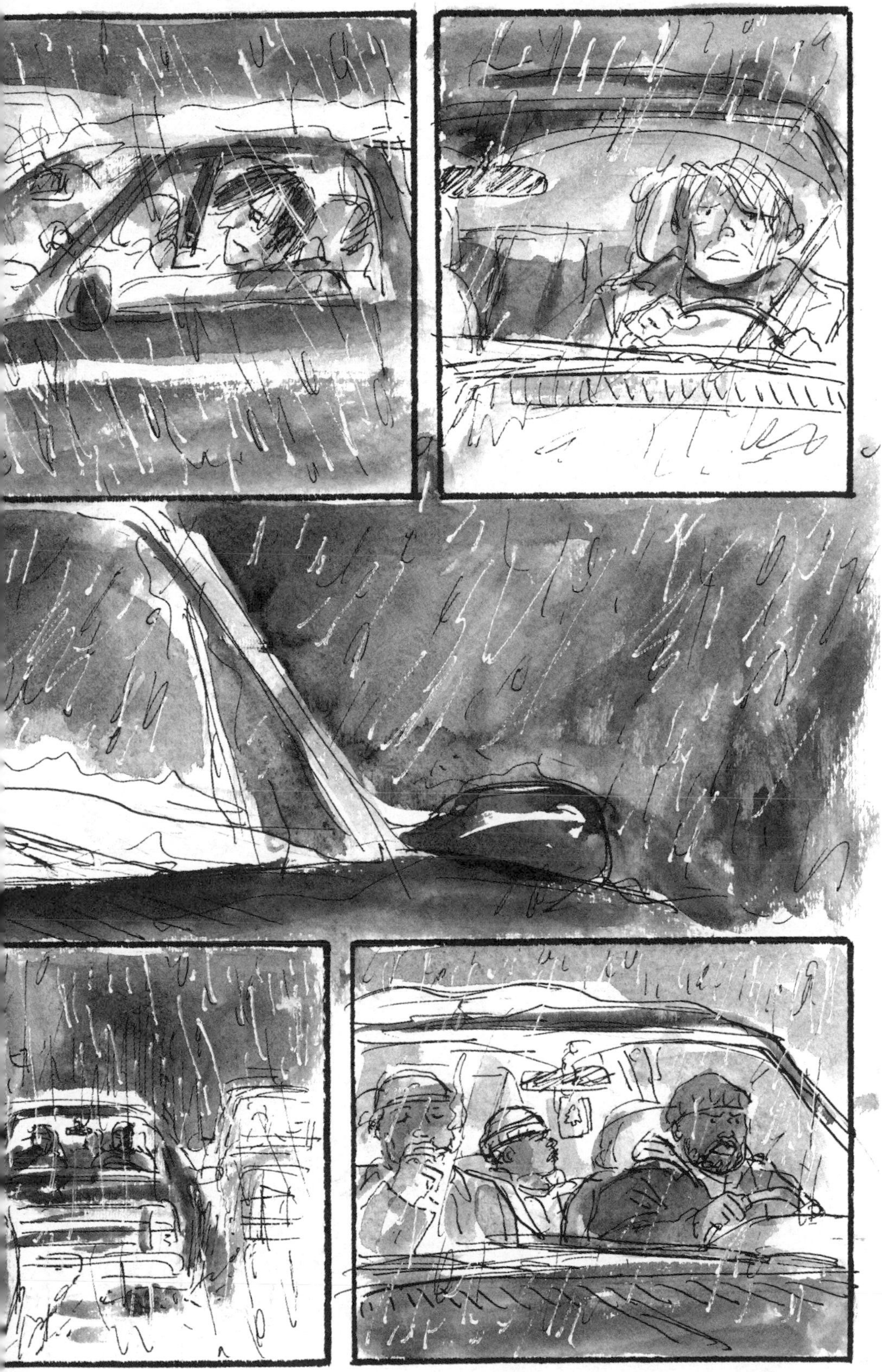

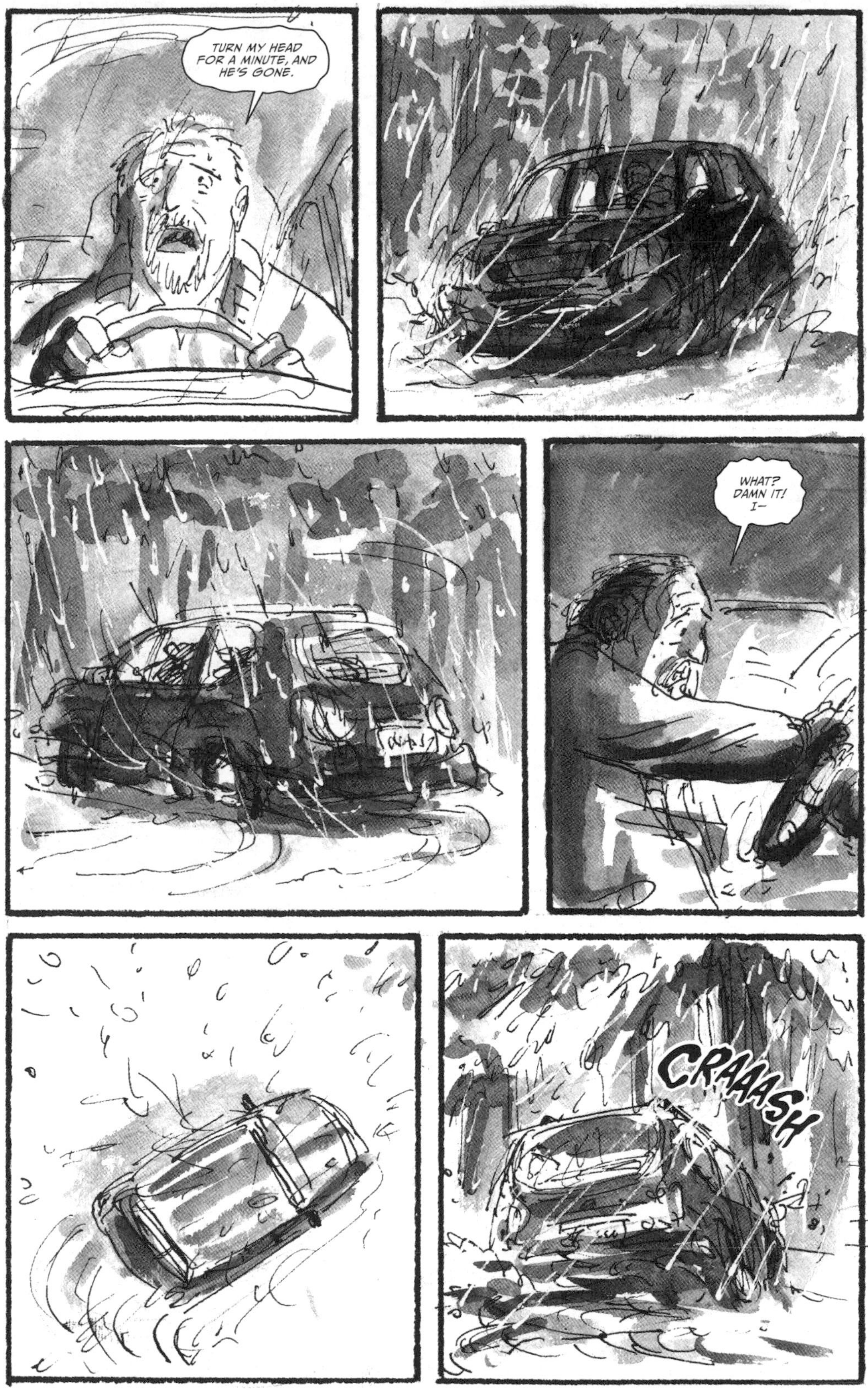
TURN MY HEAD FOR A MINUTE, AND HE'S GONE.
WHAT? DAMN IT! I--
CRAAASH

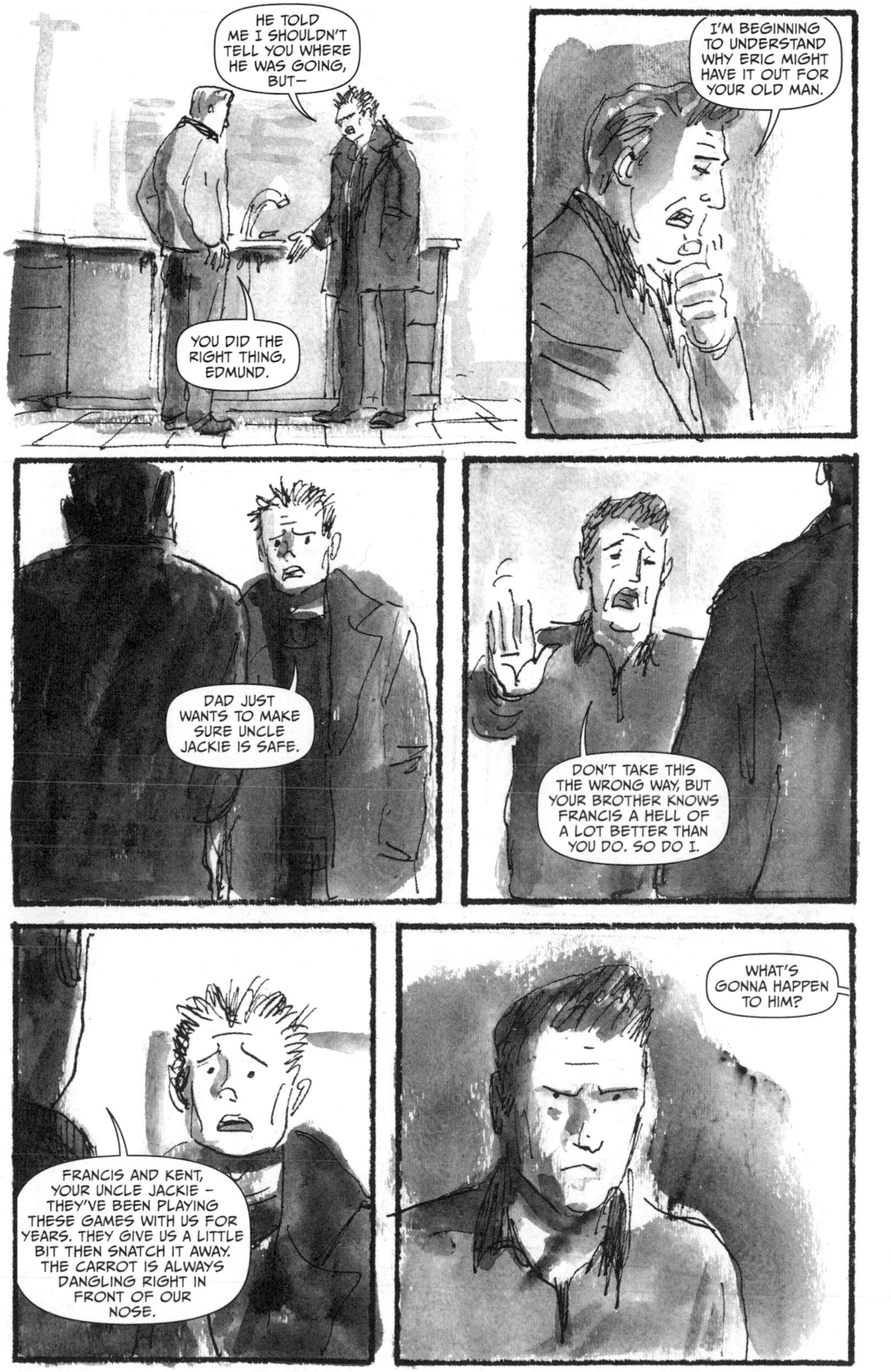
HE TOLD ME I SHOULDN'T TELL YOU WHERE HE WAS GOING, BUT–
YOU DID THE RIGHT THING, EDMUND.
I'M BEGINNING TO UNDERSTAND WHY ERIC MIGHT HAVE IT OUT FOR YOUR OLD MAN.
DAD JUST WANTS TO MAKE SURE UNCLE JACKIE IS SAFE.
DON'T TAKE THIS THE WRONG WAY, BUT YOUR BROTHER KNOWS FRANCIS A HELL OF A LOT BETTER THAN YOU DO. SO DO I.
FRANCIS AND KENT, YOUR UNCLE JACKIE – THEY'VE BEEN PLAYING THESE GAMES WITH US FOR YEARS. THEY GIVE US A LITTLE BIT THEN SNATCH IT AWAY. THE CARROT IS ALWAYS DANGLING RIGHT IN FRONT OF OUR NOSE.
WHAT'S GONNA HAPPEN TO HIM?

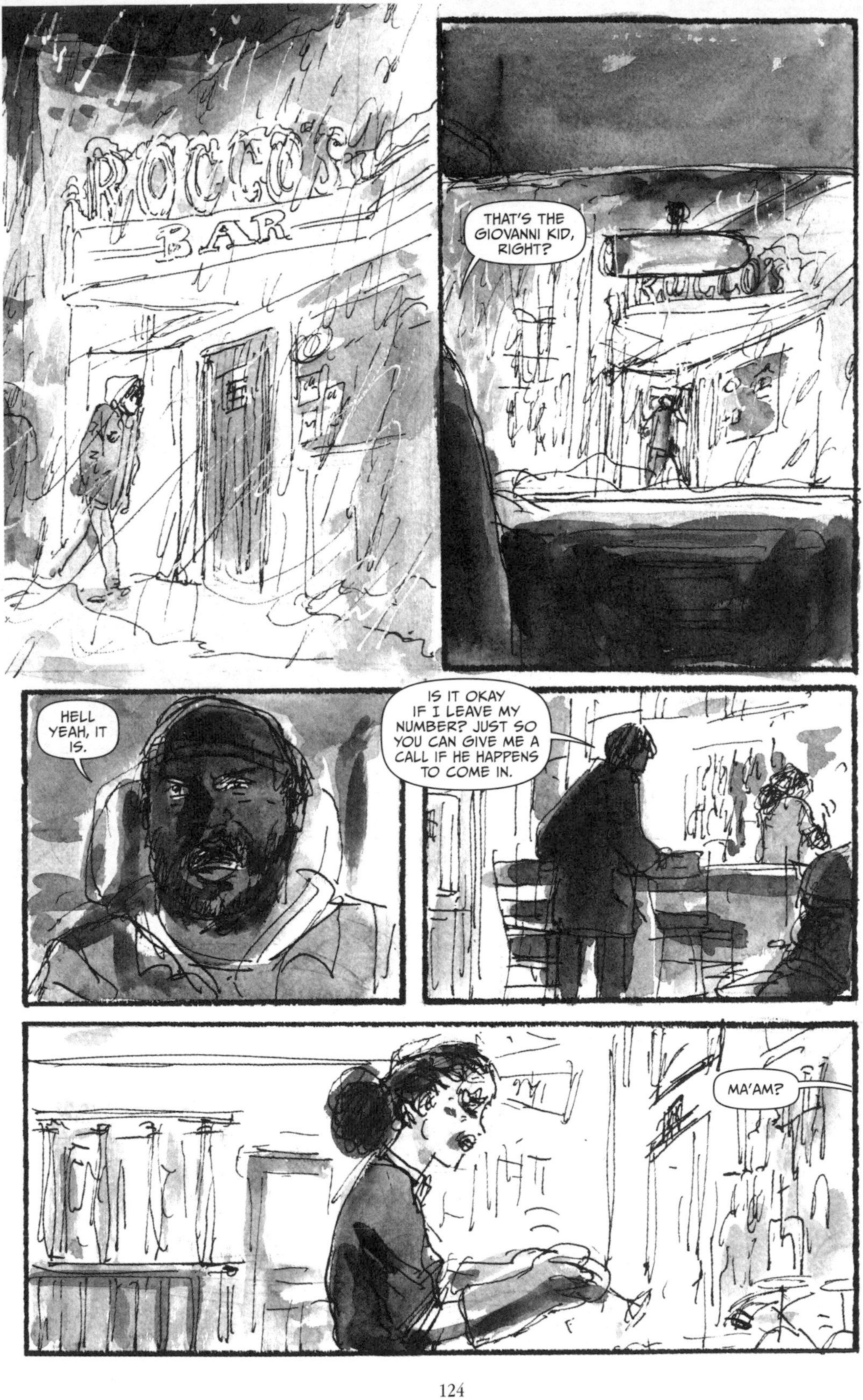
ROCCO'S
BAR
THAT'S THE GIOVANNI KID, RIGHT?
HELL YEAH, IT IS.
IS IT OKAY IF I LEAVE MY NUMBER? JUST SO YOU CAN GIVE ME A CALL IF HE HAPPENS TO COME IN.
MA'AM?

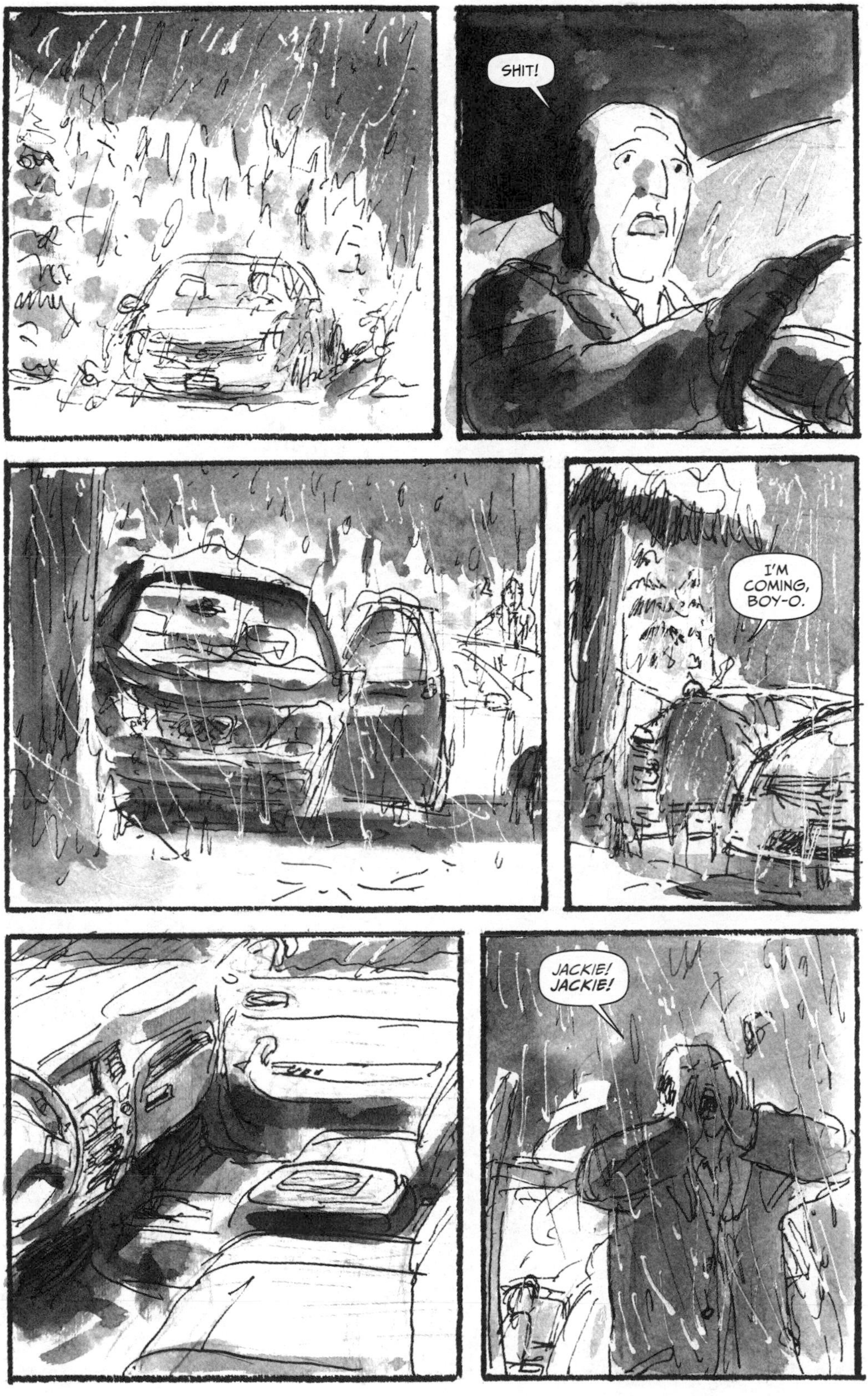
SHIT!
I'M COMING, BOY-O.
JACKIE! JACKIE!

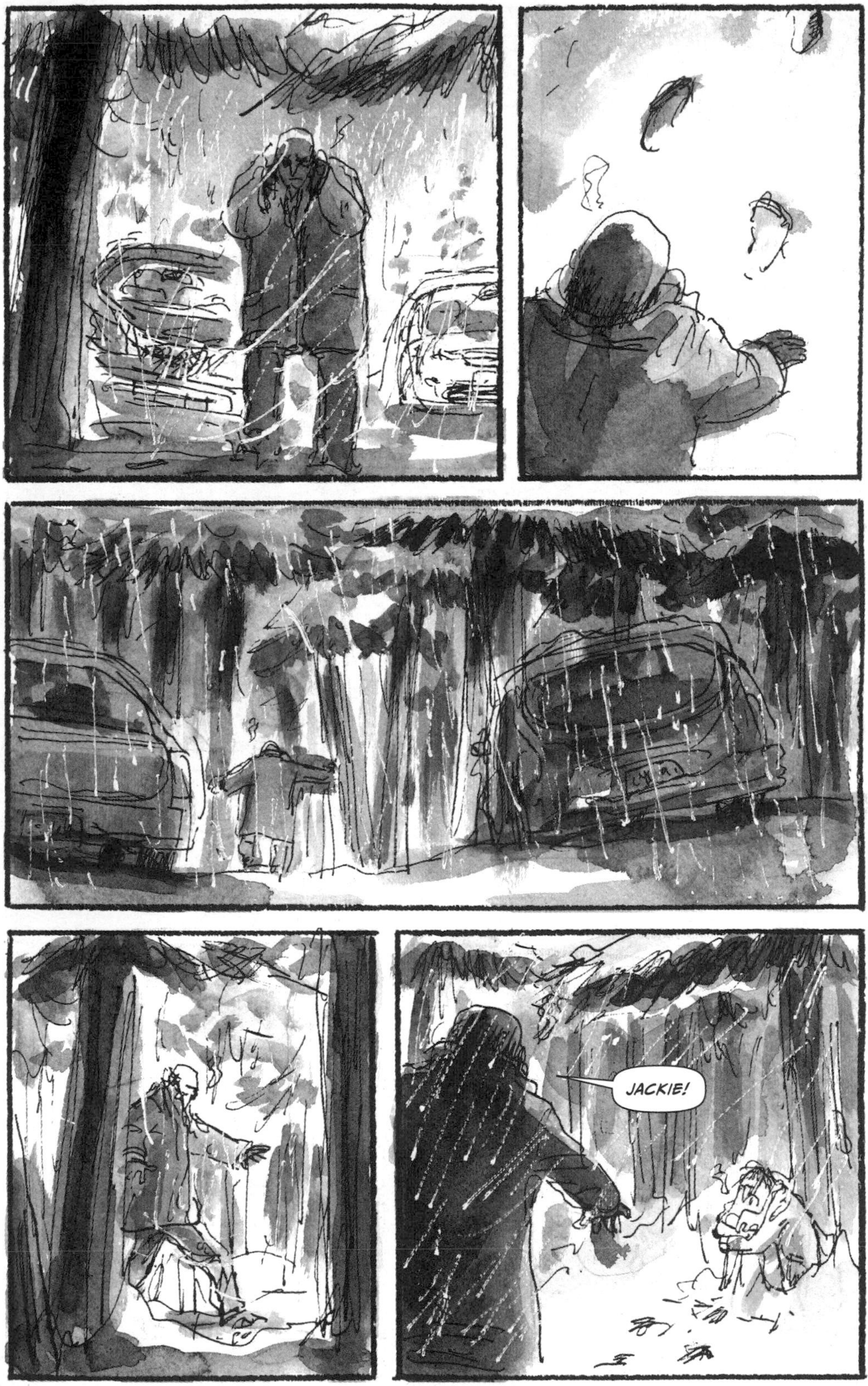
JACKIE!

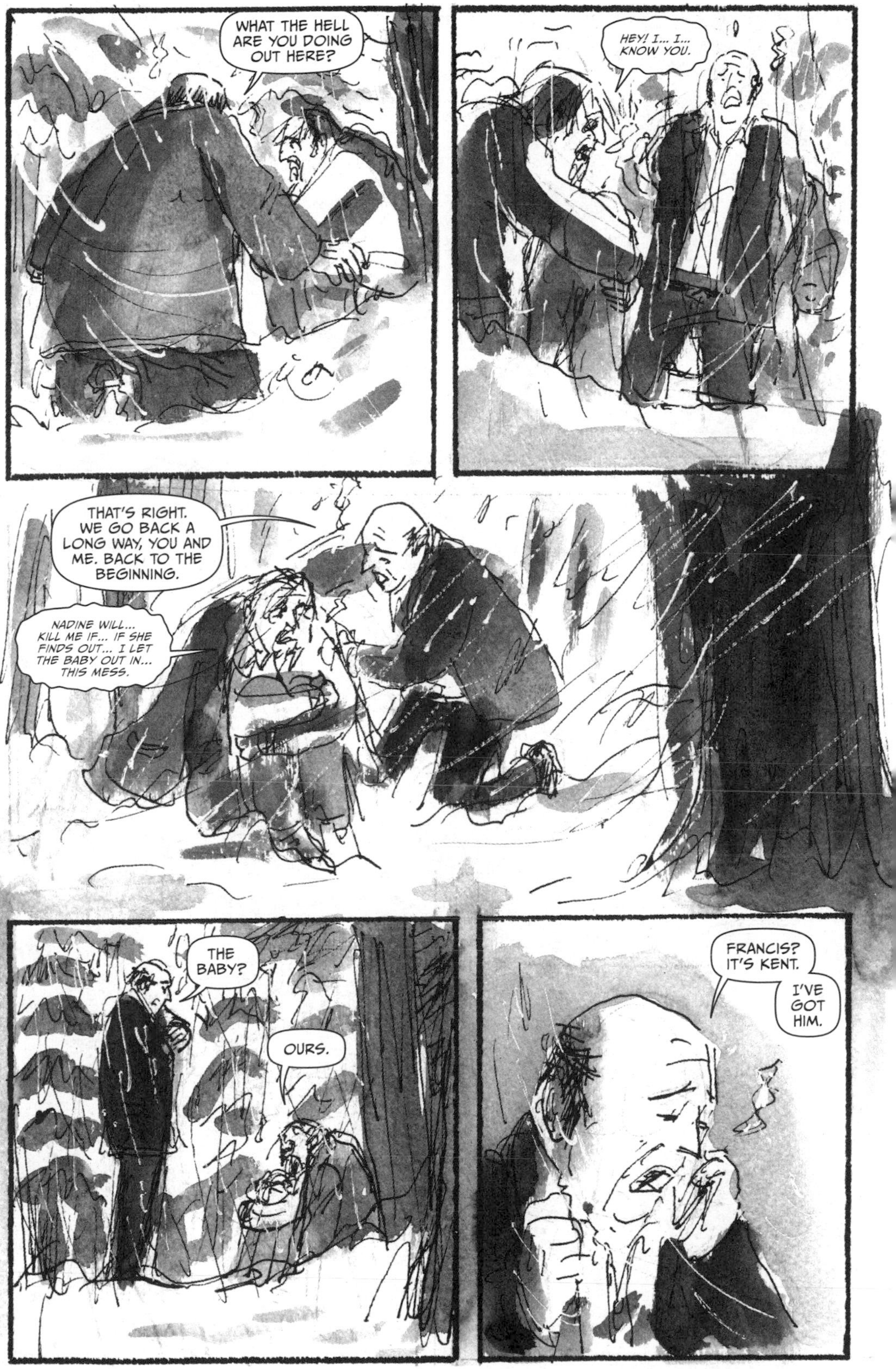
WHAT THE HELL ARE YOU DOING OUT HERE?
HEY! I... I... KNOW YOU.
THAT'S RIGHT. WE GO BACK A LONG WAY, YOU AND ME. BACK TO THE BEGINNING.
NADINE WILL... KILL ME IF... IF SHE FINDS OUT... I LET THE BABY OUT IN... THIS MESS.
THE BABY?
OURS.
FRANCIS? IT'S KENT.
I'VE GOT HIM.

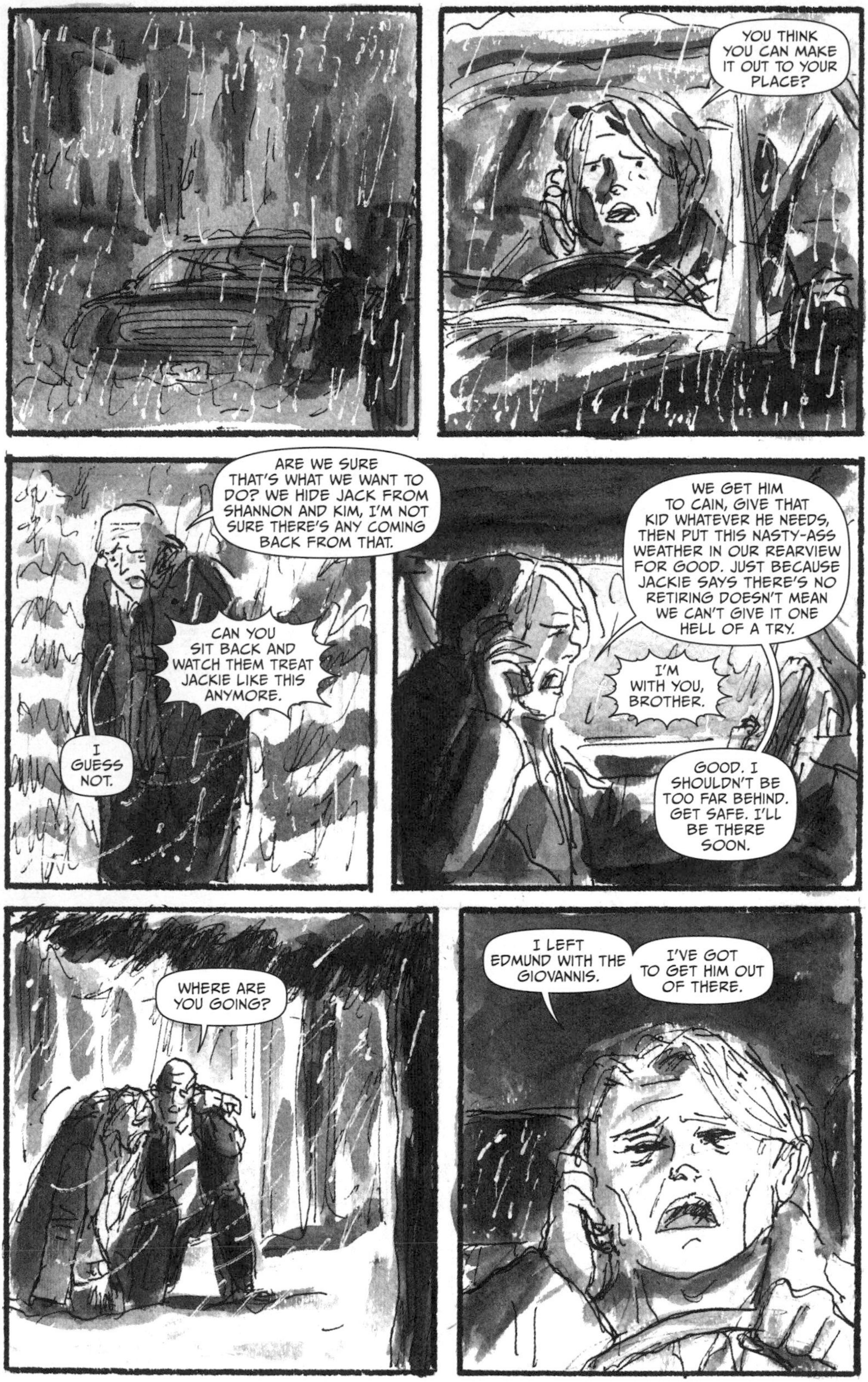
YOU THINK YOU CAN MAKE IT OUT TO YOUR PLACE?
ARE WE SURE THAT'S WHAT WE WANT TO DO? WE HIDE JACK FROM SHANNON AND KIM, I'M NOT SURE THERE'S ANY COMING BACK FROM THAT.
CAN YOU SIT BACK AND WATCH THEM TREAT JACKIE LIKE THIS ANYMORE.
I GUESS NOT.
WE GET HIM TO CAIN, GIVE THAT KID WHATEVER HE NEEDS, THEN PUT THIS NASTY-ASS WEATHER IN OUR REARVIEW FOR GOOD. JUST BECAUSE JACKIE SAYS THERE'S NO RETIRING DOESN'T MEAN WE CAN'T GIVE IT ONE HELL OF A TRY.
I'M WITH YOU, BROTHER.
GOOD. I SHOULDN'T BE TOO FAR BEHIND. GET SAFE. I'LL BE THERE SOON.
WHERE ARE YOU GOING?
I LEFT EDMUND WITH THE GIOVANNIS.
I'VE GOT TO GET HIM OUT OF THERE.

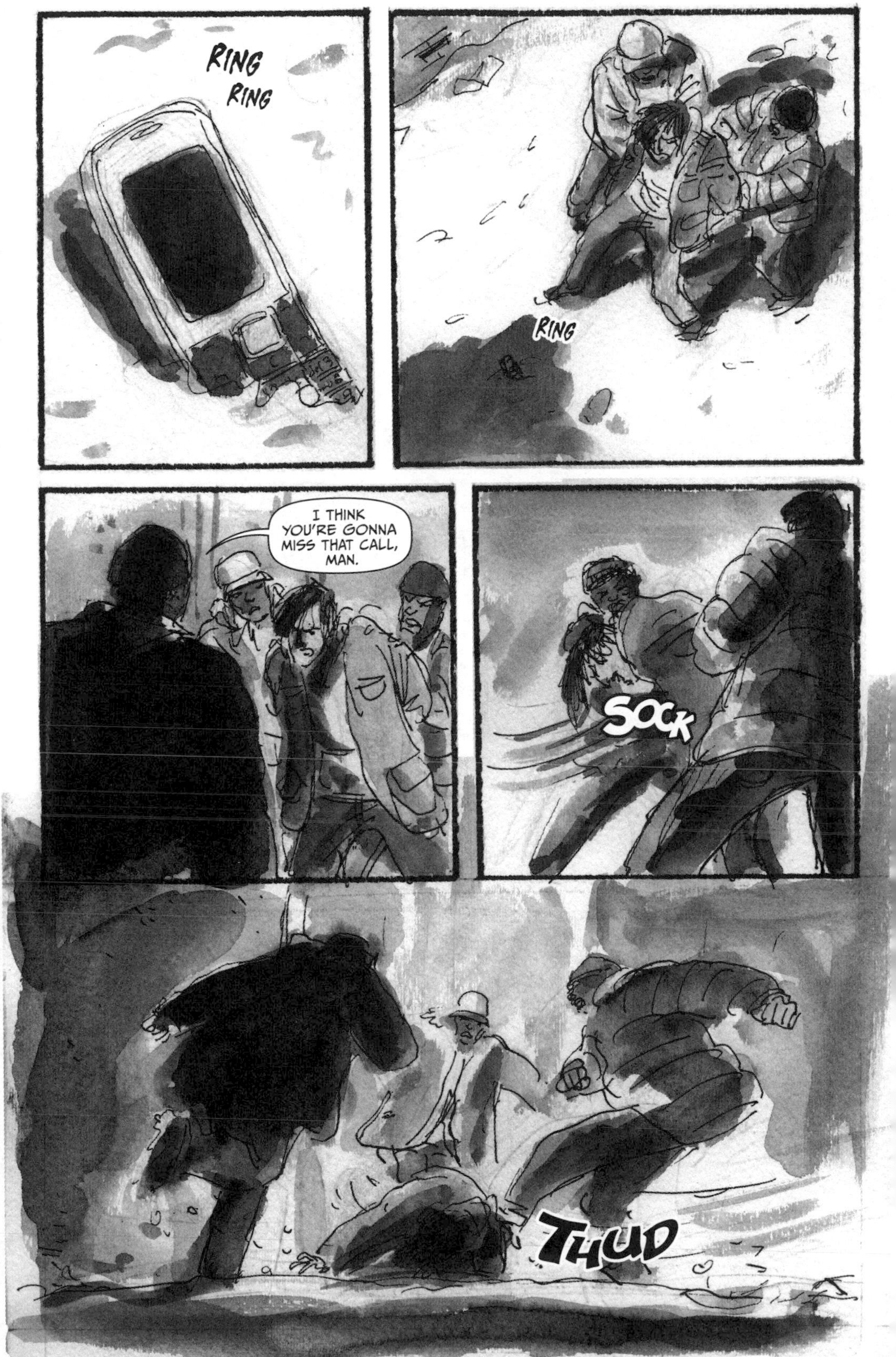
RING
RING
RING
I THINK YOU'RE GONNA MISS THAT CALL, MAN.
SOCK
THUD

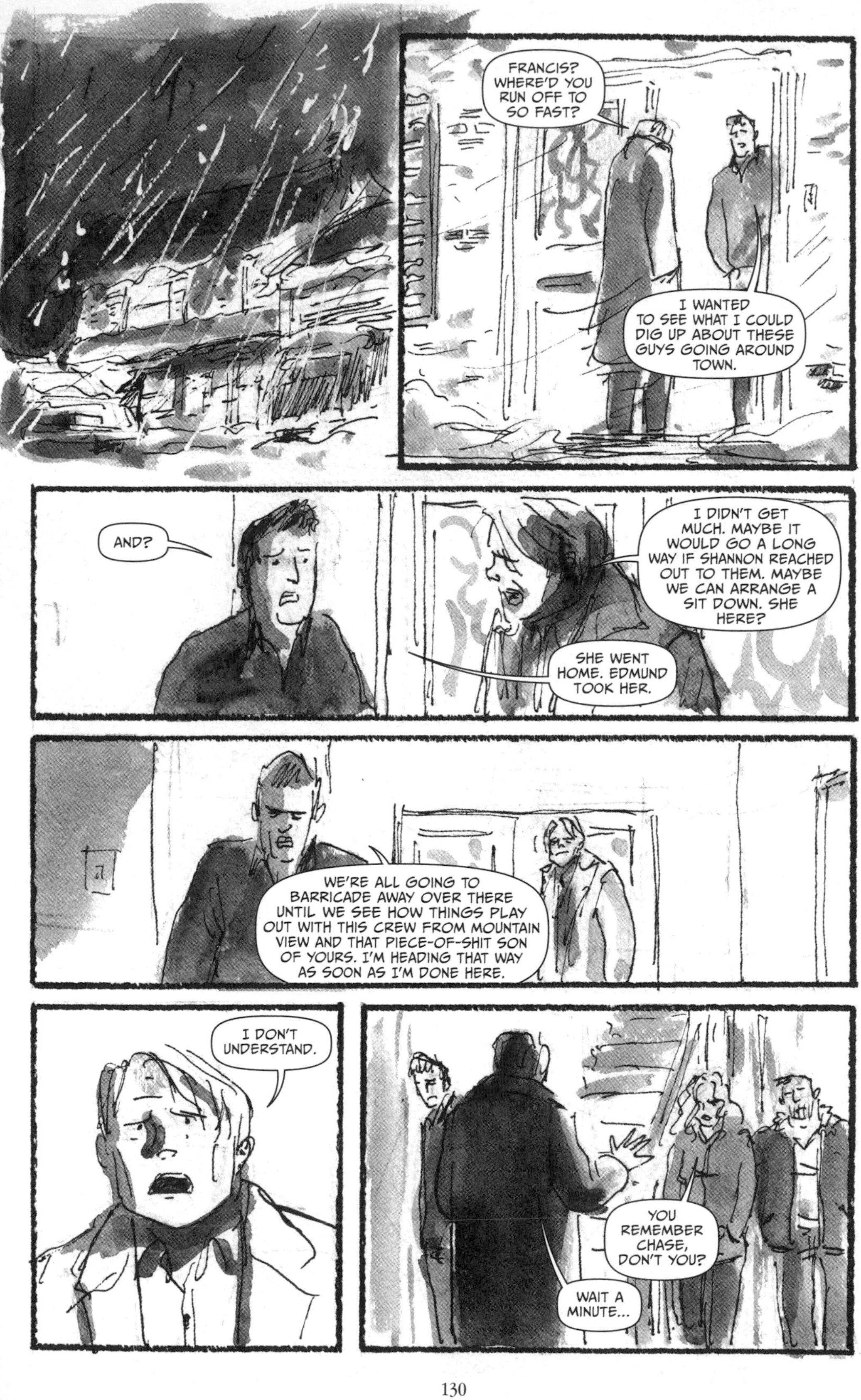
FRANCIS? WHERE'D YOU RUN OFF TO SO FAST?
I WANTED TO SEE WHAT I COULD DIG UP ABOUT THESE GUYS GOING AROUND TOWN.
AND?
I DIDN'T GET MUCH. MAYBE IT WOULD GO A LONG WAY IF SHANNON REACHED OUT TO THEM. MAYBE WE CAN ARRANGE A SIT DOWN. SHE HERE?
SHE WENT HOME. EDMUND TOOK HER.
WE'RE ALL GOING TO BARRICADE AWAY OVER THERE UNTIL WE SEE HOW THINGS PLAY OUT WITH THIS CREW FROM MOUNTAIN VIEW AND THAT PIECE-OF-SHIT SON OF YOURS. I'M HEADING THAT WAY AS SOON AS I'M DONE HERE.
I DON'T UNDERSTAND.
YOU REMEMBER CHASE, DON'T YOU?
WAIT A MINUTE...

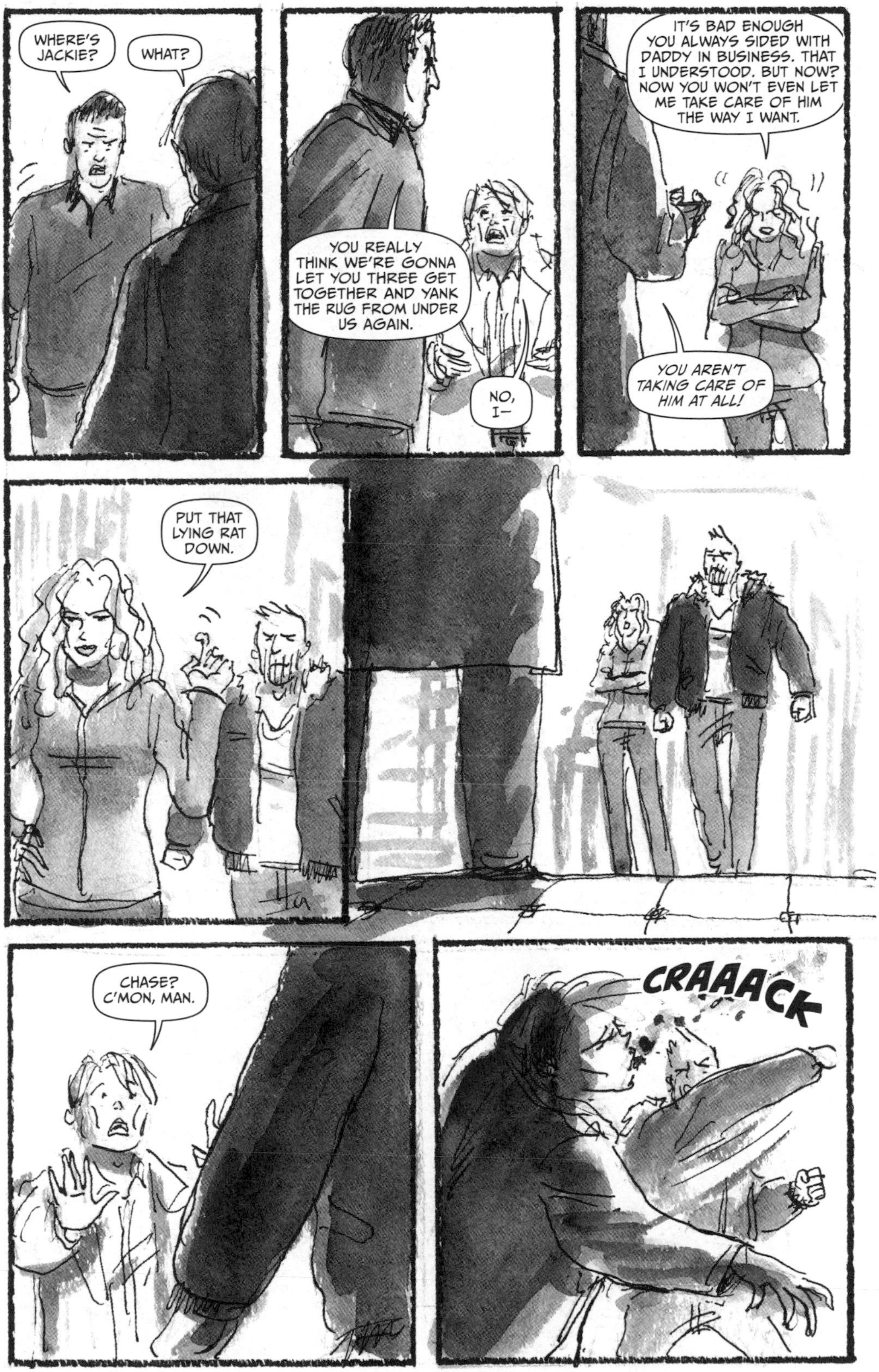

WHERE'S JACKIE?
WHAT?
YOU REALLY THINK WE'RE GONNA LET YOU THREE GET TOGETHER AND YANK THE RUG FROM UNDER US AGAIN.
NO, I—
IT'S BAD ENOUGH YOU ALWAYS SIDED WITH DADDY IN BUSINESS. THAT I UNDERSTOOD. BUT NOW? NOW YOU WON'T EVEN LET ME TAKE CARE OF HIM THE WAY I WANT.
YOU AREN'T TAKING CARE OF HIM AT ALL!
PUT THAT LYING RAT DOWN.
CHASE? C'MON, MAN.
CRAAACK

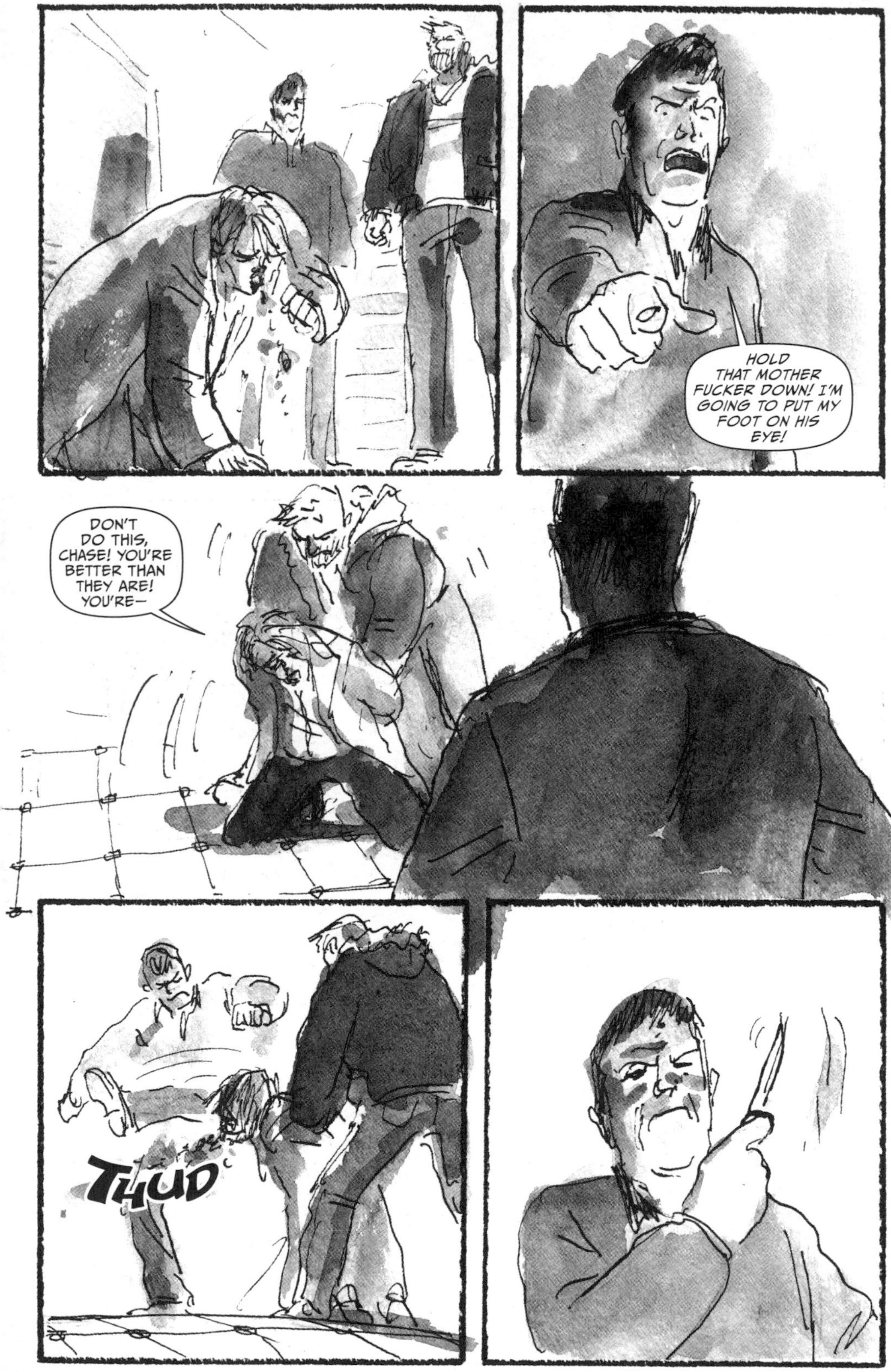
HOLD THAT MOTHER FUCKER DOWN! I'M GOING TO PUT MY FOOT ON HIS EYE!
DON'T DO THIS, CHASE! YOU'RE BETTER THAN THEY ARE! YOU'RE—
THUD

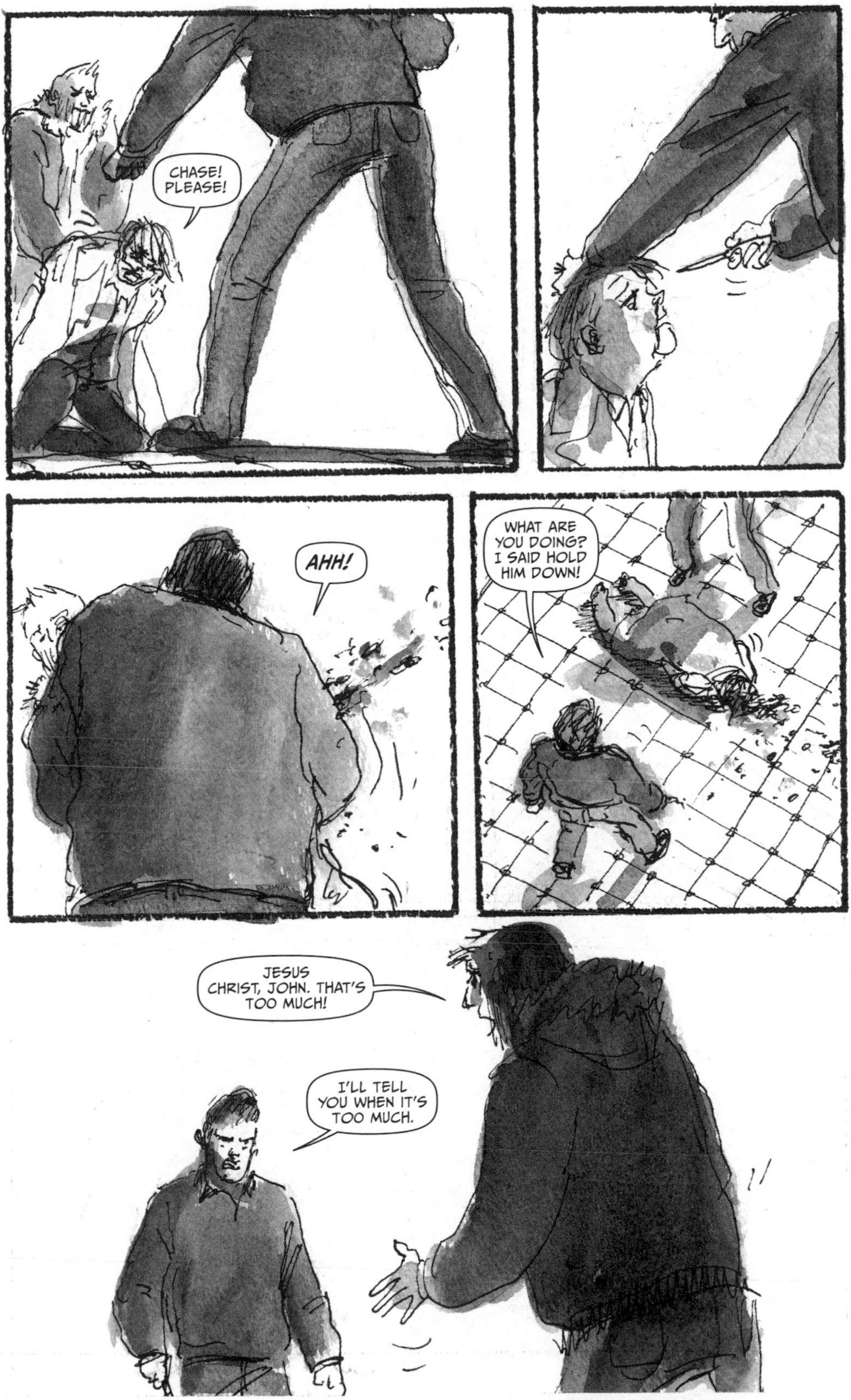
CHASE! PLEASE!
AHH!
WHAT ARE YOU DOING? I SAID HOLD HIM DOWN!
JESUS CHRIST, JOHN. THAT'S TOO MUCH!
I'LL TELL YOU WHEN IT'S TOO MUCH.

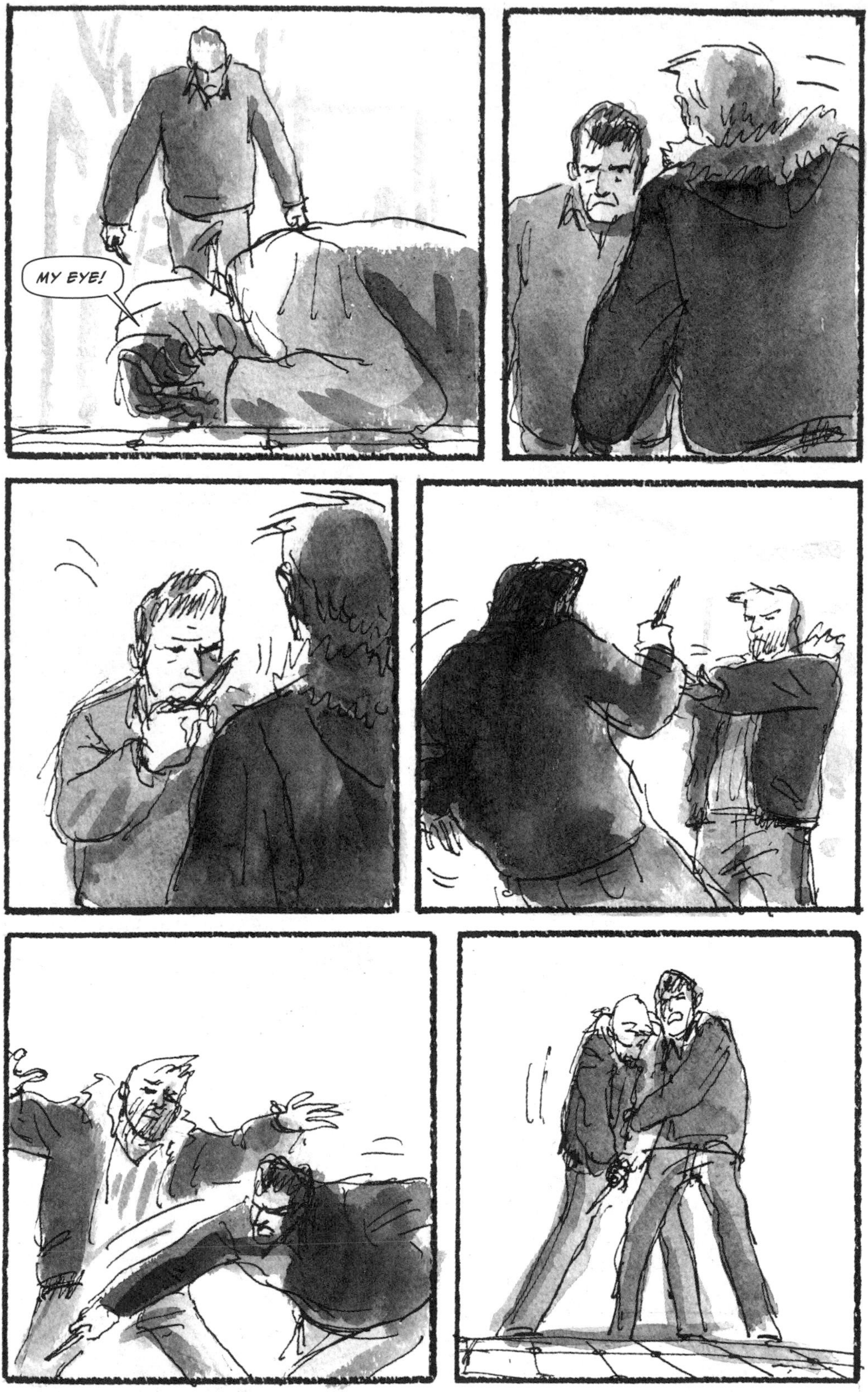
MY EYE!

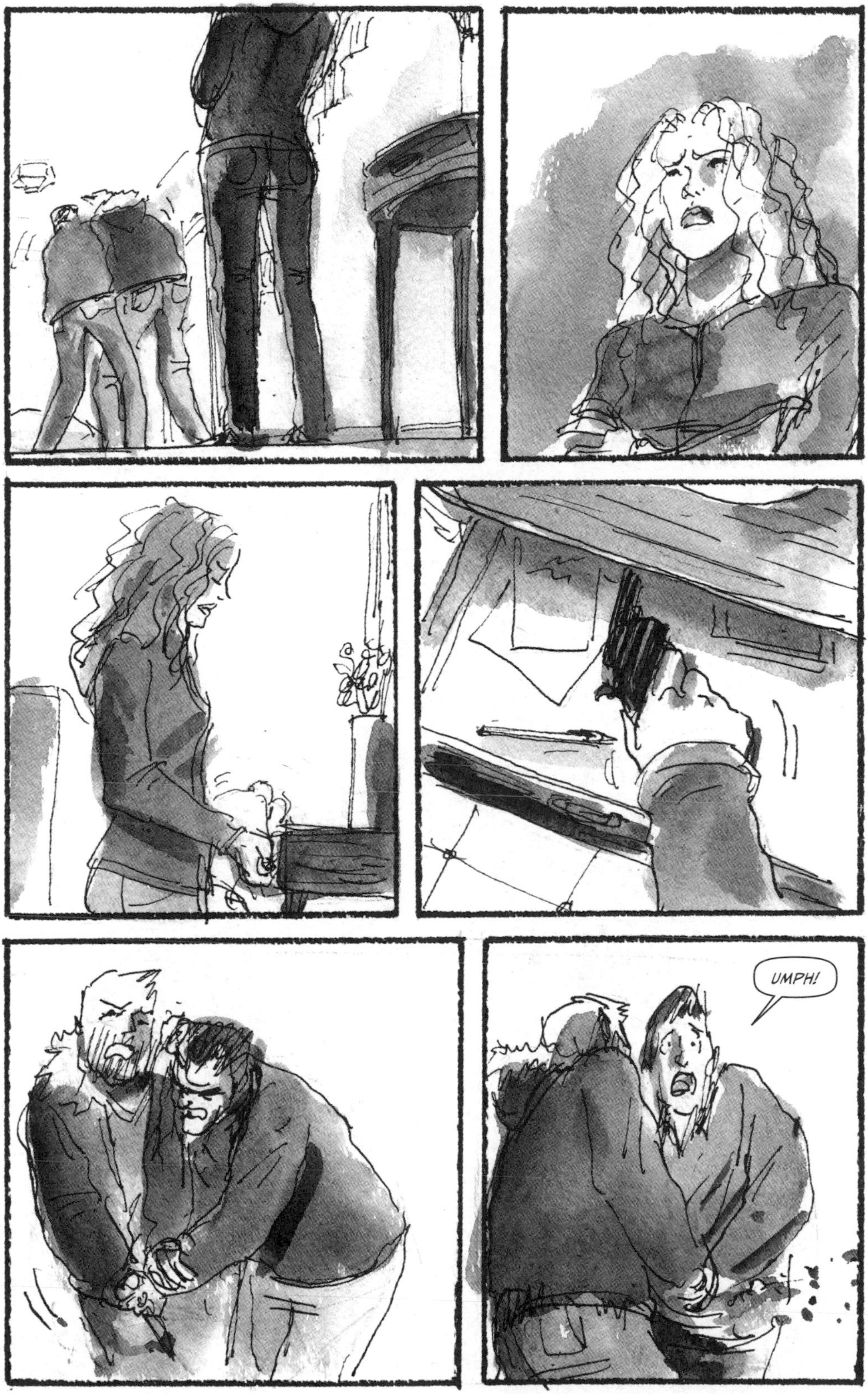
UMPH!

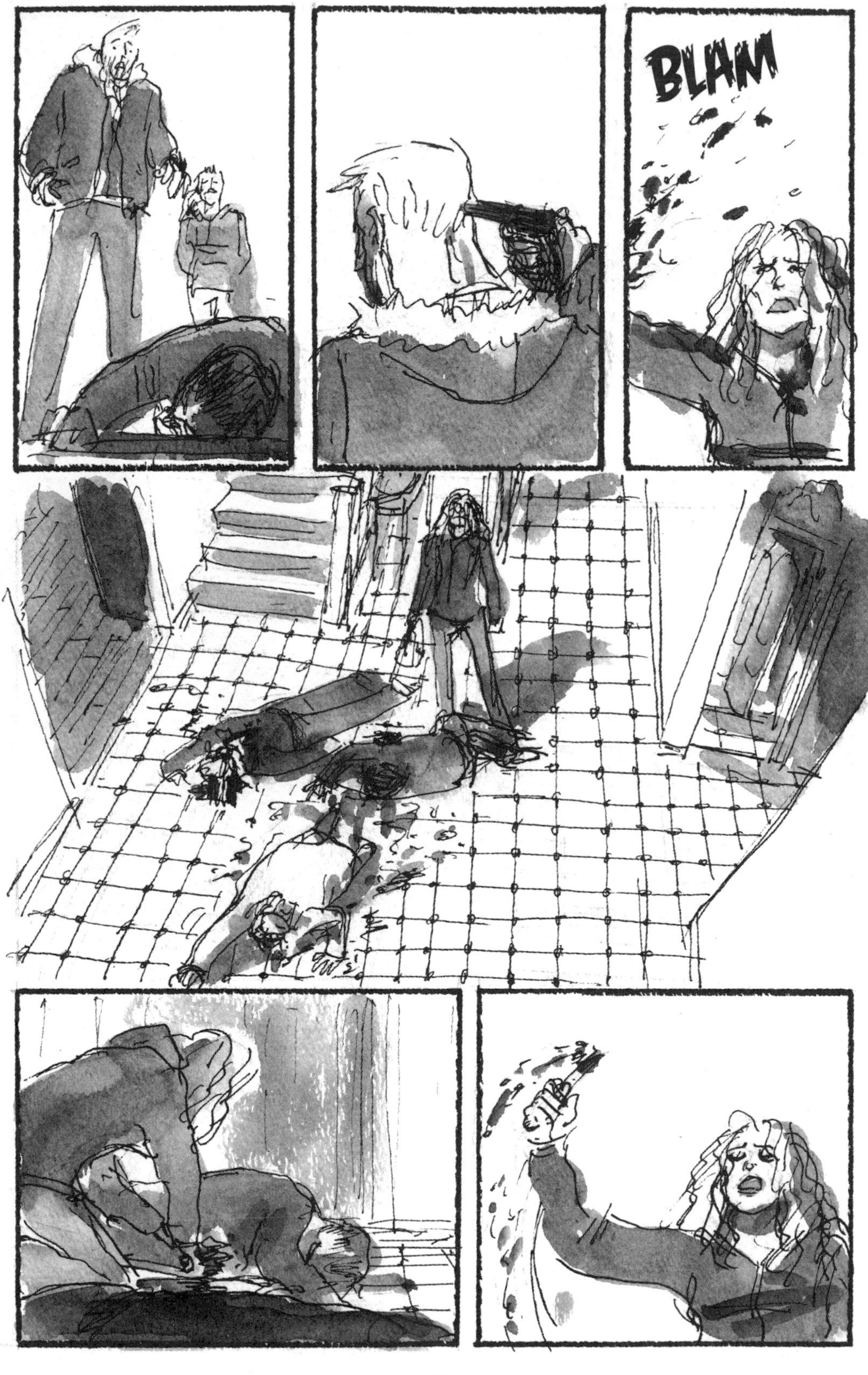
BLAM

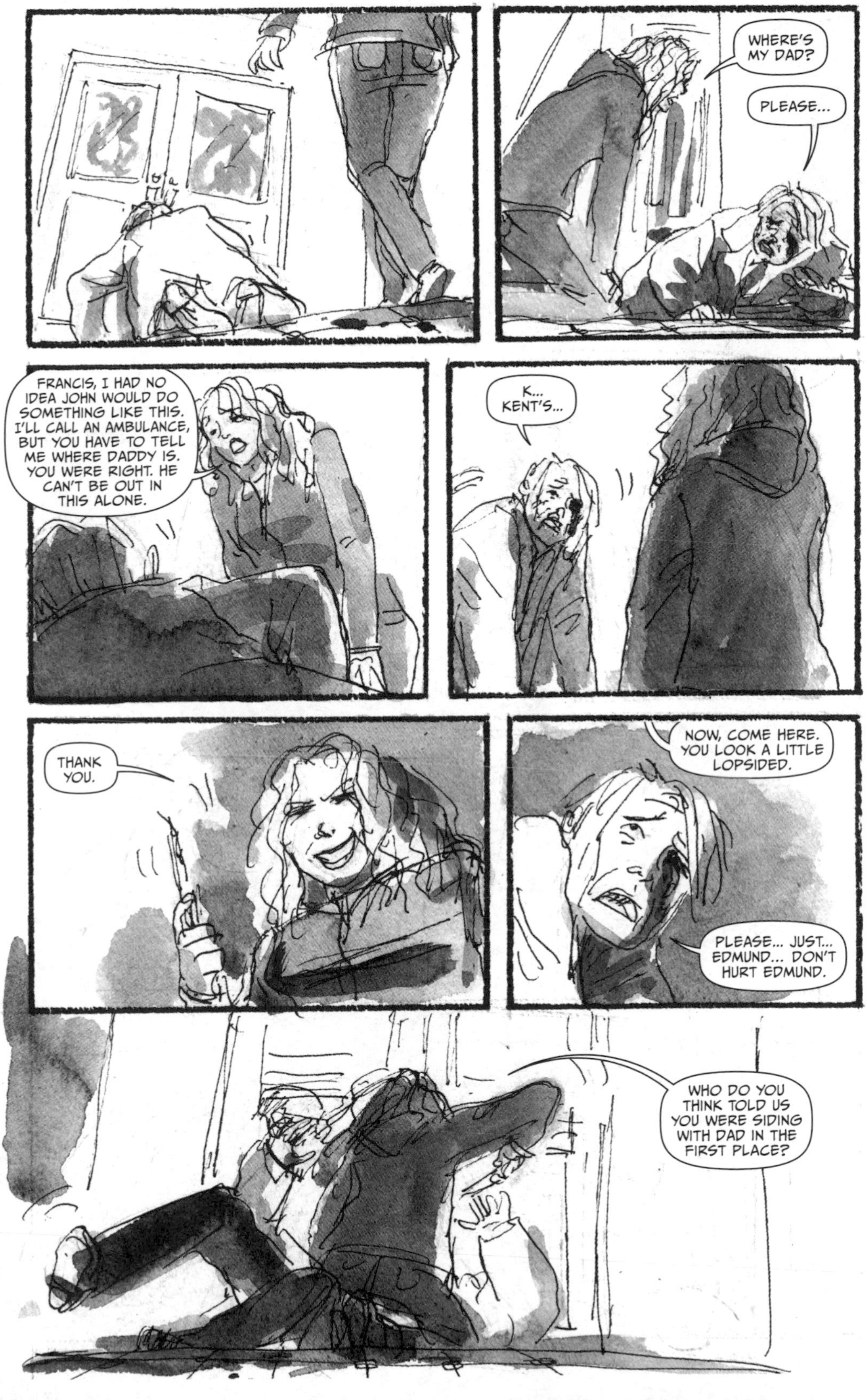
WHERE'S MY DAD?
PLEASE...
FRANCIS, I HAD NO IDEA JOHN WOULD DO SOMETHING LIKE THIS. I'LL CALL AN AMBULANCE, BUT YOU HAVE TO TELL ME WHERE DADDY IS. YOU WERE RIGHT. HE CAN'T BE OUT IN THIS ALONE.
K... KENT'S...
THANK YOU.
NOW, COME HERE. YOU LOOK A LITTLE LOPSIDED.
PLEASE... JUST... EDMUND... DON'T HURT EDMUND.
WHO DO YOU THINK TOLD US YOU WERE SIDING WITH DAD IN THE FIRST PLACE?

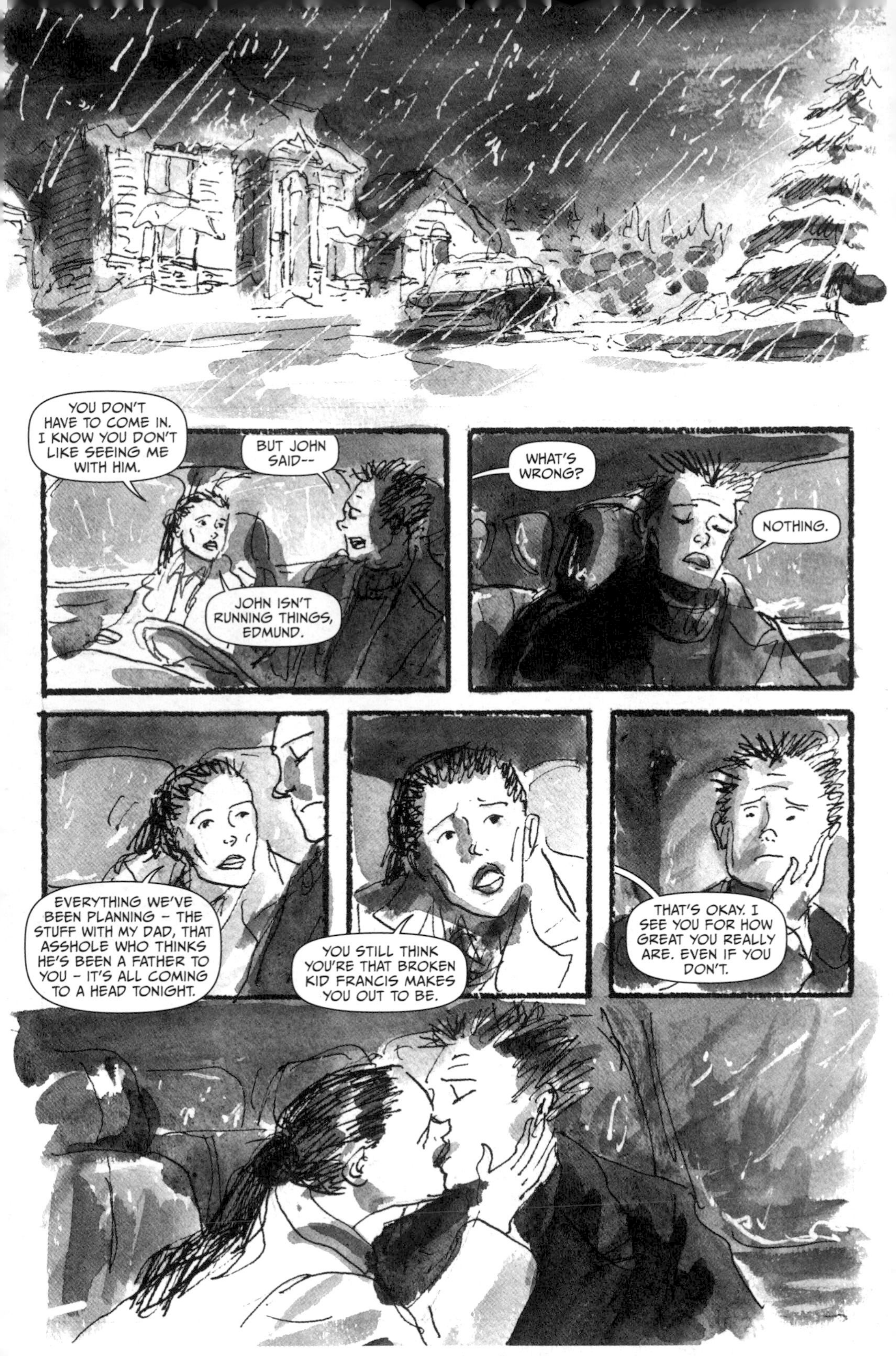
YOU DON'T HAVE TO COME IN. I KNOW YOU DON'T LIKE SEEING ME WITH HIM.
BUT JOHN SAID--
JOHN ISN'T RUNNING THINGS, EDMUND.
WHAT'S WRONG?
NOTHING.
EVERYTHING WE'VE BEEN PLANNING – THE STUFF WITH MY DAD, THAT ASSHOLE WHO THINKS HE'S BEEN A FATHER TO YOU – IT'S ALL COMING TO A HEAD TONIGHT.
YOU STILL THINK YOU'RE THAT BROKEN KID FRANCIS MAKES YOU OUT TO BE.
THAT'S OKAY. I SEE YOU FOR HOW GREAT YOU REALLY ARE. EVEN IF YOU DON'T.

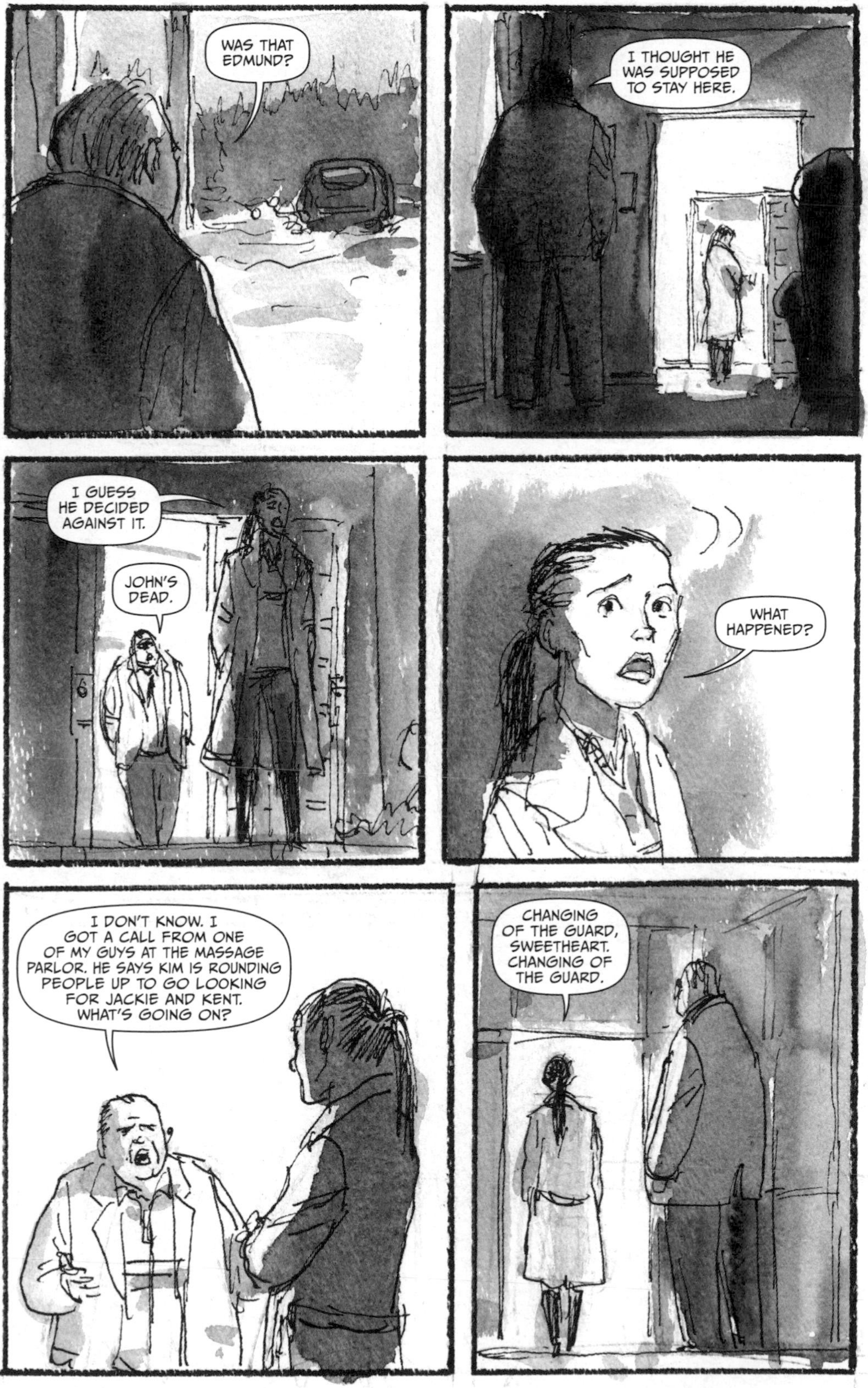
WAS THAT EDMUND?
I THOUGHT HE WAS SUPPOSED TO STAY HERE.
I GUESS HE DECIDED AGAINST IT.
JOHN'S DEAD.
WHAT HAPPENED?
I DON'T KNOW. I GOT A CALL FROM ONE OF MY GUYS AT THE MASSAGE PARLOR. HE SAYS KIM IS ROUNDING PEOPLE UP TO GO LOOKING FOR JACKIE AND KENT. WHAT'S GOING ON?
CHANGING OF THE GUARD, SWEETHEART. CHANGING OF THE GUARD.

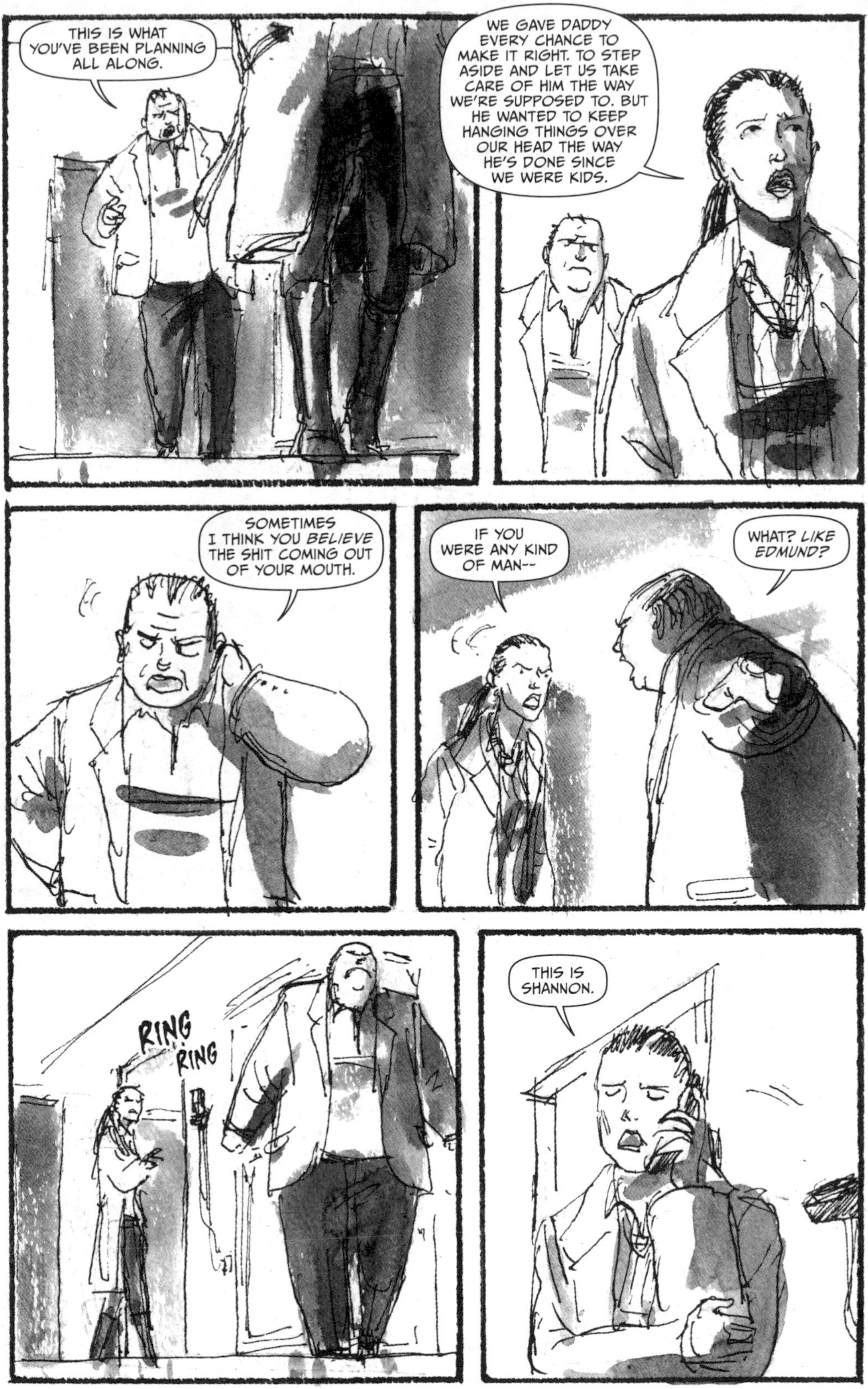
THIS IS WHAT YOU'VE BEEN PLANNING ALL ALONG.
WE GAVE DADDY EVERY CHANCE TO MAKE IT RIGHT. TO STEP ASIDE AND LET US TAKE CARE OF HIM THE WAY WE'RE SUPPOSED TO. BUT HE WANTED TO KEEP HANGING THINGS OVER OUR HEAD THE WAY HE'S DONE SINCE WE WERE KIDS.
SOMETIMES I THINK YOU *BELIEVE* THE SHIT COMING OUT OF YOUR MOUTH.
IF YOU WERE ANY KIND OF MAN--
WHAT? *LIKE* EDMUND?
RING
RING
THIS IS SHANNON.

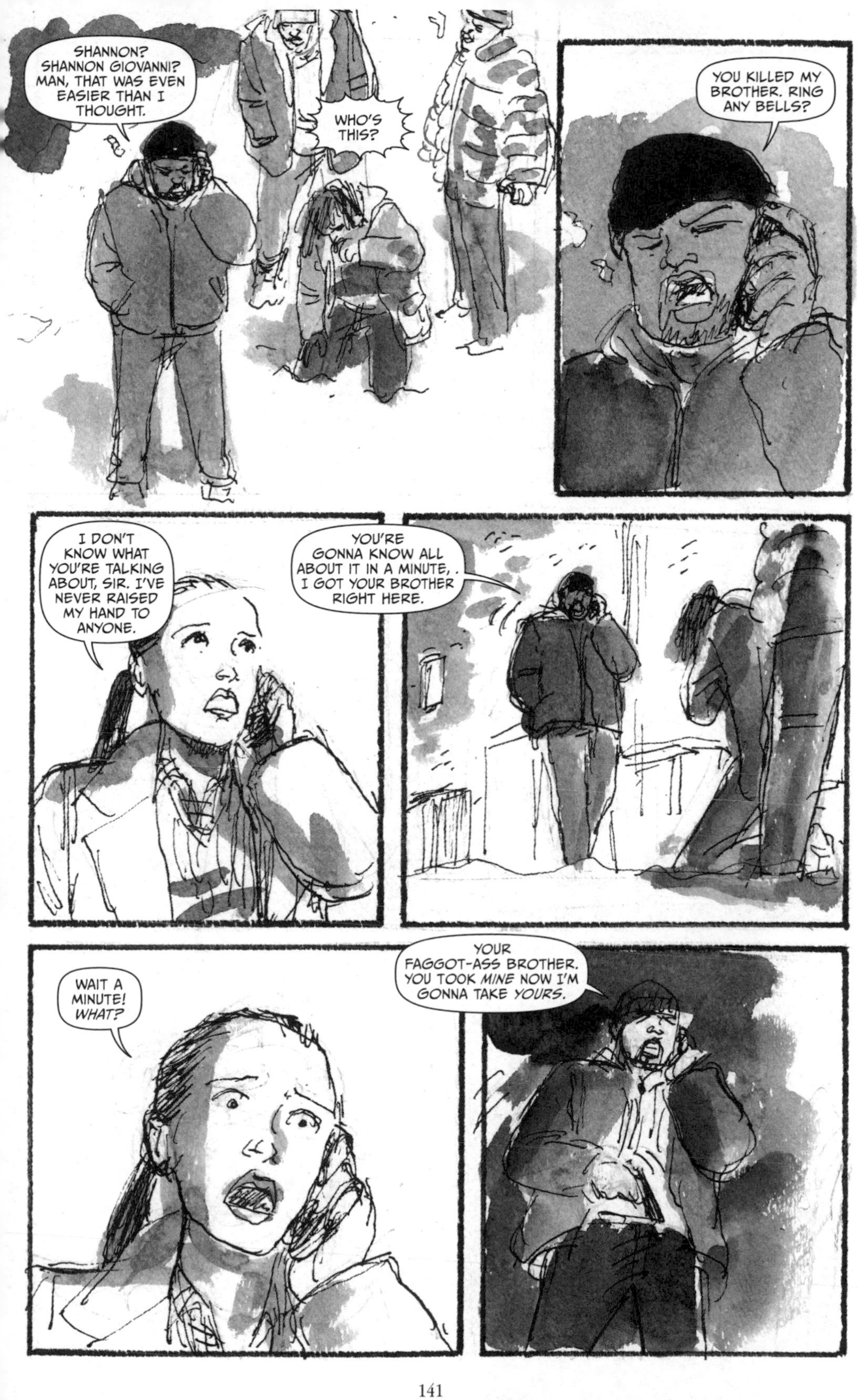
SHANNON? SHANNON GIOVANNI? MAN, THAT WAS EVEN EASIER THAN I THOUGHT.
WHO'S THIS?
YOU KILLED MY BROTHER. RING ANY BELLS?
I DON'T KNOW WHAT YOU'RE TALKING ABOUT, SIR. I'VE NEVER RAISED MY HAND TO ANYONE.
YOU'RE GONNA KNOW ALL ABOUT IT IN A MINUTE, I GOT YOUR BROTHER RIGHT HERE.
WAIT A MINUTE! *WHAT?*
YOUR FAGGOT-ASS BROTHER. YOU TOOK *MINE* NOW I'M GONNA TAKE *YOURS*.

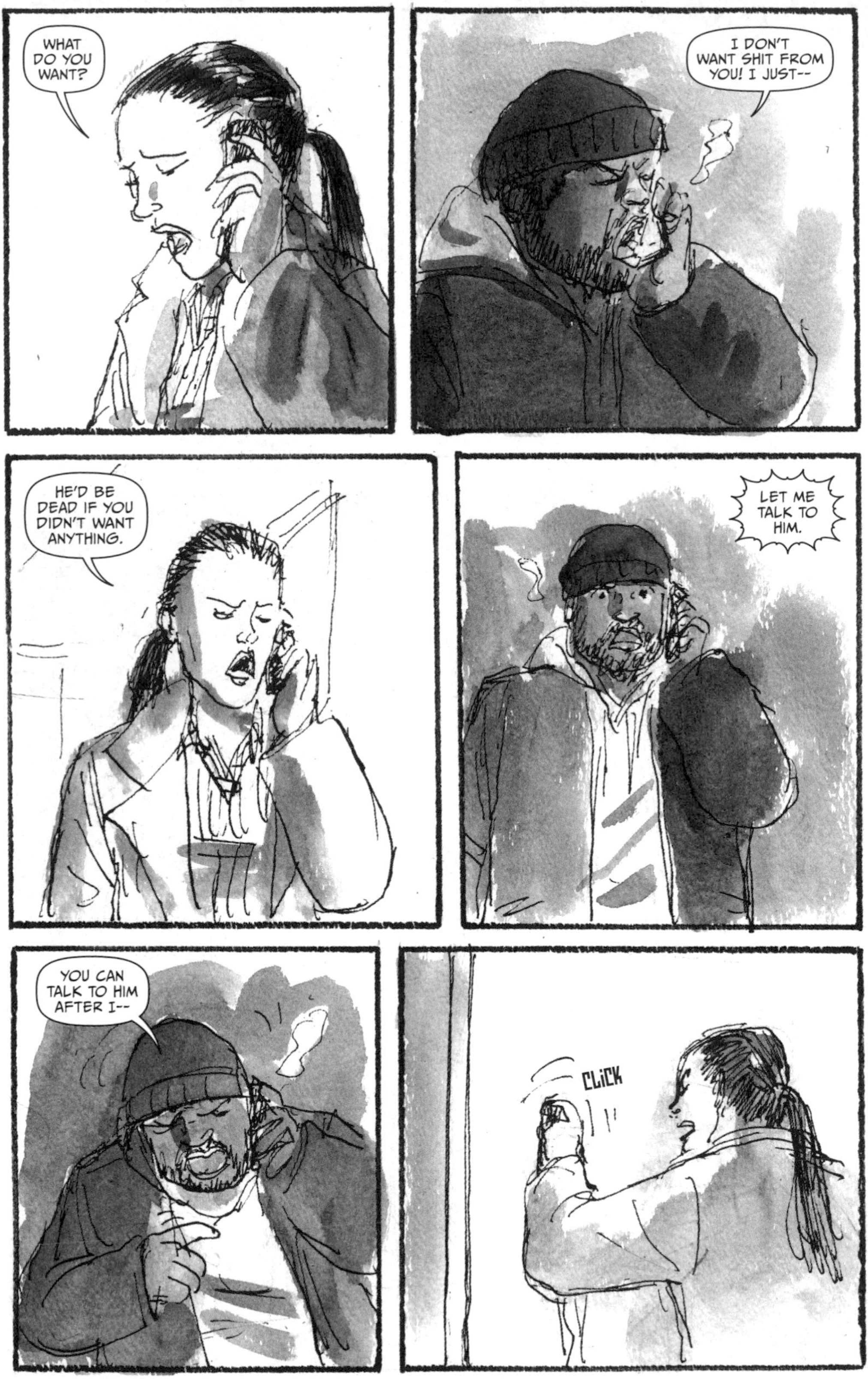
WHAT DO YOU WANT?
I DON'T WANT SHIT FROM YOU! I JUST--
HE'D BE DEAD IF YOU DIDN'T WANT ANYTHING.
LET ME TALK TO HIM.
YOU CAN TALK TO HIM AFTER I--
CLICK

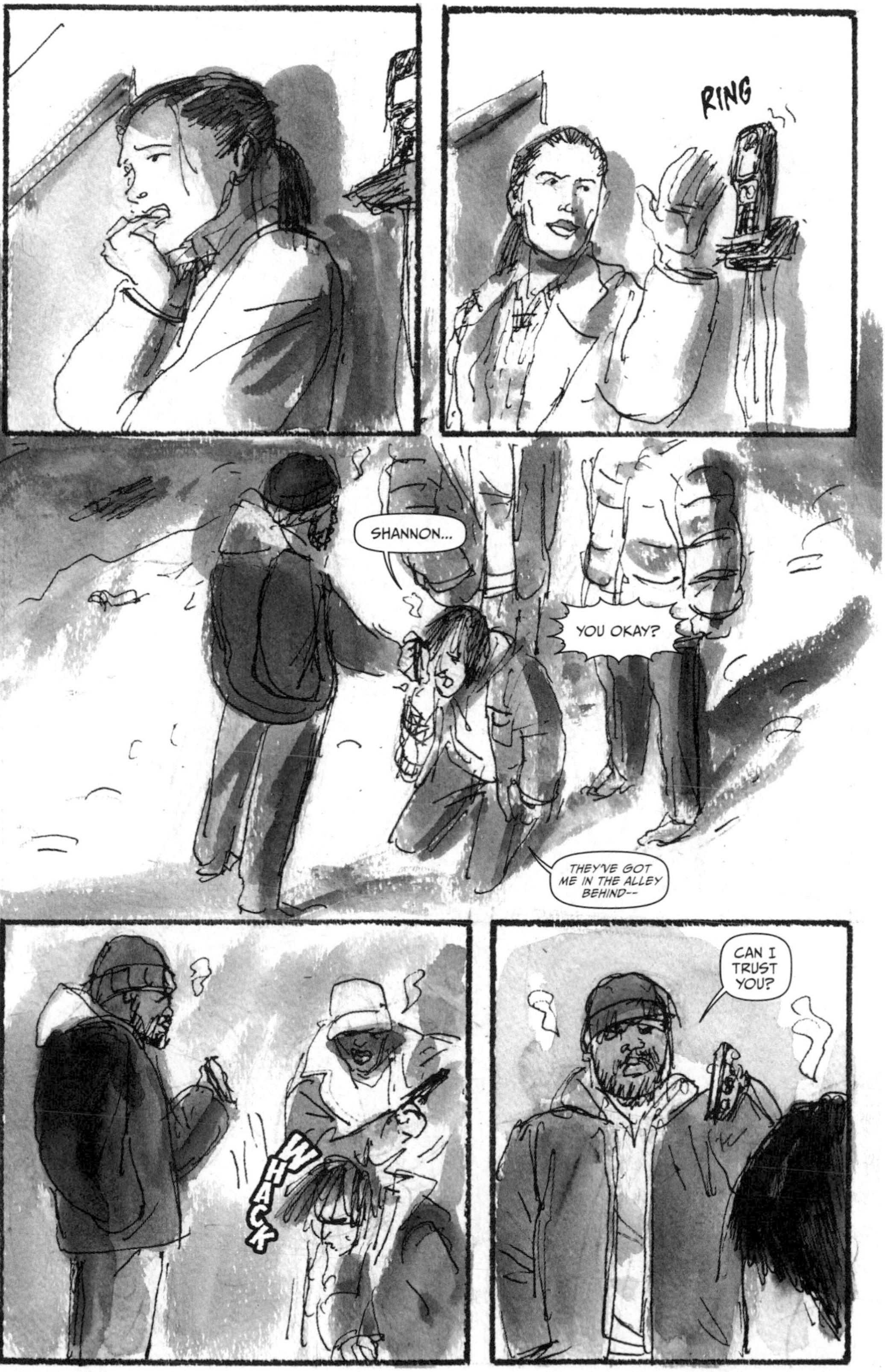
RING
SHANNON...
YOU OKAY?
THEY'VE GOT ME IN THE ALLEY BEHIND--
WHACK
CAN I TRUST YOU?

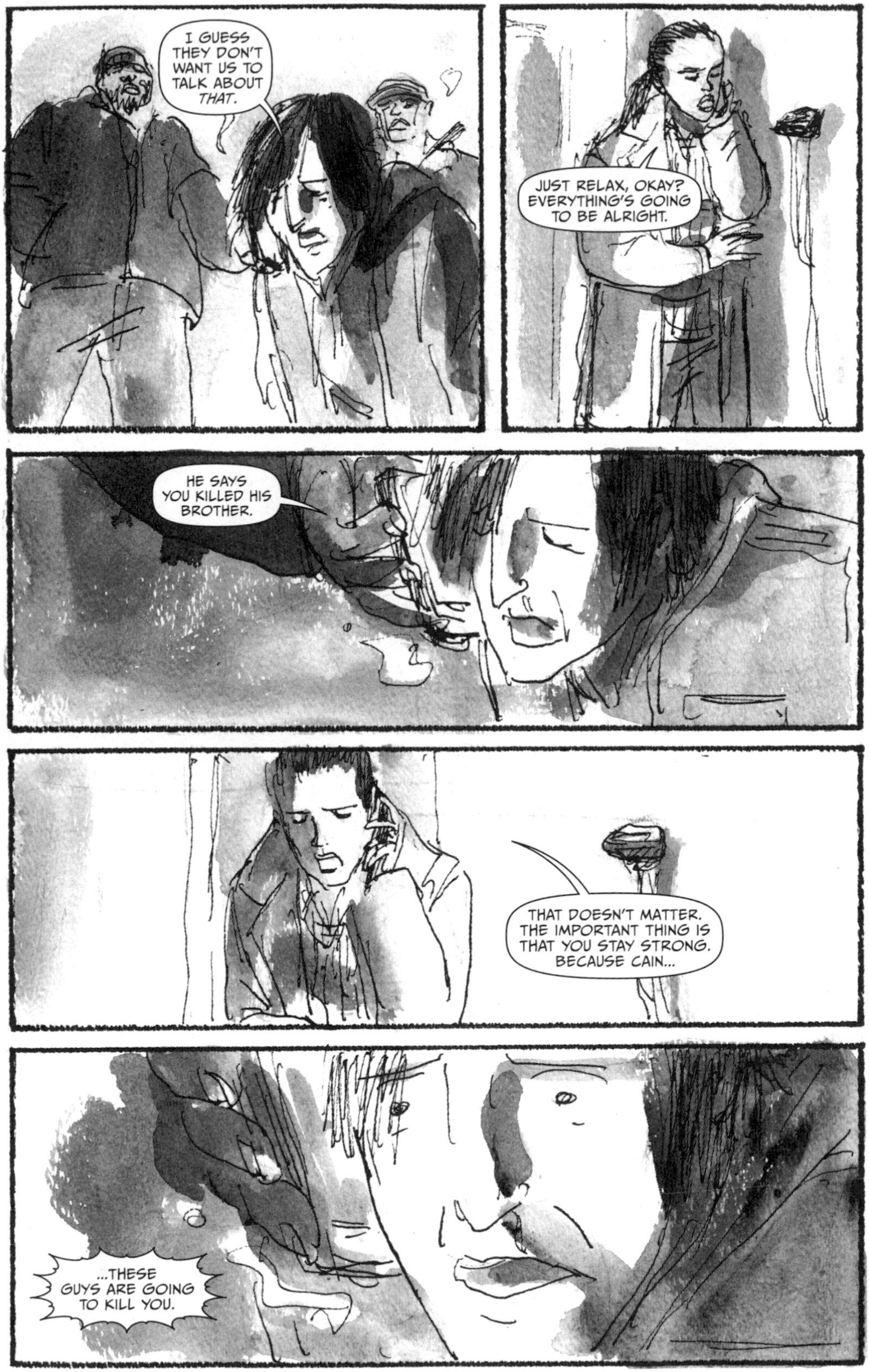
I GUESS THEY DON'T WANT US TO TALK ABOUT *THAT*.
JUST RELAX, OKAY? EVERYTHING'S GOING TO BE ALRIGHT.
HE SAYS YOU KILLED HIS BROTHER.
THAT DOESN'T MATTER. THE IMPORTANT THING IS THAT YOU STAY STRONG. BECAUSE CAIN...
...THESE GUYS ARE GOING TO KILL YOU.

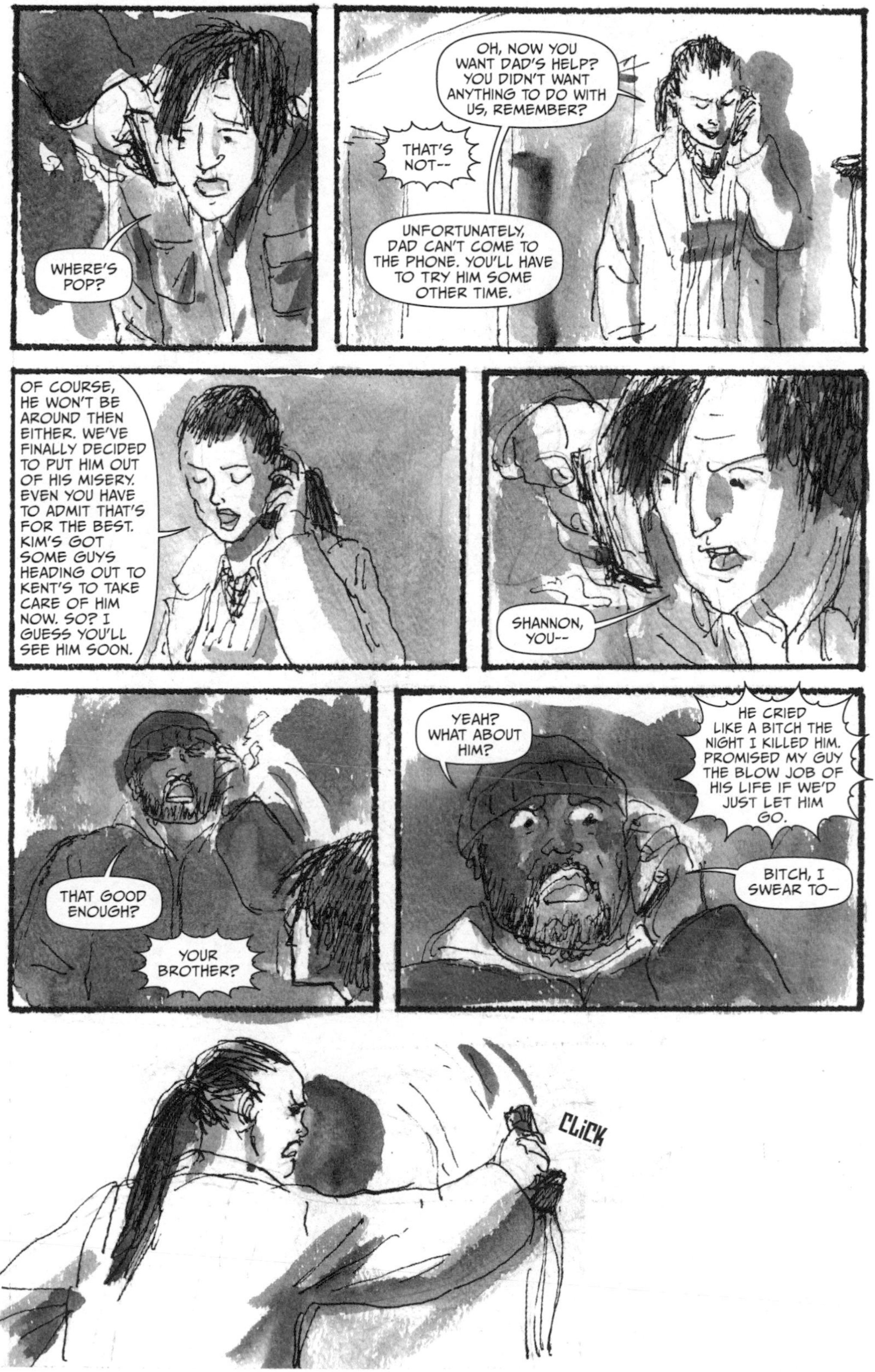
WHERE'S POP?
OH, NOW YOU WANT DAD'S HELP? YOU DIDN'T WANT ANYTHING TO DO WITH US, REMEMBER?
THAT'S NOT--
UNFORTUNATELY, DAD CAN'T COME TO THE PHONE. YOU'LL HAVE TO TRY HIM SOME OTHER TIME.
OF COURSE, HE WON'T BE AROUND THEN EITHER. WE'VE FINALLY DECIDED TO PUT HIM OUT OF HIS MISERY. EVEN YOU HAVE TO ADMIT THAT'S FOR THE BEST. KIM'S GOT SOME GUYS HEADING OUT TO KENT'S TO TAKE CARE OF HIM NOW. SO? I GUESS YOU'LL SEE HIM SOON.
SHANNON, YOU--
THAT GOOD ENOUGH?
YOUR BROTHER?
YEAH? WHAT ABOUT HIM?
HE CRIED LIKE A BITCH THE NIGHT I KILLED HIM. PROMISED MY GUY THE BLOW JOB OF HIS LIFE IF WE'D JUST LET HIM GO.
BITCH, I SWEAR TO—
CLICK

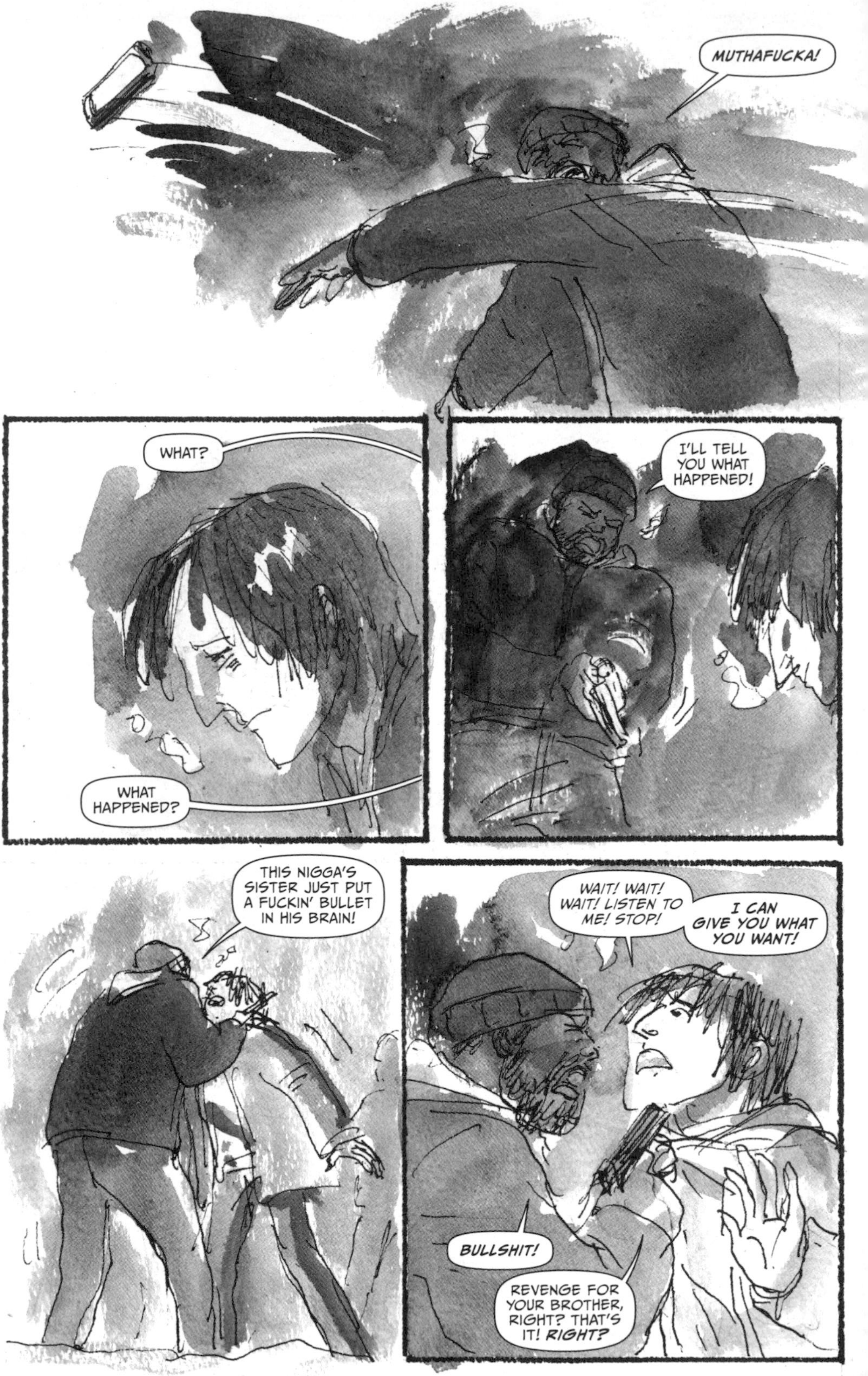
MUTHAFUCKA!
WHAT?
WHAT HAPPENED?
I'LL TELL YOU WHAT HAPPENED!
THIS NIGGA'S SISTER JUST PUT A FUCKIN' BULLET IN HIS BRAIN!
WAIT! WAIT! WAIT! LISTEN TO ME! STOP!
I CAN GIVE YOU WHAT YOU WANT!
BULLSHIT!
REVENGE FOR YOUR BROTHER, RIGHT? THAT'S IT! RIGHT?

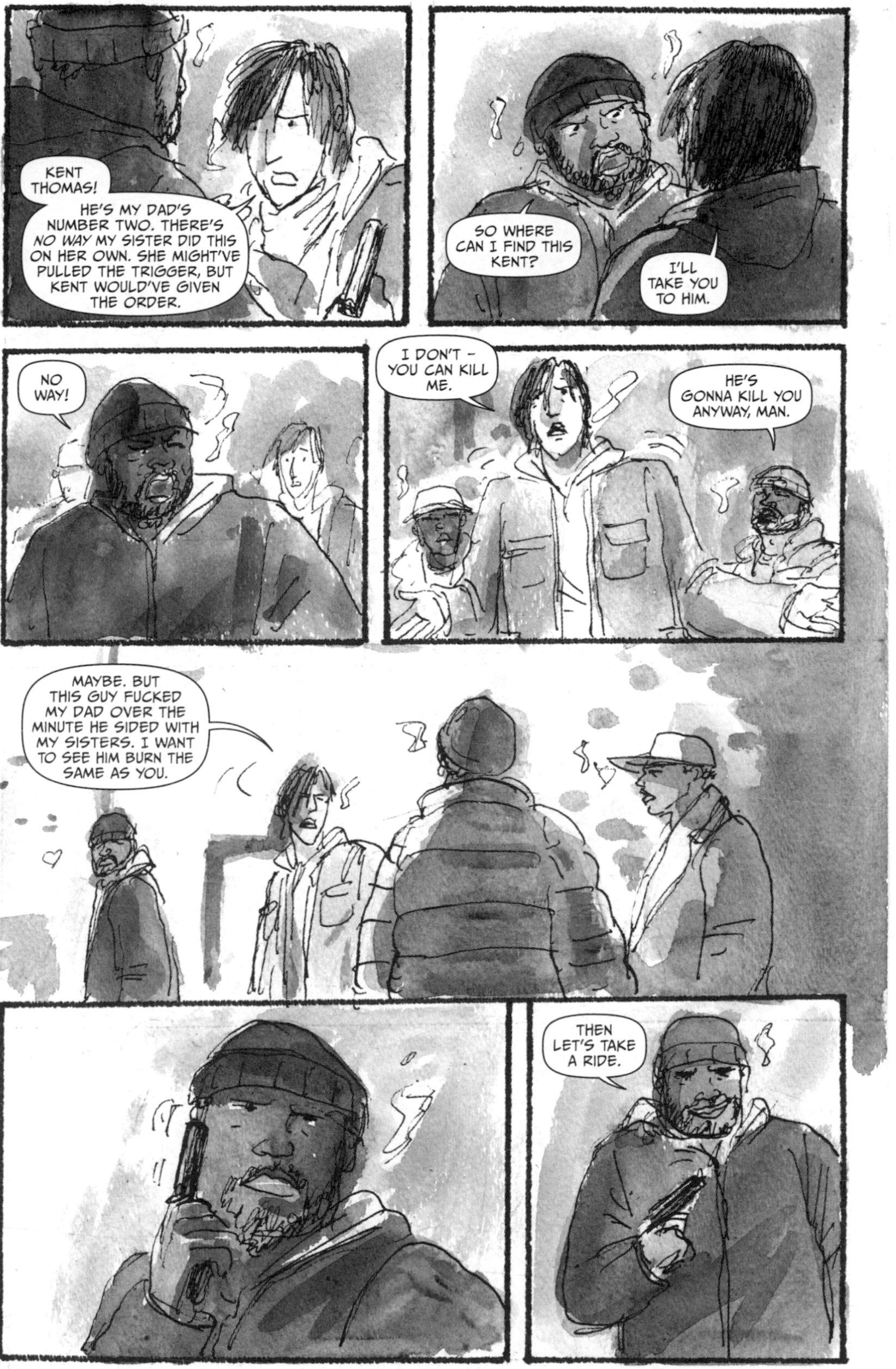
KENT THOMAS!
HE'S MY DAD'S NUMBER TWO. THERE'S *NO WAY* MY SISTER DID THIS ON HER OWN. SHE MIGHT'VE PULLED THE TRIGGER, BUT KENT WOULD'VE GIVEN THE ORDER.
SO WHERE CAN I FIND THIS KENT?
I'LL TAKE YOU TO HIM.
NO WAY!
I DON'T - YOU CAN KILL ME.
HE'S GONNA KILL YOU ANYWAY, MAN.
MAYBE. BUT THIS GUY FUCKED MY DAD OVER THE MINUTE HE SIDED WITH MY SISTERS. I WANT TO SEE HIM BURN THE SAME AS YOU.
THEN LET'S TAKE A RIDE.

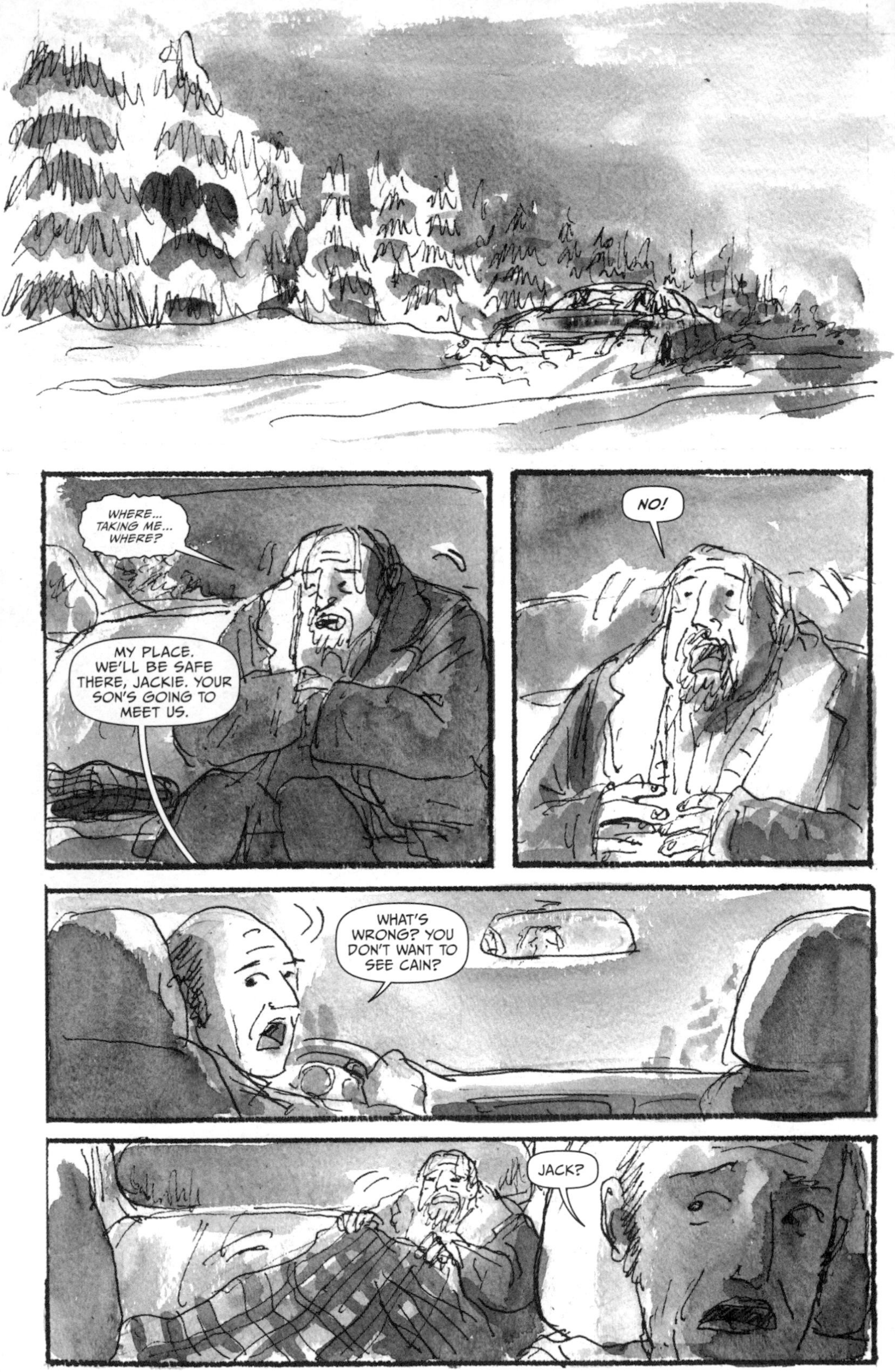
WHERE... TAKING ME... WHERE?
MY PLACE. WE'LL BE SAFE THERE, JACKIE. YOUR SON'S GOING TO MEET US.
NO!
WHAT'S WRONG? YOU DON'T WANT TO SEE CAIN?
JACK?

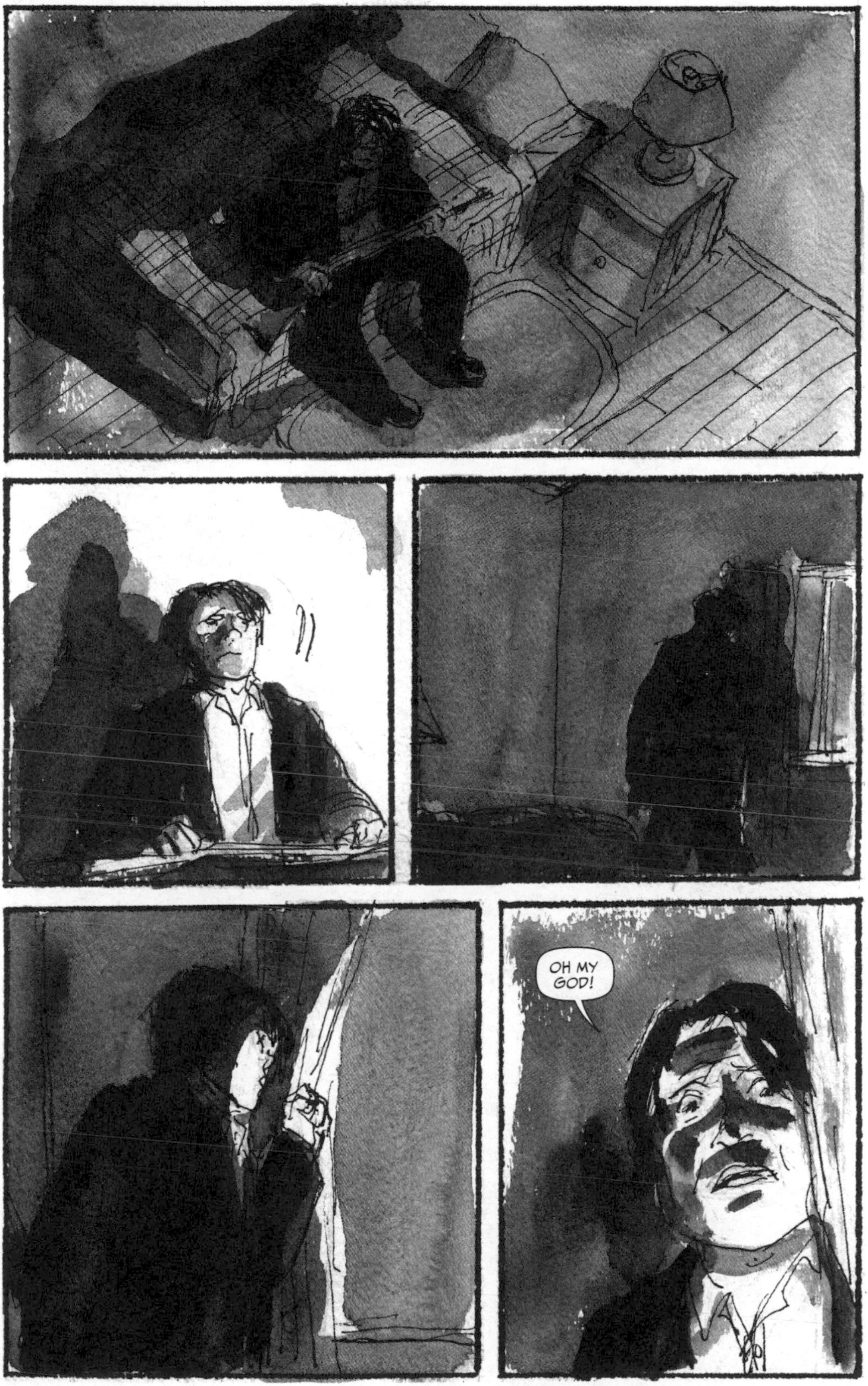
OH MY GOD!

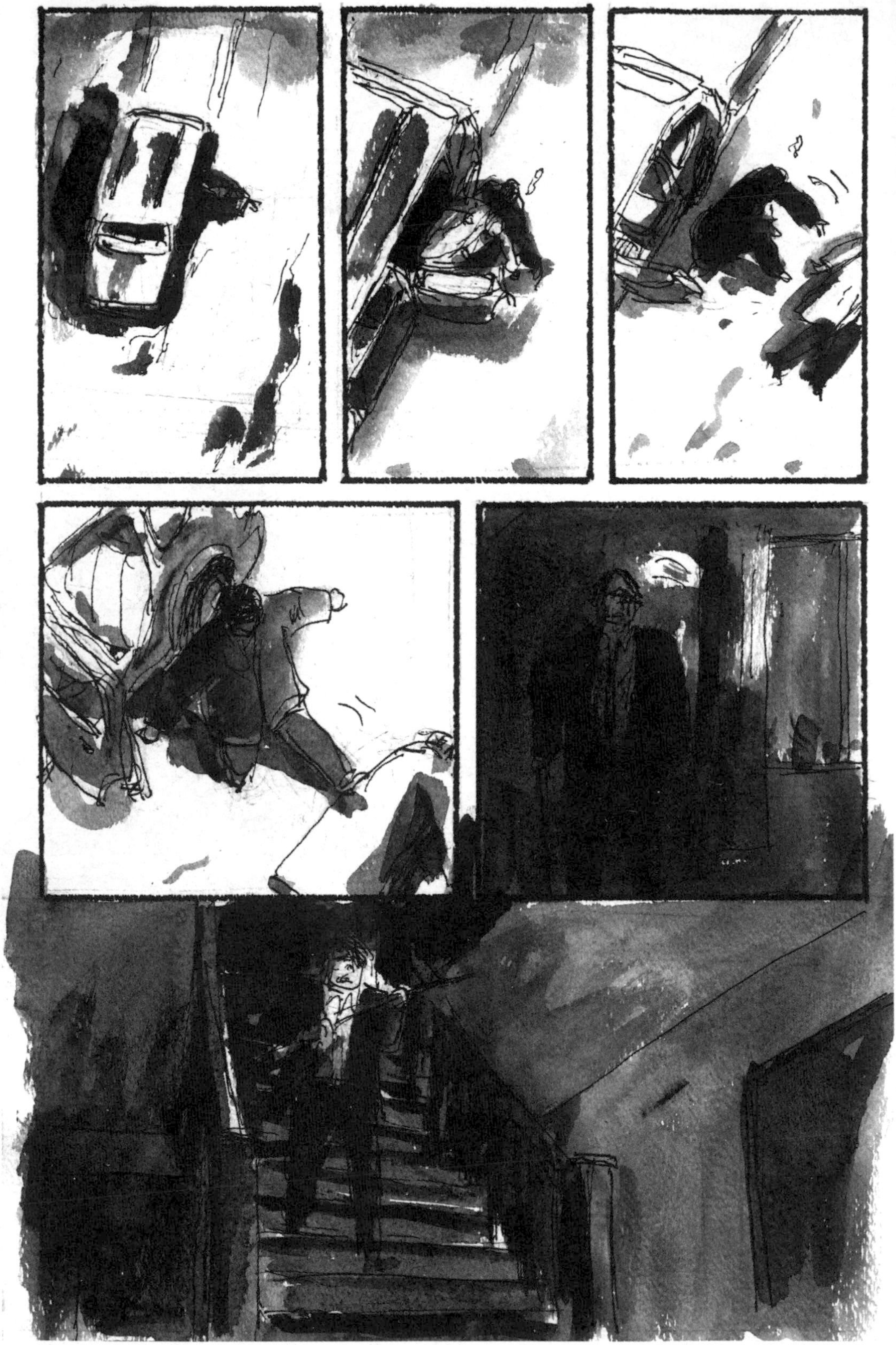

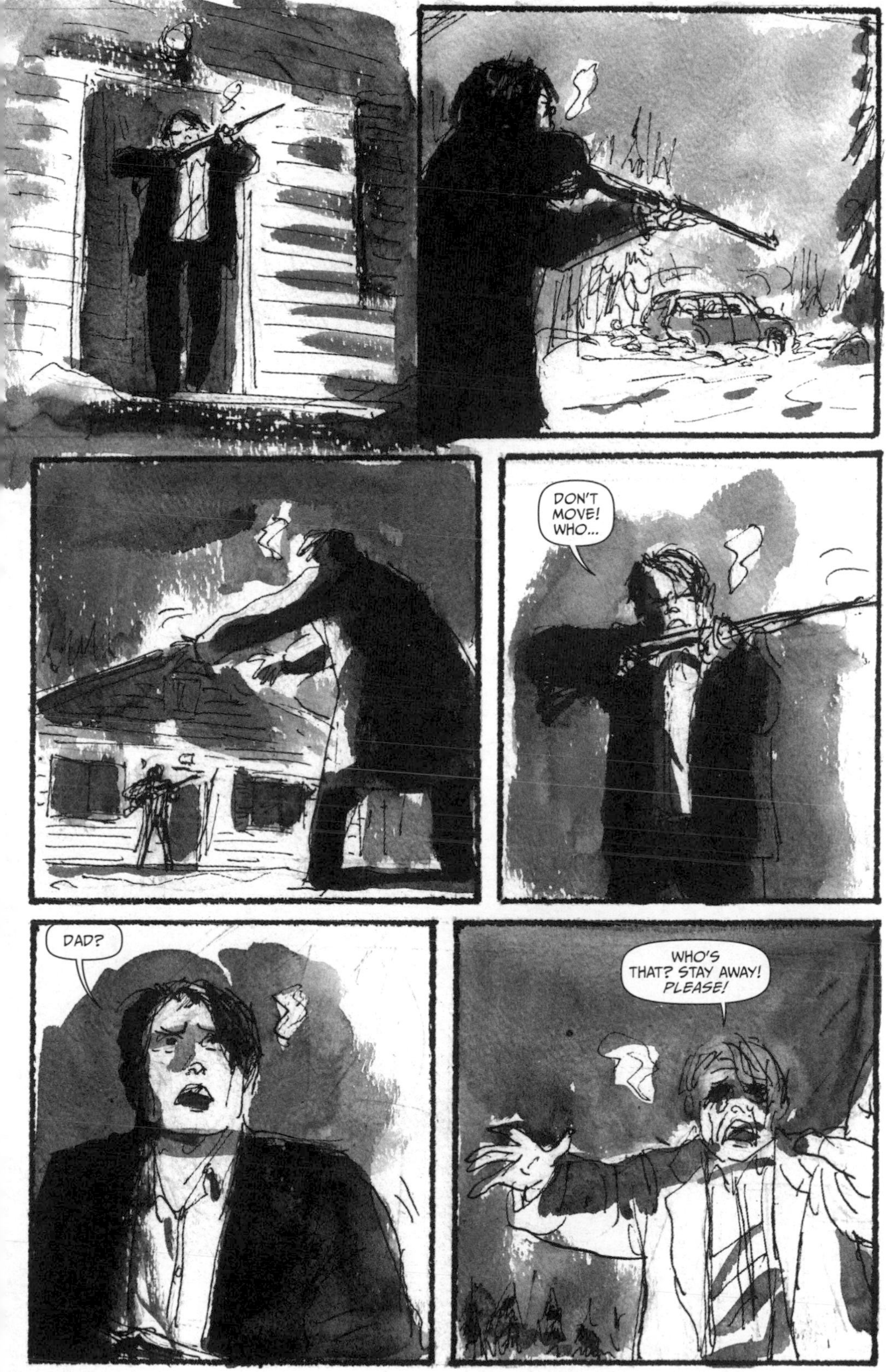
DON'T MOVE! WHO...
DAD?
WHO'S THAT? STAY AWAY! *PLEASE!*

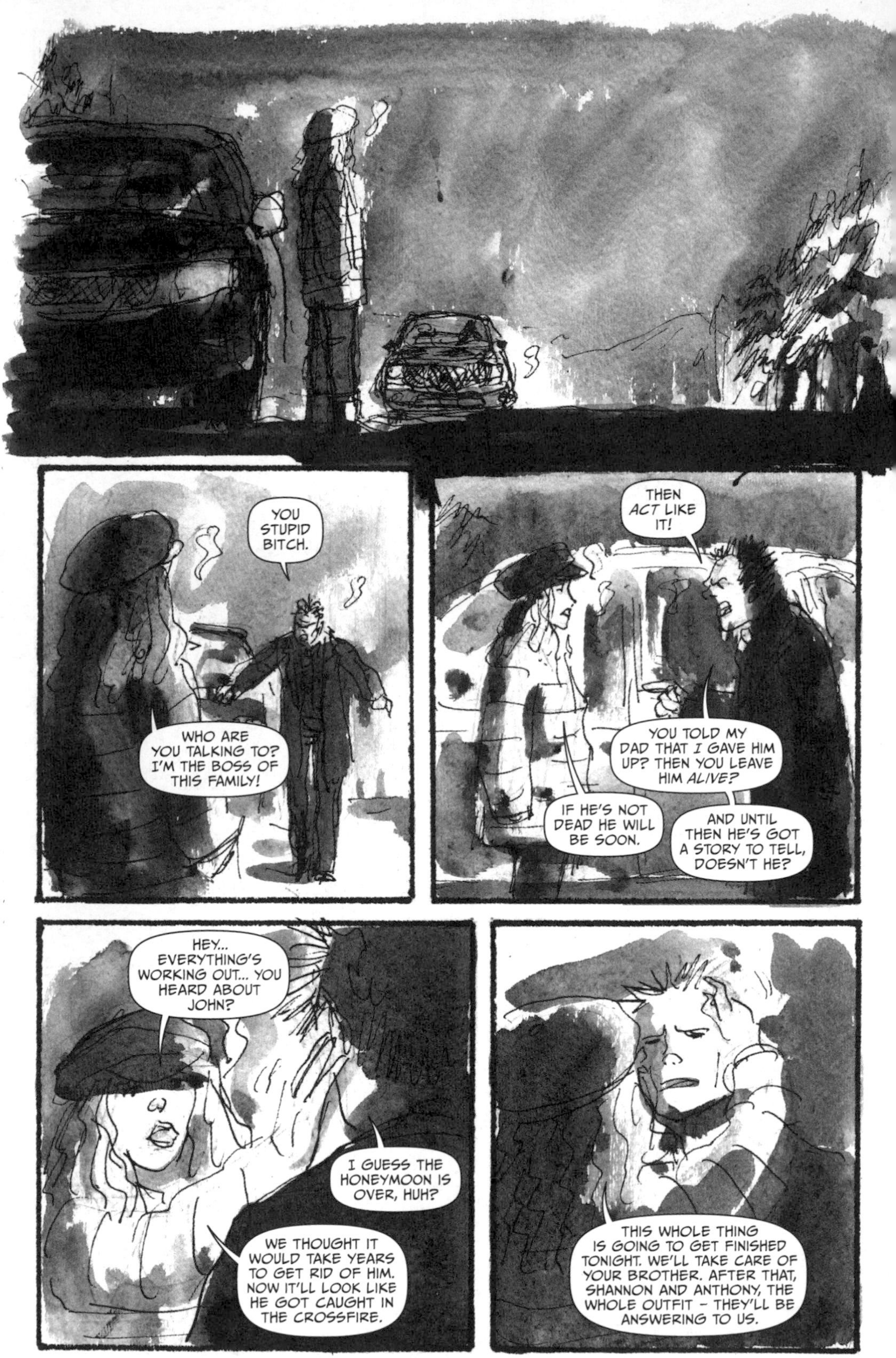
YOU STUPID BITCH.
WHO ARE YOU TALKING TO? I'M THE BOSS OF THIS FAMILY!
THEN ACT LIKE IT!
YOU TOLD MY DAD THAT I GAVE HIM UP? THEN YOU LEAVE HIM ALIVE?
IF HE'S NOT DEAD HE WILL BE SOON.
AND UNTIL THEN HE'S GOT A STORY TO TELL, DOESN'T HE?
HEY... EVERYTHING'S WORKING OUT... YOU HEARD ABOUT JOHN?
I GUESS THE HONEYMOON IS OVER, HUH?
WE THOUGHT IT WOULD TAKE YEARS TO GET RID OF HIM. NOW IT'LL LOOK LIKE HE GOT CAUGHT IN THE CROSSFIRE.
THIS WHOLE THING IS GOING TO GET FINISHED TONIGHT. WE'LL TAKE CARE OF YOUR BROTHER. AFTER THAT, SHANNON AND ANTHONY, THE WHOLE OUTFIT – THEY'LL BE ANSWERING TO US.

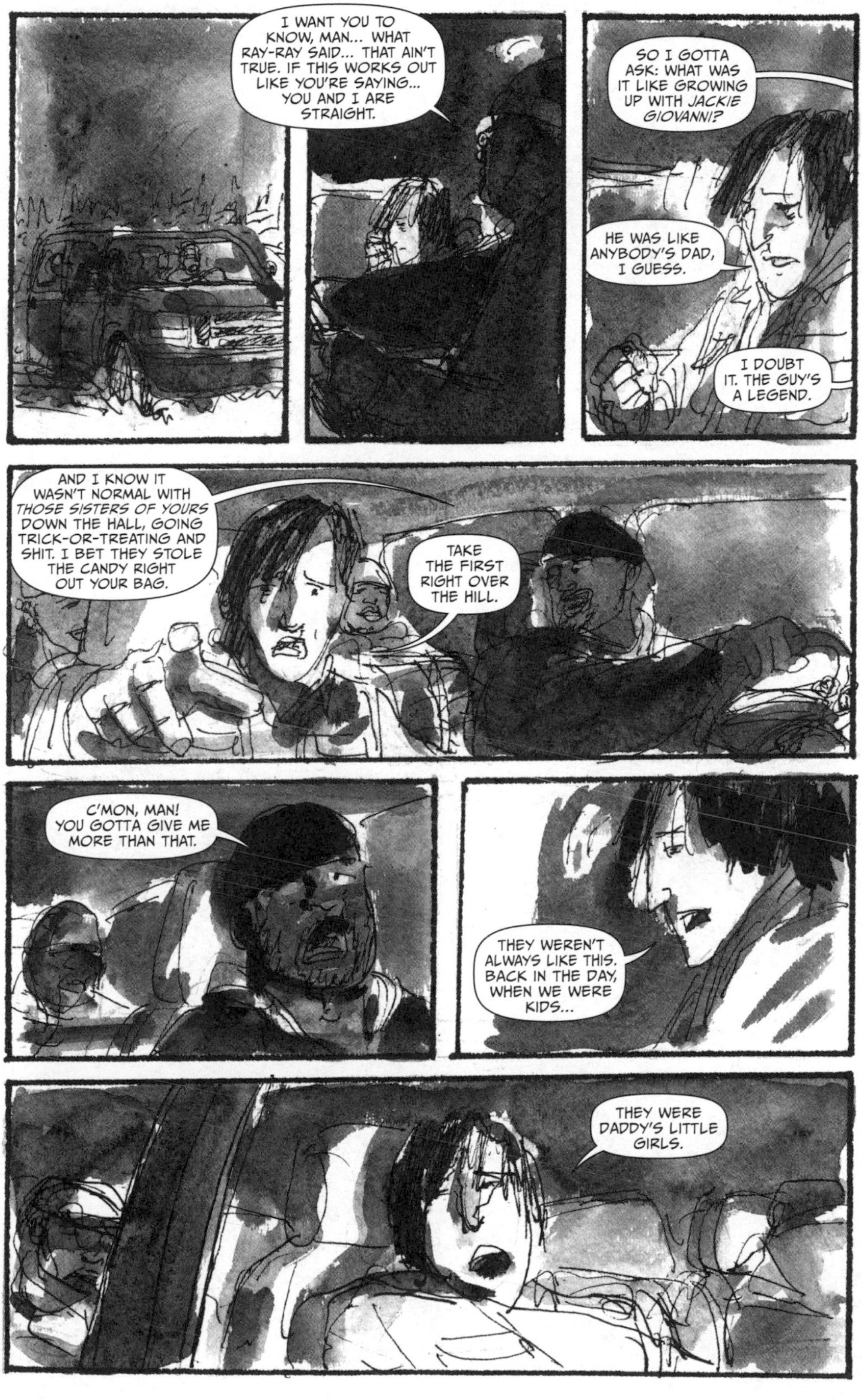
I WANT YOU TO KNOW, MAN... WHAT RAY-RAY SAID... THAT AIN'T TRUE. IF THIS WORKS OUT LIKE YOU'RE SAYING... YOU AND I ARE STRAIGHT.
SO I GOTTA ASK: WHAT WAS IT LIKE GROWING UP WITH *JACKIE GIOVANNI?*
HE WAS LIKE ANYBODY'S DAD, I GUESS.
I DOUBT IT. THE GUY'S A LEGEND.
AND I KNOW IT WASN'T NORMAL WITH *THOSE SISTERS OF YOURS* DOWN THE HALL, GOING TRICK-OR-TREATING AND SHIT. I BET THEY STOLE THE CANDY RIGHT OUT YOUR BAG.
TAKE THE FIRST RIGHT OVER THE HILL.
C'MON, MAN! YOU GOTTA GIVE ME MORE THAN THAT.
THEY WEREN'T ALWAYS LIKE THIS. BACK IN THE DAY, WHEN WE WERE KIDS...
THEY WERE DADDY'S LITTLE GIRLS.

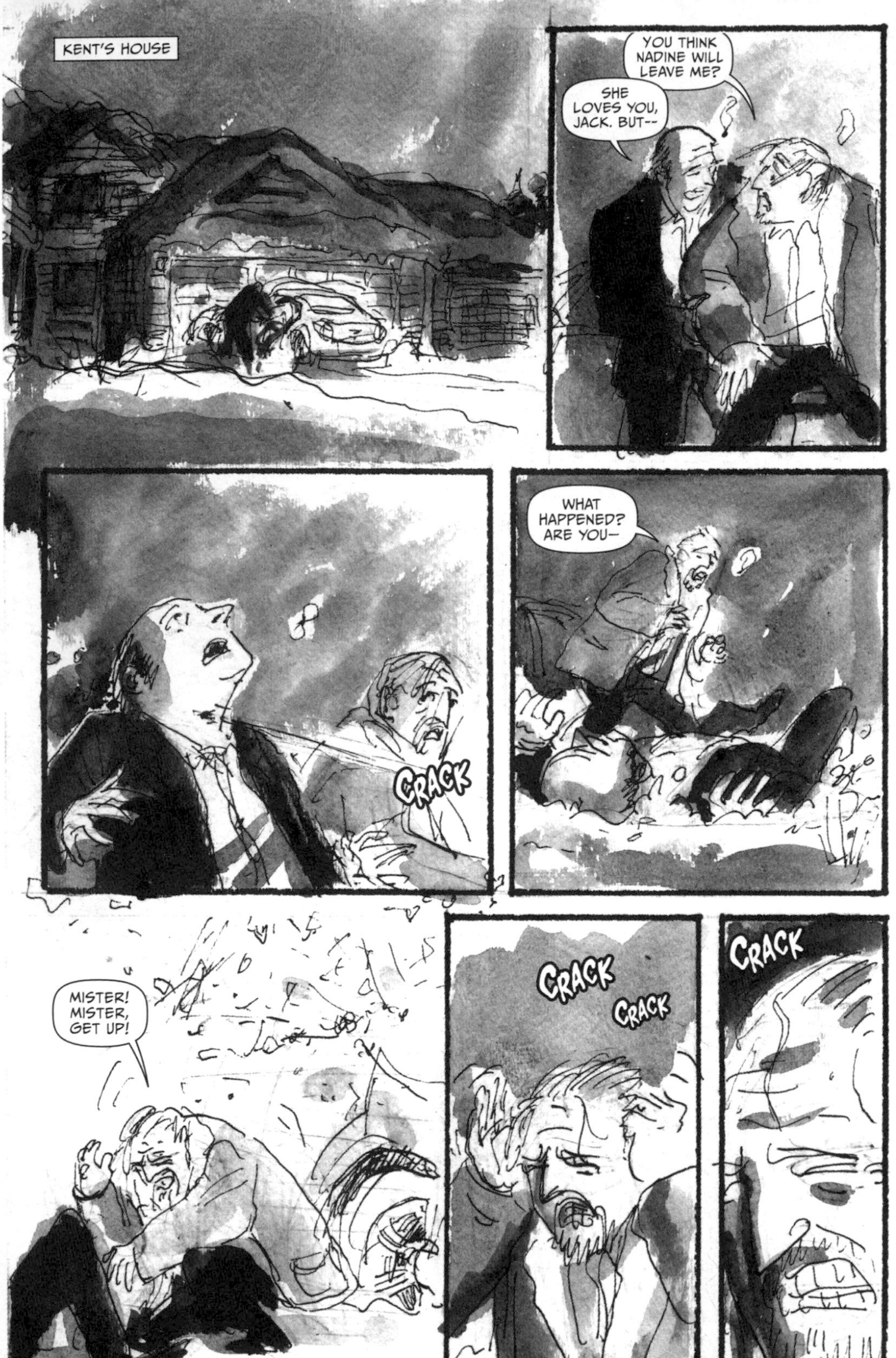
KENT'S HOUSE
YOU THINK NADINE WILL LEAVE ME?
SHE LOVES YOU, JACK. BUT--
CRACK
WHAT HAPPENED? ARE YOU—
MISTER! MISTER, GET UP!
CRACK
CRACK
CRACK

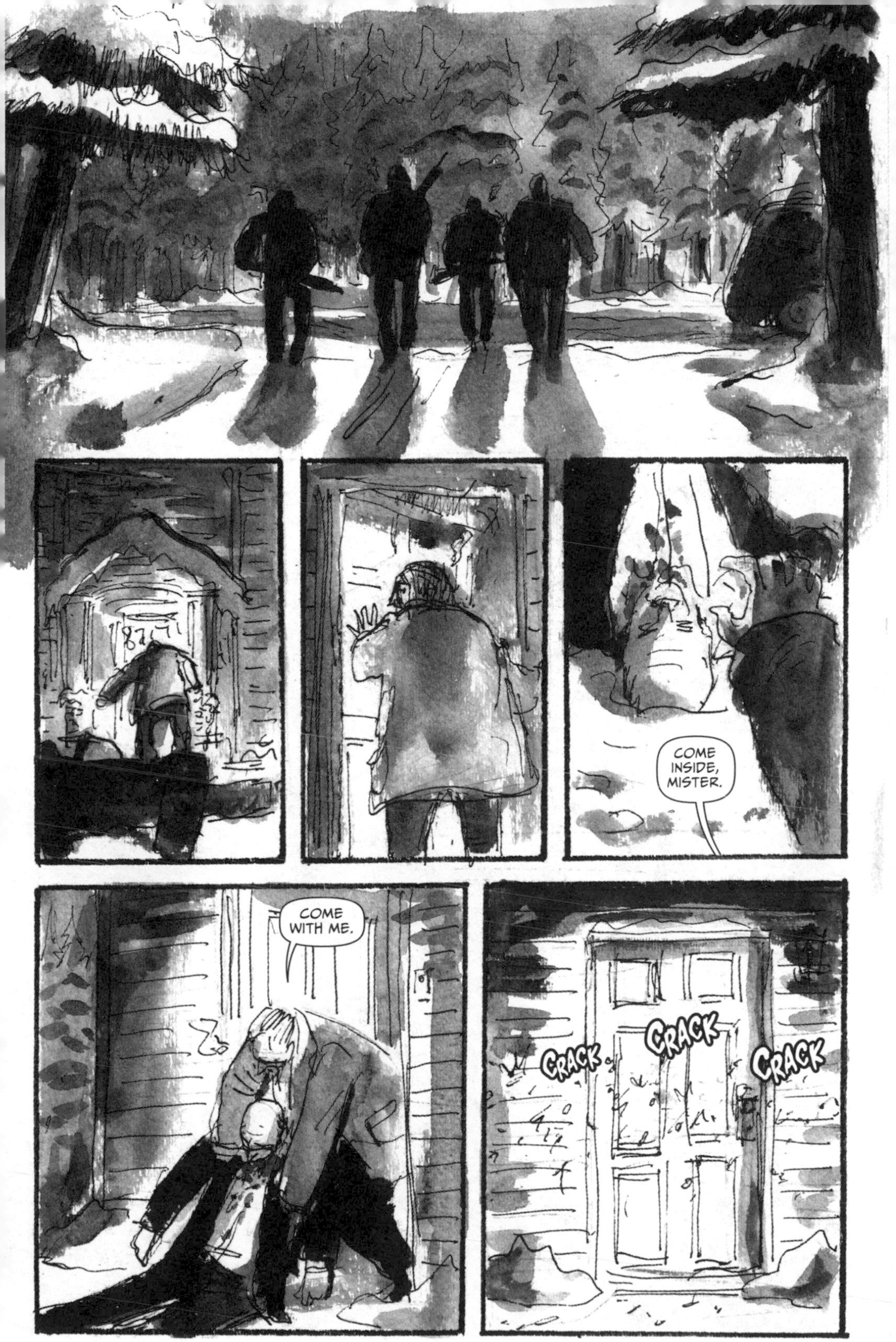
COME INSIDE, MISTER.
COME WITH ME.
CRACK
CRACK
CRACK

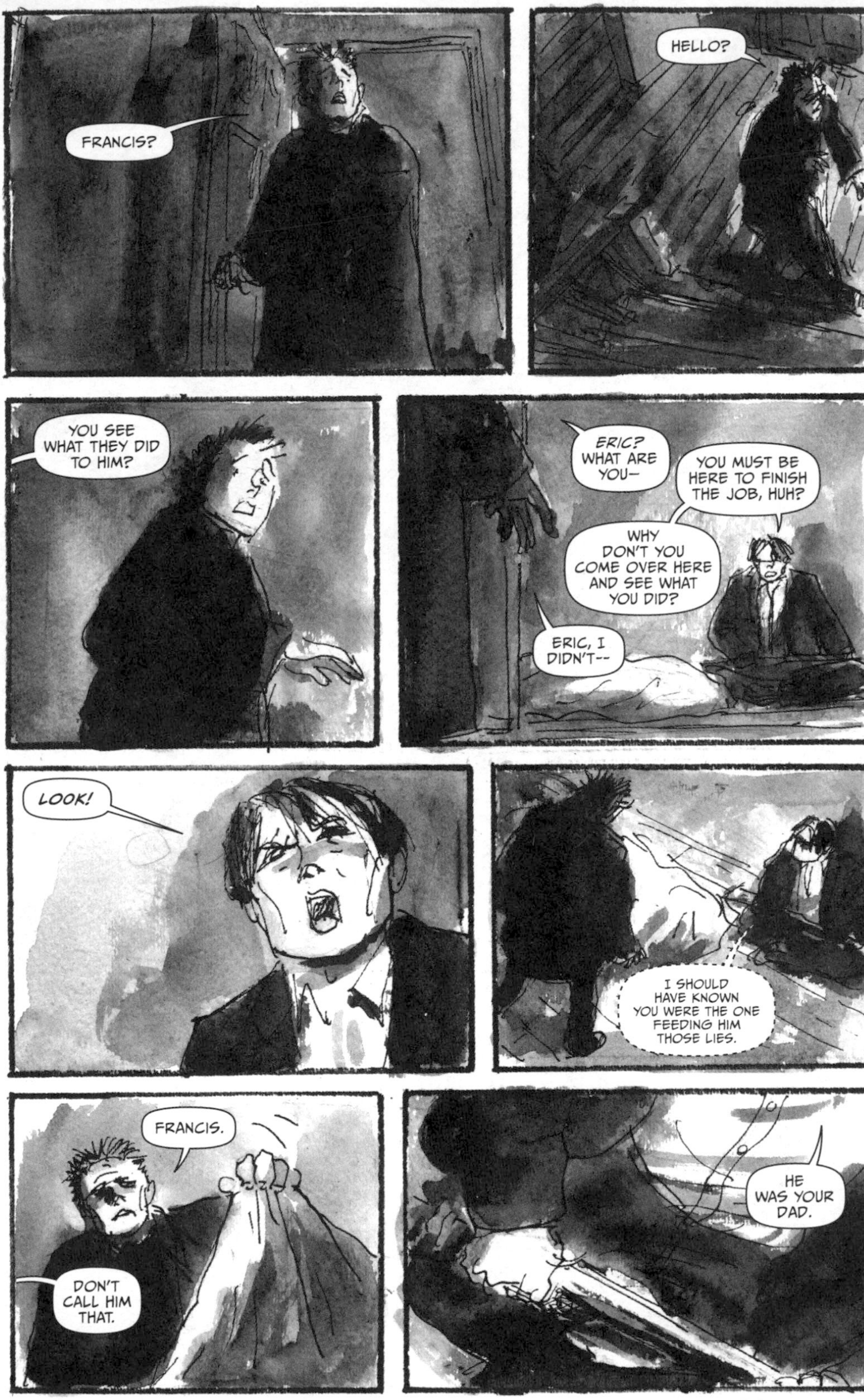
FRANCIS?
HELLO?
YOU SEE WHAT THEY DID TO HIM?
ERIC? WHAT ARE YOU—
YOU MUST BE HERE TO FINISH THE JOB, HUH?
WHY DON'T YOU COME OVER HERE AND SEE WHAT YOU DID?
ERIC, I DIDN'T--
LOOK!
I SHOULD HAVE KNOWN YOU WERE THE ONE FEEDING HIM THOSE LIES.
FRANCIS.
DON'T CALL HIM THAT.
HE WAS YOUR DAD.

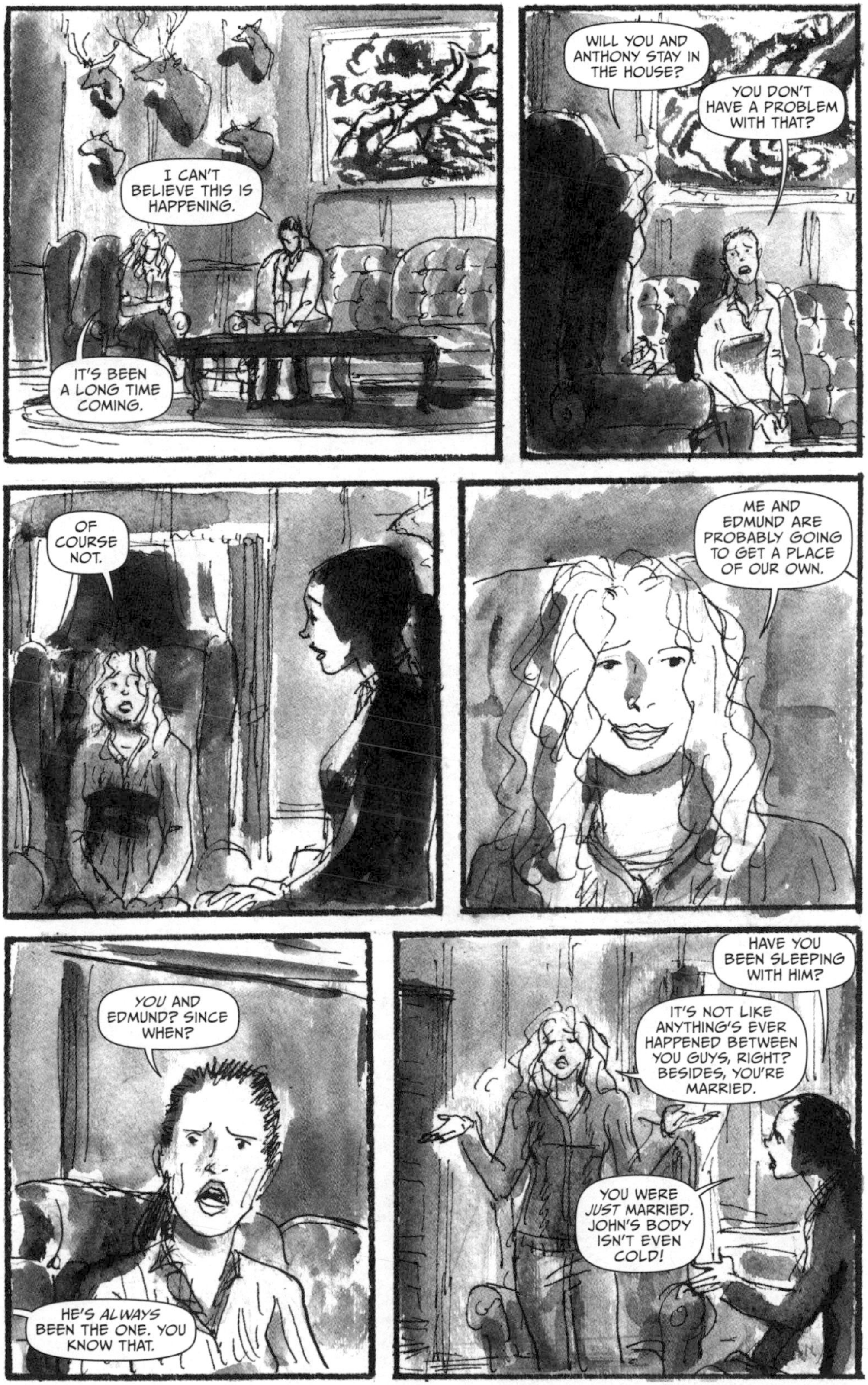
I CAN'T BELIEVE THIS IS HAPPENING.
IT'S BEEN A LONG TIME COMING.
WILL YOU AND ANTHONY STAY IN THE HOUSE?
YOU DON'T HAVE A PROBLEM WITH THAT?
OF COURSE NOT.
ME AND EDMUND ARE PROBABLY GOING TO GET A PLACE OF OUR OWN.
YOU AND EDMUND? SINCE WHEN?
HE'S *ALWAYS* BEEN THE ONE. YOU KNOW THAT.
HAVE YOU BEEN SLEEPING WITH HIM?
IT'S NOT LIKE ANYTHING'S EVER HAPPENED BETWEEN YOU GUYS, RIGHT? BESIDES, YOU'RE MARRIED.
YOU WERE *JUST* MARRIED. JOHN'S BODY ISN'T EVEN COLD!

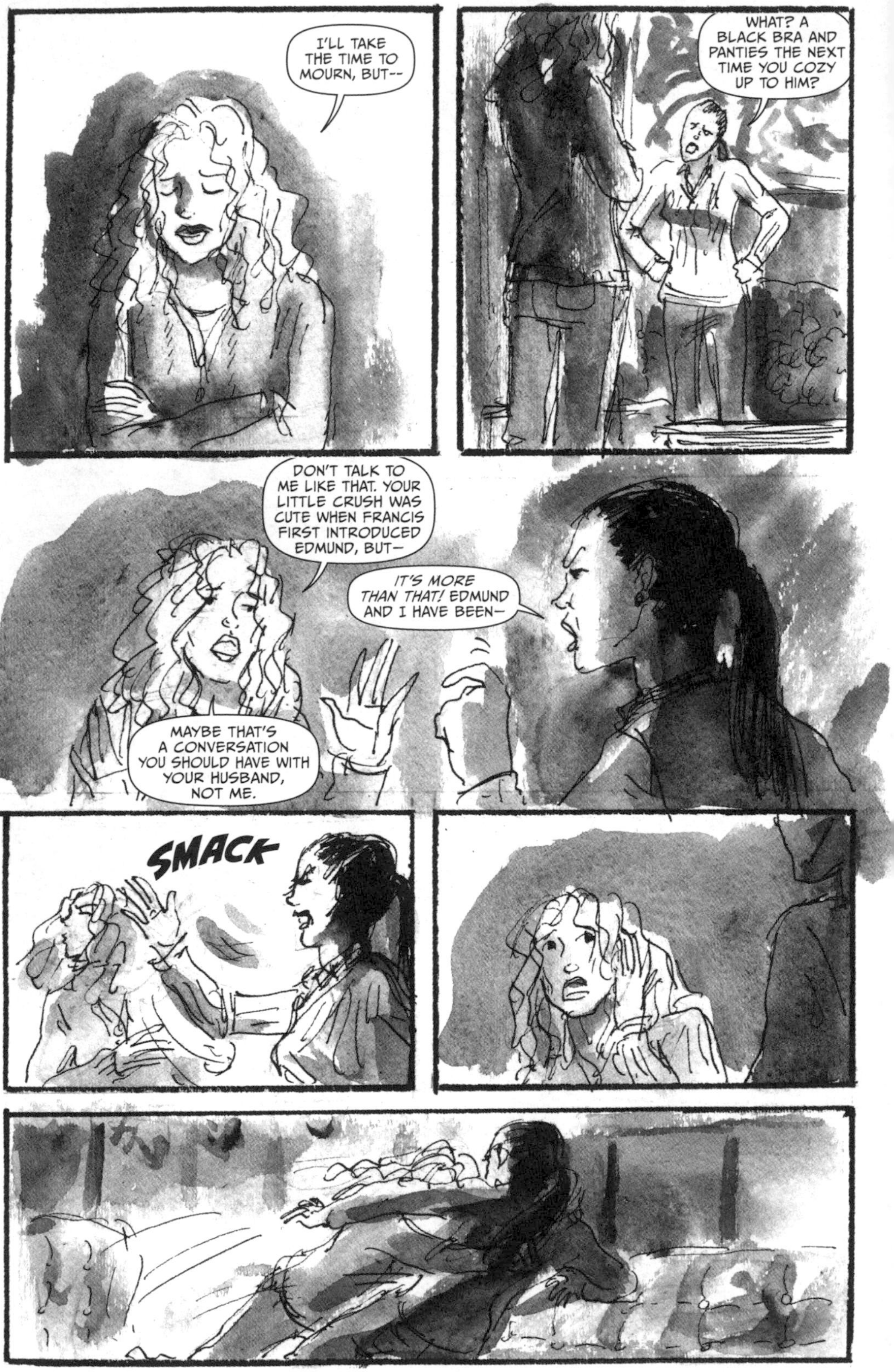
I'LL TAKE THE TIME TO MOURN, BUT--
WHAT? A BLACK BRA AND PANTIES THE NEXT TIME YOU COZY UP TO HIM?
DON'T TALK TO ME LIKE THAT. YOUR LITTLE CRUSH WAS CUTE WHEN FRANCIS FIRST INTRODUCED EDMUND, BUT—
IT'S MORE THAN THAT! EDMUND AND I HAVE BEEN—
MAYBE THAT'S A CONVERSATION YOU SHOULD HAVE WITH YOUR HUSBAND, NOT ME.
SMACK

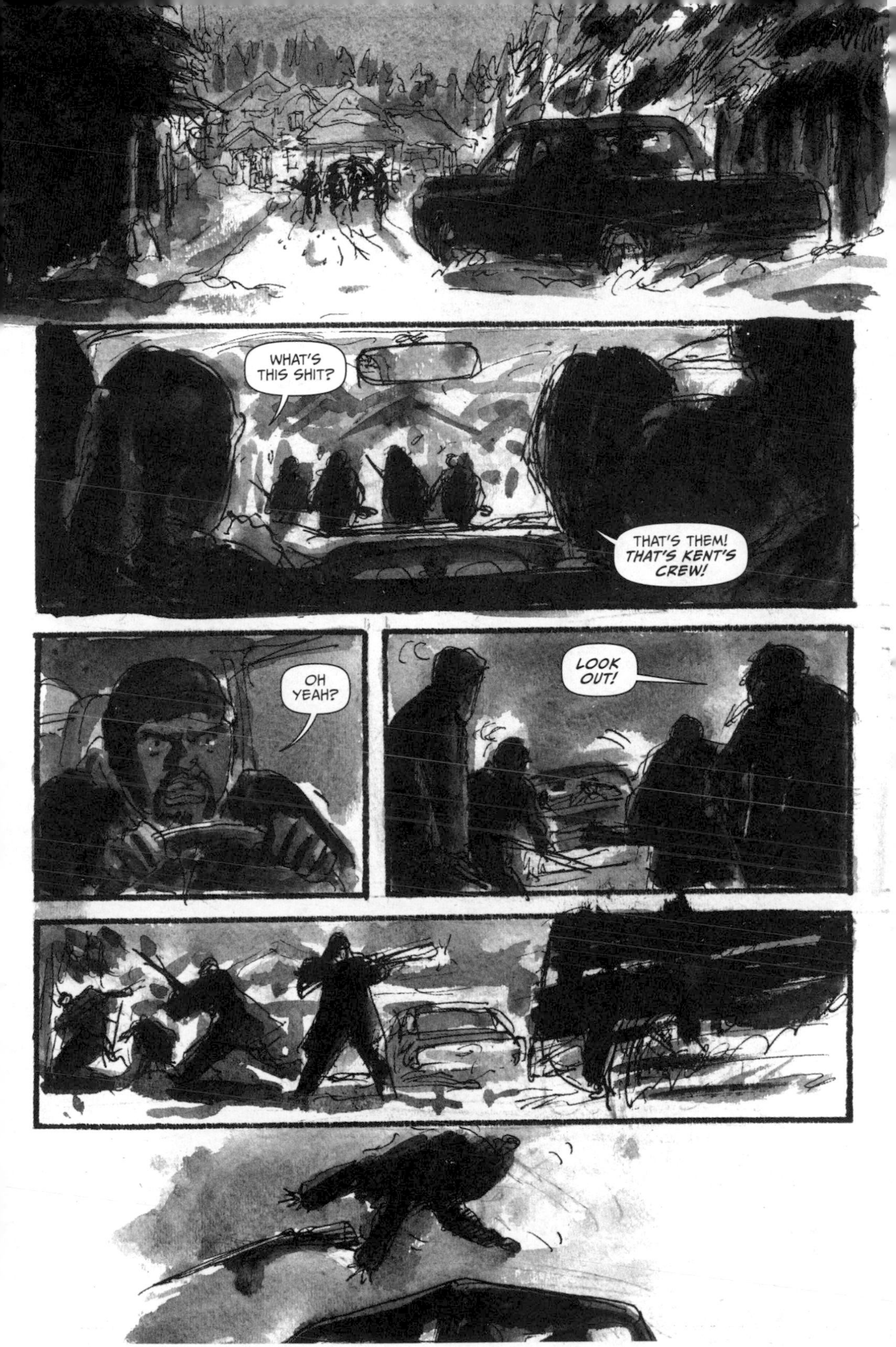
WHAT'S THIS SHIT?
THAT'S THEM! THAT'S KENT'S CREW!
OH YEAH?
LOOK OUT!

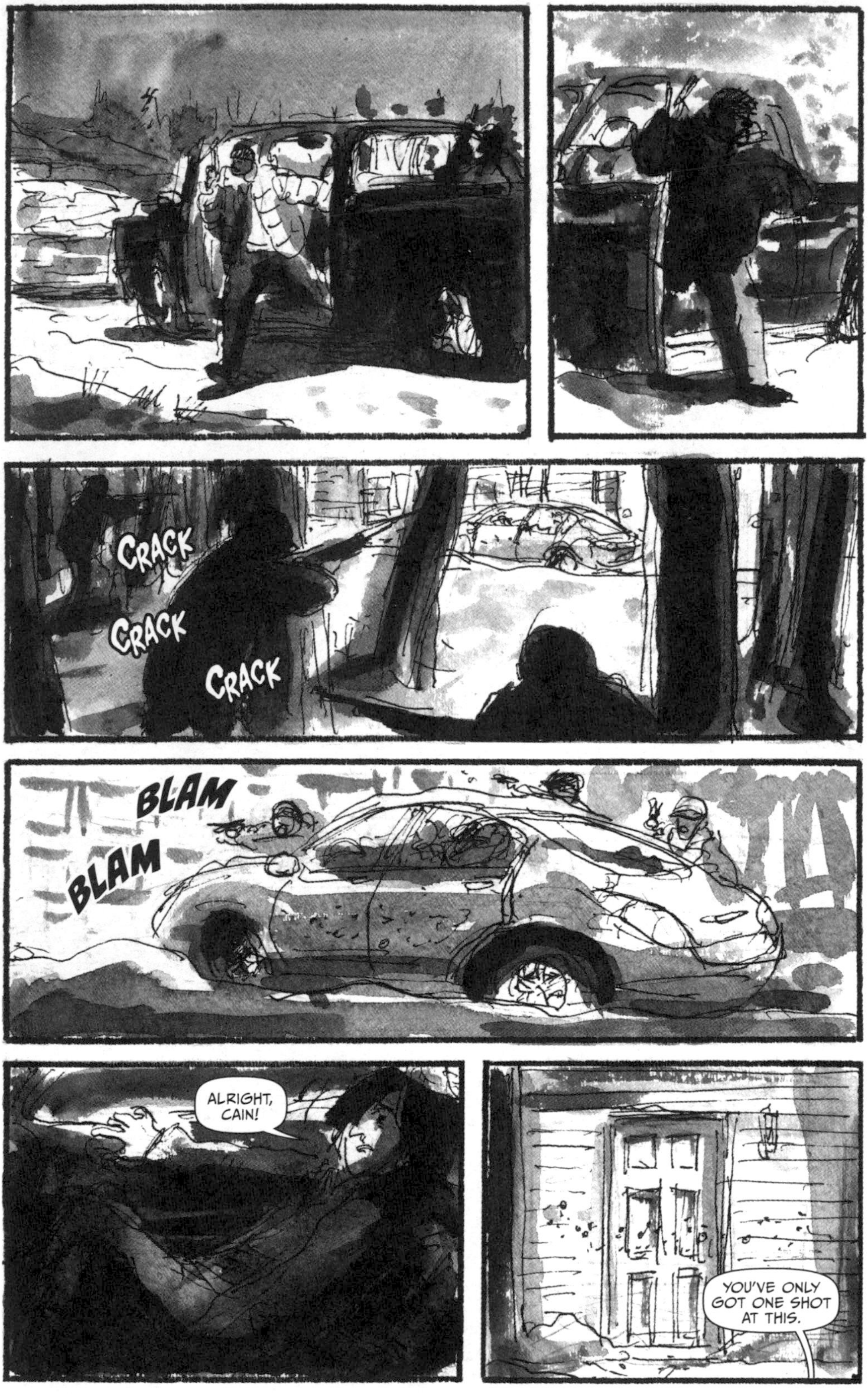
CRACK
CRACK
CRACK
BLAM
BLAM
ALRIGHT, CAIN!
YOU'VE ONLY GOT ONE SHOT AT THIS.

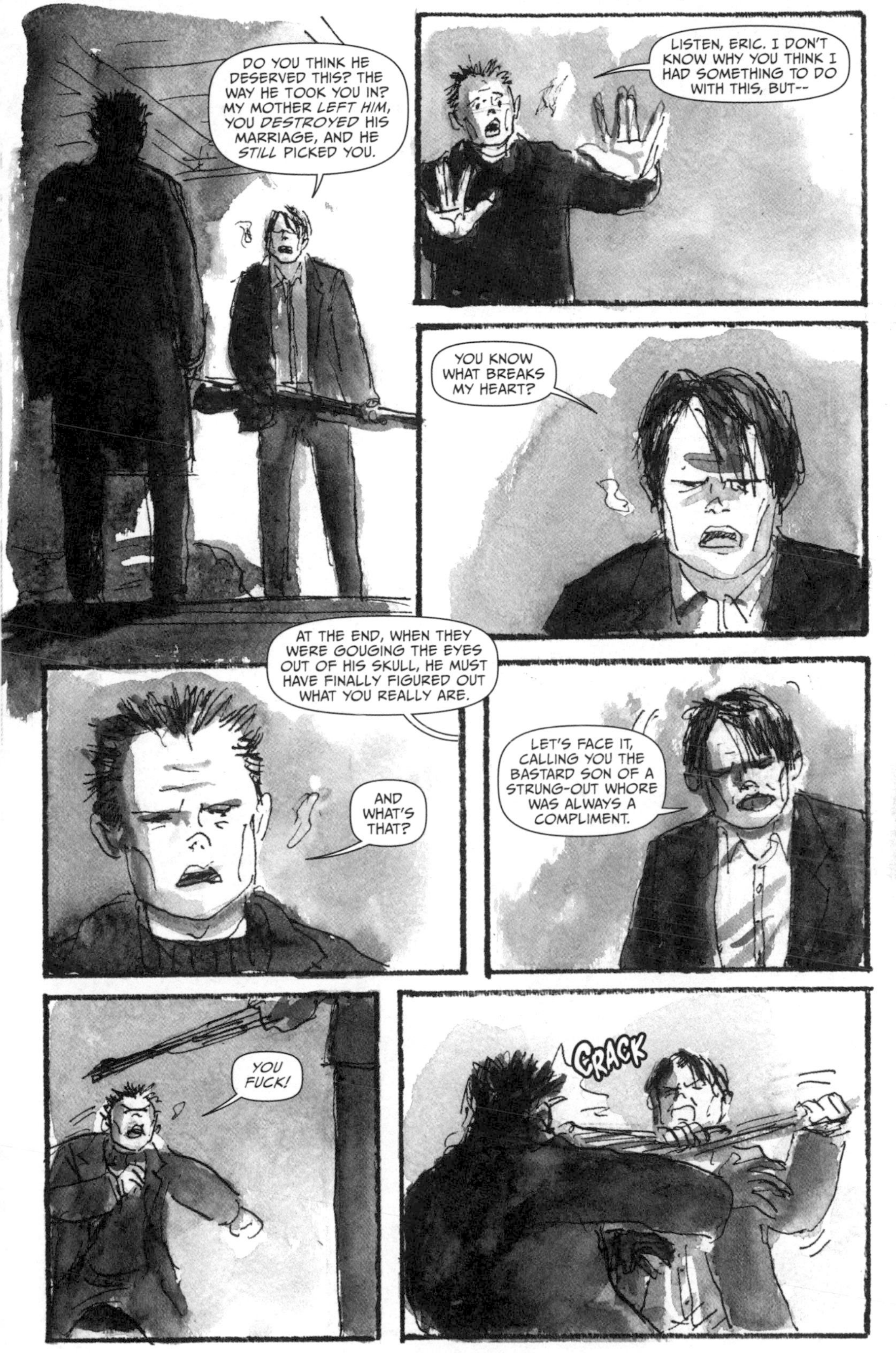
DO YOU THINK HE DESERVED THIS? THE WAY HE TOOK YOU IN? MY MOTHER *LEFT HIM*, YOU *DESTROYED* HIS MARRIAGE, AND HE *STILL* PICKED YOU.
LISTEN, ERIC. I DON'T KNOW WHY YOU THINK I HAD SOMETHING TO DO WITH THIS, BUT--
YOU KNOW WHAT BREAKS MY HEART?
AT THE END, WHEN THEY WERE GOUGING THE EYES OUT OF HIS SKULL, HE MUST HAVE FINALLY FIGURED OUT WHAT YOU REALLY ARE.
AND WHAT'S THAT?
LET'S FACE IT, CALLING YOU THE BASTARD SON OF A STRUNG-OUT WHORE WAS ALWAYS A COMPLIMENT.
YOU FUCK!
CRACK

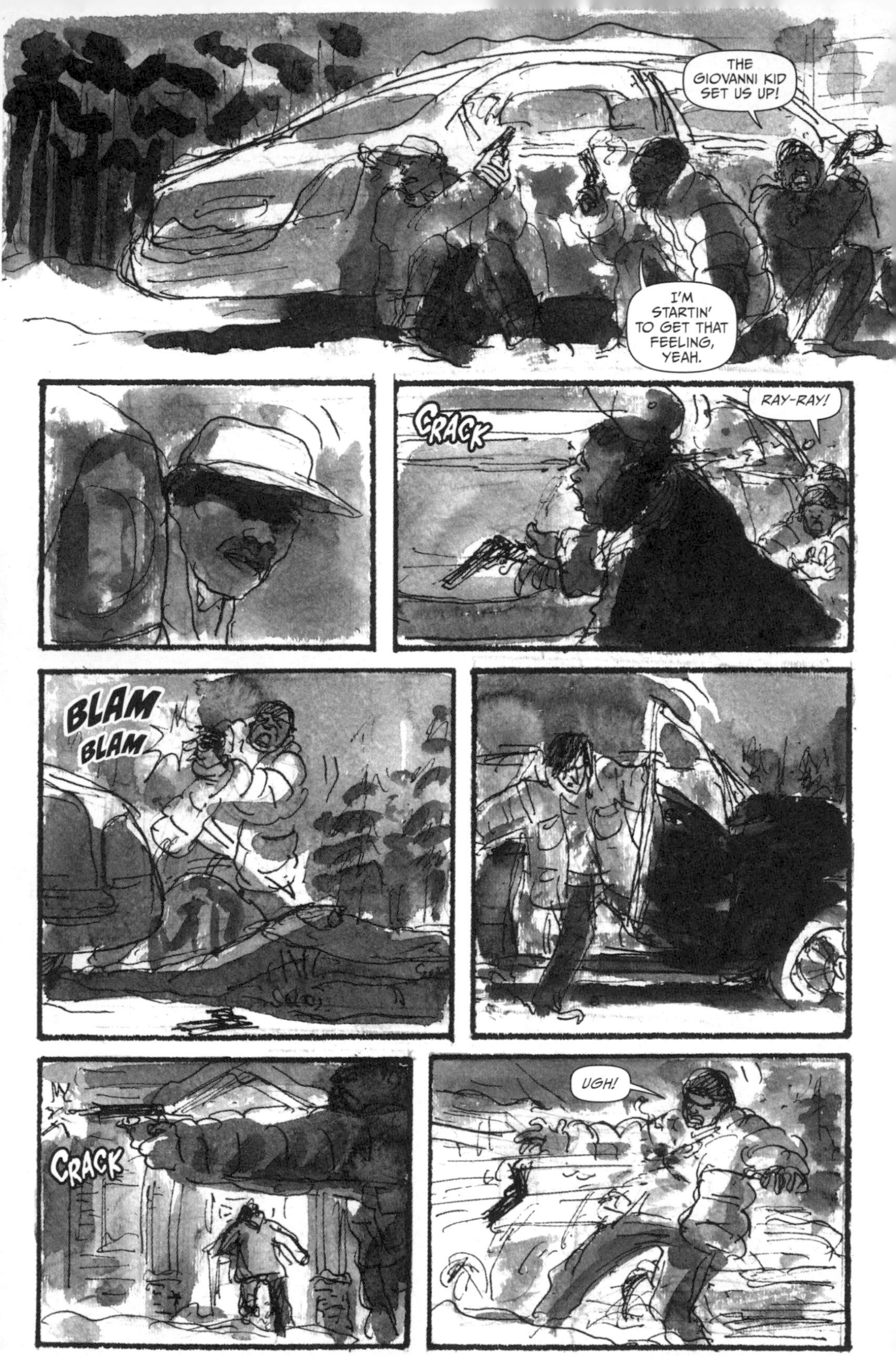
THE GIOVANNI KID SET US UP!
I'M STARTIN' TO GET THAT FEELING, YEAH.
CRACK
RAY-RAY!
BLAM
BLAM
CRACK
UGH!

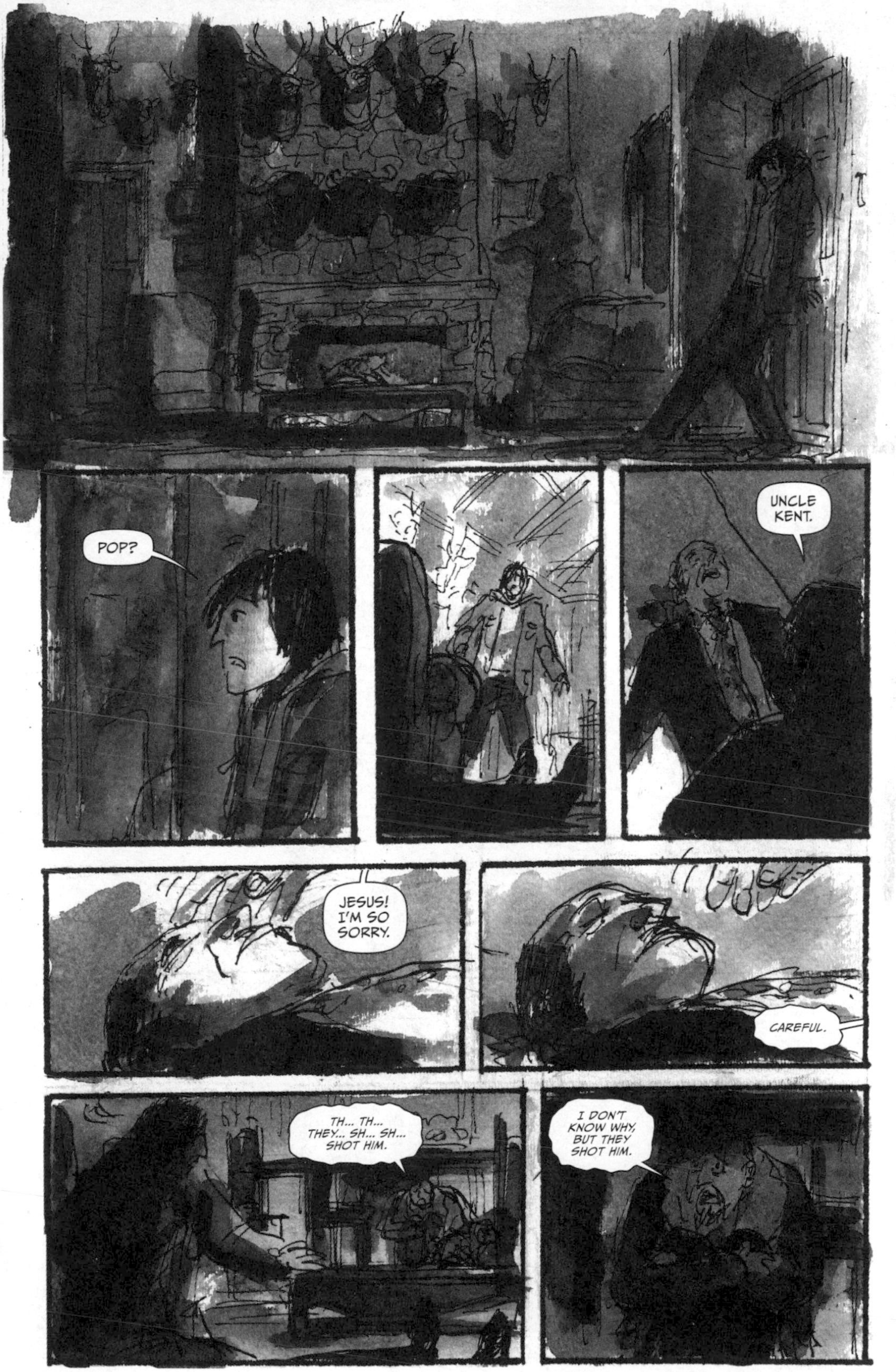
POP?
UNCLE KENT.
JESUS! I'M SO SORRY.
CAREFUL.
TH... TH... THEY... SH... SH... SHOT HIM.
I DON'T KNOW WHY, BUT THEY SHOT HIM.

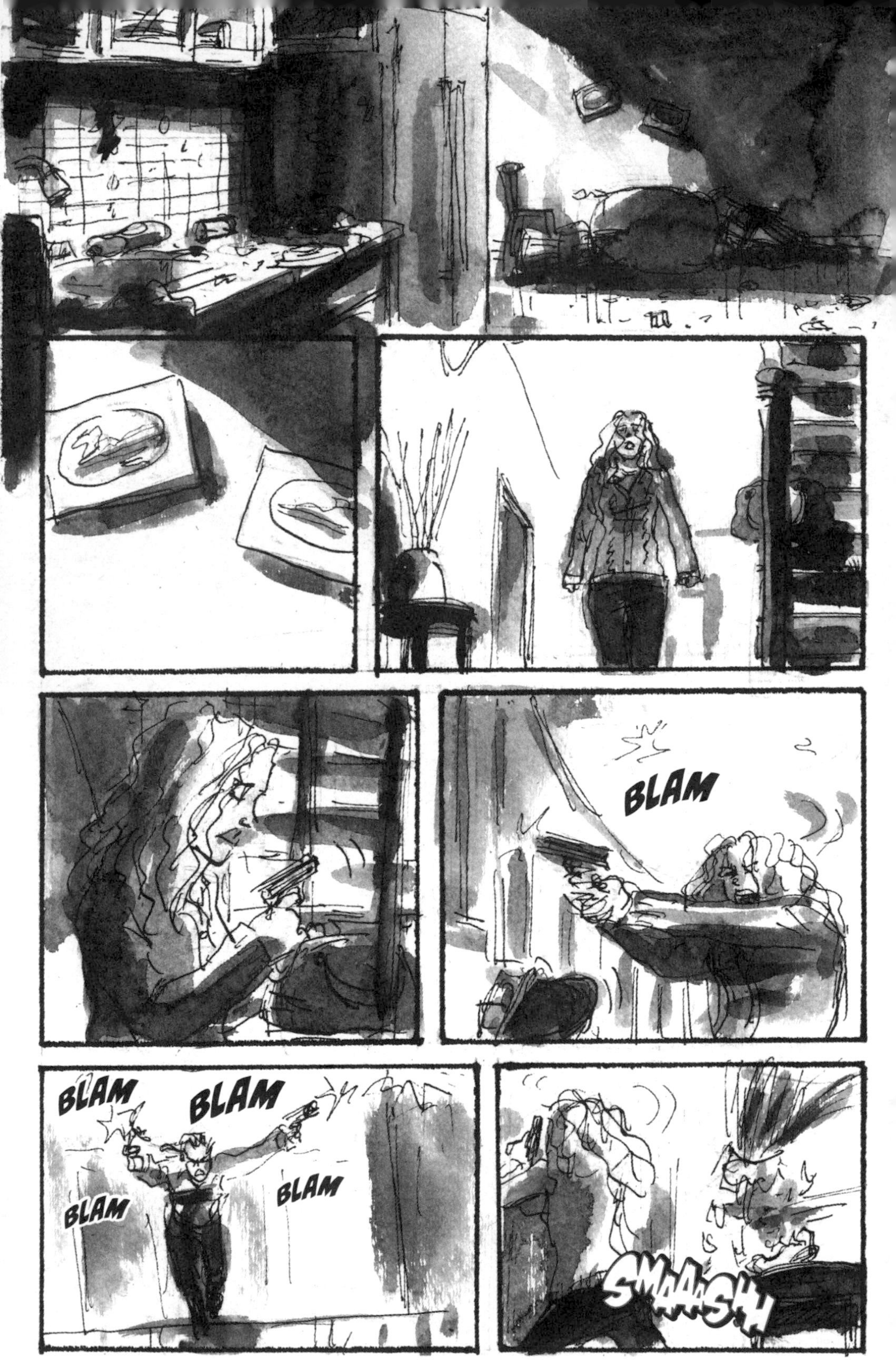
BLAM
BLAM
BLAM
BLAM
BLAM
SMAAASHH

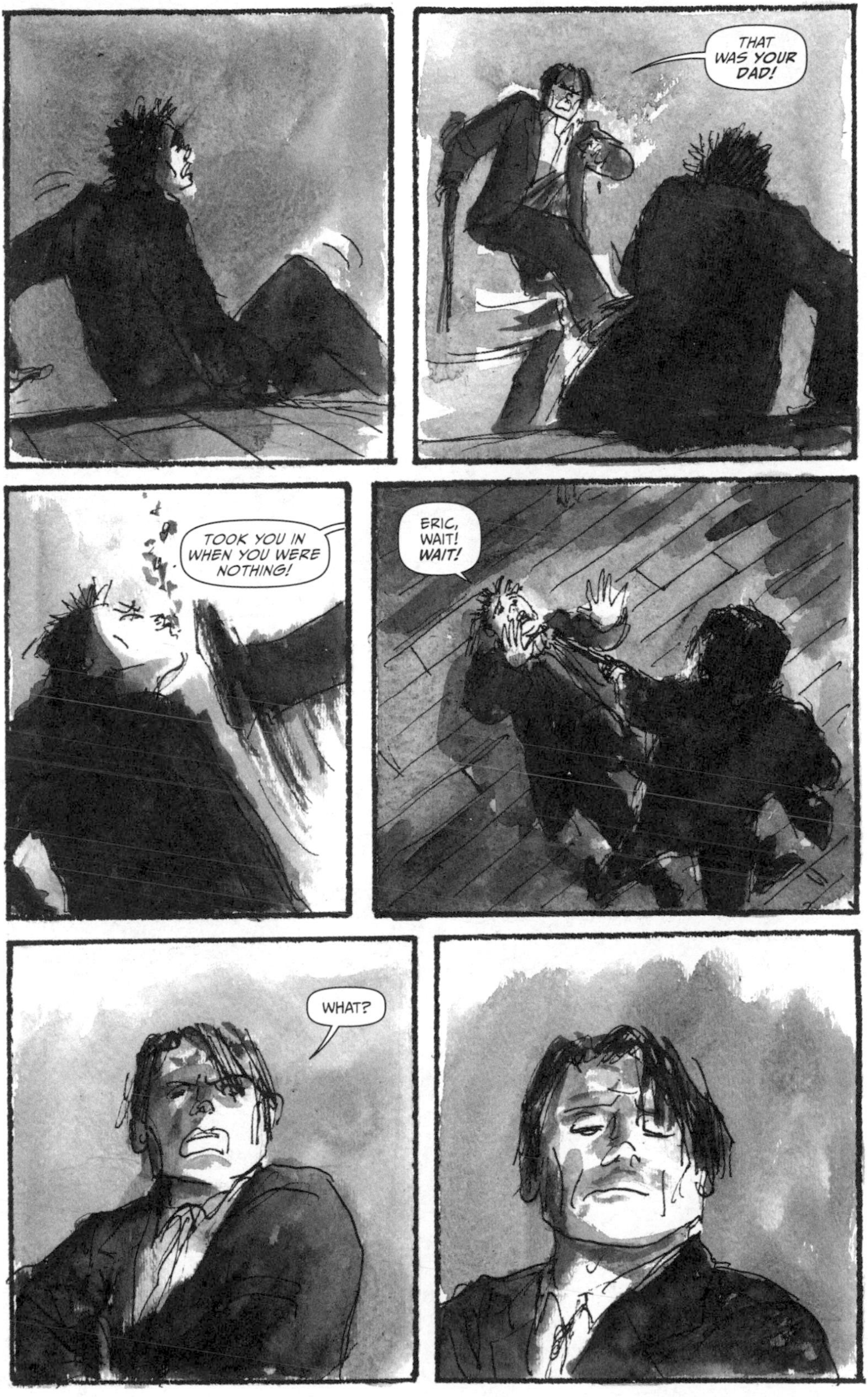
THAT WAS YOUR DAD!
TOOK YOU IN WHEN YOU WERE NOTHING!
ERIC, WAIT! WAIT!
WHAT?

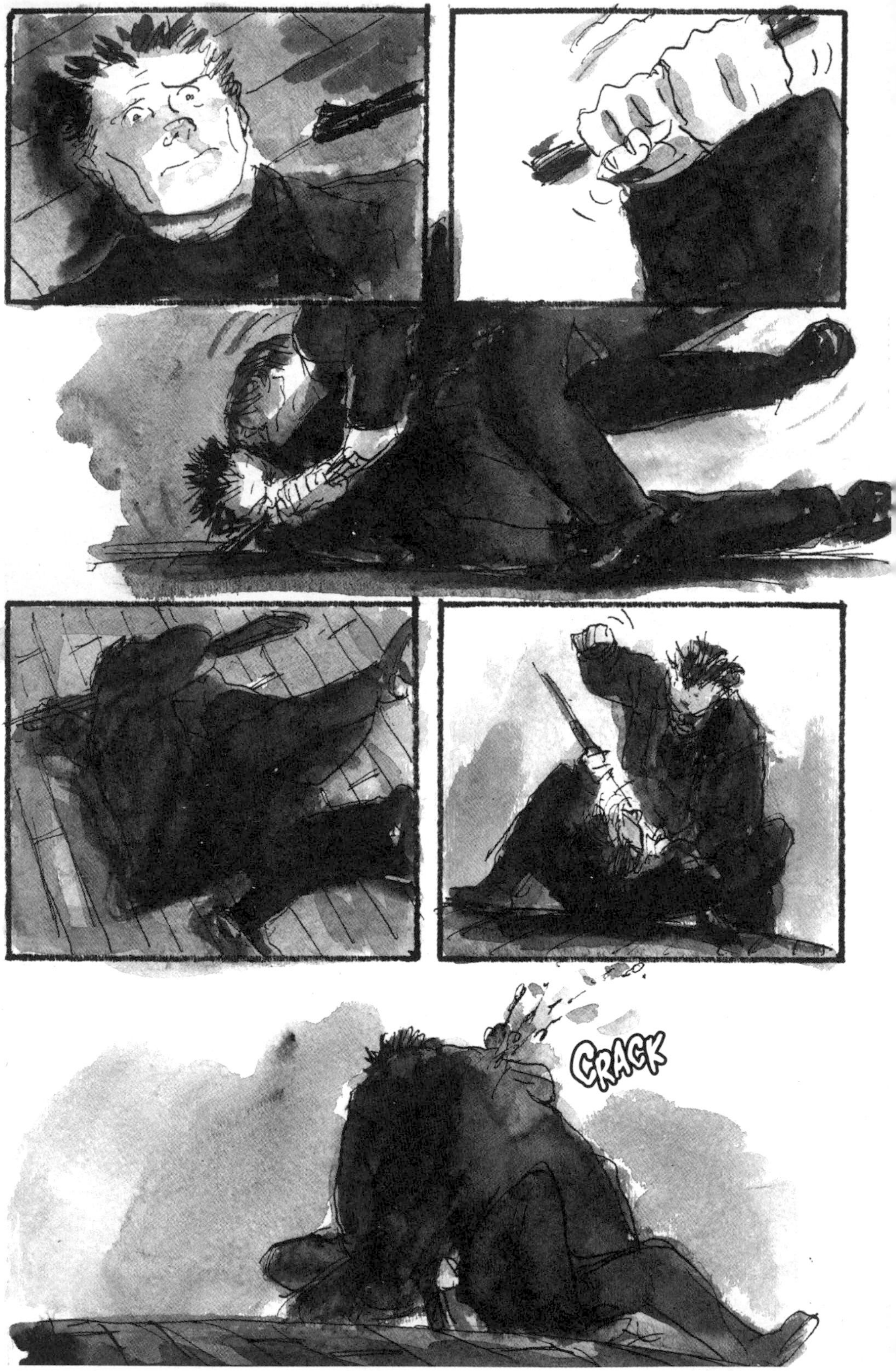
CRACK

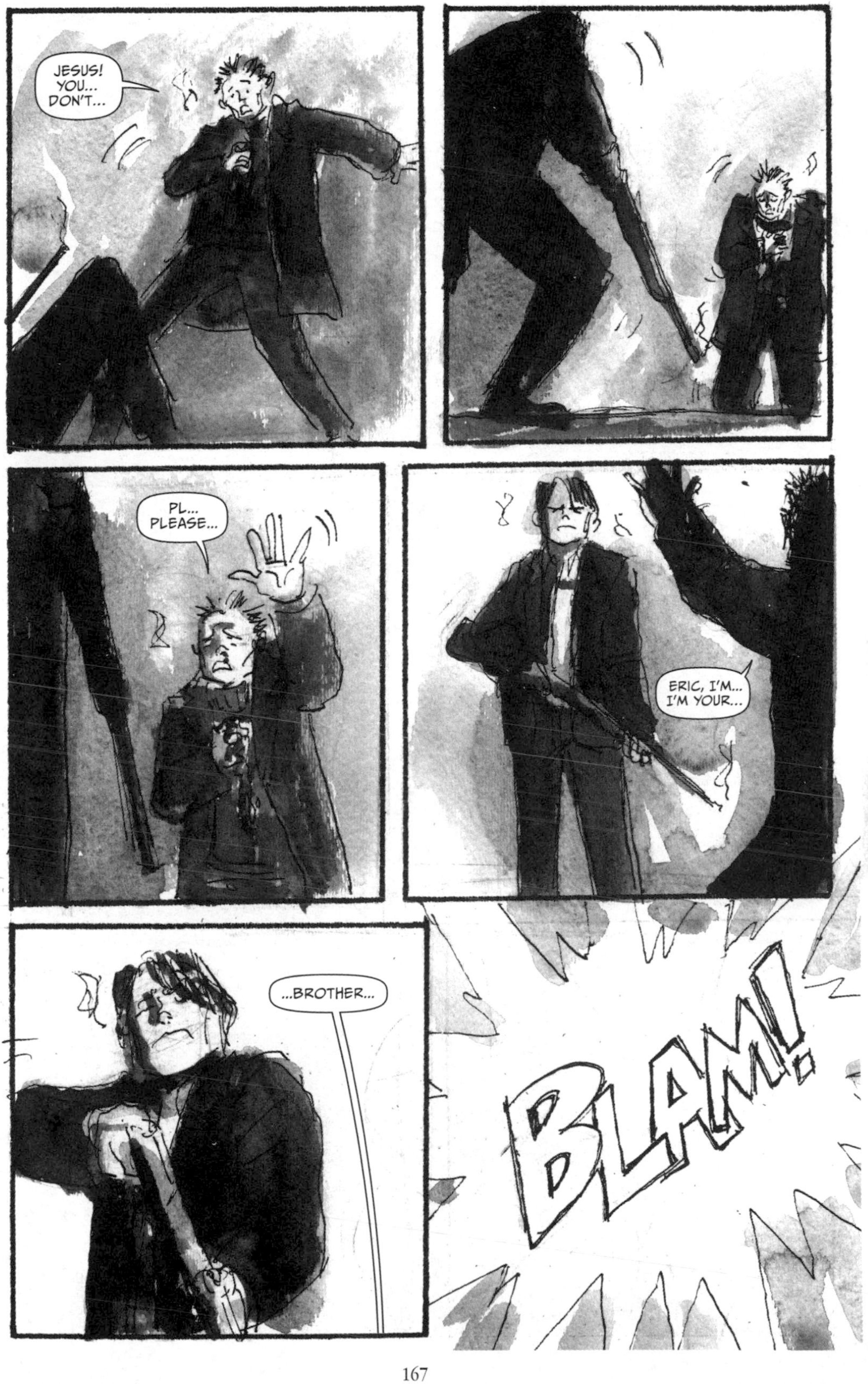
JESUS! YOU... DON'T...
PL... PLEASE...
ERIC, I'M... I'M YOUR...
...BROTHER...
BLAM!

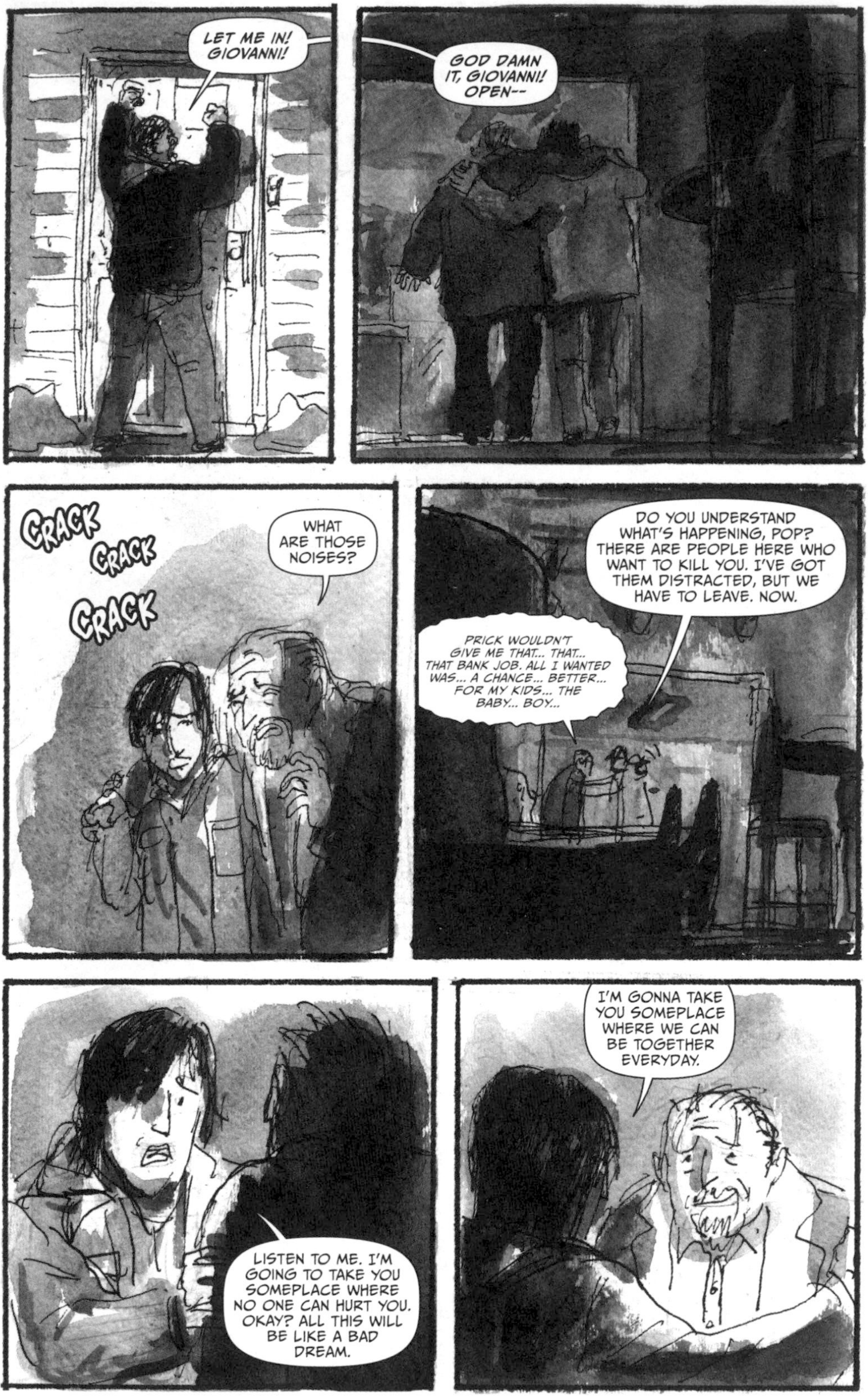

LET ME IN! GIOVANNI!
GOD DAMN IT, GIOVANNI! OPEN--
CRACK CRACK CRACK
WHAT ARE THOSE NOISES?
DO YOU UNDERSTAND WHAT'S HAPPENING, POP? THERE ARE PEOPLE HERE WHO WANT TO KILL YOU. I'VE GOT THEM DISTRACTED, BUT WE HAVE TO LEAVE. NOW.
PRICK WOULDN'T GIVE ME THAT... THAT... THAT BANK JOB. ALL I WANTED WAS... A CHANCE... BETTER... FOR MY KIDS... THE BABY... BOY...
LISTEN TO ME. I'M GOING TO TAKE YOU SOMEPLACE WHERE NO ONE CAN HURT YOU. OKAY? ALL THIS WILL BE LIKE A BAD DREAM.
I'M GONNA TAKE YOU SOMEPLACE WHERE WE CAN BE TOGETHER EVERYDAY.

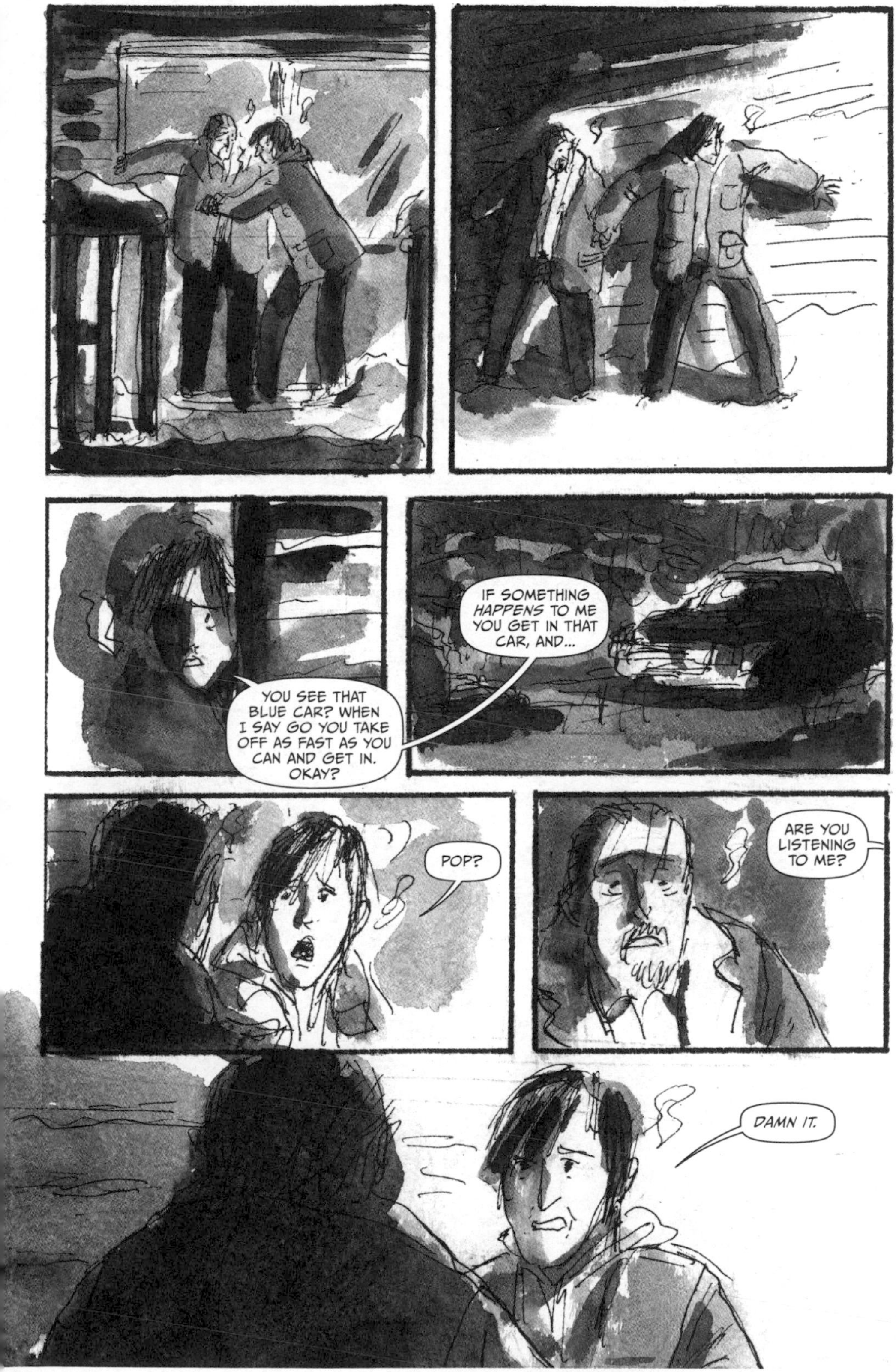
YOU SEE THAT BLUE CAR? WHEN I SAY GO YOU TAKE OFF AS FAST AS YOU CAN AND GET IN. OKAY?
IF SOMETHING HAPPENS TO ME YOU GET IN THAT CAR, AND...
POP?
ARE YOU LISTENING TO ME?
DAMN IT.

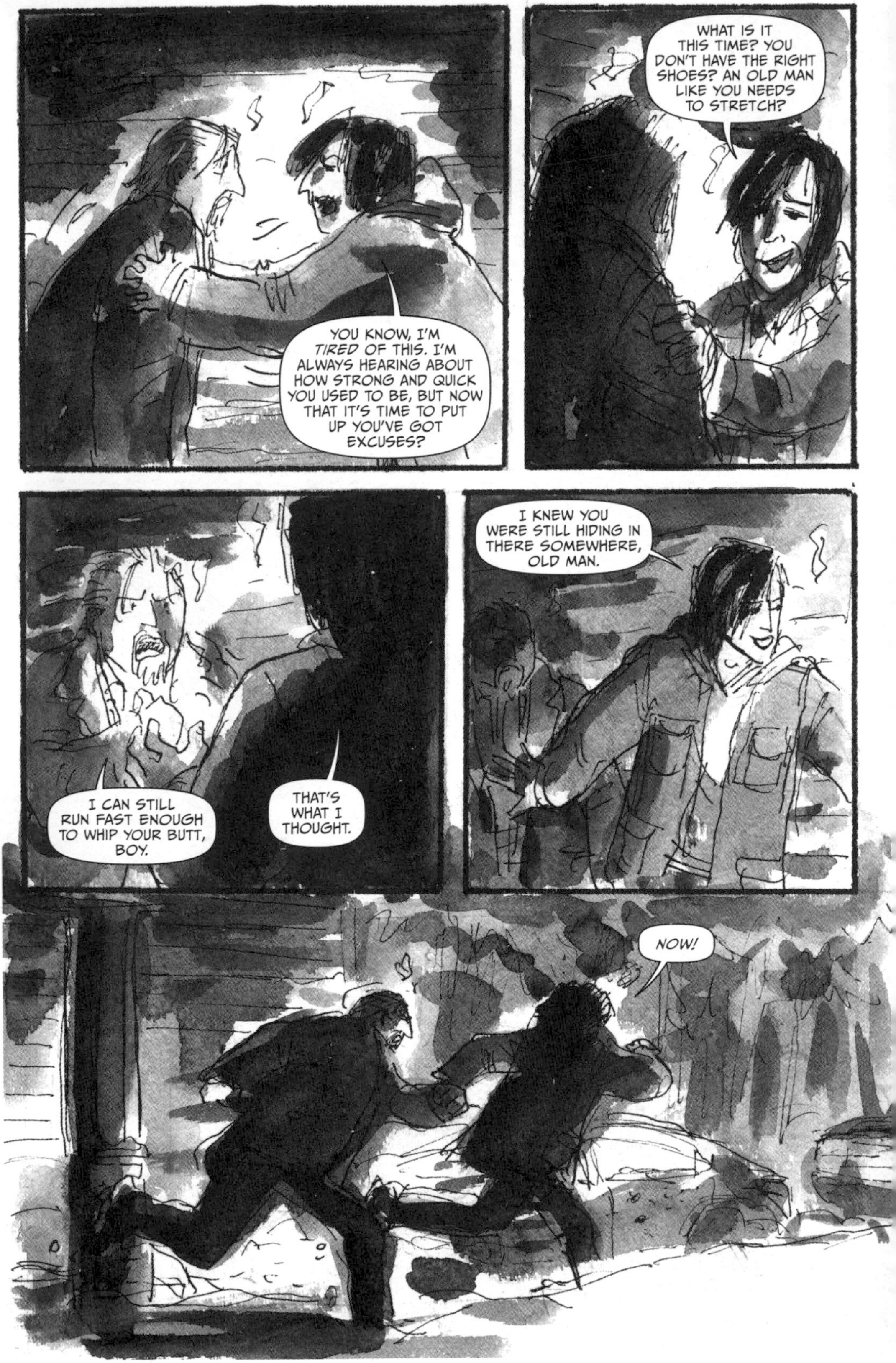
YOU KNOW, I'M *TIRED* OF THIS. I'M ALWAYS HEARING ABOUT HOW STRONG AND QUICK YOU USED TO BE, BUT NOW THAT IT'S TIME TO PUT UP YOU'VE GOT EXCUSES?
WHAT IS IT THIS TIME? YOU DON'T HAVE THE RIGHT SHOES? AN OLD MAN LIKE YOU NEEDS TO STRETCH?
I CAN STILL RUN FAST ENOUGH TO WHIP YOUR BUTT, BOY.
THAT'S WHAT I THOUGHT.
I KNEW YOU WERE STILL HIDING IN THERE SOMEWHERE, OLD MAN.
NOW!

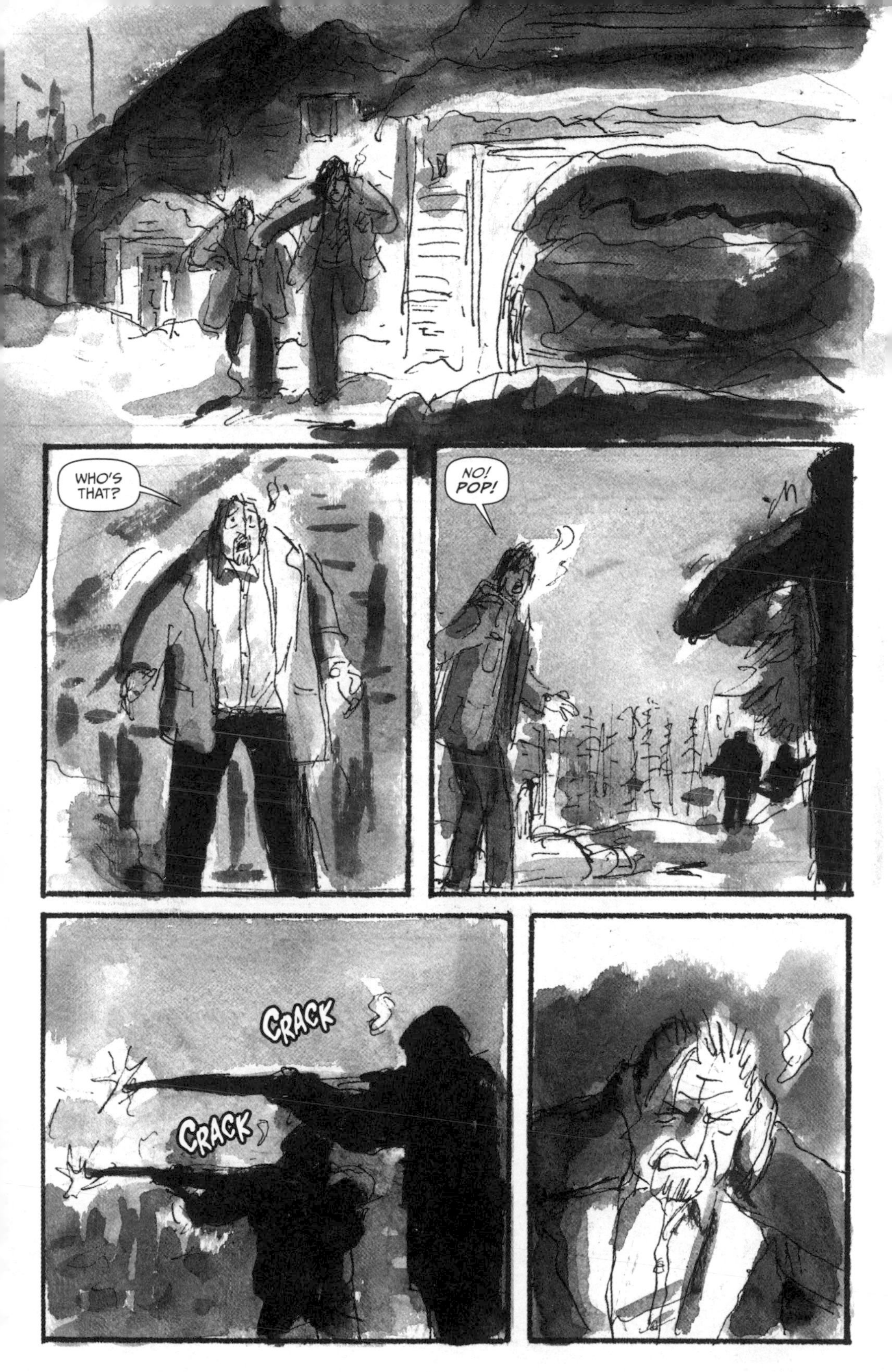
WHO'S THAT?
NO! POP!
CRACK
CRACK

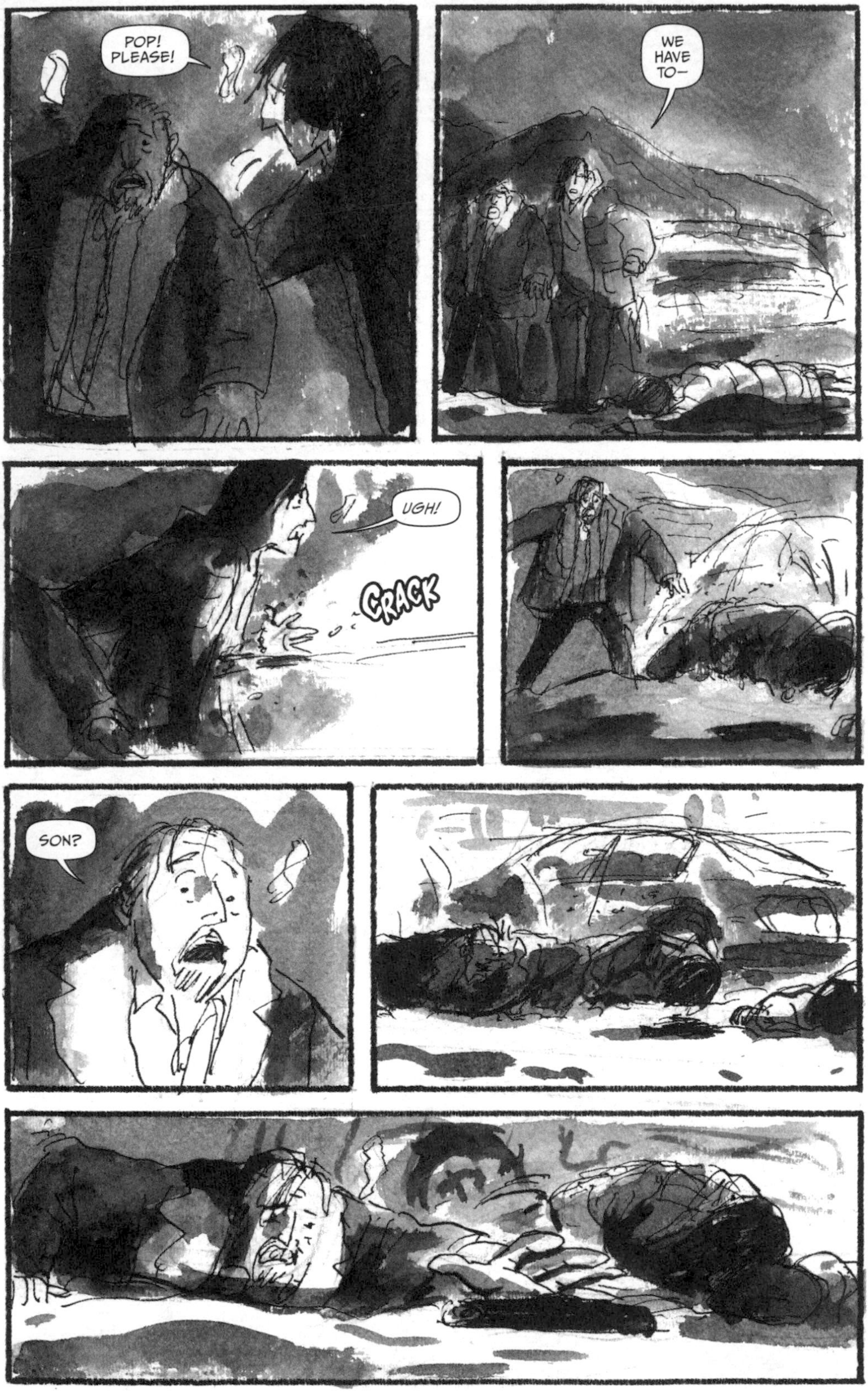
POP! PLEASE!
WE HAVE TO—
UGH!
CRACK
SON?

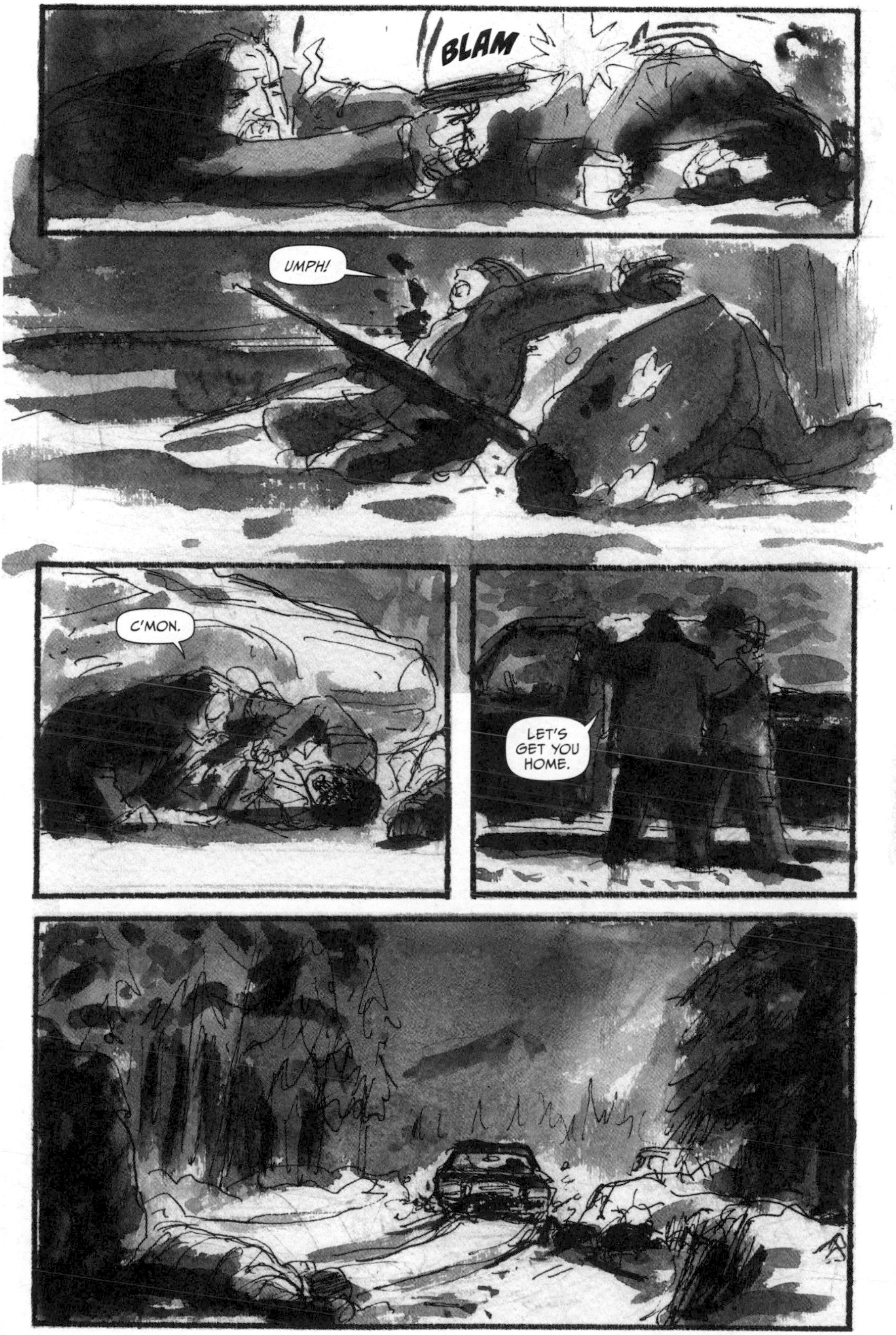
BLAM
UMPH!
C'MON.
LET'S GET YOU HOME.

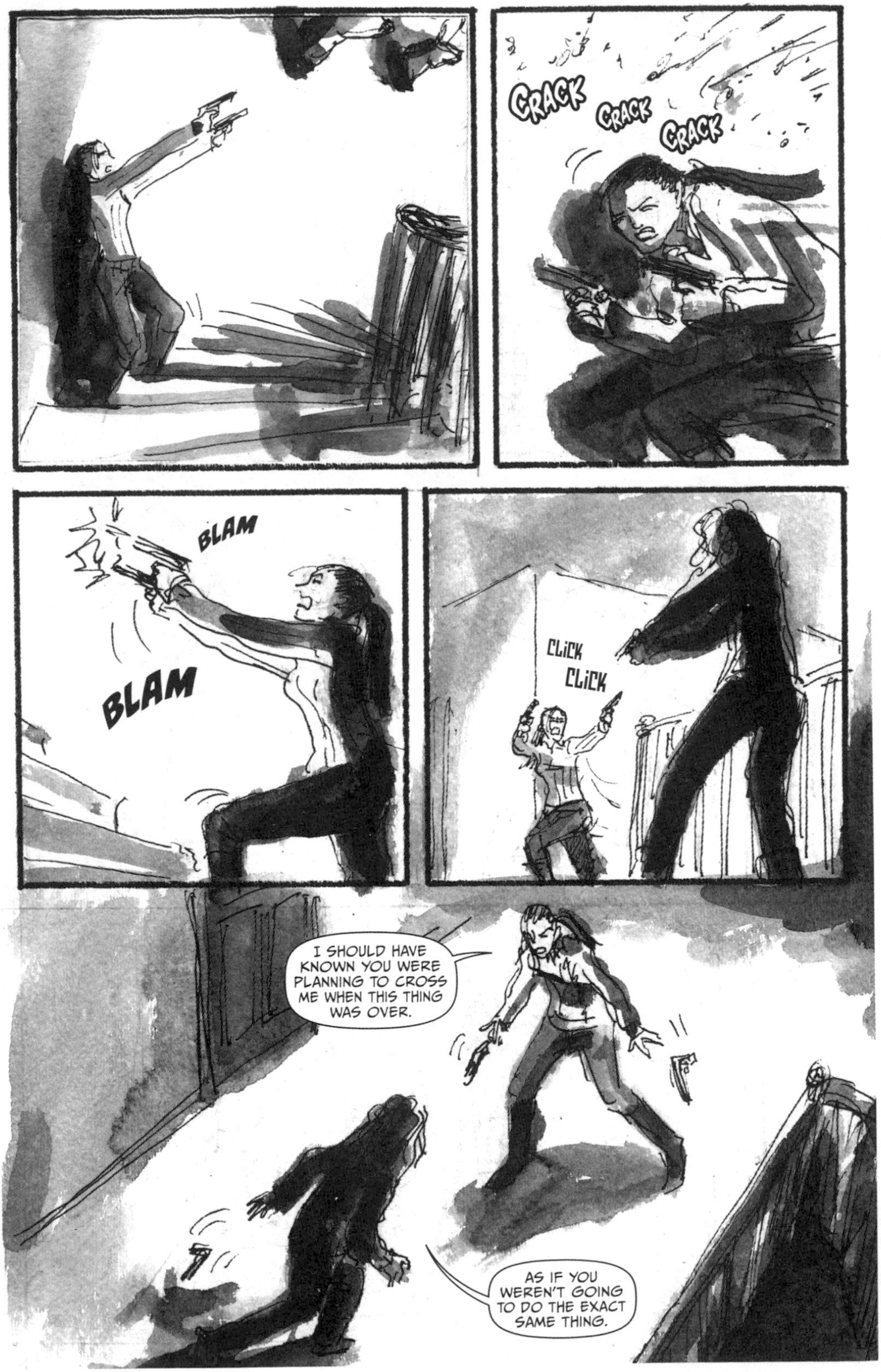
CRACK
CRACK
CRACK
BLAM
BLAM
CLICK
CLICK
I SHOULD HAVE KNOWN YOU WERE PLANNING TO CROSS ME WHEN THIS THING WAS OVER.
AS IF YOU WEREN'T GOING TO DO THE EXACT SAME THING.

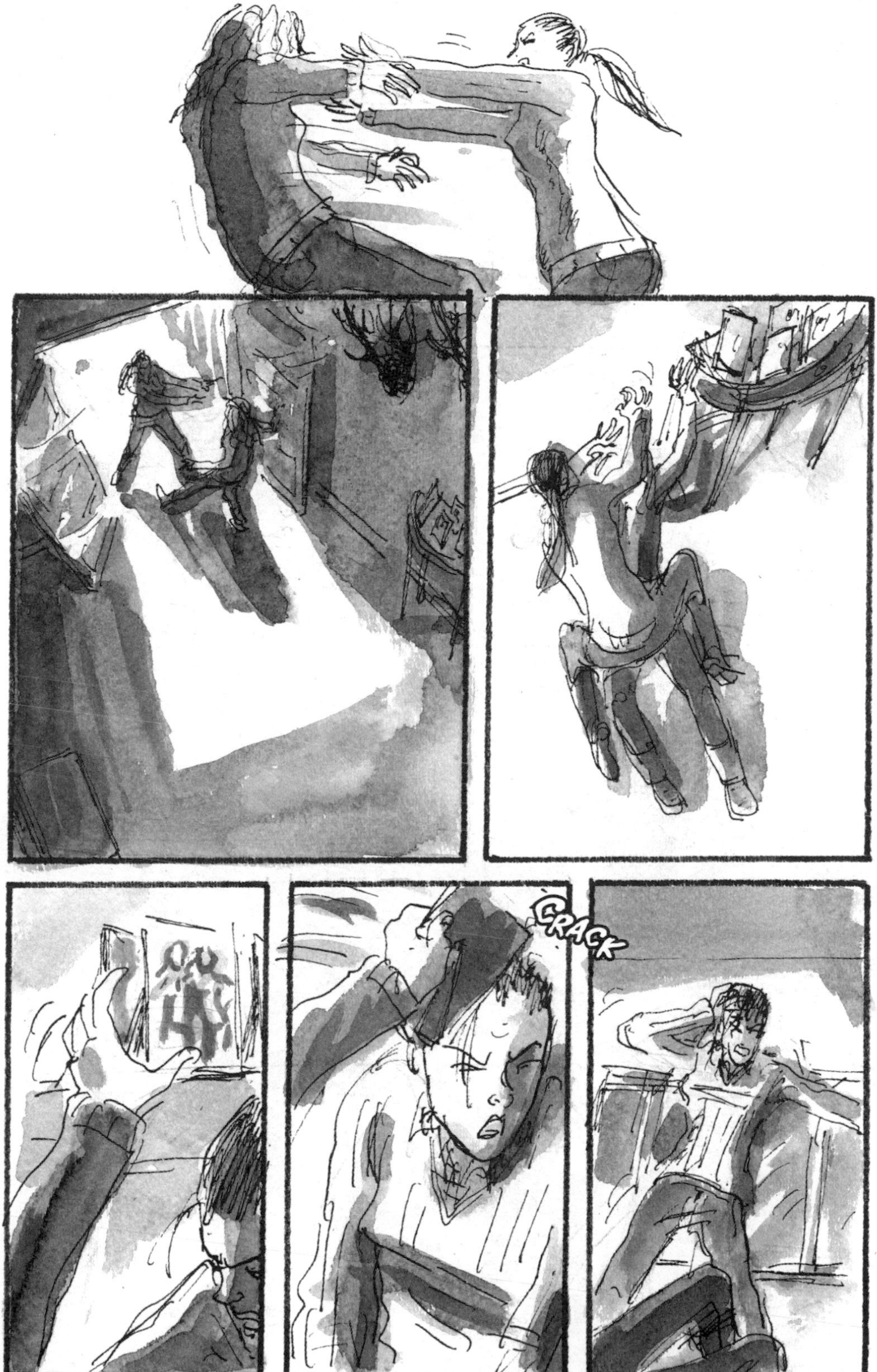
CRACK

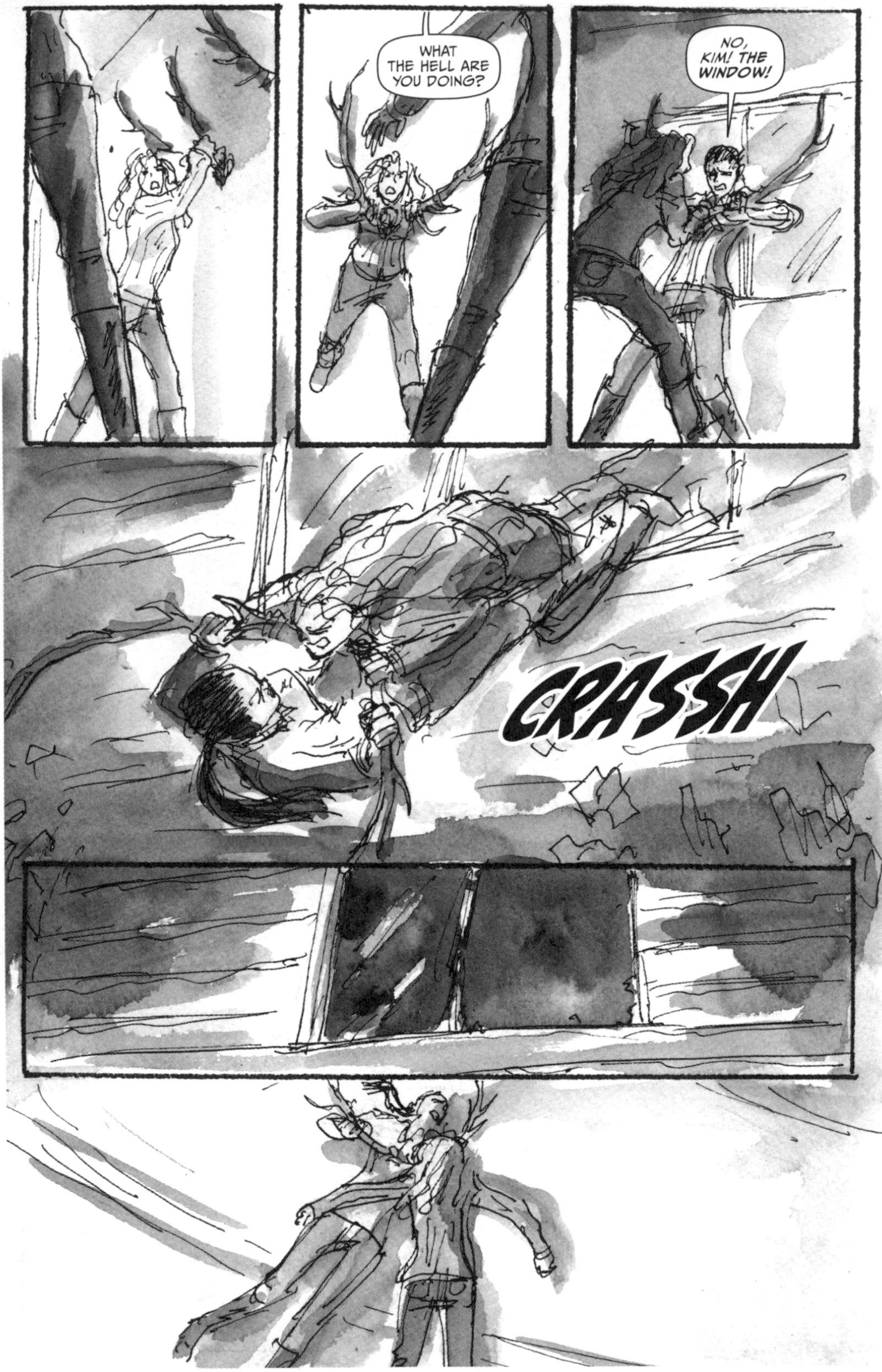
WHAT THE HELL ARE YOU DOING?
NO, KIM! THE WINDOW!
CRASSH

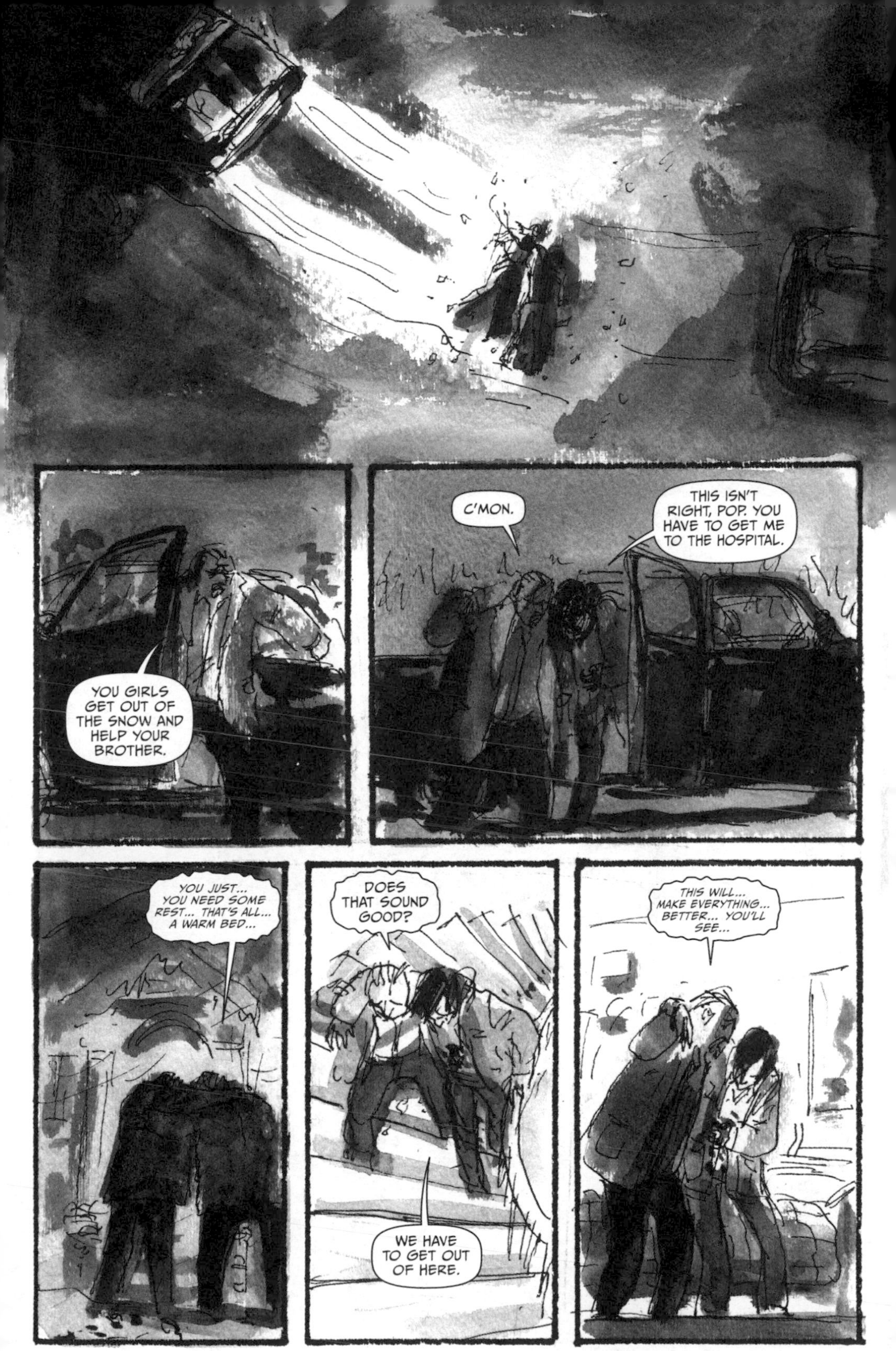
YOU GIRLS GET OUT OF THE SNOW AND HELP YOUR BROTHER.
C'MON.
THIS ISN'T RIGHT, POP. YOU HAVE TO GET ME TO THE HOSPITAL.
YOU JUST... YOU NEED SOME REST... THAT'S ALL... A WARM BED...
DOES THAT SOUND GOOD?
WE HAVE TO GET OUT OF HERE.
THIS WILL... MAKE EVERYTHING... BETTER... YOU'LL SEE...

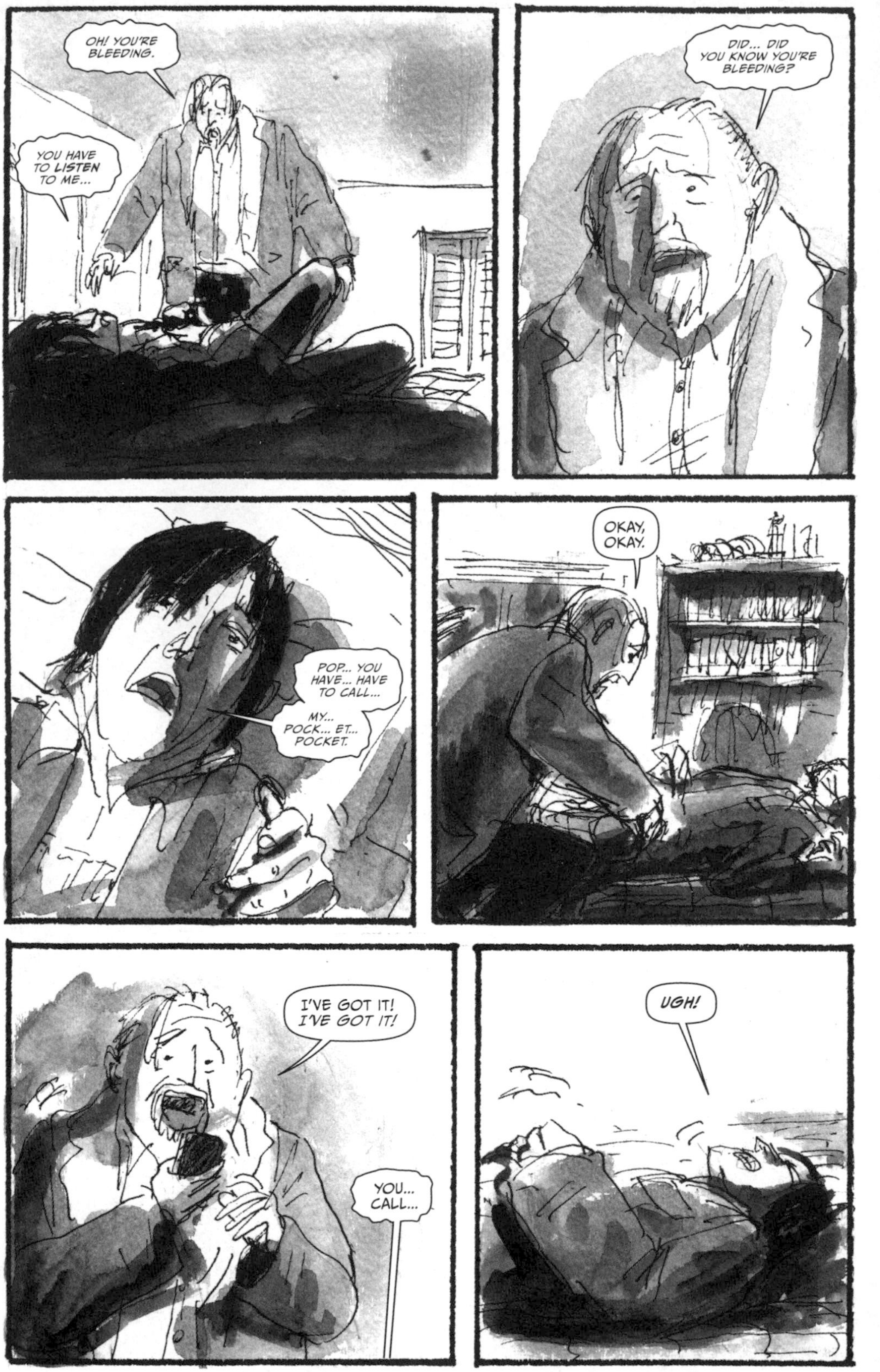
OH! YOU'RE BLEEDING.
YOU HAVE TO LISTEN TO ME...
DID... DID YOU KNOW YOU'RE BLEEDING?
POP... YOU HAVE... HAVE TO CALL...
MY... POCK... ET... POCKET.
OKAY, OKAY.
I'VE GOT IT! I'VE GOT IT!
YOU... CALL...
UGH!

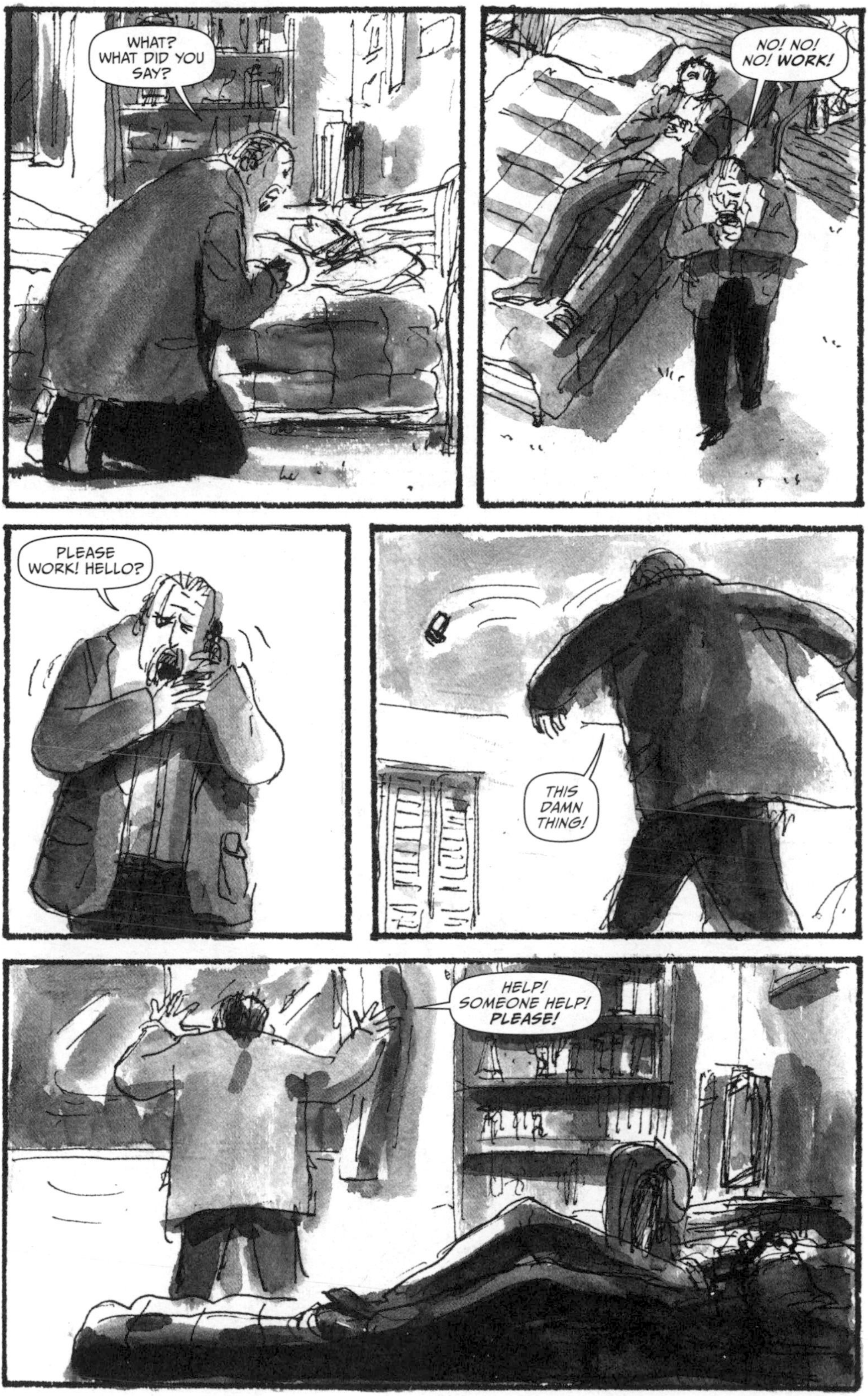
WHAT? WHAT DID YOU SAY?
NO! NO! NO! WORK!
PLEASE WORK! HELLO?
THIS DAMN THING!
HELP! SOMEONE HELP! PLEASE!

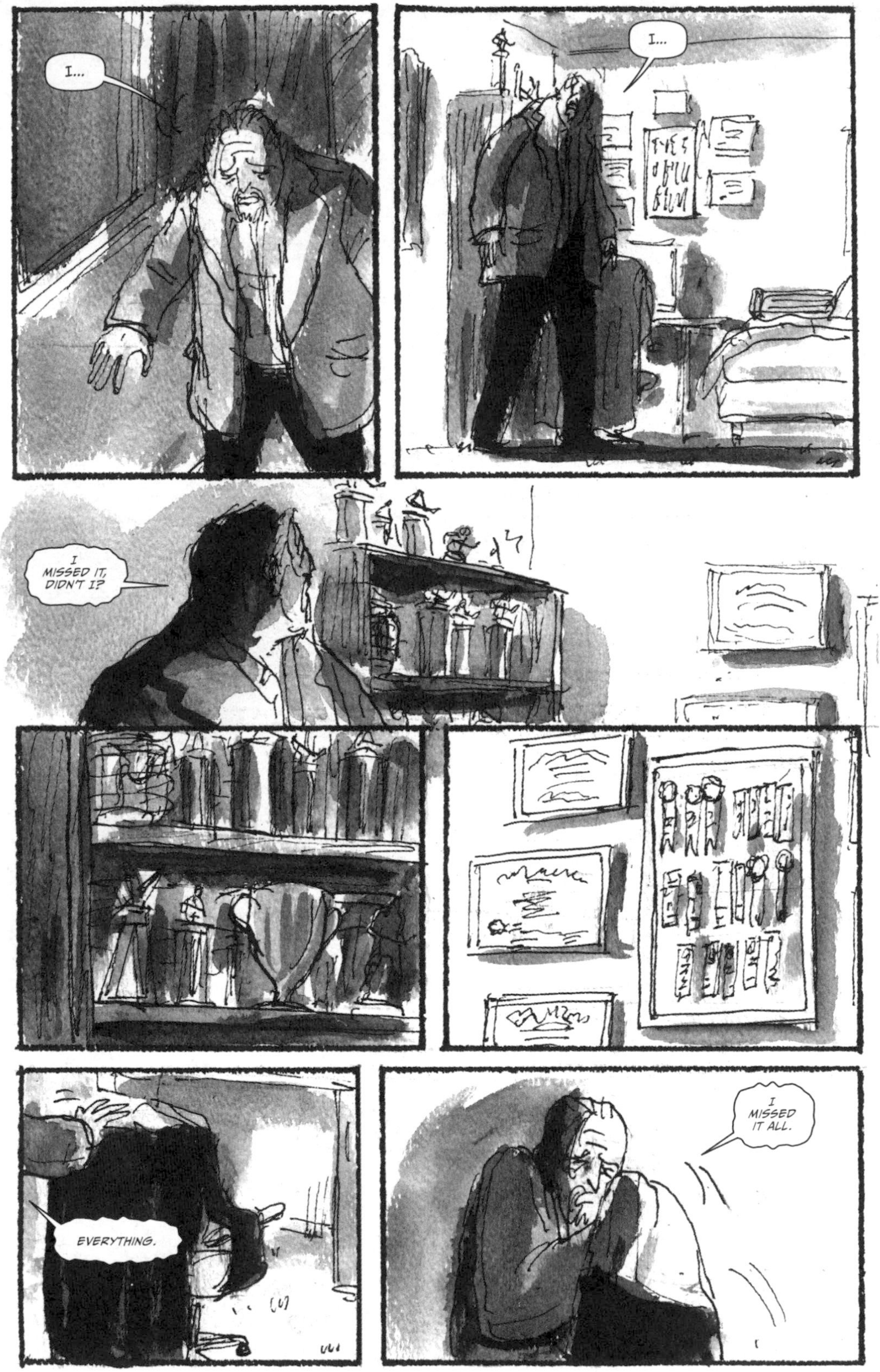
I...
I...
I MISSED IT, DIDN'T I?
EVERYTHING.
I MISSED IT ALL.

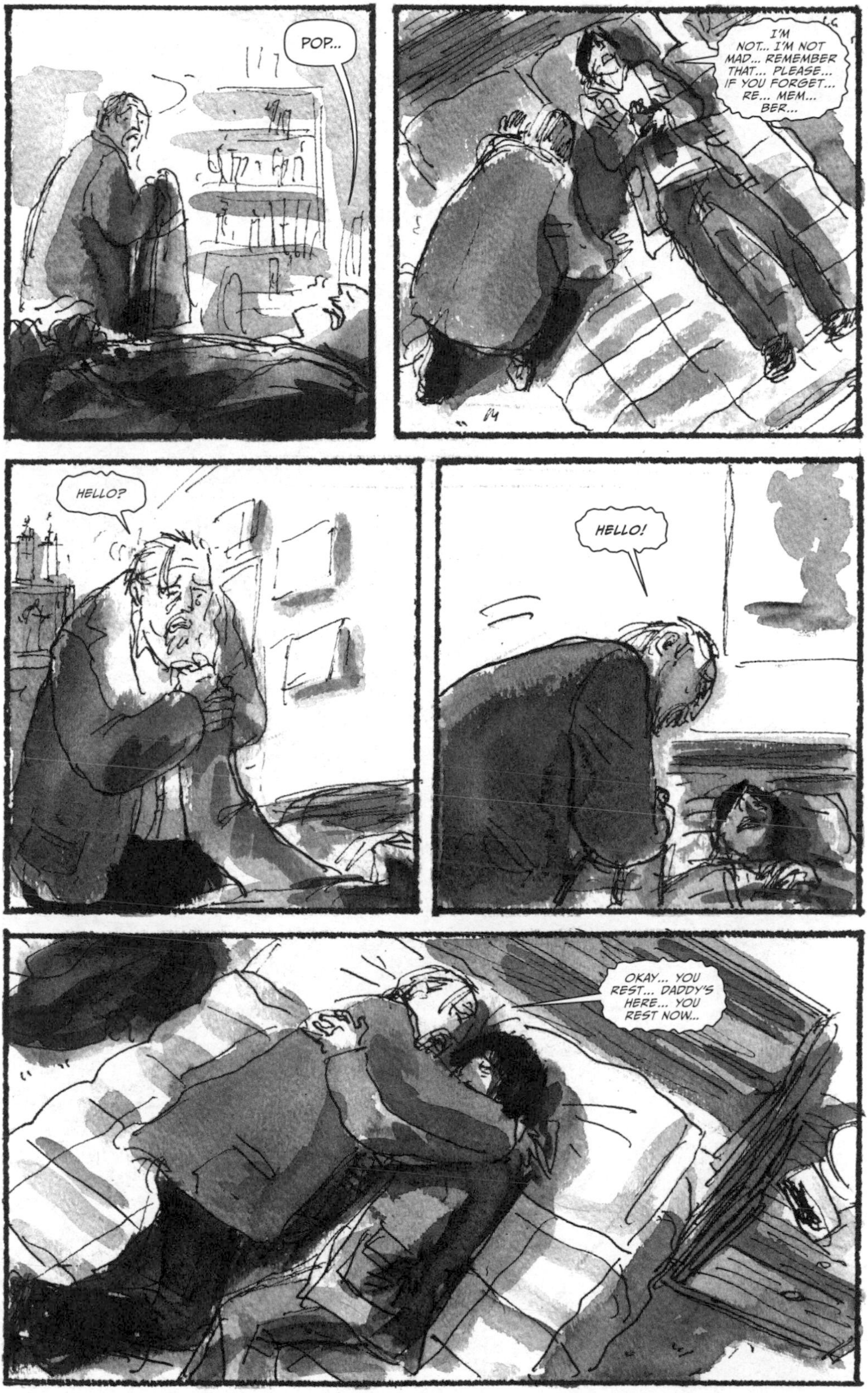
POP...
I'M NOT... I'M NOT MAD... REMEMBER THAT... PLEASE... IF YOU FORGET... RE... MEM... BER...
HELLO?
HELLO!
OKAY... YOU REST... DADDY'S HERE... YOU REST NOW...

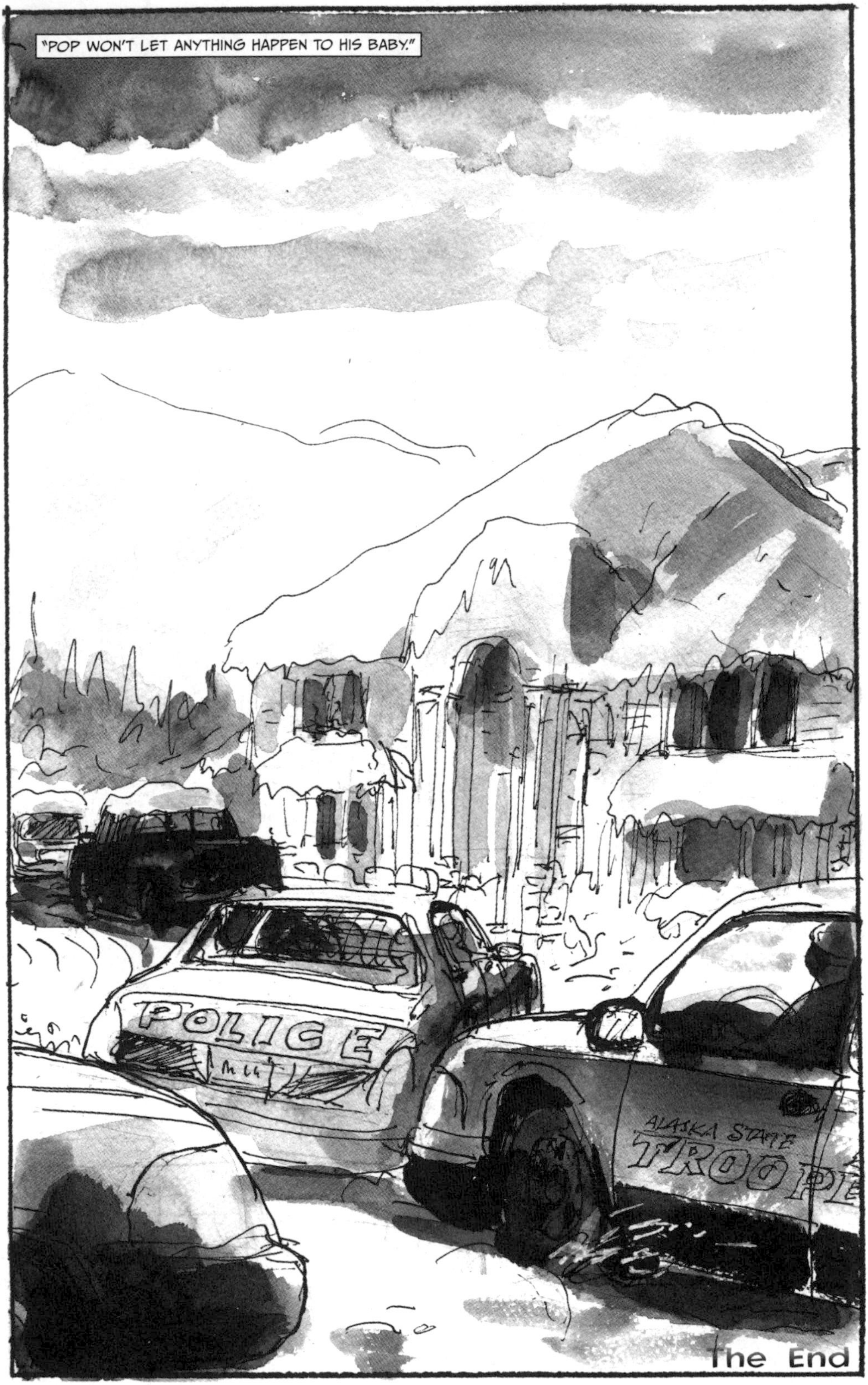
"POP WON'T LET ANYTHING HAPPEN TO HIS BABY."
POLICE
ALASKA STATE
TROOPE
The End

Also available in murder/mystery from NBM ComicsLit:
Miss Don't Touch Me, omnibus available Fall 2014, 192pp. color hc., $29.99
A Treasury of Murder, multiple volumes, by Rick Geary, $15.99 hc., 9.99, pb, $6.99 e-books

We have over 200 titles,
see our complete list at
NBMPUB.COM

NBM
160 Broadway, Suite 700, East Wing
New York, NY 10038
Catalog available by request
If ordering by mail add $4 P&H 1st item, $1 each addt'l

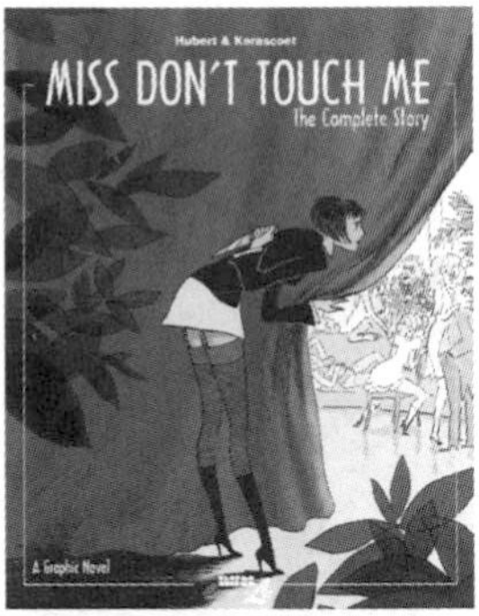
Hubert & Kerascoet
MISS DON'T TOUCH ME
The Complete Story
A Graphic Novel

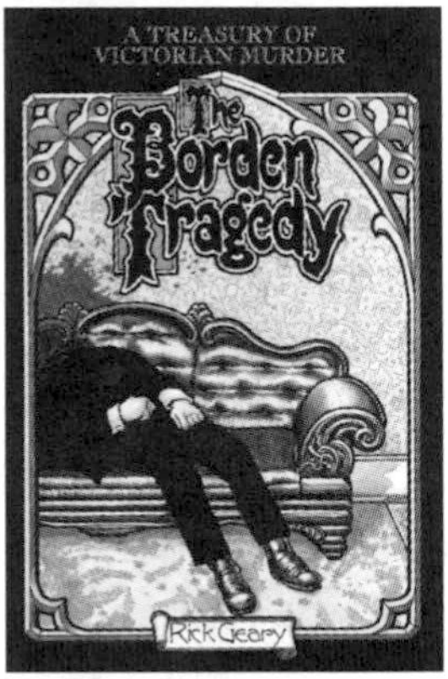
A TREASURY OF VICTORIAN MURDER
The Borden Tragedy
Rick Geary

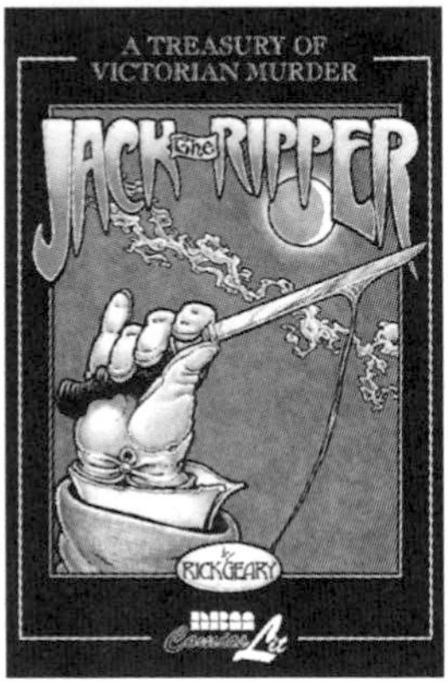
A TREASURY OF VICTORIAN MURDER
JACK the RIPPER
by RICK GEARY